# THE LIFE, LETTERS

## AND

# RELIGION OF ST. PAUL

BY

## C. T. WOOD, B.D.

FELLOW AND DEAN OF QUEENS' COLLEGE, CAMBRIDGE

EDINBURGH: T. & T. CLARK, 38 GEORGE STREET

1925

PRINTED IN GREAT BRITAIN BY
MORRISON AND GIBB LIMITED

FOR

T. & T. CLARK, EDINBURGH

LONDON : SIMPKIN, MARSHALL, HAMILTON, KENT, AND CO. LIMITED
NEW YORK : CHARLES SCRIBNER'S SONS

# PREFACE.

To write an adequate life of St. Paul would require a combination of Robert Louis Stevenson with William James, both working under the direction of a theological scholar who knew the facts and a Christian saint who could interpret them. But I think there is room for this book, which, without making any great pretensions, is meant primarily for young theological students at Cambridge and elsewhere, but which I also hope may be of interest to others and of help to masters of senior forms at schools.

Conybeare and Howson's *Life* is still the most interesting for general English readers; but it is long out of date in its information and in some of its ideas. Dr. David Smith published his *Life and Letters of St. Paul* in 1919, and it is a monument of learning. Since then we have had Dr. MacNeile's briefer *Life, Letters, and Christian Doctrine.*

In writing St. Paul's life I have tried to eschew graphic description, which needs a master-hand; neither have I thought it necessary to spoil all the stories which St. Luke tells so inimitably by " potting " them entire. In dealing with the Epistles, I have written brief introductions to each, adding a paraphrase of all except a few easy chapters, and (I hope) sufficient notes throughout on words and phrases to make the meaning clear.

But the motive which, above all, led me to publish this book was the desire to examine, as simply as possible, St. Paul's religion. Other writers of his life concentrate more on his theology : but his theology was surely built in almost every detail on his daily religious experience ; and we need books which will interpret his religion in terms which touch men's own experience of life rather than in the theological jargon which the modern mind finds both dull and unconvincing. Space has forbidden me to do this in any but a brief and fragmentary way ; and the task needs a writer of deep spirituality. But it has seemed to me worth while attempting it under my limitations. I only ask the reader's indulgence of my shortcomings, as well as his forbearance towards frank statements of personal opinion in matters of controversy.

I am greatly indebted to Canon J. H. Gray, of Queens' College, for his kindness in reading the proofs and making many valuable suggestions ; also to the Rev. J. E. Barber for some criticism of the form and contents of the book, and to Mr. V. H. Copestake for his aid in compiling the index. I should like also to express to the Publishers, Messrs. T. & T. Clark, both my gratitude for the generous way in which they have met my wishes, and my admiration for the accuracy and cleverness of the proof-reading.

C. T. WOOD.

N.B.—The view taken of the Acts of the Apostles in this book is that it is a genuine work of Luke the doctor, and is a trustworthy historical authority, especially for the life of St. Paul.

# CONTENTS.

# INTRODUCTORY NOTE.

A POSSIBLE CHRONOLOGY OF ST. PAUL'S LIFE.

(It must be understood that the dates are only approximate at the best. For the data, see the text of the book.)

| | | |
|---|---|---|
| Birth | B.C. | 1. |
| At Jerusalem under Gamaliel | A.D. | 14–18. |
| Conversion | | 32. |
| Flight from Damascus }<br>First Visit to Jerusalem (a fortnight) } | | 34. |
| Ministry in Tarsus | | 34–45. |
| Ministry in Antioch | | 45–47. |
| The Famine; Second Visit to Jerusalem | Early Spring 47. |
| First Missionary Journey | Autumn 47–49. |
| Epistle to the Galatians (from Antioch) | Winter 49–50. |
| The Council of Jerusalem; Third<br>Visit | Spring 50. |
| Second Missionary Journey | 50–53. |

[*N.B.*—Gallio was Proconsul of Achæa, July 52–July 53.]

| | | |
|---|---|---|
| 1 and 2 Thessalonians (from Corinth) | 52. |
| Third Missionary Journey | Autumn 53–May 57. |
| 1 Corinthians (from Ephesus) | Autumn 55. |
| 2 Corinthians (from Macedon) | September 56. |
| Romans (from Corinth) | January 57. |
| Riot at Jerusalem and Arrest | May 57. |
| Imprisonment at Cæsarea | June 57–59. |
| Embarkation for Rome | Early September 59. |
| Winter on Malta | November 59–February 60. |
| First Roman Imprisonment | 60 62. |
| Colossians, Ephesians, and Philemon | 61. |
| Philippians (from Rome) | 62. |
| Ministry in Spain | 63. |
| Second Roman Imprisonment and<br>Martyrdom | 67. |

# BIBLIOGRAPHY.

Books bearing on our subject are well-nigh innumerable. The following are recommended for reference.

Conybeare and Howson. *The Life and Epistles of St. Paul.* (Students' Edition, 1870).

T. Lewin. *The Life and Epistles of St. Paul* (1890). [Valuable for Archæology.]

David Smith. *The Life and Letters of St. Paul* (1919).

A. H. MacNeile. *St. Paul: His Life, Letters, and Christian Doctrine* (1920).

Lyman Abbott. *The Life and Letters of Paul the Apostle* (1898). [A popular account of his religious views.]

G. G. Findlay. Paul the Apostle (in Hastings' *Dictionary of the Bible*, vol. iii., 1904). [An invaluable summary of the facts.]
*The Epistles of Paul the Apostle.* (4th Edition). [A brief summary.]

J. Stalker. *The Life of St. Paul* (1892). [A sketch.]

W. M. Ramsay. *St. Paul the Traveller and Roman Citizen* (1896).
*The Cities and Bishoprics of Phrygia* (1897).
*The Church in the Roman Empire before 170 A.D.* (1904).
*Pauline and other Studies* (1906).
*The Cities of St. Paul* (1907).

Adolf Harnack. *The Mission and Expansion of Christianity in the First Three Centuries* (Eng. trans., 1908).
*History of Dogma*, vol. i. (Eng. trans., 1897).
*Luke the Physician* (Eng. trans., 1907).

Theodor Mommsen. *The Provinces of the Roman Empire* (Eng. trans., 1909).

Emil Schürer. *A History of the Jewish People in the Time of Jesus Christ* (5 vols., Eng. trans., 1886).

Hastings. *Dictionary of the Bible* (5 vols., 1898–1904). [Invaluable.]

*Encyclopædia Biblica.* Ed. by T. K. Cheyne and J. S. Black (3 vols., 1899).

A. E. Garvie. *Studies of Paul and his Gospel* (1911).

A. Schweitzer. *Paul and his Interpreters* (Eng. trans., 1912).

Johannes Weiss. *Paul and Jesus* (Eng. trans., 1909).

C. Anderson-Scott. *Jesus and Paul* (in "Cambridge Biblical Essays," 1909).

H. St. J. Thackeray. *The Relation of St. Paul to Contemporary Jewish Thought* (1900).

F. J. A. Hort. *Judaistic Christianity* (1894).

T. Lewin. *Fasti Sacri; or, A Key to the Chronology of the New Testament* (1865). [A mine of facts.]

James Smith. *The Voyage and Shipwreck of St. Paul* (4th Ed., 1880).

### Introductions to the New Testament.

Theodore Zahn (3 vols., Eng. trans., 1909). [Conservative.]

James Moffatt (International Theological Library, 3rd Ed., 1918).

A. S. Peake (2nd Ed., 1914). [Brief but excellent.]

### The Acts of the Apostles.

Commentaries by :—T. E. Page (1886).

R. B. Rackham (1901).

R. J. Knowling (Expositors' Greek Testament, 1901).

W. M. Furneaux (1912).

### The Several Epistles of St. Paul.

Kirsopp Lake. *The Earlier Epistles of St. Paul* (1911). [General Introduction.]

Commentaries by :—J. B. Lightfoot. *Galatians* (1892). *Colossians and Philemon* (1892). *Philippians* (1890). *Notes on the Epistles of St. Paul* (including 1 and 2 Thessalonians, 1 Corinthians 1–7, Romans 1–7), 1895.

G. Milligan. *1 and 2 Thessalonians* (1908).

H. L. Goudge. *1 Corinthians* (Westminster Commentary, 1903).

J. Armitage Robinson. *Ephesians* (1909).

R. St. J. Parry. *The Pastoral Epistles* (1920).

International Critical Commentary—

Sanday and Headlam on *Romans*.

Robertson and Plummer on *1 Corinthians*.

Plummer on *2 Corinthians*.

Burton on *Galatians*.

Abbott on *Ephesians and Colossians*.

Vincent on *Philippians and Philemon*.

Lock on *The Pastoral Epistles*.

Frame on *Thessalonians*.

Shorter Commentaries in the Cambridge Greek Testament, especially—

G. G. Findlay on *1 and 2 Thessalonians*.

R. St. J. Parry on *1 Corinthians*.

A. Plummer on *2 Corinthians*.

J. O. F. Murray on *Ephesians*.

J. H. Bernard on *The Pastoral Epistles*.

James Moffatt. *The New Testament: A New Translation* (*i.e.* in Modern English). [A valuable aid to those who are not familiar with the original Greek.]

# SOME ABBREVIATIONS EMPLOYED IN THE FOLLOWING PAGES.

---

C.H.    Conybeare and Howson's *Life and Epistles of St. Paul.*

Hast.*D.B.*    Hastings' *Dictionary of the Bible.*

E.V.    English Version of the Bible.

Lgt.    Lightfoot.

D.S.    David Smith's *Life and Letters of St. Paul.*

*T. and R.C.*    Ramsay's *St. Paul the Traveller and Roman Citizen.*

W.H.    Westcott and Hort's *Greek Text of the New Testament.*

(For abbreviations which denote Manuscripts, etc., the reader is referred to the Note at the end of the book, pp. 401–8.)

# THE LIFE, LETTERS, AND RELIGION
# OF ST. PAUL.

## CHAPTER I.

### SAUL THE PHARISEE.

1. INTRODUCTORY.—It is a very one-sided truth that
"familiarity breeds contempt." It is unhappily true,
however, that familiarity with the Bible usually blinds
us to the greatness of men like St. Paul. We know their
stories from infancy and do not stop to visualise them;
and the halo round a saint obscures reality. But a study
of St. Paul's life leaves one amazed at the bigness of the
man; and a study of his religion reveals its secret springs
and takes us into the heart of Christianity.

Biographers of great men tend to fall into one of two
extremes: either they treat them as geniuses whom nature
throws up unexpectedly, out of all relation to their environment; or, on the other hand, they present them as
merely favourable products of their age and nation, as
owing nearly all to the *Zeitgeist*. There is, of course,
truth in both extremes. A genius is still a man and cannot
be separated from the influences of heredity and environment; yet no such considerations will explain a Shake-
speare or a Paul.

In the case of the great missionary apostle, religious
theories are apt to colour the presentation of his life and

I

letters.  Older writers allow him little originality and are blind to any possible changes of opinion in him after his Conversion.  The old, rigid idea of inspiration demanded this view.

Many modern writers suffer from the swing of the pendulum.  They paint him as borrowing his views altogether from his Jewish upbringing, modified more or less considerably by the influence of Greek mystery-religions, with a modicum of fixed Christian belief ; often they treat him as the real creator of historical Christianity, who hustled the older Apostles into adopting something of his outlook !

Our task is to find the element of truth that lies in each and all of these points of view ; to trace the influence of Judaism, Greek thought, and Roman citizenship on his mind ; to see what Christianity owes to him : but beyond, far beyond, all else to connect him with the fountain-head, Jesus Christ ; and to see how the most original and most Divine religion in the world came to him from his living Lord, and worked out in his amazing life of varied circumstance.

2. TARSUS (see Phil. $3^5$, Acts $21^{39}$).—Cilicia, the country where St. Paul was born, consists of two very different tracts.  The western half is mountainous, and was at the beginning of our era a home of robber tribes ; the eastern half is a plain, lying between the great Taurus ridge of mountains and the sea, in the south-east corner of Asia Minor.  This low-lying tract was made by Pompey into a separate Roman province : but in 25 B.C. the Imperial Government joined it with Syria, which lay round the corner at a right angle, making one province of the two.  Antioch was the metropolis of Syria : Tarsus, Paul's birthplace, of Cilicia.  The town lay near the western border of the plain.  Thirty miles to the north rises the

wall of the Taurus, which was pierced there by one famous
pass, the Cilician Gates. Two miles to the north of the
city, the river Cydnus emerges from a rocky gorge ; and,
after passing it, flows ten miles to the sea.[1] The surrounding plain is fertile, sultry, marshy, malarial. Tarsus,
according to Ramsay, probably had a population of about
half a million in St. Paul's day. Its trade was considerable, for it had one famous export ; this was *cilicium*,
the hair of Cilician goats, which was much favoured for
making tents. But its intellectual fame stood higher
still. Strabo (writing in A.D. 19) says it was in his day
the chief seat of learning in the world, surpassing even
Athens and Alexandria in its devotion to Hellenic culture.[2]
It produced some leading Stoic philosophers and a few
tragic poets. In practical science it could claim the feat
of engineering the road by the Cilician Gates, which climbed
a pass in the Taurus to a height of 4300 feet. Ethnographically, its population was at the start probably a
colony of Ionian Greeks ; but the evidence of its coins
shows that the Oriental element predominated more and
more till 171 B.C. Then again there was a Greek revival ;
perhaps Antiochus Epiphanes introduced Greek settlers,
as was his way. But the East was too near its doors, and
once more slowly diluted the Hellenic strain. The city
had its own local government ; it had been made a
*libera civitas* by Rome in 42 B.C. with the right of free import and export. Probably one of the " tribes " which

[1] See Ramsay, *Cities of St. Paul*, p. 93. D.S. curiously enough gives
the distance as ¾ mile. Ramsay points out that ancient cities were
often built at some distance from the sea, to guard against the attacks
of pirates : cp. Antioch on the Orontes. At the mouth of the Cydnus
stood the port of Rhegma : the river was in those days navigable as
far up as Tarsus, for Antony and Cleopatra sailed up it.

[2] Strabo, as quoted in C.H., p. 87, n. 5. However, Dio Chrysostom,
a hundred years later, gives a very different account. Ramsay (*Cities*,
p. 89) says that Tarsus combined Hellenism with Orientalism more than
any other city in the world.

regulated local affairs was composed entirely of Jews, as we know was the case in Alexandria. Anyhow, there were many Jews living there,[1] and St. Paul was by birth a full citizen of the town. Now in 10 B.C. the Emperor Augustus instructed his old tutor, Athenodorus of Tarsus, to enact a property qualification for citizenship in the city, so as to create a bureaucratic oligarchy.[2] It follows that St. Paul's father was a man of some wealth. But not only was he a citizen of Tarsus ; he also held the coveted franchise of the Roman Empire : for his famous son tells the Roman officer that he himself was born a Roman citizen (Acts 22[28]). The Emperors bestowed this privilege on not a few leading provincials.

3. THE FAMILY, EDUCATION, AND CHARACTER OF SAUL. —The boy Saul therefore belonged to a family which formed part of an oligarchy within an oligarchy. Why or when they went to live at Tarsus, we have no means of knowing.[3] We have already seen that they must have been people of some wealth : this is confirmed by the fact that they could afford to send him, as well as his nephew after him, to Jerusalem to continue his education. There were times in St. Paul's life when he was short of money (Phil. 4[15], 2 Cor. 11[9]) ; but it is not unlikely that he inherited something later on, for the costs of his appeal to Cæsar must have been considerable.[4]

His parents gave him the Hebrew name of Saul. Now the Jews in Hellenic cities mostly used Greek names, but seem also to have borne a Hebrew name for use in private.

---

[1] " The Jew, trading with many nations and blending with none " (C.H.).

[2] Ramsay, *Cities*, p. 227.

[3] Jerome retails a tradition, which he heard at Bethlehem, that the parents escaped to Tarsus from Gischala in North Galilee when the Romans sacked the latter. But this was not till A.D. 70 !

[4] See Ramsay, *T. and R.C.*, pp. 31, 310, 312.

Thus we find " John Mark " and " Jesus Justus." Therefore it seems likely that the name " Paul " was given to our hero, not after his conversion, but at birth. " Saul Paul " is a likely combination, for assonance in names was popular. The object of St. Luke's change in the Acts, from an earlier " Saul " to a later " Paul," is no doubt to mark his new environment as Apostle to the Gentiles.

The parents were ardent Pharisees (Acts 23⁶, Rom. 4¹ 9³ 11¹, 2 Cor. 11²², Phil. 3⁵⁻⁶, 2 Tim. 1³), and taught their children the " ancestral traditions " (Acts 26⁴⁻⁵, Gal. 1¹⁴). But everything points to the fact that they had some breadth of outlook and tolerance. It is significant that they chose Gamaliel as his teacher in Jerusalem ; for whereas the stricter Palestinian Jews deprecated even the use of the Greek tongue in reciting phylacteries, Gamaliel's son tells us that his father taught a thousand boys, of whom half studied the Law, half " the wisdom of the Greeks." [1] The Jews of the Dispersion mostly took broader views than those of Palestine ; and people who were at once burgesses of Tarsus and citizens of Rome, proud of these privileges, can scarcely have belonged to the straitest sect. St. Paul's own narrowness in his Jerusalem days was probably due to a religious fanaticism which sought to drown the sense of his own shortcoming by fierce action against all heretics.

He must have been brought up to speak Aramaic [2] and Greek equally at home. He read his Old Testament both in the Hebrew and in the Greek Septuagint, if we may judge from the quotations in his Epistles.

He was born somewhere about 1 B.C., if we may trust the fourth-century tradition that he served God (as a Christian) for thirty-five years and died at the age of

---

[1] Quoted by C.H., p. 30, n. 4.

[2] His speech to the mob at Jerusalem was in Aramaic, Acts 22².

sixty-eight.[1] This harmonises with two other indica-
tions of his age : first, he was a member of the Sanhedrin
when Stephen was stoned, and therefore was over thirty
years of age ; secondly, he calls himself " Paul the aged "
when he writes to Philemon about A.D. 62.

Doubtless he followed the ordinary course of a Jewish
boy.[2] About the age of six he would begin to attend an
elementary school connected with his synagogue : after
a time he would be taught the Law by oral repetition.
When he was thirteen, he probably was taken from school
and apprenticed to a trade. For a Rabbi was not paid
as such, and Jewish parents, however wealthy, believed
in teaching every boy a trade. We know from St. Paul
himself that he learnt to make tents out of the famous
goat-hair of his native district ; and many a time in later
years it stood him in good stead that he could earn his
living in almost any city while preaching the gospel.

It was probably some two years later, say when he
was fifteen,[3] that he was sent to Jerusalem to continue his
education in the school of Gamaliel. The Rabbis of the
time were divided into two outstanding schools. Both
were Pharisaic ; but the school of Hillel, which was more
influential, upheld tradition as more binding than the
Law, as against the school of Shammai who rested everything on Scripture. Hillel's grandson was Gamaliel, a
man so highly revered that he is one of the only seven
who were ever honoured with the title of Rabban
(=Rabboni). Gamaliel, for all his traditionalism, was
no bigot, as we have already seen (p. 5). His tolerant and
wise advice to the Sanhedrin when they were taking

[1] See Ramsay, T. and R.C., Preface to Ed. II. p. xiv. The tradition
is given in the Oratio Encomiastica in Principes Apostolorum Petrum et
Paulum, which was falsely ascribed to Chrysostom.

[2] See Schürer, History of the Jewish People, ii. 2, pp. 47 ff.

[3] See D.S., p. 23, n. 1. C.H. put it at an earlier age ; but they do not
seem to leave a sufficient interval for him to learn a trade.

counsel how to punish Peter and other Apostles (Acts 5[34. 38-39]) was characteristic of the man. It was not from him that Saul learnt his fierce intolerance of heretics.[1]

The school worked in the Temple precincts. Those who, like Saul, desired to become Rabbis studied the Law. They discussed with their teacher all manner of casuistic points as to the right course of conduct in varying circumstances, or the inner meaning of the Old Testament narratives (cp. 1 Cor. 10[1-4], Gal. 4[21] 3[16]).

St. Paul exhibits a certain acquaintance with Greek literature. In addressing the Areopagus at Athens, he not only knows how to adapt his speech to his philosophical audience, but he definitely quotes, first from the philosopher Epimenides, "for in Him we live and move and have our being," and immediately after from Aratus the Cilician, "for we are kin to Him" (Acts 17[28]). He quotes from Epimenides again in Titus 1[12] (if that Epistle be Pauline). In 1 Cor. 15[33], we have an iambic line from the comedian Menander. An example of a different sort may be found in Phil. 4[8], where he apparently means, "if there be any value in the watchwords of Greek philosophy, 'virtue' and 'praise.'" Some of this knowledge he must have picked up in his youth at Tarsus and again in the school of Gamaliel, half of whose students worked at the Greek masters.[2] More of it perhaps is to be attributed to later years of travel and intercourse with men of many kinds. At the most, it was not sufficient

---

[1] So the Talmud, where we are told of three Gentile inquirers who said, "The irritability of Shammai sought to drive us from the world : the gentleness of Hillel brought us nigh under the wings of the Shekinah" (Taylor, *Pirque Aboth*, i. 16, n. 33).

[2] See Garvie, *Studies of Paul and his Gospel*, chap. i. Findlay (in Hast. *D.B.*, art. "Paul") refers to his contempt for contemporary philosophy, 1 Cor. 1[20], Col. 2[8]. He also points out that St. Paul knew some Roman law, for he speaks of "adoption" ($\upsilon\iota o\theta\epsilon\sigma\iota a$), which was not a Jewish institution.

to mould his literary style. " His vocabulary is in the main thoroughly popular and in accord with the living speech of his day." Yet he uses philosophic terms like αὐτάρκεια in the subjective sense of self-sufficiency (contentment), and συνείδησις (conscience), " which, though not unknown in the Jewish Apocrypha, first gains its full introspective moral importance in the teachings of the Stoics." [1]

Of St. Paul's personal appearance in later years we have an account in the " Acts of Paul and Thecla " (§ 3), which is generally supposed to be based on a first-century document : at any rate the account reads as true to life. It describes him as " a man small in size, bald-headed, bow-legged, strongly built, with meeting eyebrows and a rather large nose : full of grace, for at times he looked like a man and at times he had the face of an angel."

He certainly was a man of quick temper and emotion ; impulsive and nervous (cp. Acts 23[3-5]) ; but tough, buoyant, and tender. He had a quick mind and organising power, combined with humour and tact, though he could sometimes do apparently tactless things (cp. Acts 18[6-7]). Some would say that his tact occasionally led him into untruthfulness (see Acts 23[6]), but there is no sufficient warrant for such a charge. Some again would accuse him of egotism when he says " imitate me . . . " (2 Thess. 3[7, 9], 1 Cor. 4[16] 11[1] ; cp. 1 Thess. 1[6]), but an examination of the context in each case shows that he means " imitate my attitude towards Christ, my utter trust in Him, not self." [2] Sabatier well says that Paul's originality rests on the exceptional degree in which he united " dialectical power and religious inspiration." [3] We must remember

---

[1] Milligan, *The New Testament Documents*, pp. 56–7. Canon Gray points out to me that 1 Cor. 4[8] shows knowledge of Stoic doctrine.

[2] 2 Tim. 3[10] (if written by him) sounds egotistic but is not really so. For it surely means, " you have tried to follow the same *ideals* I have tried to follow."

[3] Quoted by Findlay, Hast. *D.B.*

that he had a unique preparation for his work in his cosmopolitan training combined with nationalistic fervour. From his Jewish forbears he learnt his lofty monotheism and stern moral code. From his Greek environment he acquired a mental gymnastic, utterly foreign to the Jew, which taught him to get down to the principles involved in any action. From his Roman citizenship he imbibed the conception of law and order, which enabled him to see large visions of the catholic Kingdom of God.

We have said that he was tough but nervous. His bodily strength gave him great physical endurance. But mental anxiety always told hardly upon him (see 2 Cor. 1). Besides this, he was often troubled, as we learn from his own lips, by some recurring physical weakness : he calls it his " thorn in the flesh " [1] (2 Cor. 12[7]), and it was both painful and humiliating (Gal. 4[13-15]). The view of many older commentators that he means temptations to fleshly sin has been almost universally given up. Ramsay believed that he got malaria into his system on the low coast-land of Asia Minor. But the other older view that he was subject to epileptic fits has much to be said in its favour : epilepsy is compatible with great mental endowments and bodily endurance, as we see in the cases of Julius Cæsar, King Alfred, Peter the Great, and Napoleon I., who were all subject to it. Now in Gal. 4[14] St. Paul says to the men of Lycaonia that he first entered their country because he was ill ; and that, though he looked so repulsive, they did not scorn him nor " spit out." Findlay reminds us that in that age men used to spit, when they saw an epileptic in a fit, to avert the evil from themselves ; and we are all familiar with the repulsive appearance of a person in an epileptic seizure.

St. Paul was by physical and mental constitution " psycho-pathic." He had the temperament of a mystic,

[1] Or "stake" (as R.V. mg.)

and like other great mystics he saw visions (see 2 Cor. $12^{1-4}$).
But he was, through the driving power of his religion,
first and foremost a man of action, and therein lay his
safety. Sane mystics have never deliberately encouraged
their tendency to see visions : they know well that to do
so would be to open the door to all manner of hallucinations. " Test all spirits " was the Apostle's rule : when
a vision comes, ask if it deepens one's apprehension of
God ; and if it does, thank Him for it. Thus such men
save themselves from becoming pathological victims.

4. His Religious Life before His Conversion.—
Saul was educated in the purest and loftiest monotheism
that the world had known : this became the unalterable
foundation of everything to him. Now to the Greek
mind the gods were essentially immanent—here on earth
near us and very like human beings on a magnified scale.
The Jew began at the other end ; and since the eighth
century before Christ God was to him the transcendent
ruler, the all-holy and all-high : His ways were not our
ways. So, as the centuries ran on, God seemed to recede
farther from humanity, using angels as His inter-
mediaries. This, in spite of those passages in the Old
Testament and particularly in the Psalms and deutero-
Isaiah which speak of His loving-kindness, was the trend
of Jewish religious thought.

So it was that his religion first presented God to the
young Saul, not as a present personal Friend, but as a
majestic and awful Duty-master. Drilled as he had been
in the thousand rules for life laid down by the Pharisees,
he became obsessed with the weight of it all. His conscience knew no peace : old sins dogged him, and there
was no rest from the fear of breaking some commandment. Religion was something imposed from without,
institutional : poor weak humanity was beset on all

sides by a host of evil angels seeking to hinder obedience to God.

But there was always the hope of the coming Messiah. What he should be and do, was a matter of many varied beliefs. To Saul he probably was to be, not so much a political deliverer from Rome, as a great religious law-giver acclaimed as supreme by all rival schools of Jews.

The main point, however, that needs emphasis, is that the former religion of the future Apostle was gloomy and unsatisfying. It was not something internal, which came home to dwell in a man's inmost being, satisfying his instinctive needs, an abundant source of life and joy : but it was something imposed on an evil nature, almost crushing. And he whipped himself to an ever fiercer zeal of fanaticism in the endeavour to bear the hard yoke of the Law with a conscience at rest.

## NOTE.

Two questions about St. Paul call for brief discussion, though neither of them admits of a certain answer.

(a) WAS HE EVER MARRIED ?—If so, clearly his wife was dead before his Conversion. *Later* regulations required that a member of the Sanhedrin should have been married and had at least one child : the idea was that wedlock and parenthood would produce mercy and understanding in judgment. But we have no means of knowing whether this regulation was in force as early as St. Paul's day.

It is true that the Jews regarded marriage at the age of about eighteen as almost a binding duty. But Maimonides allows celibacy even after the age of twenty to a man who wishes to give himself up to a study of the Law. Thus there is nothing to show whether St. Paul was married or not.

(b) HAD HE SEEN JESUS ?—Probably not, or we should

have some indication of the fact in his Epistles. 2 Cor. 5[16] has no bearing on the question (see note on that verse, p. 230).

But it is worth noticing that two arguments which are sometimes used to prove the negative, will not stand. First, it is said that he only claims to have seen Christ on the road to Damascus and not at any other time : but the reason for this is that the vision at his Conversion was his only first-hand *proof of the Resurrection*. Secondly, we are referred to the curious lack in his Epistles of quotations of our Lord's sayings. This omission is much more apparent than real : it is in any case quite certain that he knew a great deal of our Lord's recorded teaching. But the fact is that he was absorbed in the daily presence of Christ, and the historical aspect of His life on earth is to him secondary.

Johannes Weiss in his book *Paul and Jesus* (pp. 28–56) brings forward an ingenious but hardly convincing argument to show that Paul had seen Jesus on earth. He starts with the proposition that in visions new *facts* are not communicated to men, but only a new meaning and potency to facts already known : therefore on the road to Damascus St. Paul could not have recognised Jesus unless he already knew Him by sight. But St. Luke's narrative does not bear this out : in Acts 9[5] St. Paul asks the Lord, " *Who art Thou ?* " *i.e.* he does not recognise Jesus. We must also remember that Paul himself insists on the difference between the Conversion-appearance and his other visions of the Lord (1 Cor. 15[8] ; cp. 2 Cor. 12[1-4]) : therefore if we believe him, we cannot apply to the former appearance the limitations which may possibly regulate the ordinary visions of the mystic.

# CHAPTER II.

## THE CONVERSION AND AFTER.

1. THE DEATH OF STEPHEN (Acts 6–7).—At Jerusalem, we are told, " there arose " in the Christian Church " a murmuring of the Hellenists (or " Greek-speaking Jews ") against those that spoke Hebrew, because their widows were neglected in the daily giving of relief " (Acts 6[1]). In Judaism since the days of Solomon and Ahab there had always been two tendencies ; the one making for the absolute isolation of the " peculiar people " from foreign influences, the other seeking to throw open the door to the great world outside.   In St. Paul's age the pious in Palestine hated and dreaded everything Greek in language, thought, or manners : they clung ferociously to the Aramaic tongue, the contemporary dialect of Hebrew, and only learnt enough Greek to serve the purposes of commerce.   But in Palestine itself the foreign influence was probably much greater in the cities of the coast and of the Sea of Galilee ; while in Asia Minor and Egypt and the whole of the Eastern Mediterranean, the Jews of the Dispersion naturally spoke Greek as their mother-tongue, though Aramaic was also used in such homes as that of St. Paul.   Nor was this a mere matter of language ; it was a change of environment, which deeply affected even the conservative Jew.   St. Paul's learned contemporary, Philo, at Alexandria fell under the charm of Greek philosophy ; and, devout Jew as he was, he must needs attempt the impossible task of showing that all its truths were contained in his national

13

Scriptures. He read all sorts of mystic allegories into the Old Testament, often to the exclusion of its literal meaning : and so he came to regard even circumcision as not binding in its outward observance but only in its inward spiritual sense.

Philo is perhaps an extreme case to take ; but the same tendency was at work everywhere among Jews of the Dispersion, even those who were too keenly religious to forget the Law of their fathers. Probably a considerable number of them found their way back to live in Jerusalem from foreign lands as well as from the more Greek towns in Palestine ; and their whole outlook must have made it easier for them to accept the new light of Christianity than for their more rigid Hebrew-speaking kinsfolk. And so the cleavage, which was found among the Jews proper, spread into the Christian Church, where there has usually been a traditionalist party tending towards exclusiveness, and a progressive party seeking for inclusiveness. It is significant that one of the charges brought at his trial against the Hellenist Stephen was that of teaching that Jesus " will change the customs which Moses delivered unto us."

It was over the matter of relief for the poor that the uneasy relations of Hellenist and Hebrew Christians came to a head. The Greek-speaking minority believed that their widows were unfairly treated in the daily distribution. The Apostles were too busy to superintend it themselves ; so they asked the whole body of believers to nominate seven men, whose Christian character was above suspicion, to be in charge of poor-relief. Later ages called them the " seven deacons " (or ministers) ; St. Luke does not use the term in describing them, but they mark the beginning of a second order of church officials working under the direction of the presbyters. Their names are all Greek— a fact which suggests, though it does not prove, that the

Hebrew majority voted for seven Hellenists, in a spirit of Christian large-heartedness, hoping to allay suspicion and heal the breach. Stephen and Philip are the most famous of the seven. Stephen is marked out by St. Luke for his ardent faith and spirituality (Acts 6[5]), and he quickly came to the front as a leader in effective missionary work at Jerusalem (v.[8]). Naturally it was Hellenist Jews who were most influenced by him, or thrown into the most violent antagonism ; for it was not all of them who held tolerant views, as the case of Saul is sufficient to show.

What Saul was doing at Jerusalem, we do not know. He had probably been away during the public ministry of our Lord ; but he was back again now, apparently as a local Rabbi and member of the Sanhedrin.[1] The Jews of the Dispersion in certain parts of North Africa and Asia Minor (the provinces of Asia and *Cilicia*, Acts 6[9]) maintained a synagogue at Jerusalem ; its congregation would normally be small, except at the great Feasts when numbers came on pilgrimage. It was apparently to this synagogue that Saul was attached ; and he and other kindred spirits, unable to hold their own in argument with Stephen, began to regard him as a limb of Satan, potent for evil. Nothing is more cruel than religious enthusiasm gone awry ; but it is not consciously dishonest in the case of men like St. Paul. They must have believed they were speaking the truth when they denounced Stephen to the Sanhedrin for teaching that " Jesus of Nazareth shall destroy this place (the Temple) and shall change the customs which Moses delivered unto us " (Acts 6[14]). And all Stephen's defence before the Sanhedrin (chap. 7), though it makes dull reading to us in St. Luke's summary, is really very much

---

[1] D.S. says (p. 41), " He had come to Jerusalem for the Passover." This seems highly improbable, since he was a member of the Sanhedrin in the capital ; and after Stephen's death, he was working under the High Priest's directions.

to the point. Did they accuse him of speaking against the Temple ? In a sense it was true : he *did* teach and urge, what the Old Testament proved, that the Temple was no necessity in true worship ; for God had revealed Himself to the patriarchs in far-off lands and held commune with His people no less really before the days of Solomon than since ; and in later days prophets like Isaiah had taught that God does not live in any house made with hands (vv.[47-50]). Did they accuse him of teaching that Jesus had abolished the Law ? Yes, it was true ; He had abolished the Law, but only by fulfilling it, by giving a deeper and more intimate revelation of God. But the Jews had always tried to stand still, instead of moving forward ; they had always murdered the prophets : and when that Jesus came, whom the Law foretold (v.[37]) and who was its fulfilment, they had crucified Him too. " You who received the Law, it is you who have failed to keep it, not we " (v.[53]).

Saul the Rabbi, as he sat in the council to try this man and gnashed his teeth with fury, little dreamed that this was the message which he peculiarly among Christian Apostles was to develop and preach in many lands ; by which he was to lift Christianity out of the danger in which it stood, of becoming merely a Jewish reformed sect, into the position of a world religion such as our Lord's teaching involved. Yet so it was to be : it was Stephen's mantle which descended, with a double gift of power, upon one of the judges who murdered him. Few things in St. Paul's life can have been so indelibly stamped on his memory as the details of this scene and its terrible end ; and when he too became one of these cursed Nazarenes, it was Stephen's presentation of Christ's attitude to the Law which dominated him from the first.

The trial ended in an act of hopeless illegality : for the Sanhedrin, though it could inflict lesser penalties on Jews

for religious offences, had no power of capital punishment
without ratification by the Roman governor.  But Pilate,
in the closing years of his procuratorship (which terminated
in A.D. 35) had lost grip ; and this all happened not earlier
than 31, perhaps two years later.

Stephen had called his judges murderers and sons of
murderers ; it is little wonder that they voted him guilty
of blasphemy : but he heeded them not ; " Behold, I see the
heavens opened," he cried, " and the Son of Man [1] standing on the right hand of God."  All thoughts of legality
vanished from their minds.  They seized him and dragged
him out of the Temple courts through the streets of the
Holy City till they stood without the walls ; and there
they stoned him even while he prayed for them, " Lord,
lay not this sin to their charge."

## 2. THE CONVERSION (Acts $9^{1-9}$ $22^{3-11}$ $26^{9-18}$.  See note [2]

[1] A recognised title for the Messiah, since the writing of the " Similitudes " in the Book of Enoch nearly a hundred years earlier.

[2] We must note some apparent discrepancies between these accounts
in minor points :

(a) Acts $9^7$ states that Saul's companions *heard* the voice but saw no
man.  In $22^9$ St. Paul says that they saw the light but *heard not* the
voice.  Many attempts have been made to reconcile these two statements :  Chrysostom suggested that they did not hear Christ's words
but did hear Saul's answer.  Others try to differentiate between ἀκούω
(" to hear ") with the genitive φωνῆς in $9^7$ and with the accusative
φωνήν in $22^9$.  It is better to acknowledge that St. Luke, for all his
usual accuracy, has made a slip in one of these passages (probably $9^7$).
The light may have been a flash of lightning (ἀστραπή) as the verb in
$9^3$ and $22^6$ (περιαστράπτω) seems to suggest.

(b) *When was Paul's commission to the Gentiles given to him ?*  According
to Acts $9^{15}$ Christ announced it to Ananias : according to $22^{17-21}$ Paul
received it from Christ in a subsequent vision at Jerusalem :  according
to $26^{17-18}$ our Lord gave him this explicit commission at his Conversion,
and he expressly tells King Agrippa that his ministry abroad was in
obedience to this heavenly vision (vv.[19-20]).  Probably all three statements
are correct :  he may at his Conversion have received some intimation
of his future work which he understood more fully when Ananias spoke

below).—Saul had not only been at the trial of Stephen and voted against him ($8^1$ $22^{20}$), but in his fanatical zeal he had gone out to the place of execution and taken charge of the proceedings ($7^{58}$). So it came to pass that he heard the dying man's prayer for his judges and executioners. Many an evil man has gone to his death courageously : but this was more than courage, it was sublime love for his enemies. The young Pharisee—Saul was now about thirty-three years of age—must have asked himself what was the secret of it. But, as he himself wrote in later years, " even Satan can take on the appearance of an angel of light " (2 Cor. $11^{14}$). Was not God's Law absolute and infallible ? And " only the man who carried it out should live by it." His own haunting sense of failure and his frequent temptations were surely due to a divided heart : human pity and admiration were only weaknesses to be suppressed if they conflicted with God's revealed will. So he flogged himself on to greater ardour in this inquisition : but all the while in his subconscious self there lived the memory of Stephen's words and radiant face as he died.

Well may Augustine say, " Si Stephanus non orasset, Ecclesia Paulum non haberet " (If Stephen had not prayed, the Church would not have Paul).[1] The martyrdom

to him. But he only interpreted this as a command to work among Gentiles in Syria. Later on when he was at Jerusalem the clear call came to him to go abroad.

*Note* that the words " it is hard for thee to kick against the goads " are only found in $26^{14}$. They are a Greek proverb (see Æsch. *Agam.* 1602) which does not occur in Jewish literature, though in Eccles. $12^{11}$ we find the metaphor, " The words of the wise are as goads." Some (*e.g.* Findlay) understand " the pricks " or " goads " in St. Paul's case to mean the pricks of the Mosaic Law which Christ was using to teach him his own impotence. It probably means more generally the guidance of the Divine husbandman (cp. the passage in Ecclesiastes).

[1] August. *Serm.* 382. 11. William James, in *The Varieties of Religious Experience*, was the first psychologist to put forward the theory of what he calls " subconscious incubation " in relation to religious conversions of this type. Since his time the theories of Freud and Jung,

was the signal for an outburst of persecution of the Christians. Saul was a ready instrument in the hands of the authorities. He "laid waste" the Church at Jerusalem, entering into private houses and haling men and women off to prison ($8^3$) : he had them flogged ($22^{19}$) in his endeavour to make them blaspheme the name of Jesus ($26^{11}$, 1 Cor. $15^9$, Gal. $1^{13}$). And when he could find no more victims in Judæa, he was still "breathing out threats and slaughter against the disciples" (Acts $9^1$) : so he went to the High Priest and begged to be sent to Damascus with a commission to arrest Christians there ($9^2$).

It may be asked, What authority had the High Priest to secure the arrest of Jews living in a foreign city ? In towns founded or refounded by the Greek kings who succeeded to the Eastern empire of Alexander the Great, the Jews were allowed autonomy so far as was compatible with public order : in Antioch and Alexandria they had this freedom ; and in other Greek cities of the East [1] the Roman government guaranteed them certain privileges such as exemption from military service and the right to follow their own religion and observe the Sabbath. Experience showed that this was the easiest way of dealing with a people who were so useful and yet so obstinately attached to their national creed and customs. Unfortunately we know nothing about the government of Damascus just at this time (see below, pp. 27 ff.). All we can say is that the jurisdiction of the High Priest at Jerusalem in religious affairs extended to any Jew at Alexandria and probably in a number of other cities.

---

however extravagant some of them are, have done much to explain this "incubation" as a process commonly found in mental life, *i.e.* the repression for a time of certain thoughts or temptations which become "complexes" in the "unconscious" self and tend to break through into the conscious life at unforeseen moments.

[1] See Mommsen, *Roman Provinces*, ii. 171–3.

The journey to Damascus is about 150 miles,[1] and in all probability Saul and his men rode on ass-back.[2] Damascus stands far from the sea on the eastern foothills of the Anti-Lebanon range, in a narrow but fertile strip which lies between the mountains and the desert. Its site is 2300 feet above sea-level : well-watered by rivers which flow from the mountains, the town enjoys a delightful climate and is surrounded by rich and beautiful country, in strong contrast to the eastern desert which comes close to the walls. So it still exists to-day when Babylon and Nineveh and every other city of equal antiquity are long deserted ; and "the street called Straight" where the blinded Saul lodged with Judas the Jew (9[11]) still bears the same name.

There is no need here to tell the story of the appearance of Christ which Saul saw as he drew near Damascus about midday. St. Luke recounts it three times, so strongly does he feel that it is pivotal for the development of Christianity.

Now St. Paul saw many a vision in his lifetime (cp. 2 Cor. 12[2], and see above, p. 10). Yet he sharply differentiates the appearance of Christ to him at his Conversion from all his other visions of the Lord. In 1 Cor. 15[8] he insists that it was *the last of the Resurrection appearances, which he distinguishes from all visions as somehow being more objective and external* (cp. 1 Cor. 9[1]). This is an important witness to the fact that he himself believed in the story of the empty tomb. Visions came to him, as to many another mystic since, Christian and non-Christian,

---

[1] It would be rather less if they crossed at the ford of Jericho and kept up the road east of Jordan. But they are more likely to have chosen the western route, *i.e.* by the Samaritan hills to the Vale of Esdraelon, and then east down the Vale of Jezreel to the ford of Beth-shan. This route would bring them into places where they could carry on their inquisition for Christians.

[2] Acts 9[8], describing his entry into Damascus, says " his men led him by hand " ; but this does not prove that they were on foot.

when he was absorbed in the adoration of God in silent,
self-forgetting worship : this appearance of Christ came
to him without warning, unsought ; there was no working
up to it in his consciousness, however much it may show
an uprush from his subconscious self.[1]

All sane mystics insist that visions in themselves do not
afford any sure test of reality : they must be tried by their
effect on the practical religious life.[2] And we must admit
the same test of the appearance of Christ which Paul
believed himself to have seen on the road to Damascus.

It is quite possible that, in the midday heat, he was
attacked by some nervous or muscular trouble in the head
which made him temporarily blind, some " occipital
lesion " or whatever other polysyllabic name medical
authority may assign to it ; and that it may have caused
the instantaneous conviction that this was Christ against
whose charm he had fought so desperately in his inmost
soul.[3] This hypothesis may be true to fact ; but however

[1] See Pratt, *Religious Consciousness*, p. 403 : " These visions are
rarely true hallucinations, but are what psychologists distinguish as
pseudo-hallucinations ; the subject even during the experience knows
that it is a vision that he sees. . . . The visions of the mystics are
determined in content by their belief, and are due to the dream imagination working upon the mass of theological material which fills the mind."

[2] See Pratt, *op. cit.*, p. 463 : " The auto-suggestion and mono-ideism
of the great mystic are more nearly related to those of the man of action
than to the pathological conditions of the same name found in degener-
ates. . . . Some of the great mystics have probably had touches of
hysteria at certain crises in their careers. But if we take their lives and
activities—in short, their mysticism as a whole—they present a very
marked contrast to the hysteric. Both indeed are very suggestible ;
but the hysteric is subject to all sorts of haphazard suggestions, from
without and from within, whereas the Christian mystic is dominated
constantly by the *self*-suggestion of a determined will bent on the
pursuit of righteousness."

[3] See William James, *Varieties of Religious Experience*, Lecture I.,
p. 13 : " Medical materialism finishes up St. Paul by calling his vision
on the road to Damascus a discharging lesion of the occipital cortex,
he being an epileptic. It snuffs out Saint Teresa as an hysteric, Saint

true, it only explains the *occasion* of the appearance to him, it does not in the least test the objective truth of it. The only test of reality in such matters is the effect on a man's life ; what he did in later years, the amount of power and influence he had in changing the lives of men for the better—these are the tests and the only ultimate tests of the objectiveness of his vision. We could not legitimately appeal to St. Paul's conversion to establish our belief in God ; but starting with belief in God as the All-Father, we may unhesitatingly accept the story of the Conversion as true in essentials.

We need not tell of Saul's blindness, nor how he fasted for three days after the Jewish manner, nor how he was healed by the Jewish Christian Ananias (Acts 9¹⁰⁻¹⁹).[1] But it is interesting to note that he had not been baptized earlier in life ; for it means that he had not come under the influence of John the Baptist or his disciples. They represented non-legalistic ideas which found no favour with the more rigid Pharisees (cp. Mt. 3⁷⁻⁹).

3. THE EFFECTS OF THE CONVERSION ON SAUL'S RELIGION.—The first and most obvious conviction that his changed outlook brought to Saul was that Jesus of Nazareth was the Messiah, and in some real sense the

Francis of Assisi as an hereditary degenerate. George Fox's discontent with the shams of his age and his pining for spiritual veracity, it treats as a symptom of a disordered colon. Carlyle's organ-tones of misery it accounts for by a gastro-duodenal catarrh." Cp. also p. 10 : " Alfred believes in immortality so strongly because his temperament is so emotional. Fanny's extraordinary conscientiousness is merely a matter of over-instigated nerves. William's melancholy about the universe is due to bad digestion—probably his liver is torpid. . . . Peter would be less troubled about his soul if he would take more exercise in the open air."

[1] St. Luke, in describing the faith-cure in vv.¹⁸⁻¹⁹, uses technical medical terms (ἀπέπεσαν, λεπίδες, ἐνισχύθη ; see Hobart, *Med. Lang. of St. Luke*, p. 38). But of course he had only heard St. Paul's description of it ; it *felt* as if scales were removed from his eyes, a symbol of his own mental darkness which vanished at the touch of Christ.

" Son of God " (see Acts 9²⁰). So much is indubitable. His Messiahship had formed the text which the Apostles preached unceasingly, as St. Luke shows in the opening chapters of the Acts. Garvie maintains [1] that in the earlier stages of his Christian life this was all that Christianity meant to St. Paul, and that he says so in 2 Cor. 5¹⁶, where " knowing Christ after the flesh " means interpreting the Resurrection merely as a proof of Messiahship rather than of the Lord's abiding presence. But though it is true that the Apostle progressed and deepened his grasp of Christianity year by year, it is incredible that at first he thought of Christ as an absent Messiah. The Lord had spoken to him on the road to Damascus—spoken really and actually : He, the Son of God, the revealer of the Father, was *here*, an abiding Presence and a constant inspiration. That thought was so much to the Apostle all the rest of his life, that it overshadows in his Epistles even the words and acts of Christ on earth (except, of course, the Resurrection, which was the means of His omnipresence). Out of Christ's abiding presence came his inspiration and his new-found joy ; all his oppressive sense of sinfulness and failure vanished at it ; it loosened the shackles of sin by giving him the power of personal union with his Lord, the very keystone of all his belief. We are saved, delivered, ransomed " *in Christ*," in actual personal union with Him—so the Apostle taught again and again in every Epistle he ever wrote.[2] That was Christianity to him ; and out of that, his actual daily experience, comes all his theology.

The question is often asked, How did his conviction

---

[1] *Studies of Paul and his Gospel*, p. 54.

[2] If it was the historic Jesus rather than the risen Christ that formed the kernel of his religion, surely his first impulse would have been to go to Jerusalem and learn all he could from the Lord's companions. But that is just what, as he explains in Gal. 1¹⁶, he felt no impulse to do at first.

of Jesus' Messiahship produce his belief in the invalidation of the Mosaic Law, a belief which he always connects with the Resurrection ? [1] The older Apostles were slow to draw the inference ; how did St. Paul come to it, and is it likely that he came to it quickly ? Now he was not a systematic theologian, like a mediæval Schoolman, who sat down and argued out dogmas by some method of dialectic. True, he was a great philosopher, in a sense ; but he used his philosophy to explain his beliefs, not to construct them. [2] His theology is nearly always based immediately on his experience. [3] Next, we have to remember that he was spiritually the child of Stephen, who certainly in some sense believed that Jesus would alter the customs which Moses enjoined (see above, pp. 15–16) : it was on this very point, above all others, that he had attacked the Christian deacon as a renegade. Thus he came to Christianity associating it with the idea that the Law of Moses was not permanent or essential. He came also after a long and weary struggle to keep the Law strictly himself, and he had never known permanent peace or freedom till he forgot the demands of the Law and fixed all his thoughts on the gracious presence of the Son of God. Surely he was forced, and forced immediately by his own experience, to the conclusion that Christ was equally the Saviour of the whole world, and that the mere observance of the Law as such had never saved any man. He knew that Jesus had taught men to love God and one's neighbour, and had said that he who learned this love would instinctively keep the Law and

[1] So Schweitzer, *Paul and his Interpreters*, pp. 104–5, who assumes that Jesus Himself never contemplated the abrogation of the Law, any more than the early Church did.

[2] This, according to Hegel, is the function of all true philosophy.

[3] The most noteworthy exceptions are his Christology and his eschatology : *e.g.* his belief in our Lord's pre-existence is incapable of verification in experience.

more than the Law. " With the abrogating of the Law
for the believer, the barrier between Jew and Gentile
fell," says Dr. Garvie.[1] Years passed before St. Paul
worked out his explicit belief that justification (acquittal
before God) is by faith (*i.e.* by loving, humble trust in
Him), not by works. But we must needs believe that
from the moment of his conversion he regarded the Law
as a taskmaster from whose thraldom he had at last
escaped. The older Apostles came to Christianity in a
very different way : to them it was no sudden release
from an intolerable burden, but the slow learning of a
better and a fuller way. So it took them years to understand what Paul perceived quickly, that the Gentile world
was to come to Christ without passing through the narrow
gate of circumcision. The habits of a lifetime had taught
them to regard the Gentiles as outside the fold, untouched
by God. St. Paul had taken the same view, perhaps
even more intensely. But the sudden upheaval of his
whole life on the road to Damascus carried away many a
former prejudice ; and he learnt to think of himself as
having been in no way superior to the Gentiles, only as
having sinned against fuller light than was shed on them.

[1] *Studies of Paul and his Gospel*, p. 35.

# CHAPTER III.

## EARLY CHRISTIAN MINISTRY : TARSUS AND ANTIOCH.

1. DAMASCUS AND ARABIA (Acts $9^{19b-25}$, Gal. $1^{15-17}$).—
Saul spent " certain days " in Damascus, telling his story :
but before long he felt the need of quiet and leisure. His
whole life had been revolutionised ; he wanted to think
out what this meant, and what the future required of
him. So he " went away into Arabia " (Gal. $1^{17}$). Now
Arabia was originally the name of the Sinaitic peninsula,
in the far south ; but by this time it had been extended
to include all the region east of Jordan, as far north as
Damascus, which it included.[1] His retirement was, no
doubt, to some quiet spot near Damascus where he would
have opportunity for thought and prayer.

At any rate, it was to Damascus that he returned,
probably after a few weeks' absence. He was now as
eager to proclaim Jesus as he had formerly been to persecute Him ; and where could he do this so effectually
as at Damascus, considering the errand which had first
led him thither ? So he preached there and " increased

[1] See quotations from Pliny, Strabo, and Justin Martyr in D.S., p.
56, n. 5. Nevertheless Dr. Smith follows Lightfoot in maintaining that
St. Paul actually took the long journey to the Sinaitic peninsula, because
Arabia in Gal. $4^{25}$ refers to the south. But that is just as reasonable as
to argue that because an Englishman abroad has at one time meant the
south-east when he speaks of England, he can never mean Cumberland,
which passed into the hands of the Angles at a much later date. The
view taken above is following Ramsay (T. and R.C., p. 380).

the more in strength " (9²²). As the months passed by,[1] the Jews became more and more violently provoked against the renegade : at last they determined that he must die (9²³). With the help of the Arabs they kept a sharp look-out for him ; and some of the Jews, who knew him by sight, took their turns at watching the gates day and night (9²⁴ with 2 Cor. 11³²⁻³³).

But, as so often in old towns, there were houses built on the walls, with windows overlooking the fosse. Once the Jewish plot was known to the Christians, it was no difficult matter to put him into a large rope-basket (σαργάνη or σφυρίς) and lower it by a rope from a window.

In 2 Cor. 11³², referring to his escape, St. Paul writes : " In Damascus the ethnarch of Aretas the king guarded the city of the Damascenes in order to take me." This was Aretas IV., the native king of the Arabs in what was called Nabatæa, who had his capital in the inaccessible city of Petra, situated some distance to the south-south-east of the Dead Sea. Herod Antipas had married his daughter and divorced her in A.D. 29, which led to bitter hostility between them, breaking out into active warfare shortly before the death of the Emperor Tiberius. Herod used his influence at Rome so effectually, that the Emperor ordered Vitellius, the legate of Syria, to make a military expedition against the Arabs, and the legions were actually on the march when news came of Tiberius' death (A.D. 37).[2] His successor in the purple, Caligula, reversed his policy in many directions, and the Nabatæan undertaking was abandoned at his orders. It is even possible that he handed over Damascus to Aretas and made it part of his kingdom, just

---

[1] St. Luke in Acts does not mention the retirement in Arabia ; but he knew of it, as is clear from the contrast of " certain days " in v.¹⁹ with " many days " in v.²³. The latter phrase covers two years in 1 Kings 2³⁸⁻⁹. See Gal. 1¹⁸.

[2] See Josephus, *Antiq.* xviii. 5.

as his successor Claudius in A.D. 41 gave to the neighbouring
client-state of the Jews a king of their own in Herod Agrippa I.
We have *Roman* coins at Damascus dating from the reign
of Tiberius as late as A.D. 33–4, and again in the ninth
year of Nero, A.D. 62 ; there is no evidence at all between
those dates to show what was the government of the city.

But if Aretas ever did obtain Damascus, it cannot have
been before A.D. 37, and St. Paul's conversion therefore
cannot be dated earlier than 35 or (more probably) 36.
Such a late date seems to me very difficult to harmonise
with the chronology which the Apostle himself gives of his
second visit to Jerusalem in Gal. 2[1]. A fuller discussion
of the question who is meant by " Aretas' ethnarch " will
be found below (see note at the end of this section). Here
it must suffice to say that the Romans probably had
Damascus under their own direct administration ; but
that they allowed the Arabs in the city a certain measure
of autonomy, and that these were represented by an
Ethnarch, similar to the Ethnarch who was head of the
Jews in Alexandria.

We might ask why the Jews did not themselves arrest
St. Paul and send him bound up to the High Priest, if they
had power over all religious offences within their community.
But in the uncertainty as to the date the question is un-
answerable. If Aretas held the city, he may well have
prohibited such action without his consent : if it was in
the hands of the Romans, St. Paul might be expected to
claim his position as a Roman citizen, which would exempt
him from all Jewish jurisdiction.

It must never be forgotten, in reading the Acts, that
St. Luke is not writing a life of St. Paul, but is tracing
the development of the gospel from Jerusalem to Rome ;
though it is true that he does record more personal details
about the Apostle in the scenes at which he was actually
present himself.

### NOTE ON "THE ETHNARCH OF ARETAS."

St. Paul's language in 2 Cor. 11[32] is accepted by a large majority of historians and theologians as proving that the king of the Nabatæan Arabs was in full possession of Damascus two years after the Apostle's conversion. The evidence from the coinage is given above ; but it is merely negative : even if the Romans administered Damascus continuously from A.D. 33 to 62, there would be nothing extraordinary in the disappearance of all coins of the period.

It is usually assumed that "Ethnarch" means Viceroy ; but the word itself does not necessarily imply that. It denotes the "ruler of a nation or $ἔθνος$ living with separate laws and customs amongst those of a different race" (Headlam in Hast. *D.B.*). In Alexandria, where the Jews, as in all Seleucid cities, had a very large measure of autonomy, their chief official was known as "Ethnarch" or "Alabarch" (=Arabarch). Josephus, *Antiq.* xiv. 7. 2, quotes from the geographer Strabo these words : (At Alexandria) "there is also an Ethnarch allowed them, who governs the nation and distributes justice to them, and takes care of their contracts and of the laws to them belonging as if he were the ruler of a free republic" (Whiston's translation). For evidence that this official was sometimes called "Alabarch," see Josephus, *Antiq.* xviii. 6. 3 : this name means "head of the Arabs" in a certain locality in Egypt : as such it is used sneeringly by Juvenal, i. 130 : in an inscription from the Thebaid in South Egypt (*C.I.G.* 4751) it occurs as the title of an officer there (see Pauly-Wissowa, under "Arabarches").

The word may be illustrated by similar terms current at the time. In the Near East, as early as the days of Strabo, the diet of a Roman Province ($τὸ\ κοινόν$) was wont to elect a President, who acted as their representa-

tive with the Roman government: in Asia he was an
" Asiarch," in Lycia a " Lyciarch," and in Achæa a
" Helladarch " (see Mommsen, *Prov. of the R. Emp.* i. 347,
n. 1).

The kingdom of the Nabatæan Arabs was taken over
by the Romans in the reign of Trajan. It still maintained
its tribal organisation, and the head of each tribe was *at the
beginning of the second century* known as an " Ethnarch,"
as is proved by Greek inscriptions found in the Hauran.[1]

Thus there are, as it seems to me, two possibilities about
the " Ethnarch of Aretas " in 2 Cor. 11[32].

(1) If the Romans were in full possession of Damascus
at the time, as seems more likely in the lack of evidence to
the contrary, Aretas must have been allowed by them to
nominate an " Ethnarch " or Governor-General of the
Arabs in the city. This is approximately the view of
Ramsay, who compares the " Ethnarch " to a modern
Consul.

(2) Damascus *may never have been taken* from the
Nabatæan kings before the end of the first century A.D.
This is Mommsen's view (*op. cit.* II. 148, n. 4). He says:
" From the fact that the city struck coins with the heads of
the Roman Emperors, there follows doubtless its dependence on Rome and therewith its self-administration, but
not its non-dependence on the Roman vassal prince:
such protectorates assumed shapes so various that these
arrangements might well be compatible with each other."
He appeals also to the fact, recently established by an
inscription found there, that the district of Dmer, north-
east of Damascus on the road to Palmyra, was still under
the Nabatæan kings in A.D. 99. But this last fact proves

---

[1] See Schürer, *Studien und Kritiken*, 99. 1. But the writer of the
article " Ethnarch " in the *Encyclopædia Biblica* has no right to quote
this as proof that the tribal heads were called Ethnarchs *in Aretas'
dominions.* See Mommsen, *op. cit.* II. 154.

nothing about Damascus : the territories in Syria, under Roman rule, dovetailed into each other in extraordinary fashion, as Josephus proves. We can imagine how much puzzled a historian might be in A.D. 4000 by ascertaining that the north end of Lake Windermere had been in Lancashire !

As against Mommsen, we have further to remember that there are extant a large number of coins of Aretas IV., which apparently came from a mint at Petra ; and they all bear his bust, not that of the Roman Emperor (see G. F. Hill, *Catalogue of the Greek Coins of Arabia, Mesopotamia, and Persia in the British Museum*, pp. 5–10, xviii. and xxxvii.).

2. THE FIRST VISIT TO JERUSALEM (Acts 9²⁶⁻³⁰, Gal. 1¹⁸⁻²⁴).—" Then after three years," writes St. Paul, " I went up to Jerusalem." But we have to remember, in dealing with Biblical reckonings of time, that it is necessary to subtract one from the number given to get the modern equivalent. Our Lord was crucified on a Friday, and buried the same night : He rose again in the early dawn of Sunday. In the New Testament this is not only said to have happened " on the *third* day " where we should call it the second, but He was " three days " in the tomb (Friday, Saturday, Sunday). In some cases we need not make the deduction ; thus when St. Luke says (Acts 28³⁰), " he abode *two full* years in prison," it obviously has its modern meaning ; and there are probably other cases where the word " full " is not expressed but the meaning is the same.[1]

---

[1] Biblical reckoning is complicated by the fact that we cannot say with any certainty what reckoning of the new year St. Luke adopted, *i.e.* whether in March or in the autumn. It is noteworthy that Luke, though a Greek, apparently follows the Semitic method of counting numbers.

However, we shall not be far out if we suppose the Conversion to have happened in A.D. 32 (*i.e.* thirty-five years before his martyrdom, which was probably between 66 and the spring of 68) ; and the return to Jerusalem in the end of 34. In many ways it must have been a painful visit to him, with all his old friendships wrecked. Indeed he was incurring greater danger by going than he ever met at Damascus ; but he never recked of personal peril when he had Christ's cause in view. He did not go with any thought of remaining, for he had been told by Christ that his work was to be among Gentiles ; but he went to see and to question (ἱστορῆσαι) St. Peter, with whom he was not yet acquainted, and he stayed a fortnight (" fifteen days ") with him. He must have longed to hear reminiscences of what Jesus did and said on earth, of which he himself knew so little : he may have also discussed with the older Apostle his future sphere of work, but Gal. 1 reads as though he had already made up his mind that Christ meant him to go outside Palestine.

Except Peter, the only Apostle in Jerusalem was James the Lord's brother,[1] who was obviously resident there, and had become presiding Presbyter in the Church. The local Christians were naturally shy of their former persecutor ; but fortunately there was one who could personally vouch for Saul's stalwart work in Damascus and enable him to win their confidence. This was Barnabas, a Hellenist Jew from Cyprus and cousin to John Mark. They were of Levitic descent and people of some wealth.[2]

---

[1] Gal. 1¹⁹. He was not one of the Twelve Apostles, but bore the title in the larger sense in which it was given to an eye-witness of the Risen Christ. It is sometimes said that the Apostles had scattered from Jerusalem because of the persecution ; but, as Ramsay points out, that theory expressly contradicts Acts 8¹. They were away on missionary work.

[2] See Acts 4³⁶. The earliest Christian meetings at Jerusalem were in the house of Mark's mother, which must have been large enough to contain them.

He himself was a man of commanding appearance, if we may judge from Acts 14[11-12], and his nickname Barnabas (" Son of Consolation ") shows that he was kindly and sympathetic. It must have meant much to St. Paul at such a time to have him as sponsor. He spent part of his stay in approaching the Hellenist Jews who formed his old circle ; but their former trust had turned to bitter hatred and they began to scheme his death, probably by some legal accusation. The only thing the Church could do was to get him away at once and personally escort him as far as Cæsarea. He left the capital before he had the chance of visiting any of the other churches in Judæa, and remained unknown to them even by sight (Gal. 1[22]).

3. TARSUS AND ANTIOCH, ABOUT A.D. 35–47 (Acts 11[19-26]). —Paul decided that he would go back to his old home : so he took ship for Tarsus (9[30]), and there we lose sight of him for more than ten years. St. Luke does not record a single incident of all that time, chiefly because space forbade it.[1] The only glimpse we get is the Apostle's own statement in Gal. 1[21] : " Then I came into the regions of Syria and Cilicia." He was passing his apprenticeship for the future—preaching Christ in Tarsus, probably with occasional tours into the outlying towns and villages of Cilicia, and keeping himself all the while by his trade of tent-making. It is possible that some of the adventures to which he refers in 2 Cor. 11[23-27] befel him now, even as his vision of Christ mentioned lower down in the same passage (2 Cor. 12[1-4]) certainly falls within this period (" fourteen years ago," v.[2]). But on the whole, it is not likely that the broader-minded Jews of Tarsus were so bitterly resentful of his work as those in Damascus and

---

[1] We must remember that an ancient author was circumscribed by the necessity of getting his book into the length of a papyrus roll : see p. 401.

Jerusalem. We would fain know something of his relations with his own family, but nothing is recorded.

These years, however, were a time of great importance in
the history of Christianity. The gospel was spreading
far beyond the confines of Palestine. The persecution,
which began after Stephen's death, had scattered the
Christian community at Jerusalem far and wide ; and they
had founded churches in Phœnicia, Cyprus, and the Syrian
Antioch.

Antioch was now at the very summit of its glory, and
was known as the third city in the Roman Empire. It
had been founded little more than two hundred years
before, by the Greek dynasty of the Seleucids. Damascus
was the old Arabian capital of Syria, but was too far from
the sea to satisfy a Greek. So Seleucus Nicator had
built the town, which he called after his father Antiochus,
on the river Orontes, with a port called Seleucia 15 miles
away.[1] He gave equal citizenship to Syrians, Greeks,
and Jews, as was his way in all the cities he founded or
refounded. Partly as a result of this, there were more
Jews in Syria at this time than even in Egypt, where they
numbered 13 per cent. of the total population.[2]

The Romans made Antioch the capital of Syria ; there
was the Legate's Court, with a comparatively large circle
of Roman officials. The town was also the centre of a
vast trade, and it was famous for the learning and culture
of its inhabitants. But it was too far east to escape the
taint of Orientalism, the consecration of sexual immorality
by obscene rites of nature-worship.

So it is a landmark in the history of Christianity when

---

[1] C.H. (p. 111, n. 5) say that the journey up to Antioch by river is
41 miles; but Seleucia, which lay north of the mouth of the Orontes,
is described as 16½ miles distant by land.

[2] See Harnack, *Expansion of Christianity*, I. p. 7 (Eng. trans.). Philo,
*In Flacc.* vi. 8, gives the number of Jews in Egypt as about a million.

the Church was founded there ; and it is associated with
two new developments, of which the second is vital. It
was at Antioch that the followers of Jesus, hitherto called
Nazarenes, received the name which has come down in
history (Acts 11[26]). The word " Christian " has a Latin
termination ; it is formed after the analogy of terms like
" Pompeians," " Marians," which denoted the partisans
of Pompey and Marius in the Civil Wars. In the New
Testament it is never used by Christians of themselves, but
is always put in the mouths of opponents (Acts 26[28],
1 Pet. 4[16]). But this does not show that it was originally
a derisive nickname, as is sometimes supposed. It was
obviously coined by Gentiles, and the Church preferred
to keep for its own use its own glorious names οἱ ἅγιοι
(" the Saints "), that is, " God's consecrated men," and
οἱ ἀδελφοί (" the Brethren "). But Antioch is famous
in Christian story for a much greater development than
this. St. Luke, in recording the spread of the Gospel outside Palestine, says that they " spoke the word to none save
only to Jews. But there were some of them, men of
Cyprus and Cyrene [*i.e.* Christian Jews of the Dispersion],
who, when they were come to Antioch, spake unto *the
Greeks also* " (Acts 11[20] : see note 1 below). When the
news of this step came to Jerusalem, the Church there sent
down a delegate to report on it ; and their choice naturally
fell on Barnabas, partly because it was his fellow-Cypriots
that were responsible, and partly because of the respect
in which he was held (11[24]). He found the situation very
reassuring : not only were large numbers of Greeks being
converted, but the effect on their lives was such as to

[1] There can be no doubt that " Greeks " (῞Ελληνας), and not " Hellenists " (῾Ελληνιστάς) is the right reading. It is required by its
contrast with " Jews " (not " Hebrews ") : and there would have been
nothing new in preaching to Hellenists. ῾Ελληνιστάς, however, has the
authority of the manuscripts B and L.

make him certain that it was in accordance with God's will (" he saw the grace of God," v.$^{23}$). We must remember that all this happened after St. Peter's vision and the conversion of the centurion Cornelius (Acts 10), though the Church at Jerusalem was still hesitating.

To Barnabas the work at Antioch seemed of the greatest strategic importance : he not only resolved to stay there himself, but he looked round for some one else to come and help. His thoughts naturally turned to St. Paul, now a man of about forty-six years of age, who had been commissioned for work among the Gentiles and who was so specially well equipped for it by education. He went himself to Tarsus and fetched him (Acts 11$^{25}$). This happened one full year before the famine (*i.e.* about A.D. 45).

At this point we must stop to consider a question of importance, to which various answers have been given : when Luke says that the missionaries in Antioch preached to the Greeks, does he mean that they baptized heathen converts *without requiring of them circumcision*, or did they still insist on the Mosaic Law ? To my mind St. Luke's meaning is clear : from the first they did not regard Mosaic ordinances as binding on Gentiles. He has told us (in chap. 10) how Cornelius was baptized without circumcision. In Acts 15$^{23}$ the letter of the Church at Jerusalem is addressed to " the brethren *which are of the Gentiles* in Antioch and Syria and Cilicia," clearly uncircumcised Christians. *The inclusion of Cilicia here must refer to St. Paul's converts* won during his ten or eleven years at Tarsus. Neither they, nor those at Antioch, had been required to submit to circumcision. Again, St. Paul, in his speech to the mob at Jerusalem (Acts 22$^{17-21}$) says, " When I had returned to Jerusalem (after the Conversion), and while I prayed in the temple, I fell into a trance, and saw Him saying unto me, Make haste, and get thee quickly

out of Jerusalem ; because they will not receive of thee
testimony concerning Me. . . . Depart : for I will send
thee forth far hence unto the Gentiles." St. Luke at any
rate must have understood this to refer to the Apostle's
*first* visit to Jerusalem, and as an explanation why he did
not preach among his old circle there. Ramsay argues
that it cannot be dated at the time of the first visit, because
it was not followed by work among the heathen ;[1] but
to my mind this passage strongly confirms the view that
he did go to Tarsus to preach to Gentiles. We may add
another fact which supports the same conclusion, namely,
the large number of Gentile converts made at Antioch. For
in cities where there was a Jewish colony, there was usually
a large fringe of heathen round the synagogue ; they were
deeply attracted by the lofty monotheism which was taught
there, but not at all disposed to submit to the Mosaic
ritual which was binding on proselytes.[2] It was from this
fringe that St. Paul afterwards made the greater number
of his converts, as we shall see below ; and it was from
these people undoubtedly that the Church at Antioch
was chiefly recruited now. It is noteworthy that Tarsus
and Antioch were both towns which admitted Jews to full
franchise ; and this seems to have promoted in them a
far more tolerant and sympathetic attitude towards
foreign religions than prevailed elsewhere. The same
broad attitude is found in the Jews of Alexandria, which
also gave them citizenship. Therefore the action of the
Christians in admitting Gentile converts without circumcision did not arouse any fierce opposition : the trouble
came later, when the fact was realised in Palestine.

[1] *T. and R.C.*, pp. 60–4.

[2] Seneca, as quoted in Augustine's *City of God*, vi. 11, complains that
"the usage of the accursed race . . . is now received throughout all
lands " ; and Josephus, in his *Jewish War*, ii. 20. 2, boasts that the
women of Damascus were nearly all "attached to the Jewish
worshippers."

4. THE FAMINE : SECOND VISIT TO JERUSALEM (Acts
11²⁷⁻³⁰ 12²⁵).—The reign of the Emperor Claudius (A.D.
41–54) was marked by several famines due to the failure
of the corn crops in the Mediterranean world.[1]  So when
a Christian prophet named Agabus came from Jerusalem
to Antioch and foretold " a great famine over all the
world," the local Church made provision for it.  But it
did not need Agabus' assurance to know how severely
the scarcity would be felt by the Christians in Jerusalem,
who were very poor in financial resources ; and when the
crops failed in the ensuing summer, the Antiochenes
determined to send food to relieve their brethren in Judæa.

The exact date of this famine is uncertain.  Josephus
refers to it several times [2] : he tells how Helena, queen of
Adiabene, a recent convert to Judaism, went up to Jerusalem
to worship ; she found the suffering in the Holy City so severe
that she was moved to buy corn from Egypt and figs from
Cyprus to distribute among the sufferers.  This shows that
in Palestine the scarcity was far worse than in Northern
Syria or the Levant generally.  Josephus seems to imply
that this was in the fourth year of Claudius, i.e. A.D. 45 ;
but elsewhere he puts it in the procuratorship of Tiberius
Alexander, i.e. 46–48.  St. Paul in Gal. 2¹ puts his
second visit to Jerusalem " fourteen," that is, thirteen,
years after his first ; this suggests the spring of A.D. 47,[3]
after the failure of the harvest in 46.

Be that as it may, the Church at Antioch sent their

---

[1] See Suetonius, *Claudius*, 18.  Tacitus, *Annals*, 12. 43.

[2] *Antiq.* iii. 15. 3 ; xx. 2. 5, and 5. 2.  Josephus' language suggests
that the famine extended over two or three years.

[3] That is, assuming what is argued below : (a) that Gal. 2¹ means
fourteen years after the first visit, rather than after the Conversion ;
(b) that the visit to Jerusalem mentioned there is his second visit, when
he carried the famine relief, and not his third visit for the Council of
Jerusalem.  On the date, see further, D.S., p. 646, and Turner in Hast.
*D.B.*, art. " New Testament Chronology."

relief in kind by the hands of Barnabas and Saul, who handed it over to the presbyters at Jerusalem (v.[30]). Lightfoot thought that the mention of the presbyters implied the absence of the Apostles : but it does not follow, for the board of presbyters were the executive body in any case. St. James was probably in Jerusalem (see 12[17]).

5. IDENTITY OF THIS VISIT TO JERUSALEM WITH THAT RECORDED IN GAL. 2[1-10].—In the opening section of his letter to the Galatians, St. Paul is trying to show that his apostleship was derived straight from Christ Himself, and not from the older Apostles nor the Church at Jerusalem. He had never been near Jerusalem, he says, till " three " years after his Conversion, and then only for a fortnight ; and it was " fourteen " years more before he went there again.

It certainly seems, at first sight, as if he were recounting *all* his visits to the city up till the time of writing, or at least up till the time when a concordat was reached on the question of admitting Gentile converts without circumcision. It would surely have been fatal to his whole purpose if he had omitted any visit at all. If on his second journey to Jerusalem at the time of the famine, the older Apostles had all been absent, would he not certainly have written, " I went up, but I did not see any of the Apostles " ? To omit all mention of a visit would have been to place himself in a very equivocal position.

Yet Lightfoot and others suppose that in Galatians he leaves out the famine visit altogether, because the Apostles were absent ; and that Gal. 2 refers to the time of the Council of Jerusalem (Acts 15) which ultimately settled the question of circumcision.

It is therefore necessary to examine the account given in Gal. 2[1-10] carefully. St. Paul says there (1) that he and Barnabas went up " in pursuance of a revelation " ;

(2) that he laid before the older Apostles "the gospel which I preach," in a *private* conference ; (3) that he resisted the urgent demands of some Jewish Christians for the circumcision of Titus ; (4) that Peter, James, and John agreed with his own attitude towards Gentile converts ; but the older Apostles were going to preach mainly to Jews, and therefore would go on observing the Mosaic Law ; (5) that they begged him to remember how poor the Christians of Jerusalem were, and to collect funds for their aid from the wealthier Gentiles.

Now, there is not a word in this which is out of harmony with the circumstances of the famine-relief visit. Indeed his statement in Gal. 2 that he and Barnabas went up " in pursuance of a revelation " strongly suggests Agabus' prophecy mentioned in Acts 11[28]. If we identify the two visits, it is clear that Paul and Barnabas had a second object in making the long journey to Jerusalem ; besides conveying the famine-relief, they wished to hold a private conference with the older Apostles and come to an explicit understanding on the admission of Gentiles without circumcision ("the gospel which I preach, lest I should run or have run, in vain "). Their thoughts were already turning to an extended missionary tour along the coast of Asia Minor : it was vital that they should get a clear agreement with the leaders at Jerusalem on the course which they had already followed and meant to follow in the future. This explains what otherwise is surely something of a puzzle, why the Church at Antioch should have parted with its two most effective missionaries merely in order to convey the relief to Jerusalem.

It must be noticed (see point 2 above) that the conference of Paul and Barnabas with James, Peter, and John was entirely private : whereas the Council of Jerusalem was a public assembly of the whole local Church to settle the Judaistic question. Of course it is possible that the Council was immediately preceded by a private discussion. But if its decrees had been published when St. Paul wrote " Galatians," it is hard to understand why he does not quote them in the Epistle : it would make his position far stronger to quote the public utterance of the Apostles at the Council and the formal decision which followed, than merely to appeal to a private agreement with the three leaders. Finally, in Gal. $2^{11}$ we learn that Peter at Antioch vacillated about the Judaistic question and led Barnabas to do the same. This is intelligible after a private conference at Jerusalem : it is almost impossible after the Council, where St. Peter had committed himself in a public speech, and after the first missionary journey, where Barnabas had taken up a final attitude towards the question of circumcision.

The reason for this vacillation is often forgotten : for it had an intelligible reason and was not sheer weakness. At the private discussion the position reached was this : the Apostles would observe the Mosaic Law strictly when they were in a community of Jews, as St. Paul himself did afterwards (cp. 1 Cor. $9^{20}$) ; but would not observe it among Gentiles (this is implied in Gal. $2^{7-10}$). Peter was at Antioch, shortly before the first missionary journey of Barnabas and Paul, as we suppose, and shared in the Agape or Love-Feast with uncircumcised Christians ; then came certain narrow Jewish-Christians who were shocked at his neglect of the Law, and he fell in with their scruples, on the principle of not offending them.[1] Paul points out to Peter (Gal. $2^{14-21}$) that, according to their common conviction, salvation came only through faith in Christ, and therefore that the Mosaic rites were matters of indifference one way or the other : they both

[1] We might compare the position of an Anglican clergyman in some foreign town who takes the Holy Communion with Dissenters until some more rigid Anglicans arrive, who are shocked at his action.

kept the Law at Jerusalem to show that they did not wish to disown their nationality : to do so was not in any way to prevaricate about their principles ; it was a concession to sentiment and to old associations. But to insist on Jewish practices at Antioch, where Gentiles predominated, would be false to the root principle of salvation by faith. Thus the whole position implied in Gal. 2¹¹ is that a private agreement had been reached.

6. RÉSUMÉ OF THE JUDAISTIC QUESTION.—Judaism was becoming more and more a missionary religion,[1] but pagans always submitted to circumcision with extreme reluctance. A very large number of earnest Gentiles were repelled by the crudity and even immorality of much in Greek and Latin mythology ; and in their restless scepticism they found in the grand monotheism of the Jews a great revelation ; they were drawn to the synagogue in large numbers. But, side by side with the Jewish conception of God was the rather repulsive ritual of the Law and tradition. Full proselytes had to submit to immersion and circumcision, and even then they remained inferior to a born son of Abraham, at any rate in the first generation. After circumcision, they were forbidden to intermarry or hold free intercourse with their own people : thus they were cut off from family and race, only to be treated as inferiors in their new environment. It is no wonder that full proselytes were few even while a large number of Gentiles formed a fringe of the synagogue. The latter are called by St. Luke " God-fearers " (οἱ φοβούμενοι or σεβόμενοι τὸν Θεόν) :[2] in later ages than this, the Jews distinguished them as " proselytes of the

---

[1] See Harnack, *Expansion of Christianity*, I. pp. 11–12.

[2] Among these " God-fearers " women were especially prominent. See the quotation from Josephus given on p. 37, n. 2 ; and cp. Acts 13⁵⁰ (Pisidian Antioch), 17⁴ (Thessalonica), and 17¹² (Berœa).

gate " from the " proselytes of the sanctuary." Josephus
says (*Bell. Jud.* vii. 3. 3): " The Jews continued to attract
a large number of Greeks to their services, making them in a
sense part of themselves." It was naturally among these
" God-fearers " that St. Paul made the majority of his
converts : they were fruit ready to be plucked. And it
was equally natural that the Jews were infuriated when
the great missionary came and admitted them to full
Church membership on what the Jews regarded as easy
and immoral terms. They looked on the Apostle much
as a modern missionary, who was obstinately refusing to
baptize a heathen chief until he gave up polygamy, would
look on another who came along and incontinently
baptized the polygamist ! Thus the Judaistic question
centred round the terms on which heathen converts were
admitted.

We must now trace briefly the development of the
question in the Christian Church up to this time.

(*a*) Christ Himself told His Apostles to confine their
preaching to Jews in His own lifetime, because He adopted
an intensive rather than an extensive method. But even
the most strongly Judaistic of the Gospels, that according
to St. Matthew, represents His last words to His Apostles
on earth as an injunction to make disciples among all
nations and to baptize them ; there is no mention of
circumcision (see Mt. 28[19]). Some may reject this evidence
on the ground that it is coloured by the standpoint of the
second generation of Christians. Yet we cannot doubt
that it rightly interprets our Lord's mind. His own
attitude to such Samaritans, Greeks, and Latins as crossed
His path is alone enough to prove this. His central
teaching, that all the Law and the prophets is summed
up and superseded by the golden rule of love to God and
one's neighbour, places His attitude beyond question.

(*b*) Philip, Peter, and John had all preached in Samaria :

but probably they only admitted converts who were circumcised. Philip's eunuch was doubtless a proselyte.

(c) Stephen, however, had taken up a more definite
attitude to the Law : he regarded it as fulfilled in Christ
and superseded ; henceforth it was no longer essential.
And it is important to notice that his teaching was not
disowned by the older Apostles ; it created no sort of
crisis within the Church at Jerusalem, though it might have
done so if he had proceeded to give up the practice of the
Mosaic ritual himself.

(d) St. Peter's attitude towards Cornelius shows that
he and the other Apostles, however much in theory they
were in agreement with Stephen, were not ready to put
it into practice. But his vision led him to baptize the
centurion and thus forced his hands. Some commentators
(e.g. Dr. Lake) think that the Apostles regarded the case
of Cornelius as an example of God's "uncovenanted grace,"
and therefore as unique, not to be taken as a precedent.
Fortunately, this theory is definitely refuted by Peter's
speech at the Council of Jerusalem (Acts 15⁷⁻⁹), where he
clearly stated that the incident of Cornelius had revealed
to him, and through him to the Church, that God only
required faith in Christ from Gentile converts. Once
more we must insist that Peter's vacillation at Antioch
(Gal. 2¹¹) was not a repudiation of this teaching, but was
due to his hesitation about the right course when in the
presence of rigid Jewish Christians.

(e) Paul had admitted Gentiles without circumcision both
at Tarsus and Antioch. At first there was no opposition ;
but by degrees, as the Palestinian Christians learned of it,
the narrower and more conservative among them became
sorely troubled. By A.D. 46 the question was becoming
acute at Antioch, and that at a time when Paul and
Barnabas were contemplating an extensive missionary
tour through Gentile cities. It was imperative that they

should come to some clear understanding with the older Apostles. So when some one was needed to go up to Jerusalem with the food which the Antiochenes wished to send, they saw in it a chance of achieving their object without too much publicity. They resolved to take with them one of their Greek converts, and their choice fell on Titus.[1]

At Jerusalem strong pressure was exerted on Paul to enforce Titus' circumcision ; but he felt that a vital principle was at stake and steadily refused. He speaks as if he had felt half inclined to yield what was asked as a favour, but was prevented by the knowledge that a secret mission had been sent to Antioch from Jerusalem to " spy out their freedom " and so make trouble (Gal. $2^{3-5}$). In face of this, he could not consent to what was asked, as it would be compromising on a point of principle. But his private conference with James, Peter, and John was entirely satisfactory ; they agreed with him absolutely about the terms on which he admitted Gentile converts. Once sure of his ground with them, Paul went on with his plan for a missionary tour over new territory. It only remained for Barnabas and him to return to Antioch and report : then they would be free to start.

---

[1] We know very little about Titus' early history because, strangely enough, St. Luke never mentions him. Ramsay suggests that this silence is deliberate, because he was a close relation of the historian. This is not improbable, for Luke himself came of a Greek family connected with Antioch.

# CHAPTER IV.

## THE FIRST MISSIONARY JOURNEY
### (ACTS 13–14).

1. THE PREPARATION.—It is strange how God guides His Church. In every age she seems fearfully to look backwards ; but the Divine hand draws her on : else she had ceased to exist long ago. So, from one point of view, she seems to have stumbled into her world-wide mission ; and having stumbled, to have found the man uniquely fitted to fulfil her destiny.

When Barnabas and Saul got back to Antioch, they laid their plan for a foreign missionary tour before the Church there ; for it was to Antioch, rather than to Jerusalem, that they belonged. The governing body was apparently not modelled after the Jewish system into a board of presbyters ; the leaders were " prophets and teachers " (13[1]), men whose religious gifts brought them to the front rather than men of age and experience. But though they were essentially a " charismatic " ministry, this does not mean that there was any lack of organisation ; for when they recognised that it was God's will that they should give up their two leaders for the work, they consecrated them for it by the symbolic " laying on of hands." This act had come into usage, on the one hand, as an appeal for the bestowal of God's special gifts for the work ahead, on the other as a sign of the Church's authorisation.[1]

---

[1] Lightfoot (*Galatians*, p. 96) regards this ceremony as their consecration to be Apostles. Ramsay, however (*T. and R.C.*, p. 67), justly points

The two missionaries had brought with them from Jerusalem Barnabas' cousin, John Mark. His mother, Mary, was a leading Christian at Jerusalem (cp. Acts 12¹²⁻¹⁷, where we find the Christian community assembled at her house). Her son seems to have known our Lord personally and followed Him after His arrest (see Mark 14⁵¹⁻⁵², where the "young man" is probably St. Mark himself). If so, he would be about thirty-five years of age now, or rather more than ten years younger than St. Paul. Barnabas and Saul took him as their assistant (ὑπηρέτης, 13⁵), probably to act as amanuensis, to baptize converts, and to help generally.

2. CYPRUS. — Apparently they planned to visit the great trading cities on the coast of Asia Minor (see note 1 below), and particularly on the west. They do not seem to have contemplated a journey into the interior : that development, as we shall see, was probably the result of an illness of St. Paul. The island of Cyprus, from which Barnabas came and where there was already a Christian Church, lay practically on their way. It was only 70 miles' sail from Seleucia, the port of Antioch, to the west-south-west.

They landed on the east coast, where the town of Salamis lies in the middle of a vast bay or indentation, and preached only in the Jewish synagogues, in accordance

out that this statement is inconsistent with Gal. 1, where St. Paul emphatically insists that he derived his apostleship from Christ and not from any human authority (see 1¹).

In Acts 13³ the Codex Bezæ inserts " all " (πάντες) as the subject to "laid hands upon." This has no claim to be original, but it is interesting as a second-century interpretation.

¹ Asia Minor is a modern term, and is used for the sake of convenience in this book. But the reader should notice that where we use the word "Asia" alone, we intend it in its *ancient* sense, *i.e.* to designate the Roman province which occupied the western part (about one-third) of Asia Minor.

with their determination to approach the Jews first.
For among those of the Dispersion there was always hope
that they might receive a welcome. From Salamis they
made a missionary tour of "the whole island" (v.[6]), a
phrase which probably means the south coast, where
nearly all the towns lay, south of the mountain ridge of
Olympus. Presently they came to the capital, Paphos,
on the south-west coast. It was the seat of the
Roman Governor ; the centre also, as Athanasius tells
us, of the " deification of lust "—that is to say, of the
Phœnician worship of Ashtarte under the Greek name of
Aphrodite.

Now Augustus had divided the provinces into two
classes. The more peaceable districts, where no troops
were needed to preserve order, were handed over to the
Senate to administer ; and were ruled by a *Proconsul*
($\dot{a}\nu\theta\dot{\upsilon}\pi\alpha\tau\sigma\varsigma$, cp. Achæa, Acts 18[12], and Ephesus, Acts 19[38]),
who had lictors with the " fasces " or rods for scourging,
but no military power ; they held rule for one year only,
coming into office in July. The more difficult provinces,
however, were retained by the Emperor under his own
direct administration ; for he wished to hold in his hands
the reins of all the imperial military power. These were
ruled by a *Proprætor* ($\dot{a}\nu\tau\iota\sigma\tau\rho\dot{a}\tau\eta\gamma\sigma\varsigma$), who was more
often called *Legatus*, while under him each district was
administered by a *Procurator* ($\dot{\epsilon}\pi\dot{\iota}\tau\rho\sigma\pi\sigma\varsigma$) : thus Syria had
its Legate (Luke 2[2]), and Judæa its Procurator, who is
designated in the New Testament by the general term
$\dot{\eta}\gamma\epsilon\mu\dot{\omega}\nu$.

St. Luke's accuracy in the designation of officials is
remarkable. Cyprus was only handed over to the Senate
in A.D. 22 ; but the historian correctly calls its governor
in A.D. 47 by the name of Proconsul. The present officer
was named Sergius Paulus—perhaps the same man whom
Pliny quotes as one of his authorities for his *Natural*

*History,* which includes notes on Cyprus.[1]   St. Luke (13⁷)
calls him a " shrewd " man (συνετός), one who had practical
ability.

Science in those days, as indeed for fifteen hundred
years afterwards, was a strange mixture of real knowledge
and the wildest credulity ;  and it opened the door to all
sorts of quacks who preyed on the superstitions of men,
as to some extent it still does !   The astrologers or magi
were sometimes honest in their convictions, sometimes mere
rogues, often a mixture of both.   They claimed to foretell
the future by their horoscopes.   Sergius Paulus had an
astrologer, who was a Jew named Bar-Jesus (son of Jesus),
and whose second name " Elymas " probably means " the
wise man " (see v.⁸), being connected with a root found in
Arabic.   The Proconsul invited Barnabas and Paul to give
a lecture in his presence, regarding them as travelling
sophists or professors of philosophy :  and he was obviously
interested in what they had to say.   The astrologer, however, grew uneasy ;  perhaps he felt that such teaching
might shake his ascendancy over the Proconsul, perhaps he
was merely jealous :  at any rate, he argued hotly against
them.   St. Paul read the man's mind, and fixing an intense
look on him, he said :  " You son of the devil, you enemy
of all righteousness, full of all manner of cunning and
rascality, will you not cease . . . ? " and he told him he
should lose his sight for a time.   He was struck blind at
once ;  and the Proconsul, already " deeply impressed by
the teaching of the Lord " (v.¹²), forthwith hesitated no
longer and professed conversion.

It was the missionaries' first contact with a Roman
official in predominantly heathen society, the first indication that opposition would come not so much from the
ruling power as from adversaries whose material interests

[1] See ii. 90, 97, 112 ;  xviii. 12, 57 (I borrow these references from
D.S., p. 84).

were threatened : so Luke records the scene in detail. Any one who feels doubt about the historical truth of it should remember that St. Paul unquestionably believed himself to have the power of producing bodily disability in others (see 1 Cor. 5⁵). Whether he was right ever to use such a power is a different question ; but that he once or twice did so, seems indubitable. We are told that witch-doctors in African villages possess similar powers, which depend for their working on the belief of their victims.

St. Luke at this point writes " Saul, who is also Paul," and henceforward discards the Hebrew name. Some have inferred that the Apostle took the name of the Proconsul ; but that is highly unlikely. Probably he had always been " Paul " in Gentile society, but Luke had heard him called " Saul " at Antioch. The change of name is due to the historian's personal reminiscences (see further p. 5 above). But we must note another significant change in Luke's narrative at this point : till now he has spoken of " Barnabas and Saul " ; after this, the order is inverted and we have " Paul and Barnabas," except at the Council of Jerusalem, where he keeps the old order (15¹². ²⁵, though contrast v.²²). This again reflects personal reminiscence : the changed order marks the time when the great Apostle took the lead.

3. PERGA.—From Cyprus they sailed in a north-westerly direction to the mainland of Asia Minor. About the middle of the south coast is the large Gulf of Attalia. In Western Cilicia, the haunt of pirates then and often since, a ridge of the Taurus Mountains runs down into the sea. West of it again is the Gulf, where the mountains recede inland and leave the plain that was called Pamphylia. Perga was its capital, standing some miles inland from the port of Attalia ; and here our missionaries left

the sea and struck up inland. Here too John Mark deserted them and went back, we are not told why.

Clearly Paul and Barnabas had formed some plan for their tour. If they originally meant to go to Lycaonia, they would naturally have gone overland through Cilicia. Their voyage to Cyprus and Attalia strongly suggests that their original intention was to go on coasting vessels round to the great ports on the west of Asia Minor, such as Ephesus. Yet as soon as they reach the mainland, we find them making inland across Pamphylia and over rough mountain paths for a long distance, to the plateau of Lycaonia. How can we explain this apparent change of plan ?

Now malaria, that neglected factor in history, is the scourge of the coast of Asia Minor : and Ramsay suggests that at least one of them, St. Paul, succumbed to a bad attack, and decided to go up into the healthier climate of the hinterland plateau.[1] That he was suffering from some illness seems highly probable ; and the conjecture is strongly confirmed by a passage in Galatians (assuming that this Epistle was written to the Christians of Lycaonia and Pisidian Antioch) : for he writes in Gal. 4[13], " Ye know that *because of an infirmity of the flesh* I preached the gospel unto you on my former visit," and he goes on to remind them of their affectionate care of him ; " ye despised not that which was a temptation to you in my flesh " (*i.e.* the repulsive nature of his illness), " nor did ye spit out." But at this point we must remind the reader of what was said above (p. 9), that men used to spit, when they saw an epileptic in a fit, to avert the evil from themselves. Therefore, though Ramsay is possibly right in suggesting malaria,[2] the evidence on the

[1] See Ramsay, *Historical Commentary on Galatians*, pp. 422 ff.
[2] We may add that malaria does not make its victim repulsive to the onlooker, as epilepsy does : therefore Ramsay's suggestion does not explain St. Paul's strong language in Gal. 4[14].

whole points to epilepsy, from which St. Paul probably suffered at intervals all his life. Something, we may suppose, had brought on a succession of fits at this time ; and the doctors may well have advised him to avoid the excitement of crowded cities for a time.

Be that as it may, John Mark's desertion [1] is to be attributed to the change of route. Perhaps it involved a longer period away from home than he was prepared to face ; or perhaps he was daunted by the rough and dangerous journey over mountains infested by robbers (cp. 2 Cor. 11[26]).[2]

We do not know whether Paul and Barnabas stopped in Perga (see Acts 13[13]). It may be that Paul was too ill ; or else they met with no adventure there which Luke found room to record. They pushed on northwards over the mountains for 100 miles till they had crossed the whole district known as Pisidia.

4. PISIDIAN ANTIOCH (Acts 13[14-52]).—The town of Antioch lay, strictly speaking, outside the boundary of Pisidia. Ethnographically it belonged to the old Phrygian stock, politically to the Roman province of Galatia. It had been founded by one of the Greek Seleucid kings, and called Antioch after Antiochus, father of Seleucus I.[3] But in order to distinguish it from the other cities of the same name, it was known as ἡ πρὸς Πισιδίᾳ, i.e. " that on the Pisidian border." St. Luke in Acts 13[14] calls it " Antioch of Pisidia " ; but in 14[24] he correctly speaks of it as outside Pisidia.

---

[1] That it was a desertion is clear from Acts 15[38].

[2] It has often been pointed out how appropriate to this district is the mention of " perils of rivers and perils of robbers." See C.H., pp. 132–4, and illustrative inscriptions in Ramsay, *The Church in the Roman Empire*, pp. 23–4.

[3] We know of five Antiochs in Syria founded by the Seleucids, and one in Asia.

It lay 3500 feet above sea-level, surrounded by mountain ridges and large lakes; and an important trade route passed through it, though it lay a short distance to the south of the great artery of Asia Minor, the road which ran from Ephesus to the Far East. Originally the Seleucids had conferred full citizenship on all the chief races who settled there, including the Jews (as at Tarsus, and Syrian Antioch); but in 25 B.C., when the Romans formed the province of Galatia, they made it into a Roman "colony"—that is to say, a miniature of the Imperial City. A "colony" was primarily a military post on some frontier or in a disaffected district. Most of the "coloni" were veteran soldiers, who were pensioned off in this way. They were made the ruling caste in the town [1] and were entirely free from the jurisdiction of the provincial governor; they elected their own magistrates, whose proper designation was "duumviri," though they loved the courtesy title of "Prætors" (cp. Acts 16[20. 22. 35]). Such was the constitution of Pisidian Antioch, and again of Philippi and Corinth. But the population of Antioch was predominantly Phrygian, and followed the old orgiastic religious cults of their race. They worshipped the moon-god Mên as supreme; but their chief attachment was to an old goddess of the Artemis-Cybele class—that is to say, she bore the Greek name of Artemis the Virgin-goddess, but had the attributes of Cybele, who was anything but a virgin. For the foul obscenities which have always been the cancer of Oriental cults prevailed here. As Ramsay puts it,[2] this worship was the antithesis of Hellenism, because it held that social life based on marriage was an outrage on freedom. Thus there was a veneer of Greek culture, but it was thin; while

[1] The citizenship was originally confined to the colonists, but it was gradually extended to influential pro-Roman natives.

[2] T. and R.C., p. 138.

the aristocratic minority of Romans held themselves apart. St. Luke has the local atmosphere when he distinguishes the "plebs" of v.[45] from the citizen caste of v.[50].

On the first Sabbath day after their arrival in the city, Paul and Barnabas attended the synagogue, and the scene is full of interest. When the two Lessons had been read (from the Law and the Prophets respectively), the rulers of the synagogue sent a message to them, inviting them to address the assembly; for this was often done to strangers of some education. The Jewish preacher sat while he spoke; but Paul, standing up in the Greek manner, and with a characteristic wave of his hand, began an address. Luke, although he had probably already met the Apostle in Syrian Antioch, was not with him on this first tour; so the sermon, which is here recorded, cannot be transcribed from the historian's shorthand notes. But he had often heard St. Paul give an opening address in a synagogue, and he knew quite well the general line which he took in such cases; and so in all probability he sketches it in here. It is not meant to be more than an outline, as is clear, for instance, from the abrupt introduction of a new topic in vv.[38]-[39] without further explanation.

The Apostle addresses his congregation as " Jews and God-fearers " (vv.[16, 26]) : he reminds them of the great succession of leaders whom God had given to Israel; David was their culmination, and God promised spiritual salvation through one of his descendants. Jesus of Nazareth was this Saviour; men crucified Him, but He rose again, as indeed David had foretold[1] in Pss. 2[7] and 16[10]. The position then was this, that through the Christ forgiveness of sins or "justification" (a favourite

---

[1] Such prophecies would satisfy that uncritical age, though they would convince few in our times.

word with St. Paul) was offered to men, releasing them from the sins "from which ye could not be justified by the Law of Moses." He does not expressly draw the inference that the Law is abrogated; he merely says that they have now something much more complete.

The Jews do not seem to have been thrown into violent antagonism by this address : indeed, he was invited to tell them more in the synagogue on the "next Sabbath" (for this is clearly the sense of μεταξύ in v.⁴²) [1] : and not a few Jews and "devout proselytes" (which probably denotes "God-fearers") followed him out of the building for further discussion.

On the next Saturday the synagogue was crowded with Gentiles, and the Jewish leaders were furiously jealous. They contradicted him so savagely that he decided, now for the first time, to give up going to the synagogue and to gather the Gentiles elsewhere. This procedure did not placate the Jews, who saw their "God-fearers" flocking after him more and more ; they worked on certain leading ladies, who no doubt attended the synagogue, and were drawn from the citizen caste, to approach their husbands and induce them to expel the Christian missionaries from the city. It is not unlikely that Paul and Barnabas were first scourged by the lictors (so Ramsay) ; for in 2 Cor. 11²⁵ we read, "thrice was I scourged with the lictors' rods" : this punishment was only possible in a Roman "colony," and when he wrote these words St. Paul had, as far as we know, only preached in three colonies—Pisidian Antioch, Lystra, and Philippi (though he had passed through Troas).

---

[1] Josephus uses μεταξύ to mean "succeeding" ; cf. *de Bell. Jud.* v. 4. 2, "David and Solomon as well as the kings μεταξὺ τούτων," where it cannot mean "between them." The Codex Bezæ here substitutes ἑξῆς, to make the meaning clear.

## NOTE ON THE HISTORICITY OF THE SPEECHES
## RECORDED IN THE ACTS.

Thucydides was the greatest classical historian of ancient Greece ; and almost the most valuable portions of his work are the speeches which he records, because they give us a unique insight into the mentality of the great city-statesmen.  Yet it is universally agreed that he had before him, when he wrote, at most an outline record of what they said—in other words, the speeches as we have them are his own compositions.  It is obvious that the value of such a record depends mainly on the insight and intelligence of the historian.  Now in St. Luke, as in Thucydides, we have a writer of masterly ability.  It seems highly probable that in the early chapters of the Acts he pursued the same method as the great Athenian ; that is to say, he only had access to rough reminiscences of what was said on any occasion, and he composes the speeches himself.  For instance, he puts into the mouth of Gamaliel (Acts 5[36]) a glaring anachronism in the reference to Theudas, whose rebellion did not take place till some ten years after Gamaliel spoke (see Burkitt, *The Gospel History and its Transmission*, pp. 107–8).  But the case is quite different when we come on to St. Paul's life.  From the second missionary journey onwards he was himself with St. Paul most of the time, and he probably took shorthand notes ; for in his time there was more than one system of shorthand in vogue (see Milligan, *The New Testament Documents*, Appendix C., p. 241), and he was a highly educated man.  Where he was not himself present, as at Athens, he had St. Paul's own record of what happened and what was said.  That this is so, seems to me to be proved by the fact that the chapters in the Acts which deal with St. Paul's adventures in St. Luke's absence are marked by exactly the same accuracy of detail as those which record the writer's first-hand experience.

5. ICONIUM (Acts 14[1-7]).—The great central trade road of Asia Minor, starting from Ephesus, ran up the Mæander valley and thence due eastwards for many a league, passing a few miles north of Pisidian Antioch. Farther on, where it crossed the plateau of Lycaonia, a branch road ran southwards to Iconium and beyond. But the traveller going from Antioch to Iconium had the chance of a short cut, for the Romans had built a military road south-eastwards across the mountains to Lystra, some 60 miles away, and on to Derbe, which lay on the south-east extremity of the Lycaonian plateau, near a mountain region infested by lawless highland clans. In all probability this was the route by which the two missionaries now left Antioch : before reaching Lystra they would take a track to the left which led straight over to Iconium.[1]

The plateau of South Lycaonia was bounded on the west by a well-watered mountain ridge, on the lower slopes of which stood Iconium and Lystra : away to the south the great heights of the Taurus towered up.

All Lycaonia was now part of the Roman Province of Galatia (Ramsay, *Cities*, pp. 334-5). Iconium was then, as it is now,[2] the most important city in the whole region. But though it was included in Lycaonia for administrative purposes, ethnographically it belonged to Phrygia on the west ; and its inhabitants were Phrygian in all their ways and probably clung to their national sentiments. Thus when St. Luke (14[6]) says that Paul and Barnabas fled from

---

[1] See Ramsay, *The Church in the Roman Empire*, pp. 28-36. The " Acts of Paul and Thecla," a third-century romance but based apparently on some early traditions, represents them as taking this route.

[2] From the eleventh to the fourteenth century it was the capital of the Seljuk Turks, and so played no small part in the growth of the Ottoman Empire.

Iconium " unto the cities of Lycaonia "—as if Iconium was outside the latter country—he is reflecting popular speech, not official status.[1]  The people cherished the old worship of all central Asia Minor, the nature-cult of the goddess-mother Cybele, with its obscene rites ; at Iconium they called her Athena, for they prided themselves on their Greek culture, and Luke calls them " Hellenes " (14[1]), a word he never uses of any other Galatians.

The town stands at a height of 3370 feet above sea-level, and receives a plentiful water-supply from the mountains on the west.  The country round is naturally rich and fertile, though Turkish misgovernment has now for so long devastated it.  Under the Roman Empire Lycaonia was shown much favour by the Government, for it stood as an outpost over against the turbulent mountaineers beyond.  So Iconium was strongly pro-Roman in its sympathies, and was allowed to retain its constitution as a Greek city with a popular assembly (cf. 14[4, 5]) and a Senate.

Paul and Barnabas met with much the same experiences here as at Antioch : but they stayed longer, probably for several months, and made a large number of converts, both Jewish and " Greek."  And all the while the Jewish community was trying in vain to find some means of stopping them ; for there was no bureaucracy here, as at Antioch.

Party spirit, however, runs high in the life of all free cities, and people must needs take sides over everything, even where there are no daily newspapers.  It is a witness to the success of the missionaries that their preaching became at last something of a public event in the life of the place ; but this gave the Jews their chance.  Accom-

---

[1] Ramsay (Church in Roman Empire, p. 39) quotes an inscription of Hierax, a Christian of Iconium, who calls Iconium " Phrygian " in A.D. 163.

panied by the " archons," which perhaps means members
of the Senate, they made a public demonstration against
the Christians ; the mob soon came to blows, and stones
were thrown. So the Apostles deemed it wise to with-
draw from the city for a time, meaning to return when
public feeling had died down and some new matter
absorbed the general interest.

6. LYSTRA (Acts 14[8-20]).—Lystra, where they went
next, lay off the main road up a side valley at a height
of 3750 feet. Though it had a plentiful water-supply
like Iconium, it was not commercially so important.
But as a military post it was of great moment ; therefore
it had been made a Roman " colony," like Pisidian Antioch.
Its population was not large ; it consisted merely of the
Roman " coloni " and the Anatolian population who
spoke the old Lycaonian language.

But it is of extraordinary interest, in view of the scene
depicted in the Acts, to realise that a famous Greek myth
was connected with this neighbourhood. It was said
that Zeus and Hermes once came down in disguise and
wandered about the country in the garb of artisans.
In vain they sought food and shelter from the rich and
fashionable, but at last they were welcomed in the humble
cottage of Philemon and Baucis.[1]

So it was that, when Paul cured the lame cripple in the
streets of Lystra, the people cried out that Zeus had come
again with Hermes, spokesman of the gods.[2] They were
simple folk and credulous ; and they spoke the old speech
of Lycaonia, so that their cries would be unintelligible to
the Apostles. The city boasted a Temple of Zeus, which
stood outside the walls, like the Temple of Artemis at

---

[1] See Ovid, *Metamorphoses*, viii. 611 ff.
[2] Compare the language of Gal. 4[14], where he is referring to this visit ;
" ye received me," he says, " as a messenger (angel) of God."

Ephesus.  The priest hurried off to fetch sacrificial bulls
crowned with garlands, to do honour to the gods who had
come down among them once more.  The solemn pro-
cession was entering the gateway [1] of the city, when the
Apostles saw and understood.  In dismay they rushed
forward to protest against the sacrifice to themselves,
crying out, " We too are men of like passions to yourselves."
Most of the people would understand Greek, which was
necessary for trade ; and St. Paul, as the crowd stood
round in confusion, went on to make them a speech.  St.
Luke gives a short outline of what he said, no doubt as
an example of the way in which the Apostle usually
approached a heathen audience untouched by Judaism ;
and it is of extraordinary interest to us.  It is on the
same lines, though of course it is much more simple, as
his address to the Areopagus at Athens (Acts 17[30] : cp.
also Rom. 3[25]).  He appeals to what his audience know
of God, and starts from that.  The wonderful world,
which He has made, bears witness to His might and
wisdom ; the " rain and fruitful seasons," to His great
love for us.  Men misconceived God in their blindness—
this was spoken to a people familiar with the obscene rites
of nature-worship—and God had " suffered " it for long

---

[1] τοὺς πυλῶνας, 14[13].  A πυλών is a gateway ; it denotes the entrance
of a private house in Matt. 26[71], Luke 16[20], Acts 10[17] and 12[13].  But
in all these passages it is used in the singular, and here we have the
plural.  In Apocalypse 21[12-15] it stands for the twelve gateways of the
New Jerusalem, and of course is in the plural.  The use of the plural
in our present passage points to a gatehouse, with an inner and an
outer gateway ; i.e. either the main gateway of the city (so Blass),
or that of the temple (so Ramsay).  But as the cure took place inside
the city (perhaps in a public square just inside the gate), it seems more
natural to suppose that the city gateway is meant.  Sometimes medical
missionaries among simple peoples to-day have to meet similar misunderstandings.  Their cures are attributed to the possession of a potent
magic ; and it is distressing when (for instance) a poor mother brings a
dead baby in her arms, entreating the doctor to bring it back to life,
and refusing to believe that he cannot.

to be so ; but at last He had given a supreme revelation of Himself, calling men to turn " from these vain things unto the living God."

For a time—one gets the impression that it was but a few weeks—they preached their gospel at Lystra unimpeded. Among those they won over (see 1 Tim. 1¹, 2 Tim. 3¹¹) was a family, consisting of grandmother, mother, and son. The first two were Jewesses, Loïs and Eunice (2 Tim. 1⁵), the latter of whom had married a Greek who was now dead (note the imperfect ὑπῆρχεν in Acts 16³). The son, Timothy, had never been circumcised, though he was probably brought up to the Jewish religion.[1]

But though there were few Jews in Lystra, the fierce enmity of those in Antioch and Iconium pursued the Apostles there. Psychological reaction produces curious results : the same people who had lately hailed the strangers as gods, were easily worked up to fury against them as impostors. One day the mob attacked them and stoned St. Paul till he was unconscious ; then they dragged his supposed corpse outside the city and hurled him down to rot there. It was a very narrow escape : but he was not seriously hurt, for he was able to start for Derbe next day.

7. DERBE AND BACK HOME (Acts 14²¹⁻²⁸).—Derbe was a small remote frontier town, 50 miles from Lystra, on the extreme south-east of the plateau. It was a mere military outpost : but it offered the missionaries a secure refuge till it was possible to retrace their steps to the three cities where they had suffered violence [2] ; and they

[1] We may fairly take the evidence of the Pastoral Epistles as to historical facts, even though they are probably not, in their present form, St. Paul's own compositions.

[2] In the new year, new magistrates would come into office in these cities (Ramsay, *Church in Roman Empire*, pp. 70-2). This offered the Apostles some opening.

made many converts in this out-of-the-world spot. Unless it was winter, they might have travelled home overland by the Cilician Gates ; but that would be to leave their Galatian converts unorganised and unhelped. The least exercise of imagination enables us to realise something of the dangers which they faced in going back as they had come : it was a decision of superb pluck.

As it turned out, they suffered no further ill-usage. In each town they cheered up the Christians to meet persecution bravely, and they organised the Church by appointing[1] elders, after the Jewish system. They preached in Pisidia and in Perga on the way back : St. Paul had probably been too ill to do so on the outward journey. From the port of Attalia they got a ship straight for Seleucia, from where a day's march would bring them to Antioch. The mother-Church[2] was cheered by hearing how " God had opened a door of faith unto the Gentiles " ; and Paul and Barnabas took a much-needed rest after all they had gone through. St. Luke merely says that they spent " no little time " there ; probably it was six or eight months, over the winter.

8. WHAT ACCOUNT OF CHRIST'S LIFE DID THEY GIVE THEIR CONVERTS ?—We may pause at this point to ask if we know anything more about the conditions in which they had left their Gentile converts to face the new Christian life. Each Church had, as we have seen, a

[1] St. Luke's word is χειροτονεῖν, which properly means " to elect by a show of hands " ; but sometimes it is used loosely for " appoint," cp. 10[41]. We have no means of deciding whether they nominated the elders themselves or left the choice to popular election.

[2] ἐκκλησία (" Church ") in v.[27] is used in its earlier sense, which denotes the Christian community in a certain place. The word implies that the members were a self-governing body like a Greek city. But St. Paul came more and more, as time went on, to use the word " Church " of the one body of believers everywhere : we find it so used as early as Gal. 1[13]. St. Luke in the Acts shows both usages.

governing board of elders. But had they no account of
what Jesus taught and did, as a guide to His principles
and a standard for gauging new situations ? St. Luke
does not tell us ; but a careful reading of St. Paul's
Epistles makes it clear that they had some information
(see 1 Thess. $4^{1.15}$, 1 Cor. $6^2$ $7^{10}$ $8^{12}$ $9^{14}$ $11^{23}$, Gal. $5^{14}$,
Rom. $13^{8-9}$, etc.). St. Paul appeals to the Corinthians
more than once to keep the Christian " traditions " which
he " handed over " to them (1 Cor. $11^2$). As for their
knowledge of the events of Jesus' life, probably Paul and
his companions simply related to them some outstanding
events, such as some of His miracles and, above all, the
story of His crucifixion and resurrection. For it is not
likely that, as yet, any historical account of Jesus' life
had been written or even drawn up : the Apostles told
of it, as far as we can judge, casually as need arose, rather
than systematically, particularly in the early days when
they expected the Second Coming to occur very soon.
St. Mark's Gospel is believed to be practically the life of
Christ as Peter preached it in his later years, when the
Apostles began to realise the need of a life-story.

On the other hand, the surpassing value to the world
of knowing exactly what Jesus *said* and *taught* became
apparent at an early date, as we see from St. Paul, though
he usually refers to, rather than quotes, our Lord's sayings.
He " handed on " the teaching of Jesus to His converts,
whether in written or oral form is impossible to determine.
So far as we know, the earliest written account of the
words of Jesus was that collected by Matthew the Apostle
in Aramaic, as Papias tells us ; and clearly this involved
the co-operation of the apostolic circle at Jerusalem.
Everything points to an early, rather than a late, date
for this ; and it is not improbable that this was what
St. Paul " handed on " to his converts.

# CHAPTER V.

## THE EPISTLE TO THE GALATIANS.

(See p. 51 above, and especially p. 39, § 5.)

1. WHO ARE MEANT BY "THE GALATIANS"?—Is the term used *ethnographically* of those who are Galatians by blood, or *politically* of those who live in the Roman province of Galatia?

(*a*) The country of Galatia proper had a curious history. In the fourth and third centuries B.C. a great wave of nomad Celtic tribes or Gauls moved west across mid-Europe. In 390 a horde of them attacked Rome, when the Capitol was only saved by the cackling of geese. Large numbers settled on the Atlantic coast, and gave their name to the country of Gaul; but others retained their nomad ways and moved slowly eastwards again. Soon after 300 we find them invading Northern Greece till repulsed at sacred Delphi. About 275 more than twenty thousand of them crossed the Hellespont into Asia, where for forty years they carried all before them. In 230, however, Attalus I. of Pergamus made headway against them and drove them out of the rich cities of the west coast up into the high plateaus of the interior. Here they settled down to an agricultural life in the district which came to be called Galatia or the country of the Gauls. It stretched from south-west to north-east for 200 miles, with its southern boundary almost in the centre of Asia Minor; its breadth was about 100 miles. Its inhabitants were essentially country folk and there were few towns.[1] In all history a conquering people, like the Vandals in Africa or the Normans in England, is nearly always a minority in numbers, and absorbs the culture of the conquered. So it was in this case : the original inhabitants, who were akin to the Phrygians, taught them the ways of settled life. It is true that the Gallic language was spoken till about 400 A.D., and the Druids probably retained something of their priestly rule ; but the nature-worship of Cybele, in which there was also a strong element of priest-rule, became dominant.

(b) When the Roman eagles came, the Galatians were left in the interior much in the position of a native state in India under English rule : for they acted as a check on the turbulent hill-tribes of the south. The last king, Amyntas, pushed his borders down as far as the Taurus. At last, in 25 B.C., Augustus made a Roman province of Galatia. Using the country of that name as a nucleus, he added, on the north-east part of the old country of Pontus, a district which was afterwards known as Pontus Galaticus ; on the south-west, part of Phrygia, which similarly came to be called Phrygia Galatica ; and finally on the south, most of Lycaonia. These southern districts were, politically and commercially, far the most important part of the province, as they were well provided with roads.

Now in 1 Pet. 1[1] " Galatia " is indisputably used to denote the Roman province. Is it not likely that St. Paul, with his keen sense of Roman citizenship, would also use it in the same sense ? " Galatians " is the only word which would embrace at once the people of Pisidian Antioch, of Iconium, of Lystra and Derbe ; and, as was mentioned above, these people were strongly pro-Roman

[1] The most important was Ancyra, which to-day, under its modern name of Angora, is regarded as the home of Turkish nationalism.

in feeling, so that the title would not wound their pride.[1]

Modern opinion is on the whole with Ramsay in favour of the province-theory, *i.e.* what is known as the " South-Galatian " theory, because it maintains that in his Epistle St. Paul is addressing the Christians of the southern districts. But some leading scholars (*e.g.* Bishop Chase and Dr. Moffatt) still follow Lightfoot and the older commentators in holding the " North-Galatian " theory, *i.e.* that the Epistle was sent to the country of Galatia.

*Summary of the Arguments.*—(1) The date of the Epistle is important in this connexion : for if we are right in the conclusion, reached below on other grounds, that Galatians was written before the Council of Jerusalem, Southern Galatia must be its destination. It is certain that St. Paul did not go north of Lycaonia on the first tour. However, the doubt about the date of the Epistle leaves this argument indecisive.

(2) Barnabas is mentioned in Gal. 2 as if he were well known to the readers ; but he was not with Paul after the first missionary journey. This fact favours the South-Galatian theory.

(3) On the second missionary journey St. Paul began to ask his well-to-do Gentile converts to save up money for the relief of the poor at Jerusalem. He regarded it as a matter of prime importance, not only for the actual relief it would bring, but even more as a mark of unity and a link between the new Gentile Churches and the mother-Church at Jerusalem. He collected the money on the third missionary journey, and the amount was considerable. He had to exercise the most scrupulous care in the matter, for his enemies had accused him of all

---

[1] Ramsay, *Cities*, p. 351, quotes the inscription on a third-century A.D. tombstone, where Apollonia in Pisidian Phrygia is called the " fatherland of *the Galatians.*"

sorts of underhand dodges to make money ; therefore he would not handle this fund himself but insisted on the election of delegates to administer it. In 1 Cor. 16³⁻⁴ he requests the Church at Corinth to choose their representatives ; in 2 Cor. 8¹⁸⁻²¹ he refers to an unnamed delegate who had been elected by the " Churches." In Rom. 15²⁶ he speaks of the contributions made to the fund by Macedonia and Achæa, the two *provinces* of Greece ; in 1 Cor. 16¹ of the subscriptions given by the Churches of *Galatia*.

Now we must turn to the list of those who actually conveyed the money with him to Jerusalem—that is, the elected delegates. It is given in Acts 20⁴. We find mentioned :

(*a*) One representative of *Achœa* (Sopater of Berœa). It is strange if Corinth was not directly represented ; and in view of 2 Cor. 8¹⁸⁻¹⁹, it seems natural to suppose that St. Luke himself acted as their delegate. In this case the province of Achæa sent two representatives.

(*b*) Two representatives of *Macedonia*, both from Thessalonica.

(*c*) Two representatives of *Asia*.

(*d*) Gaius of Derbe and Timothy of Lystra, presumably acting also as representatives of a province. But *their province was Galatia*, and 1 Cor. 16¹ proves that Galatia had contributed. The inference seems certain that in the latter passage the word denotes the province, not the country ; and that it was represented by two Lycaonians.

(4) We have left to the last the two passages where St. Luke uses the phrase " Galatian country," because their evidence is so uncertain. These are Acts 16⁶, on the second tour ; and Acts 18²³, on the third tour.

On the South-Galatian theory, let us see what these passages mean. In 16⁶ St. Paul, on leaving Lycaonia and Pisidian Antioch, makes a missionary journey through τὴν Φρυγίαν καὶ Γαλατικὴν χώραν—that is, " the Phrygian-Galatian region " ; we may follow Ramsay in interpreting

it to mean " that part of Phrygia which was in the province
of Galatia," [1] or may take it loosely as equivalent to the
borders of Phrygia and Galatia (see note on p. 99).   In
18[23] he goes from Syrian Antioch on a journey " right
through the Galatian region and Phrygia " (τὴν Γαλατικὴν
χώραν καὶ Φρυγίαν)—that is, probably through the whole
district of South Galatia into Phrygia proper, which was
in the province of Asia.

On the North-Galatian theory, 16[6] means that he went
from Pisidian Antioch into Phrygia and then north-
eastwards across the inland steppes into the *country* of
Galatia, which he had never visited before ; and 18[23] means
that he went through Lycaonia north into the country of
Galatia and then retraced his steps into Phrygia.

Linguistically there is nothing against this interpretation, except that it is odd to find " the Galatian region "
where he might more simply have said " Galatia."   Also
we must admit that, if St. Paul visited the north-central
steppes for the first time, St. Luke would not necessarily
record his adventures there ; for, as we have pointed out
already, an ancient author had to compress his subject-
matter within the limits imposed by the length of a papyrus
roll (which was not more than 30 feet at most).   Nor,
again, is it true to say that the country of Galatia was very
difficult of access ; for it was touched by several roads.[2]

The real difficulties in supposing that Luke meant the
*country* of Galatia in these two passages are twofold :
first, it is hard, on this theory, to interpret naturally the
language of Acts 16[7].   St. Paul was in the " Galatian
region," and he came " over against Mysia, making to
enter Bithynia."   A glance at the map will show that

---

[1] There is an inscription, found at Pisidian Antioch, where χώρα
(" region ") designates a " district " in the province of Galatia.   See
Ramsay, *T. and R. C.*, p. 103.

[2] See Ramsay, *Hist. Geog. of Asia Minor*, p. 237.

he must have been going north (as on the South-Galatian theory he was), not west (as apparently he would be on the North-Galatian theory).

Secondly, in 18²³ the North-Galatian theory makes his journey incredibly complex. His objective was Ephesus, and he visited his old converts on the way there. The great trade route from the East ran straight down to Ephesus ; on the South-Galatian theory, he got on to it a few miles from Pisidian Antioch, and continued to go due west down to the sea : it is a straight course. But on the North-Galatian theory he goes from Pisidian Antioch north-east for some 150 miles, and then has almost to retrace his steps to get to Ephesus.

We conclude, then, that a strong convergence of probabilities points to the identification of the " Galatians " with the Christian converts of his first missionary journey.[1]

2. THE OCCASION OF WRITING.—The events which led up to the letter are quite clear. He had met with great success on his first visit [2] to Galatia, and they had shown him warm affection and loyalty. But now he has heard of a swift and surprising change in them (1⁶) which

---

[1] Some commentators state that the Epistle makes no reference to the persecutions of the first missionary journey, and consider this a serious argument against the conclusions reached above. But (a) St. Paul does refer to his own sufferings, in Gal. 6¹⁷ (" the stigmata of Jesus "). (b) It is quite likely that the Jews had ceased from active persecution of the Galatian Christians while they hoped to induce them to keep the Law (cp. Gal. 4¹⁷).

[2] See 4¹³. The words τὸ πρότερον may mean (1) " on the former of my two visits," or (2) more loosely, " formerly." New Testament usage and that of contemporary Greek shows a predominance of the second meaning. Nevertheless, the first sense is more likely here. " Because of an illness I preached to you formerly," would require the tacit contrast, " but in health I am preaching to you now " ; as the latter is not true, the meaning will not hold good. Moreover, in 1⁹ and 5³ he speaks of having given them certain warnings, which seems to presuppose at least two visits. Finally, we must remember that he had visited them *twice on the first missionary journey*.

arouses his whole soul to passionate protest. Some Jewish Christians in Galatia have joined with the Jews in teaching the Gentile converts that they cannot hope to win the help of God unless they are prepared to carry out His ordained rite of circumcision. We can imagine how such an argument might appeal to a young Christian community in hours of depression and difficulty, with no leaders to advise them. Bred to priestcraft as they were, then attracted by the monotheism of the synagogue where they would constantly be told that circumcision was God's only covenanted entrance into the fold, would they not feel, when their first enthusiasm was somewhat spent, and they had to face the discipline of life in heathen surroundings, that there might be truth in the Jewish contention ? The appeal to authority is always attractive to men in hours of weakness or discouragement.

St. Paul had taught them otherwise ; but then it was said that he was not possessed of full apostolic authority, as he had not been with the Lord. He could only derive his authority from the older Apostles, and where was the proof that he had their approval ? He was a time-server, a mere opportunist who changed his tone with his audience ($1^{10}$) ; he observed the Law in Jerusalem ; but when he thought it would pay him, he was ready not to insist on circumcision.

_16_. DATE OF THE EPISTLE.—Commentators have assigned to Galatians almost every conceivable date between the end of the first missionary journey and the middle of the third. Two points, however, seem to stand out pre-eminently as carrying weight.

On the one hand, we have the argument of Lightfoot, who shows conclusively the close resemblance in language and teaching between Galatians and Romans, as well as its affinity with the two Epistles to the Corinthians.

Therefore he assigns it to the period of the Apostle's stay at Ephesus on the third tour, or thereabouts.

On the other hand, if we neglect the literary argument, there is much to be said for putting the Epistle before the Council of Jerusalem, *i.e.* during St. Paul's residence at Antioch after his first tour. First, St. Luke expressly tells us in Acts 16⁴ that the Apostle distributed the decrees of the Council to the Christians of South Galatia—decrees which laid down, in the name of the Church at Jerusalem, that circumcision was not to be required of the Gentiles. After this, how could the Judaistic party find any ground for their argument ? And if they had tried, is it not utterly incredible that St. Paul should have avoided all reference to the decrees when it would have shattered his opponents' case at one blow ?

Secondly, in Gal. 1–2 it looks as if he were recording all his visits to Jerusalem, and his intercourse with the older Apostles up to the date of writing. But we have seen that chap. 2 probably refers to the time of the famine : why should he omit all mention of going to the Council if it had already taken place ? And if Lightfoot's date be accepted, why does he not record his fourth visit to Jerusalem ?

Thirdly, we know that on the second missionary journey St. Paul was urging the Galatians to join in the collection for the poor at Jerusalem (see above, p. 66, § 3). The Epistles of the third journey, Romans and 1 and 2 Corinthians, are full of references to the fund. Why, then, does he never even mention it in Galatians ? In 6¹⁰ the context calls aloud for such mention, if the scheme was then in existence.

No one can doubt the resemblance of Galatians to the Epistles of the third tour : but after all, it does not prove absolute contemporaneity. If the same man writes two letters on the same subject with an interval of six years between them, is it not certain that we shall find community of thought and expression in them ? (St. Paul reached Antioch, after his first tour, probably towards the end of A.D. 49 : his stay at Ephesus was probably from the autumn of 53 to the summer of 56, and he wrote Romans in the following winter.)

Perhaps the most striking resemblances of Galatians with the Epistles of the third journey are to be found in the thought that we are " crucified with Christ " (Gal. 2$^{19}$ 6$^{14}$), and that baptism implies " putting on Christ " (3$^{27}$). The same conception is expanded in Rom. 6$^{3-11}$. But these phrases do not mark any new development in his thought. They spring straight out of his favourite and central idea, that the spiritual life of each Christian is fed by his union with the living Lord ; and the words " in Christ," by which he expresses this union, occur just as frequently in 1 Thessalonians (which apart from Galatians is his earliest letter) as in Galatians (six times in each). There is nothing whatever to show that he developed the conception at a later stage : it belonged, on the contrary, to the very essence of his Christian belief, and goes right back to his Conversion.

Nor is there any other trace in Galatians of ideas which belong distinctively to his later ministry, such as his developed eschatology. It is true that there is a world of difference between Galatians and the letters to the Thessalonians. The former is complex and difficult : the latter deal very simply with Christ as the Coming Judge. But we do not know enough about the Galatian Churches to explain how St. Paul expected them to follow his argument. Whether he wrote in 49, or in 55 or 56, makes little difference on this point. It is less a difference in date than in the mentality of his readers.[1]

We conclude, then, that after the first missionary

[1] It is worth calling attention to the resemblance between Gal. 2$^3$ and 1 Thess. 3$^5$.

journey when St. Paul was at Antioch, news reached him
that a vehement endeavour was being made to persuade
his Gentile converts in Galatia to submit to circumcision.
The Jews who had driven him through their bitter enmity
out of Pisidian Antioch, Iconium, and Lystra, were not
men to let grass grow under their feet ; they lost no time
in launching a counter-attack which, if it were successful,
would do much to restore their " God-fearers " to them ;
and they managed to enlist the help of some Jewish
Christians who denied St. Paul's apostolic authority.
The news probably reached the Apostle in the spring
after his return—that is, early in A.D. 50.  It would be after
the beginning of March, for ships did not sail before
February.  In hot indignation he wrote his letter, which
is unique among his Epistles in containing no word of
praise.  After the opening address ($1^{1-5}$) he plunges straight
into reproach of his readers for their quick change of front.


4. MYSTIC UNION WITH CHRIST.—We must insist again
that union with the ever-present Christ is the pivot of
his religion, and therefore of his theology.  It is vital to
grasp this ; for only so shall we be safe from misunderstanding his belief.  In every Epistle he writes, and ever
more frequently as time goes on, we find the constant
refrain " in Christ."  The same characteristic marks
the writings of St. John, though there is a slight difference in expression : see our Lord's words as given in
John $17^{21.\ 23.\ 26}$.

Let us try to fathom his meaning.  Comradeship
between two human beings, resting on sympathetic affection, is the greatest thing in the world.  The nearer it
reaches perfection, the more do their souls interpenetrate,
the more do the two become one, thinking, willing, and
dreaming alike : each may be said to be " in " the other
by mystic union, each made at one with (" atoned " to)

the other. At his conversion St. Paul realised that the risen Lord was henceforth to be his ever-present friend and guide. Christ, free from all taint of selfishness or sin, Christ who has the mind and heart of the Divine Father, offers to weak feeble man His perfect friendship, to be " in " them as they may be " in " Him (cp. Gal. 4¹⁹). His life becomes in us eternal life, for He pours it into us : His " blood " (which to the Hebrew mind always denotes the sacred principle of life), shed sacramentally on Calvary for our sakes, becomes our spiritual food. " In Him " we are at-oned with God the Father : men always become like what they love.[1]

In saying this, we have purposely avoided St. Paul's own language. He develops the conception (which, be it noted, rests on his constant experience) under many different similes. Sometimes he borrows metaphors familiar in the Greek Old Testament, such as that of " redemption," or buying some one out of slavery (even as Jehovah is said to have " redeemed " the Hebrews out of Egypt). Sometimes he uses words taken from the current religious language and aspirations of the Hellenistic world, such as " salvation " (that is, rescue from evil). There is always a danger of pressing these metaphors too far, and getting out of them more than they were ever meant to convey ; as when men infer from St. Paul that Christ's atoning work was the result of some mysterious transaction between God the Father and Himself. We shall have to say something of these various terms as

---

[1] Since the above was written, there has been published an English translation of lectures given in 1923 at Selly Oak, by Professor Adolf Deissmann of Berlin, under the title *The Religion of Jesus and the Faith of Paul.* He discusses fully the phrase " in Christ " (see esp. pp. 164 ff.) and takes much the same view as is given here. For a different view see Headlam, *St. Paul and Christianity.* He writes, p. 146 : " No logical expression (of this religious experience) is possible ; there is no analogy in ordinary experience."

they meet us in the Epistles. Here it must suffice to insist on the fact that his religion and all his theology are based on his daily experience of mystic union with Christ : this is the clue to the true interpretation of his language.

Finally, this also explains what is a rather startling fact about his Epistles, namely, the paucity of his references to the sayings and deeds of Jesus on earth, other than the Crucifixion and Resurrection. We find such references here and there, though they usually do not amount to direct quotation (but see the references given in § 8, p. 63). The fact is that he was preoccupied with the daily presence of the Risen Lord. Historical Christianity was to him the basis on which this communion rested ; but it faded into the background before the present reality.

For the linguistic use of ἐν in the phrase " in Christ," cf. the Greek adjective ἔνθεος, "inspired by a god " : and in the N.T. ἐν πνεύματι ἀκαθάρτῳ, "dominated by an evil spirit," Mk. 5² ; and St. Paul's phrase ἐν σαρκί, "dominated by the flesh," Rom. 8⁸.

5. PARAPHRASE OF THE EPISTLE.—[Note that in the Epistles the most difficult and important passages are put between asterisks.]

1¹⁻⁵. THE SALUTATION.—" I, Paul, an Apostle of Christ, *who received my apostleship not from men but directly from Jesus Christ Himself*, send greeting to the Churches of Galatia. May God give you His grace and peace, and the Lord Jesus Christ, who saved us by giving Himself, *and not by any external ritual.*"

1⁶⁻¹². HIS INDIGNANT WONDER AT THEIR FICKLENESS. —(Note that in this Epistle alone he plunges straight into his upbraiding ; in every other letter he first says such courteous things of his readers as he truthfully can.)

" I am amazed at your quick change of front, which amounts to a departure from Christ, adhesion to a different

way of salvation ; *different*, I say, not a second and as you
think a more profitable way ; *different*, because it relies
not on Christ but on institutional rites. [Circumcision is
itself a matter of indifference, $6^{15}$ ; but to make it binding
is to deny Christ, $5^{3-4}$]. Such teaching is accursed.

" I know you accuse me of shiftiness, because I sometimes
keep the Mosaic Law and sometimes neglect it. What
I have written above is at any rate plain : no one can now
accuse me of temporising."

(Note that in v.$^{10}$ we have what is called a zeugma : he
means, " Am I trying to persuade men, or thinking solely
of God's will ? ")

$1^{11}$–$2^{21}$. HE TRACES HIS OWN HISTORY TO SHOW THAT
THE OLDER APOSTLES NEITHER CONFERRED AUTHORITY
ON HIM NOR SOUGHT TO DO SO. HE RECORDS ALL HIS
VISITS TO JERUSALEM FROM THE TIME OF HIS CONVERSION
UP TO THE DATE OF WRITING, TO PROVE HIS POINT. THEN
IN $2^{11-21}$ HE TELLS THEM HOW AT ANTIOCH HE HAD BEEN
DRIVEN TO REBUKE EVEN PETER FOR HIS INCONSISTENCY
IN THIS MATTER OF THE LAW.—" The message I preach is
not a human affair : it came to me straight from Jesus
Christ Himself. It is not mine, to alter as I will. (vv.$^{13-14}$)
You have heard of my life before my conversion, what
a zealot I was for all the Jewish traditions, and how it led
me to ' lay waste ' the Church of God. (v.$^{15}$) When
God, by a special revelation, led me to conversion, He
showed me that He had marked me out, before ever I was
born, to preach to the Gentiles. My commission was so
clear that I felt no need of consulting with the older
Apostles nor of seeking their authorisation. (v.$^{18}$) It was
two years before I ever went to Jerusalem, and then I went
for a fortnight only to stay with Peter and get information from him [about the life of Jesus]. I did not even see
any other Apostle except James the Lord's brother. And
after that I went away to preach in Tarsus and Antioch,

before I was even known by sight to Judæan Christians outside Jerusalem, though they had heard of my wonderful conversion.

(2¹) " Thirteen years later I went again to Jerusalem with Barnabas, taking with me an uncircumcised Gentile convert, Titus, to introduce him to the older Apostles. My reason for going was simply the result of a Divine revelation, not of any human behest. But I took the opportunity of a private discussion with the older Apostles on this very subject of admitting Gentiles without insisting on the Mosaic Law. I wanted to come to an understanding with them, lest the work of evangelisation should suffer. *(v.³) There was great pressure put on me by some to circumcise Titus ; but I felt bound to refuse, because some false brethren had come to Antioch like spies and made complaints about my free admission of the Gentiles, wishing to enslave us to the Mosaic Law. (v.⁵) Therefore I could not give way, even for an hour, for a central principle of the gospel was at stake. The older Apostles, justly revered as they are, though that is of small account to me in this matter where Christ's command to me is clear—they, I say, neither gave me authorisation nor caused me to change my methods : nay, they recognised that I had been sent to the Gentiles, though they felt their first call to be to the Jews, Christ having so ordered for us both.* And when they had seen how wonderfully God had blessed my mission, the leaders, James, Peter, and John, gave me their pledge of fellowship and their absolute consent to my method. They only begged me always to remember how needy the Christians of Jerusalem were, if I could help in any way."

[*Note.*—Some commentators believe that Titus *was* circumcised ; they translate 2³, " he was not *compelled* (it was done voluntarily)," and v.⁵, " we gave way (but by way of courtesy), not subjection." It is supposed that

St. Paul was in an awkward position because he had allowed Titus' circumcision : it looked like inconsistency. But this theory does violence to the Greek, where there is no stress on "was compelled . . . by way of subjection." And it is incredible that St. Paul should have consented to circumcise a Gentile under the circumstances. v.⁶ does not convey a slighting reference to the older Apostles. He means, " however great they are, I had to obey Christ, not them."]

2¹¹. " So far was I from receiving any new charge from the older Apostles, that when, after our conference at Jerusalem, Peter came to Antioch, I actually upbraided him for inconsistency. At first he joined in the common meal [Agape] with our uncircumcised Gentiles : but later on some Jewish Christians came on a commission from James ; and Peter [who had resolved that *among Jews* he would observe the Law] wished to absent himself from the meal : other Jewish Christians, including even Barnabas, were led away by his inconsistent argument. *(v.¹⁴) So I said to Peter before them all, ' Why do you make this sudden change ? You consented to accept the Gentile Christian standard by eating with them ; now you are as good as asking them to adopt the Mosaic Law. (vv.¹⁵⁻¹⁶) You and I were, to start with, strict Jews, priding ourselves on being righteous in God's eyes, and looking down on all Gentiles as sinners. We were both taught to see that we were ourselves sinners, and that the Law gave us no escape : we found freedom only by faith in Jesus Christ, apart from any covenantal rite. (v.¹⁷) Our whole experience in Christ showed us that we were on exactly the same level as Gentile " sinners," with the same way of escape that they have. If you *now* mean to imply that neglect of the Law is sin, then we were led into sin and by Christ Himself ! (v.¹⁸) The real sin in us [he says " I " from courtesy, but he means St. Peter] is any looking back, any attempt to erect again the fence which Christ taught us to demolish. (v.[19]) The impotence of the Law brought me to Christ in my weakness : I found deliverance in my union with Him, and therefore the Law is a dead thing in my life. My life is now no longer mine, but that of Christ in me. (v.[21]) If the Law can make us righteous in God's sight, then Christ's death and suffering were surely superfluous.' "*

[*Note on* 2[11-21].—This is a difficult and important passage, admitting of several various interpretations. In the above paraphrase, the whole passage is regarded as a summary of St. Paul's argument with St. Peter; and *primâ facie* this view has everything in its favour. W.H. mark a new paragraph at v.[15], as if it and the following verses gave St. Paul's expansion to his readers of his meaning in 14[b]. But v.[18] seems almost meaningless unless addressed to St. Peter. The chief difficulty in the view, which I have taken, is the " for " in v.[18], where we should expect " nay rather."]

3[1-5]. APPEAL TO THEIR CHRISTIAN EXPERIENCE.—" You foolish Galatians, who has hypnotised [1] you ? I placarded Jesus Christ before your eyes as the crucified (cp. 1 Cor. 2[2]). When you were converted and received the Spirit, was it because you had earned it by what you did [ritual and moral], or because the message gave you *faith* in Him ? Your first steps in Christ were purely spiritual ; now you are trusting for progress to things outward and fleshly. Can the persecutions you endured [from the Jews] be really in vain ? God has richly dowered you with His Spirit and worked miracles among you ; was it because you kept the Law or because the message brought you faith ? "

[*Note on* v.[1].—The Crucifixion is central to St. Paul, but chiefly as followed by the Resurrection. In itself, however, it is the supreme proof of God's inalienable

---

[1] ἐβάσκανεν means, " charmed with the evil eye, as a snake fascinates a rabbit." The English " fascinate " is the same word.

love for us : love alone can redeem, and the price that it
has to pay is suffering.]

3⁶⁻²². THE CLASSIC CASE OF ABRAHAM, WHOSE " FAITH "
WAS " COUNTED TO HIM FOR RIGHTEOUSNESS " (Gen. 15⁶).
—" The language of Genesis is clear. Those who base
all on *faith* are Abraham's spiritual descendants. This
is the true meaning of God's promise to him, ' *in thee shall
ALL THE NATIONS (Gentiles) be blessed.*' If you trust to
your performance of the Law to commend you to God,
remember that the Old Testament pronounces a curse
on every one who does not keep *every* command of the
Law. The Law can set no human being right with God,
as is clear from the passage in Habakkuk which says,
' *the righteous man shall get life by faith.*' (v.¹²) This is
not the principle of the Law, of which it is said, ' *the man
who carries out its commands shall get life by them.*' Christ
ransomed us from the curse which we inherited by our
failure to keep the Law ; by becoming Himself a very
curse for us (for Deuteronomy pronounces a curse on every
one who is hanged on a tree) : He did this that in Him we
might inherit Abraham's blessing, Gentiles and all, that
by faith in Him we might receive the promised Spirit."

[*Note.*—The question whether salvation comes by
" faith " or " works " was probably discussed by the
contemporary Rabbinic schools ; and it is not unlikely
that both sides quoted in favour of their own opinion
the case of Abraham, the father of the Jewish race. But if
the Epistle of St. James was written before this time, as
seems quite likely, St. Paul probably takes from it the
case of Abraham. St. James 2²¹ asks, " Was not Abraham
our father justified by works, in that he offered up Isaac ? "
He goes on to argue that faith and works interact, each
stimulating the other : so (v.²³) " the scripture was
fulfilled which saith, ' and Abraham had faith in God,
and it was reckoned unto him for righteousness.' " St.

Paul discusses the case of Abraham here and in Rom. 4. In Gal. 3⁶⁻¹⁴ he takes St. James's quotation and points out that its very wording ("had *faith* in God ") contradicts the conclusion which it is adduced to confirm.

The apparent contradiction between St. Paul and St. James is discussed below (p. 91). They clearly mean different things by "faith." St. Paul means, "wholehearted *trust* in God "; St. James, intellectual assent.

It is vital that the words "justify " and "justification " should be clearly understood. To "justify " does *not* mean "to make righteous," but "to acquit, to consider or treat as righteous." "To be justified " is much what old-fashioned writers mean by "being put right with God."

The question between justification by faith or by works is vital to religion. Are we to think first of morality, and of God as a help ? or are we to think first of God, trusting that He will so fill us with His Spirit that our morality can look after itself ? But "salvation by works " in St. Paul has a further reference than to morality: "works" includes all outward actions, and in particular the performance of institutional rites and external ceremonies which, as it were, bind God to His covenant with His people.]

[*Introductory Note to* 3¹⁵⁻²².—This section is difficult. In order to understand it, we must bear in mind that διαθήκη (" covenant ") was used (1) for a covenant, in the sense of a contract between two parties, binding on both, as the Law was ; (2) for a last will and testament, disposing of one's property at death, *i.e.* an unconditional gift or promise. St. Paul insists that God's promises to Abraham were absolutely unconditioned by his observance of any Law : they were a free and irrevocable gift. *But Genesis* 15¹⁸ *calls them a* διαθήκη (" *covenant* "). Yes, says the Apostle, but this was not a contract with conditions attached ; it was like a will, giving an inheritance without conditions. The Mosaic Law was a contract ;

6

but as it was not given till 430 years after the " covenant "
to Abraham, it cannot annul the latter. The whole
story of Gen. $15^{17-21}$ where God alone symbolically passes
between the animal victims, implies that Abraham did
not pledge himself to anything ; but God gave His promise
unconditionally because Abraham had faith in Him.
$v.^{16}$ is a parenthesis.]

$*3^{15}$. " Take an analogy from ordinary human life. Any
contract or testamentary disposition, once it has been
ratified, cannot be annulled or added to. $(v.^{16})$ (In
Abraham's case we are told that the promises were made
to him ' and to his seed.' Now seed is a collective
noun ; you cannot say ' seeds ' : it implies that his heirs
shall have some bond of unity which is found in Christ.)
$(v.^{17})$ But to return to my analogy : a testament was
ratified by God to Abraham 430 years before the Mosaic
Law was given; therefore the Law cannot annul the
promise. $(v.^{18})$ Now there is a complete difference
between the two common forms of ' testament,' namely,
a legal contract and a gift by will : one is a covenant,
resting on legal conditions which bind both parties ; the
other is a free promise, binding only him who makes it.
The second is what God in His goodness gave to Abraham.
$(v.^{19})$ You will say, ' What use was the Law if the promise
is independent of it ? ' It was given to make men
conscious of sin, so that they longed for the promised
Saviour. The Law, which, as tradition tells us, was brought
to Moses by angels, was a conditional contract between
God and man, Moses acting as the mediator or attorney.
$(v.^{20})$ The word ' mediator ' implies two parties ; but
in Abraham's case God acted alone.*

$(v.^{21})$ " Yet, though Law and promise rest on two different principles, the Law was not simply contrary to the
promises. If any conceivable Law could have given life
to men, it would have been the Mosaic Law. $(v.^{22})$ But

Law inevitably makes men conscious of sin and failure : they thus learn to long for some compelling *inward* force to make them fit recipients of the promise, and the only such force is faith in Jesus Christ."

3²³-4⁷. CONTINUED DISCUSSION OF THE USE OF THE LAW : ITS CONTRAST WITH THE FREEDOM OF THE GOSPEL. —(v.²³) " The Law thus served an educational purpose. Just as children have a tutor,¹ so the Law was to us, fitting us for the freedom which Christ was to bring later, when loyal faith was to supersede rules. (v.²⁶) For God gives us real freedom as His sons through faith—gives it us in our union with Christ Jesus. Baptism *into Christ* means putting on the spirit of Christ : for those who have done that, *there cannot be* any more distinctions between one nation or class or sex and another. For the living Christ is in all of you ; therefore you are one in Him, apart from any possible differences in your outward conditions. And as Christ is Abraham's seed (see v.¹⁶), you are in Him the inheritors of the promises."

4¹. " But to return to my metaphor of a child [*i.e.* to 3²⁵], as long as the heir is a minor, he is treated like any slave ; he is subject to men who control his person and his goods, until the day named in his father's will ² that he should come into his inheritance. Just in the same way we, when we were spiritual minors, were kept in slavery to the ' rudiments of the world ' (see note 1 below), till Christ came to ransom us from slavery into adoption as the sons of God. (v.⁶) Our sonship is now proved by the Spirit within us, which makes us cry ' Abba, Father.' And because we are God's sons, we inherit His promises."

[*Notes.*—(1) 4³ : τα στοιχεῖα τοῦ κόσμου occurs here and

---

¹ παιδαγωγός, a slave who looked after a child out of school hours.

² Roman Law apparently allowed the father to fix the age of his son's majority in certain cases. But we do not know what system of law St. Paul is using.

in v.[9] ; and elsewhere only in Col. 2[8] where the elaborate
and burdensome demon or angel cult of the Colossians is
said to be "according to the rudiments of the world."
Now στοιχεῖα, "rudiments," means (a) the letters of
the alphabet ; (b) the elements of nature ; (c) the root
principles or groundwork ; (d) in *mediæval* Greek,
"spirits" supposed to inhabit and rule the world of
nature—a development of (b). In Col. 2[8] (d) would suit
the Colossians' beliefs attacked by St. Paul : but there is
no instance of the word bearing this meaning in Hellenistic
or earlier Greek ; and the meaning is utterly unsuitable
in Gal. 4[3, 9]. So we seem forced to adopt (c) in all
three Pauline passages ; *i.e.* "according to the basic
principles of the world of men."

(2) 4[6] : "Abba" is the Aramaic for "Father." "Abba,
Father" is thus a bilingual phrase used in Palestine ; see
Mark 14[36], Rom. 8[15].]

4[8-20]. IT IS ABSURD TO TURN BACK TO CHILDISH THINGS.
AFFECTIONATE APPEAL TO THEIR EARLY FERVOUR.—
(v.[8]) "You Galatians were once heathen, slaves of demons
who were no real gods. Now you have recognised what
God is, or, to speak more truly, you have been recognised
by God, treated as His friends. How can you return to
the weak and beggarly principles, which are of the same
order as the rites which once burdened your lives, to
reliance on the observance of Sabbaths and new-moon
feasts, annual feasts and sacred years ? You make me
fear that my work has been in vain among you.

(v.[12]) "Base your religion on Christ Himself as I do. You
never did me any wrong. I first came to Galatia because
I was very ill ; and though I looked repulsive and you must
have been tempted to despise me, you did not ; you never
'spat out' when you saw me [see p. 9, 51], but you received
me as a messenger of God [see Acts 14[12ff.]] and not as one
demon-possessed. (v.[15]) You called yourselves happy to

hear me : you would have dug out your own eyes and given them to me. Have I become your enemy through dealing honestly with you ? (v.[17]) My opponents flatter you with an evil object : they want to shut you out of the larger brotherhood, that you may flatter their pride. I am not jealous, believe me, at your receiving their attention in my absence, as long as it aims at your good. I brought you once to the birth, my little children ; now it seems as if I must endure again the travail pangs for you, until [suddenly inverting the metaphor and making them the mother] Christ takes form within you."

[For the inversion of the metaphor in the middle of a passage, cp. 2 Cor. 3[13-15], 1 Thess. 2[7] (W.H. text), and 5[2-4] (W.H. text).]

4[21-31]. THE ALLEGORY OF ABRAHAM'S TWO WIVES.— (v.[21]) " You wish to accept the Mosaic Law ; but in the Law itself I can show you the way of slavery and the way of freedom. Abraham had two sons ; the first, Ishmael, was his son by a slave, the second, Isaac, by a freewoman. The first was born in the order of natural law ; the second by a special promise of God. This story is to be interpreted allegorically. Hagar corresponds to the old covenant —she came from Mount Sinai, a mountain in Arabia, the land of slaves, and she bears children for slavery ; she corresponds to the earthly Jerusalem. Sarah, the free-born, bears the son of promise into freedom, corresponding to the heavenly, ideal Jerusalem ; and we, like Isaac, are free children of the promise. (v.[29]) We read [Gen. 21[9]] that Ishmael persecuted [1] the babe Isaac : even so do the Jews to us. Yet God said that the slave-woman and her child were to be cast out. Remember that we are in the succession of the freewoman, not the slave."

---

[1] So the R.V., " mocking." Modern commentators usually explain otherwise—that Ishmael was " sporting," *i.e.* taking part in the games at the weaning feast.

[*Note*.—Such arguments sound very strange to the modern reader, but they are thoroughly Rabbinic in style and are a reminder to us of St. Paul's upbringing. Fortunately, he does not often use them ; for by such methods one could prove anything ! His famous contemporary, Philo, the philosophic Jew of Alexandria, is driven in his loyal defence of the Old Testament not only to allegorise some of the stories but even to deny their historical truth. St. Paul only looks for an eternal truth in human story.

For to the Jew at this time it had become a maxim that there exists a heavenly archetype to all good things on earth (cp. " the Jerusalem which is above," v.²⁶—cp. Heb. 8⁵ 9²³). So to the Jew the Messiah was existing archetypally in heaven : this does not mean personal pre-existence, but rather the perfect idea as existing in the mind of God. Everything good is a piece of Divine revelation. Philo elaborated this under Platonic and Stoic influence.]

5¹⁻¹². CHRIST OFFERS FREEDOM : THERE IS NO OTHER ROAD TO IT.—(v.¹) " Christ veritably gave us freedom : therefore do not again be entangled in the yoke of slavery. I tell you solemnly that any man who seeks circumcision contracts to fulfil the whole Law. If you rely on your performance of the Law to put you right with God, you are losing sight of His grace and Christ is become nothing to you. Faith longingly waits for God to give us the righteousness we hope for. (v.⁶) To the man who is in Christ circumcision or uncircumcision are mere matters of indifference : *faith which is translated into action by love* is everything. (v.⁷) You were making good progress : who has hindered you ? God, who is always calling you, is not behind him. ' A little leaven leavens the whole lump.' I am confident that you will come to my way of thinking. The man who is unsettling you, will have to bear his judgment whoever he is. As for me, you say that I temporise about circumcision [1] ; if so, why do the Jews persecute me ? In that case the cross of Christ, which offends the Jews, has lost its sting ! Oh, I wish those who disturb you would mutilate themselves outright (like the devotees of Cybele)."

5[13-15]. WARNING THAT LIBERTY DOES NOT MEAN LICENCE.—" You were called, I say, for freedom. But take care not to use your freedom so that it plunges you into the lusts of the flesh. Let love make you *slaves to one another*. For (as Christ taught) the whole law is fulfilled in the one command to love your neighbour as yourself. If like animals you bite and devour each other, you may be altogether destroyed."

[*Note.*—We see from Romans and 1 Corinthians how easily the heathen world turned the doctrine of free forgiveness into " Antinomianism," *i.e.* the attitude that *all* moral laws are indifferent to the Christian. Here we have only a brief reference to the man who presumes on his liberty.]

5[16-25]. THE ONLY SURE PROTECTION AGAINST WORKS OF THE FLESH IS TO FILL YOURSELF WITH THE SPIRIT.—(v.[16]) " Do not simply resist evil, a negative course which will never bring victory. Fill your life with active goodness, the inspiration and enthusiasm which the Holy Spirit will give you, and so effectually drive out the evil passion. (v.[17]) For the flesh and the spirit are in human life ever opposed to one another [not because the flesh is necessarily evil, but because it is evil when it is allowed to dominate] : so that you must expect temptation."

Then follow two lists, the " works of the flesh " (vv.[20-21]), which, it is worth noting, include a great deal more besides what we call " fleshly sins " ; and secondly, the " works of the Spirit (vv.[22-23]). v.[24] gives the assurance of victory : life in Christ gives the death-blow to lust, though it may seem slow in dying. v.[25] is a reminder that the test of spiritual life is living spiritually.

[1] Possibly he had already circumcised Timothy, who was a " Galatian."

[*Note.*—v.[16] is one of the most profound truths ever uttered, a truth which modern psychology is emphasising as a new discovery of our age. We find it also in the Gospels, Luke 11[21-26].][1]

5[26]–6[10]. SOME WAYS OF CARRYING INTO LIFE THE CHRISTIAN SPIRIT.—The section needs no paraphrase. The apparent contradiction in the English between 6[2] and 6[5] is not in the Greek. The " burdens " of v.[2] ($\beta\acute{a}\rho\eta$) are the loads which come at times, sorrow, and failure, and poverty : love bids us share these with our neighbour, and so lighten his load. The " burden " ($\phi o \rho \tau \acute{\iota} o \nu$) in v.[5] is like a ship's cargo, that which each man bears through his life's voyage, his individual responsibility to God, of which no man can relieve him. v.[9] is an epigram in Greek : " let us not feel evil (*i.e.* be discouraged) in doing good." (So 2 Thess. 3[13].)

6[11-18]. AUTOGRAPH SECTION, added by St. Paul in his own writing. He has dictated the previous part of the letter as was his custom. Cp. 2 Thess. 3[17].

(v.[11]) " Look at my own large writing [in contrast with the copy-book hand of the amanuensis]! Those who are trying to force you into circumcision, want to make an outward show of piety, simply to avoid persecution for the Cross of Christ. (v.[13]) Even the circumcision party themselves are not able to keep the Law, but they want you to be in the same position that they may glory in your outward respectability. God forbid that I should

---

[1] " We may take as an example of this the familiar experience which is heard again and again in the testimony of religious converts who say, ' I struggled against such-and-such a sin, but its power over me simply grew greater. Then I realised that I could not conquer in my own strength, and I gave up struggling and left it in the hands of the Lord, and the burden of my sin rolled away ' " (Thouless, *Introduction to the Psychology of Religion*, p. 172). The psychological explanation is to be found in what the new Nancy school call " the Law of Reversed Effort " (see Baudouin, *Suggestion and Auto-Suggestion*) ; namely, that conscious opposition to a sin focuses the mind upon the temptation.

glory in anything but the Cross : by Christ I am crucified to the world, and the world to me. Circumcision and uncircumcision matter nothing in themselves ; all that matters is that I should be a ' new creature ' [a Rabbinic term]. To those of you who will adopt this standard only, may there be peace and mercy, for they are the true Israel.

(v.[17]) " Oh, do not give me trouble ! Remember what I have suffered for you : I bear in my body the brand-marks of Jesus [the " stigmata " were marks branded on runaway slaves, etc.]. The grace of our Lord Jesus Christ be with your spirit, my brothers. Amen."

[*Note on v.*[11] (" See with how large letters . . .").— Kenyon, *Textual Criticism of the New Testament*, p. 30, says of this : " Exact analogies may be found in many Egyptian papyri, where the body of a document is written by a friend or a clerk, and the principal appends his ratifica-tion in a large hand at the end ; . . . the phrase implies that the body of the Epistle was written in a hand of small or medium size."]

### 6. THE RELIGIOUS PRINCIPLES INVOLVED IN " JUSTI-FICATION BY FAITH."

(1) There always are in every religious community men who by temperament are very conservative of tradition. Their preoccupation is to secure continuity with the past. In their wish to preserve against corruption the religion revealed to their forefathers, they regard as sacred the very forms in which it is enshrined : not only its creeds, but all details of liturgy or ritual, must be preserved as a hedge against the despoiler. To their minds, God's people stand to Him in a special covenantal relationship ; and the rites which mark inclusion within the Covenant are sacred to the last degree.

Such minds are often strong in emphasising the social aspects of religion and " salvation by works " ; but they are apt to forget God's inward voice with which He speaks to each of His children.

Now it was this type of religion in which St. Paul had been brought up, and he naturally had a strong revulsion at his Conversion. To him as a Christian the personal life " in Christ," the intimate communion, became everything. He had once been obsessed by his frequent failures to keep God's commands ; now he is content to leave all that, because he has the daily joy of intercourse with God " in Christ " : therefore he preaches with insistence " justification by faith,"—that is, God's acceptance of him through simple, childlike trust.

Such a religion has one main danger, that of excessive individualism ; but from that St. Paul is quite free. He is never preoccupied with his own personal salvation, and he lays great stress on the importance of the corporate life and convictions of the Church. Again and again he insists that no one has true " faith " unless his life shows the fruit of it in Christian act. In Gal. 5⁶ he defines his ideal as πίστις δι' ἀγάπης ἐνεργουμένη, " faith realised in action through love." In Rom. 2¹³ he states emphatically, " Not the hearers of the law are declared innocent before God, but the doers of the law." And in 1 Cor. 13² he writes, " If I have all faith so as to move mountains, but have not love, I am nothing." " Faith " to him means the sort of faith on which all friendship rests— whole-hearted trust : it is an active, warm, inspiring motive, which *must* produce " works," and better works than any other motive can. A child may love father or mother passionately : yet in the home its actions will often be imperfect, sometimes even wrong. But father or mother can read the child's heart, and show a trustful understanding, which day by day will give the child more insight into their ideals and more power of good act. No deeper analysis of the Christian religion has ever been made : St. Paul gets down to the very heart of Christ's teaching.

(2) St. Paul and St. James compared.—St. James, in his Epistle, approaches the question from a different standpoint and a different experience. Though always a devout Jew, he was not of the traditionalist type against whom St. Paul writes : indeed he, like St. Paul, is attacking much in contemporary Pharisaism, though from a different angle. He has in mind the hypocritical religion which our Lord denounces—that of men who " say and do not." " By their fruits ye shall know them," said Christ : by their works ye shall know them, said James.

He draws from this the conclusion that it is " by " works that a man is justified, and " not only by faith." It is obvious that by " faith " he really understands mere intellectual assent. In $2^{22}$ he states the obvious, but none the less important, truth that mental conviction must express itself in action, and that so morality and religion strengthen each other.

No one can question the soundness of his practical teaching, though Luther styles his letter an " epistle of straw." But St. James was a thorough Jew, with a genius for intuitive grasp of the right : he lacked St. Paul's Greek training, which enabled the great missionary to get down to root principles. St. Paul points out that it is not " *by* " works that a man is justified, but by an inward disposition which necessarily shows itself in works and so is itself confirmed. His analysis is more penetrating than St. James' : it goes deeper into the teaching of Him who bids us, when we have done our utmost, still to say " we are unprofitable servants." The man who regards his own moral life with complacency, comparing it favourably with that of his neighbours, is a long way from Christianity. Needless to say, St. James was not such a man : but he leaves the door open to him.

# CHAPTER VI.

## THE CONGRESS AT JERUSALEM.

1. THE OCCASION.—We gather from Acts 15[1. 5] that there was in Jerusalem a party of Christians who had previously belonged to the sect of the Pharisees, and who could not reconcile themselves to the admission of Gentiles without circumcision. James, the Lord's brother, who was the presiding elder in the Church of Jerusalem, was clearly not on their side (see Gal. 2[9]); but with his strong Jewish sympathies he retained their confidence and sometimes used their services in communicating with distant Churches (Gal. 2[12]). At Antioch these pious but stupid bigots brought on a storm, as some of them had lately done in South Galatia. In each instance, they probably fraternised with the more narrow-minded of the Jews. If Christianity was to be merely a form of Judaism which identified Jesus of Nazareth with the Messiah, there was not much to keep the two from making common cause.

It was vital to get the Judaistic question settled once for all by a public conference. Jerusalem was recognised as the administrative centre; and Paul and Barnabas were sent there as representatives of the Church of Antioch to confer with the apostles and elders.[1] A public congress was at once summoned, to which all the Jerusalem

---

[1] Note that in Acts 15[3] it is said that, on their way to Jerusalem, they told of the conversion of the Gentiles abroad to the churches in Phœnicia and Samaria, but there is no mention of the churches of Judæa.

Christians were invited (15[22]). After a discussion in which various opinions were expressed (v.[7]), Peter rose to speak in favour of Paul's view, arguing mainly from his own vision at Cæsarea (Acts 10). " Barnabas and Paul " (Barnabas has still the pre-eminence in Jerusalem) told the tale of their marvellous success on their missionary tour. Finally, James, revered of both parties, backed up Peter (note that he calls him by his Aramaic name Symeon), first on the ground of the vision at Cæsarea (v.[14]), and secondly on the basis of an old prophecy of Amos, where (according to the Greek Septuagint, not the Hebrew text) it is foretold that the Gentiles are to seek after Jehovah. It is singular that neither St. Peter nor St. James refers to any such saying of Jesus Christ as is recorded in Matt. 28[19], Luke 24[47]. It may be argued that our Lord says nothing explicit about the terms on which the Gentiles are to be admitted, but neither does Amos ! We seem driven to the inference that Jesus never said anything definite and conclusive about preaching to the Gentiles, though we may be quite sure that Matt. 28[19] is a legitimate interpretation of His words and is in accordance with His mind and will.

2. THE DECREES.—St. James advised that the Congress should publish a letter stating definitely that circumcision was unnecessary for Gentile converts, but urging them to keep strictly certain rules which were deemed to be incumbent on all Christians. Unfortunately our manuscripts and the early Fathers give two very different versions of these necessary observances, both in recording St. James' speech (v.[20]) and in the text of the letter (v.[29]).

(a) The mass of manuscripts agrees with the Alexandrian type of text which is translated in the English Version. According to this reading Gentile Christians are bidden to abstain from—

(i) " the pollutions of idols," or (v.[29]) " things sacrificed to idols " ;

(ii) or (iv) " fornication " ;

(iii–iv) or (iii–ii) " from what is strangled " and " from blood."

(b) The Codex Bezæ (D), backed up by the weighty authority of Irenæus (Asia Minor and South Gaul, second century), Tertullian and Cyprian (North Africa, third century), as well as by the later Ambrosiaster, omits " what is strangled " (πνικτοῦ, πνικτῶν) ; and most of them add to the Decrees the negative form of the Golden Rule (" What ye do not wish to be done to yourselves, avoid doing to others "). Ambrosiaster definitely says that the insertion of the words " and what is strangled " was the work of some one who misunderstood the prohibition of " blood."

Moreover, the testimony of this group is all the stronger because in the second and third centuries Christians in Gaul and North Africa did actually observe the Jewish taboo of eating meat with the blood in it : their reason was probably that the practice of consuming blood was mixed up with certain heathen rites. At any rate Irenæus, Tertullian, and Cyprian are just the people of all others from whom we should expect support for the insertion of " things strangled," and they definitely omit it.

(a) certainly has all the best manuscripts behind it : the evidence of the Codex Bezæ is worth very little. Moreover, it might seem that St. James' words in v.[21] prove the inclusion of at least one point peculiar to the Jewish law in the previous v.[20].

If we accept the inclusion of " things strangled " the Decrees are a compromise. The Mosaic Law is not binding on Gentile converts, except in one point : they are to abstain from eating meat except when the blood has been carefully drained off in accordance with the Mosaic Code ;

for (v.²¹) daily intercourse between Jewish and Gentile Christians, especially in the Agape or common meal which preceded the Eucharist, will be made much easier by observing this taboo.

If this is the right version, then presumably what happened afterwards is that *both sides* claimed the decision as a victory. The Judaisers said that the Mosaic Law was upheld in one vital point though the Gentiles were excused circumcision as a concession to their weakness ; but that it *was* a concession to weakness, and that those who kept the whole Law were obviously much stronger for it. On this showing, the Decrees accomplished nothing ; and the Christian Church as a whole, being against the Judaistic party, quietly dropped the command to avoid things strangled ! In this way perhaps we can explain St. Paul's absolute silence about the Decrees in later years.

(*b*), however, has much to be said in its favour. It is hard to believe that St. Paul or indeed the others would couple as " essentials " (v.²⁸) fornication and this food law ! It is important to notice that the omission of " things strangled " changes the whole colour of the prohibitions. They are no longer partly ethical, partly ritual ; but are *entirely ethical*. Gentile converts are reminded that, though all the Mosaic ritual is made un-necessary for them, yet this does not mean the sweeping away of all the Ten Commandments (see the reference to Moses in v.²¹). They must keep the great moral laws *against idolatry, fornication, and bloodshed* (for with this reading that is clearly the meaning of αἵματος). More-over, from the standpoint of textual criticism it is extremely likely that Ambrosiaster is right. Some one, who mis-understood αἵματος to mean " blood in meat," wrote in the margin πνικτοῦ (" that is, what is strangled "), and so later on it found its way into the text. For if one thinks of it, " avoid what is strangled " is not a full equivalent to the Levitic Law [1]; indeed, no Jewish source prohibits strangling an animal; and beasts killed in other ways still would not satisfy the Jewish taboo.

The conclusion would seem to be that (b), in spite of its weak attestation in the manuscripts, is more likely to be the original form of the Decrees.[2]  St. Paul's views conquered all along the line, and the Judaistic question, as such, was dead in the Christian Church. The party of Judaistic Christians was anything but extinguished : egged on by the Jews, they were all the more hostile to St. Paul—at any rate the " die-hards " among them.  But, granted the early date of " Galatians," there is nothing to prove that the imposition of circumcision on the Gentiles ever again came within the scope of practical politics—" Romans " indeed deals with the question, but in a calm atmosphere which shows that there was no longer any storm-cloud surrounding it.

3. THE IMPORTANCE OF THE DECISION ABOUT CIRCUMCISION is hard to overestimate : it entails nothing less than the catholicity of Christianity, which has ever since been accepted in theory by the Christian Church, though so often nullified in practice by other methods of exclusiveness.

Had the Mosaic Law been retained as an integral part of Christianity, the Church would have been but a Jewish sect, and Christ in time might have been regarded merely as the greatest of the prophets (if indeed it is loyal to God to discuss such " might-have-beens ").  As it was, the decision made a cleavage between Jew and Christian

---

[1] See Hort, *Judaistic Christianity*, p. 73.

[2] Whether we should include also in the text the negative form of the Golden Rule is a more difficult question.  It certainly sums up admirably the three preceding ethical commands.

which persecution soon widened into a gulf. A year or two later St. Paul writes to the Thessalonians (1 Thess. 2$^{14\text{-}15}$) : "You have suffered at the hands of your own countrymen the same things as the Christian churches in Judæa did at the hands of the Jews : for the Jews killed the Lord Jesus as they had killed their prophets, and they drove us out ; they do not please God, and are hostile to all men, forbidding us to carry the message of salvation to the Gentiles."

So Christianity shook off its shackles and was free to become the religion of a world which would never have accepted the Jewish Law.

4. AFTER THE CONGRESS.—The Conference appointed two well-known *Jewish* Christians, both of them " prophets " (*i.e.* men of spiritual insight), to carry the letter and its decrees to Antioch with Barnabas and Paul. One of these was Judas Barsabbas, probably a brother of that Joseph Barsabbas whose name had been mentioned for election to the apostolic circle after the suicide of Judas Iscariot (Acts 1$^{23}$) and who therefore had seen the Risen Lord. The second was Silas, who showed such qualities on this mission that Paul secured him later as his partner in the second missionary journey, after his rupture with Barnabas. Silas is an abbreviation of the Latin name Silvanus (see 1 and 2 Thess. 1$^1$) ; and, like St. Paul, he had the proud privilege of Roman citizenship (Acts 16$^{37\text{-}38}$). Even the most bigoted Judaiser at Antioch could not question the authenticity of a letter brought by two such men. When they had achieved their object, they both returned to Jerusalem (15$^{33}$).

# CHAPTER VII.

## THE SECOND MISSIONARY JOURNEY.

1. THE FIRST STAGE OVER OLD GROUND (Acts $15^{36}$–$16^5$).
—After a time Paul suggested to Barnabas that they should
go to visit the Christian communities which they had
founded abroad. Barnabas at once consented; but unfortunately a question cropped up on which they could
come to no agreement. Barnabas wished to give his
cousin, John Mark, a second trial, hoping that this time
he would prove his grit. The very fact that Mark wanted
to join them was in his favour; and in later years he
amply proved his worth to St. Paul himself, when he came
to Rome and served the Apostle during his first imprisonment there (Col. $4^{10}$; cp. 2 Tim. $4^{11}$). We do not know
why Paul was now so strenuously opposed to taking
Mark, that he severed his connexion with his old friend
rather than yield. He felt bitter about the former desertion; the man who had forsaken him at a time he was
ill and sorely needed assistance was not one in whom he
could place reliance in moments of danger, as when facing
an angry mob. So much we must recognise. Yet Barnabas
was right in trusting his cousin.

So the two missionaries agreed to part. Barnabas
took Mark and went to Cyprus, where, according to tradition, he spent the rest of his life. Paul sent to Jerusalem
and asked Silas to take his place: later on, at Lystra, he
enrolled the services of Timothy in place of Mark. He
and Silas started overland for Galatia, leaving copies of

the Council Decrees in Syria and Cilicia. This was probably in the summer of A.D. 50 : the pass of the Cilician
Gates was open after May ; so they crossed the Taurus
into South Galatia. The apostolic letter (Acts 15²³) was
only addressed to the Gentile Christians of Syria and
Cilicia, probably out of courtesy to St. Paul, who was in
charge of Galatia ; but the position was such that he
thought it wise to distribute copies of the letter here
also (16⁴). At Lystra he performed an act of marked
tact and courtesy ; he circumcised the half-Jew Timothy,
probably feeling that he could now do it without any risk
of misunderstanding.

2. ON TO TROAS (Acts 16⁶⁻¹⁰).—North of Pisidian Antioch
the missionaries struck the great trade-road which ran
due west down to Ephesus and so communicated with
the busy seaports of the coast. They meant to follow it
to the sea, but it was not to be. On the borders of the
province of Asia, they were " prevented by the Holy Spirit "
from proceeding.[1] They turned north by a road making
for the seaports of the north or Black Sea coast in the
province of Bithynia-Pontus. But as they reached the
border, they were again stopped by the " Spirit of Jesus "
(16⁷). So they turned west through Mysia, without
preaching on the way (see παρελθόντες, v.⁸), and reached
the sea at Troas. This was a port of considerable importance, though no great antiquity : it lay south of the
ancient Troy and was a Roman " colony."

There, as Paul wondered whither God was leading him,

---

[1] διῆλθον κωλυθέντες in 16⁶ can only mean, either, " made a tour after
having been stopped," or " while being stopped " (as in ἔφη κελεύσας,
23³⁵). κωλυθέντες can scarcely be *subsequent* in time to διῆλθον, as
Ramsay seems to take it. It implies that when they turned north,
they were at first in the " Phrygian-Galatian " region (see p. 67).
Therefore the latter phrase probably denotes the part of Phrygia
included in the province of Galatia.

he saw a night vision of a man of Macedon saying, " Come over and help us." The question is sometimes asked, who was the dream-figure ? Some conjecture that he was a doctor from Philippi, now practising at Troas and in attendance on St. Paul—namely, Luke, who almost certainly joined him at this point (see § 3). Others suppose that in the port the Apostle had seen many Macedonians clad in the Greek dress, and this turned his thoughts to the country which had so profoundly influenced human culture. Be this as it may, Paul took his dream as the guiding hand of God and sailed for Europe.

3. St. Luke.—We here come to the first " we " section in the Acts [1] ; *i.e.* the verbs, which have hitherto been in the third person (" they came," etc.), in $16^{10\text{ff.}}$ are in the first person (" *we* made a straight course," v.[11], etc.). This shows that Luke joined Paul for the first time at Troas and went with him to Philippi. The " we " of the first person is not found again till Acts $20^5$, from which point it keeps recurring to the end of the book. The inference is that Luke stayed at Philippi for some years, till Paul came there again on his third missionary journey : from that time on, he shared his leader's fortunes, in the last visit to Jerusalem and the eventful voyage to Rome.

A tradition tells us that Luke was one of the seventy disciples whom our Lord sent to preach during His ministry : this seems to be mere legend.[2] But another and better attested tradition is found in Eusebius, Jerome, and Euthalius. The first of these, in his *Ecclesiastical History* (iii. 4) says : " Luke was by race of those from

---

[1] D reads " we " in Acts $11^{28}$ (" when we were gathered together "), in recording events at Antioch before the famine.

[2] Col. $4^{11.14}$ proves that Luke was not a Jew. His Gospel is clearly not the work of an eye-witness : the phrase, " *I followed up* all the events from the first " (Luke $1^3$) means " investigated."

Antioch and by training a doctor." Jerome is more explicit : he was " a doctor, by race a Syrian of Antioch."

There seems to be no reason to doubt this tradition. Ramsay, indeed, questions it (*T. and R.C.* 389, *Luke the Physician*, 65) on the ground that the historian gives us such scanty details about events at Antioch. But Luke's way is to keep himself and his own interests in the background : he is not writing an early Church history but an account of the Church's spread from Palestine to Rome. Ramsay sees in Eusebius' words (" *of those from Antioch* ") a statement not that he belonged to an Antiochene family, but that some of them had settled in Antioch. He conjectures that Luke was a Philippian doctor on the grounds mentioned above (at the end of § 2).[1]

4. PHILIPPI (Acts 16[11-40]).—The missionary party had favouring winds : they reached the Isle of Samothrace, to the north-west, in one day, and the morrow brought them to the port of Neapolis, in Macedon (contrast 20[6], where the reverse journey took four days with a head-wind). Thence they proceeded to cross the high ridge of hills which lay between the sea and Philippi. This town was about 10 miles inland on a small river which ran into the Strymon. It had long been an important place because of its gold and silver mines, and as such had been refounded by Philip of Macedon, father of Alexander the Great, who renamed it after himself. Here Augustus had fought and won the battle which made him the first Emperor of Rome : subsequently he had raised the place to the dignity of a Roman " colony." It stood on the

[1] As against Ramsay's view, note (1) that there is good reason to connect Titus with Antioch (Gal. 2[1]), and Ramsay himself suggests that Titus was closely related by family to St. Luke ; (2) that Ramsay and most commentators interpret Luke's *numbers* as conforming to the Semitic method of reckoning (*i.e.* " three years " as equivalent to what a Greek would call " two ").

great road, the Via Egnatia, which the Romans had built from the Hellespont to Dyrrachium on the Adriatic, and the road brought it trade and added importance.

Luke styles it (16¹²) "the first city of that part of Macedon," words which have exercised the commentators; for though the Romans had divided Macedon into four parts ($\mu\epsilon\rho\acute{\iota}\delta\epsilon\varsigma$), yet the capital of the eastern district was not Philippi but Amphipolis. However, Philippi was actually the larger and more important place, and its inhabitants no doubt ranked it as the "first city," as Luke knew from his long stay there: indeed at a later time (see Ramsay, *T. and R.C.*, p. 207) it became so by general consent.

Luke also calls it a "colony" (16¹²): its magistrates he styles first loosely $\H{a}\rho\chi o\nu\tau\epsilon\varsigma$, a Greek title, in v.¹⁹; but later $\sigma\tau\rho\alpha\tau\eta\gamma o\acute{\iota}$ or "prætors" in v.²⁰, etc. Their official designation was "duumviri," but by courtesy they were often called "prætors" in a colony. They were attended by "lictors" ($\dot\rho\alpha\beta\delta o\hat{\upsilon}\chi o\iota$, Acts 16³⁵, ³⁸), who bore the terrible "rods" for scourging.

On the first Sabbath Paul and Silas sought out the meeting-place of the Jews. The narrative makes it clear that there were very few of them at Philippi: only women were present at the service, probably Jewesses who had married heathen, and a few God-fearers. Apparently they had no regular synagogue but met near the river in the open air.¹ In Macedon, as in Asia Minor, women were allowed much more freedom than in Palestine or Southern Greece. Among them was a well-to-do woman from Thyatira in Lydia (province of Asia): her birthplace

---

¹ See 16¹³, "where we *thought* there was a meeting for prayer"; $\epsilon\nu o\mu\acute{\iota}\zeta o\mu\epsilon\nu$ suggests that they had inquired but could not learn with certainty. $\Pi\rho o\sigma\epsilon\upsilon\chi\acute{\eta}$ is sometimes the Greek term for a synagogue (cp. Josephus, *Life*, 54); but in view of New Testament usage it seems unlikely that a building is intended here.

produced a famous purple which was used to dye fabrics woven in the neighbourhood — "Lydia" was the name given to its finest class of export, a purple garment woven whole. So the purple-seller of Philippi, the "God-fearer" who was St. Paul's first convert, no doubt took her name from her stock-in-trade. She entertained the missionaries in her house till they left Philippi. In a place like this no one much minded what religion was taught : Paul and Silas had a free field for a time. But it was inevitable in such a town (as to-day in many parts of the mission field and at home) that Christian evangelists should sooner or later come up against vested interests. At one of the side-shows in the street some men exhibited a half-demented slave-girl, a "Python" or ventriloquist who probably told fortunes.[1] For ventriloquism was in those days attributed to demon-possession and therefore supposed to carry with it the power of forecasting the future. Even to-day in countries such as China and South India, where people believe in demon-possession, those suffering from neurasthenia or some mental complex easily come to believe that they are possessed, and the belief not only produces corresponding action but aggravates the malady. Cures are still effected by suggestion, particularly in its most potent form of religious conviction.[2] Such was the slave-girl of Philippi, who used to call out in the streets after Paul and Silas as they went by and repeat in a child-like way phrases which she had heard them utter. For some days they hesitated to interfere, but at last they could stand it no longer : Paul turned and ordered the spirit to come out of her. The cure was instantaneous. But her

[1] Plutarch says that ventriloquists ($\dot{\epsilon}\gamma\gamma\alpha\sigma\tau\rho\dot{\iota}\mu\nu\theta\sigma\iota$) were called "Pythons." The word is probably connected with Pytho, the Delphic oracle of the Pythian Apollo. In v.[16] the translation is uncertain : either "a Python having a spirit," or "having a Python spirit."

[2] Modern examples may be found in *Pastor Hsi*, by Mrs. Harold Taylor (for China), and in *The Light of India*, by Harold Begbie.

infuriated owners seized the missionaries and dragged
them to the "prætors'" court in the market-place. Jews
have an unfortunate gift for rousing suspicion against
themselves in Europe : probably in this very year (A.D. 50)
there had been Messianic riots at Rome which led Claudius
to expel all Jews from the capital. So the "prætors" of
Philippi turned a ready ear to the charge that these "Jews"
were "disturbing" the city by preaching customs which
were contrary to Roman law. They promptly ordered
Paul and Silas to be flogged and put in jail.[1]

Now the victims were both of them Roman citizens and
it was "treason" to scourge them. At Jerusalem (Acts
22[26]) St. Paul successfully claimed his right of exemption :
at Philippi there was no possible reason to deter him from
doing the same.[2] But the "prætors," to judge from
Acts 16[37] (where ἀκατακρίτους means "without hearing
the case"), condemned the prisoners without listening to a
word they had to say. At any rate, scourged they were
and put in jail. The jailer placed them in a cell opening
off the lock-up, with their feet in stocks (v.[24]) and their
hands chained to the wall (v.[26]). Luke must have seen
Paul next morning and heard what happened. About
midnight they were singing hymns, when there was an
earthquake shock ; it loosened the staples of their chains
and wrenched away the bars fastening the doors. The
cells would be in black darkness, but in the outer lock-up
with its larger windows there would be more light. So
St. Paul looking out saw the jailer on the point of com-

[1] In v.[22] περιρήξαντες αὐτῶν τὰ ἱμάτια may mean (a) "rent their
own clothes" : so Ramsay, in accordance with the usual meaning of
the words. But there is no evidence that Greeks or Romans ever did
such a thing. Or (b) "tearing off the prisoners' clothes" (as C.H. and
D.S.). The phrase is used in 2 Mac. 4[38] of King Antiochus having a
murderer stripped.

[2] Among Jews, to put forward such a claim for exemption would
be to incur violent hostility ; but there were few Jews at Philippi.

mitting suicide in the conviction that his prisoners had escaped.[1] If the Apostle had let things take their course, he and Silas would have been free ; but instinctively he did the Christian thing, he cried out, " Do yourself no harm, for we are all here." The man was moved by his generosity, even if the other prisoners did not exactly welcome it. He took the missionaries to his own apartments, washed their wounds, and gave them supper ; and he and his whole household were baptized.

Next morning the lictors came round to say that the two prisoners might be released. There is no reason to suppose (as in the reading of D) that the " prætors " were terrified by the earthquake. Paul and Silas resolved to give them a lesson against hasty judgments : they told the lictors that they were Roman citizens, condemned off-hand to an illegal punishment : they refused to go unless the magistrates came in person to offer an apology. It was a serious offence under Roman law to scourge a citizen ; so these worthies hastened to comply in a state of considerable perturbation. But they added an earnest request that they would leave Philippi in the interests of public peace, at any rate till the mob feeling had died down. Paul decided to go ; not from fear of his own safety, though there is nothing uglier to face than an excited crowd. He had by this time proved in many a street riot that his times were in God's hand. Yet ordinary prudence made him comply : to stay at Philippi would be to invite danger for their converts. But he decided to leave Luke there, for the Christians were too raw as yet to be left to their own devices. This action was more than justified later ; for no other church which St. Paul founded had such a happy history as that of Philippi.

[1] Under Roman law a jailer who allowed prisoners to escape had to undergo the punishment to which they were sentenced.

5. THESSALONICA (Acts 17$^{1-9}$).—Paul and Silas pushed on westwards along the Egnatian road ($\delta\iota o\delta\epsilon\acute{v}\sigma a\nu\tau\epsilon\varsigma$, 17$^1$) through Amphipolis and Apollonia to Thessalonica. They do not seem to have stopped at either of the two former towns, probably because they did not want to embarrass Luke's work at Philippi by preaching in its neighbourhood, and partly because St. Paul made a practice of establishing centres at some distance apart and leaving his converts to fill up the intervening gaps (as he made Ephesus his Asian headquarters and left the towns of the Lycus valley and the other ports on the coast).

Thessalonica was 100 miles from Philippi. It was at this time the largest and most important city in Macedon, capital of a second "district" in the province. It is the outlet of a long corridor which runs north into the Balkan mountains (a fact to which it owed its strategic importance in the war of 1914–18). Luke's historical accuracy once more comes out in the narrative : for it was a self-governing Greek city, with a popular assembly ($\delta\hat{\eta}\mu os$, 17$^5$) ; and it has been proved by inscriptions extant in the town that its magistrates were called by the very uncommon title of "politarchs," as Luke designates them in vv.$^{6.\ 8}$. In another particular, however, he shows less than his usual care. He tells us in v.$^2$ that St. Paul preached in the synagogue for three Sabbaths.[1] On a cursory reading that would seem to imply that he was only three weeks in the place. But there is ample proof that he stayed on for a considerable time after the synagogue was closed to him. For he made a large number of converts (v.$^4$) among the God-fearers, including some of the leading women in the town. The Epistles to the Thessalonians presuppose a ministry of some months at least : thus, for instance, 1 Thess. 2$^9$ tells us that when the Apostle was at

---

[1] The summary of his teaching in the synagogue (v.$^3$) follows the same lines as his address at Pisidian Antioch (13$^{16ff\cdot}$).

Thessalonica he had worked hard to support himself by his trade of tent-making : he refused to accept hospitality from the local church because he did not want to burden them.   The Christians of Philippi twice sent him a present of money while he was at Thessalonica (Phil. 4¹⁶).  All this clearly implies a stay of some duration.

But the Jews as usual dogged his steps and at last made the place too hot for him.   They aroused the rabble to attack the house of Jason, a convert with whom the missionaries were lodging.   Paul and Silas were out at the time ;  but their host and some others were seized and dragged before the politarchs.   St. Paul's preaching at Thessalonica, as the Epistles to the Thessalonians prove, had centred largely on the imminence of the Parousia, that is, our Lord's second coming to judge the world ;  and their converts had seized on this point and magnified it out of all proportion (see below, pp. 127 (b) and 132, § 4).   This gave an easy handle to their opponents : Jason has received men " who have turned the world upside down," and who " all act contrary to the decrees of Cæsar, saying that there is another king, one Jesus."   It was a dangerous accusation, now made for the first time since Pilate signed our Lord's death-warrant on that very charge.

But the politarchs showed more discrimination than the pompous prætors of Philippi.   They merely bound over the defendants to keep the peace, and made them deposit a sum of money as guarantee.   This meant that St. Paul might get his host into serious trouble unless he left the place.   He went most unwillingly, with heart-searching anxiety about his converts (1 Thess. 3⁵).   He meant to return as soon as new magistrates came into office ;  but in this he was disappointed : see 1 Thess. 2¹⁸, " we wanted to come to you—I, Paul, more than once—but Satan hindered us."   He must have heard that his return, even in the following year, would cause trouble and make Jason and the others liable.

6. BERŒA (Acts 17[10-15]).—Paul and Silas left Thessalonica by night, and turning to the left off the Egnatian road, they went west-south-west for 42 miles to Berœa. This was a populous and well-watered town, and the number of the converts they made there suggests a ministry of some months. They found the Jews more open-minded than at Thessalonica and more ready to discuss the Old Testament prophecies in which the early Church found predictions of the Crucifixion and Resurrection. But they were still too near Thessalonica and there was trouble again ; once more St. Paul had to move on south.

He left Silas and Timothy behind to settle affairs in the young church, but as soon as he reached Athens he felt the urgent need of companionship and help in a strange city (cp. 1 Thess. 3[1]), and sent word for them to rejoin him at once. Yet he was full of anxiety about the people he had left : he sent Timothy back again from Athens to Thessalonica to see how they were progressing (1 Thess. 3[1, 5]), and probably Silas on a similar errand to Berœa. They both rejoined him at Corinth (Acts 18[5]) with tidings which made his mind more easy about the loyalty and progress of the two churches (1 Thess. 3[6]).

For some reason he had decided not to preach anywhere in Thessaly, which lay between Berœa and Athens. It was obviously better to put a good deal of ground between himself and the enemies who dogged his footsteps ; and we have noted above (beginning of § 5) his strategic policy of spacing out his churches : also he must have felt the lure of Athens and Corinth.

We do not know how he reached Athens. The reading in Acts 17[14] of the majority of manuscripts, including the

best, is that he journeyed from Berœa ἕως ἐπὶ τὴν θάλασσαν
(" right as far as the sea "), implying that he took ship
to Athens. But the ἕως sounds superfluous, and the
language of v.[15a] (ἤγαγον, " conducted ") comports better
with an overland journey. There is therefore much to
be said for the reading ὡς (instead of ἕως) in v.[14], " as if
making for the sea," i.e. in order to mislead his enemies.
But however he went, he now left the province of Macedon
and entered a new field in the southerly province of
Achæa.


7. ATHENS (Acts 17[16-34]).—Athens [1] was unquestionably the most beautiful city in Europe, with its magni-
ficent views of sea and mountain and its unrivalled
temples of Pentelican marble.  As centres of Greek culture,
Alexandria and Tarsus might vie with her ; yet about
her there lingered the romance of a past far beyond anything they could boast.  St. Paul could truthfully say
to his Athenian audience (17[22]), " I perceive that you
are very religious " : the satirist Petronius with pardonable exaggeration says that it was easier to find a god
there than a man.  But the religion of the people was
æsthetic and dramatic : there was little moral earnestness or deep conviction.  St. Luke hits off an Athenian
characteristic admirably when he says (v.[21]), " the Athenians spent their time in nothing else but in telling or
hearing something new."

Philosophy still flourished there, though it was long
past its zenith.  Its centres were the Stoa or Porch in
the market-place, from which the Stoics took their name

---

[1] By constitution Athens was a " free " town (see note 2 on p. 147).
Commercially she was in decay and very poor, and her population was
small.  In the reign of Augustus the Piræus (her port) was a small
village which travellers merely visited in order to see the pictures in
the temples (Mommsen, Roman Provinces, i. 278).

and where they taught their austere but self-centred ethics ; and, hard by, the garden of Epicurus, where his followers proclaimed the ideal of a life of pleasure far removed from passion and all things ugly.  In all Greek towns the itinerant philosopher was a familiar figure—a man who lectured without charge, in the hope of securing a permanent opening, but nowhere else so much as in the Agora (market-place) at Athens, though the ancient court of the Areopagus was charged with the control of all lectures lest the people be corrupted by strange and immoral teaching.[1]

We may be pardoned for quoting from Conybeare and Howson a singularly interesting passage in the *Life* of Apollonius of Tyana, who had been educated at Tarsus about the same time as St. Paul : " Having come to anchor in the Piræus, he went up from the harbour to the city [of Athens].  Advancing onward he met several of the philosophers.  In his first conversation, finding the Athenians *much devoted to religion*, he discoursed on sacred subjects.  This was at Athens, where also *altars of Unknown Divinities* are set up." [2]

The custom referred to in the last clause and in Acts 17[23] was not unknown elsewhere in the Greek world ; for instance, an altar with this inscription has been found at Pergamus in Asia.  But it was so common at Athens that a legend had been invented to account for it.[3]  It is not quite certain what the real meaning of the inscription was.  Some (*e.g.* Professor Myres of Oxford) suppose that when prehistoric altars were unearthed with their inscriptions undecipherable, they were dedicated " to the un-

[1] Ramsay points out how true to local customs are St. Luke's statements that at Athens Paul taught in the Agora, but at Ephesus he hired the school of Tyrannus (19[9]).

[2] C.H., p. 266 (Philostratus' *Life of Apollonius*).  The italics are mine.

[3] Given by D.S., p. 11, from Diogenes Lært., i. 110.

known god." A more plausible explanation is this : different gods had control of different actions (as with the Christian saints in some countries to-day) ; to dedicate an altar to the wrong deity would be to risk the wrath of the right : it was safer to write " to the unknown god." St. Paul probably had never before in his life seen such an inscription : to him it came with all the pathos of a man who longed for God and knew Him not.

To return to his adventures at Athens, he taught in the Agora, and there he encountered Epicurean and Stoic philosophers. The former were still the selfish hedonists they had always been ; their creed was " get away from all things ugly as the gods do," though it is just to add that they regarded evil passions as ugly. Their belief was materialistic. Stoicism, on the other hand, with its austere ideas of duty and self-control, produced the noblest type of character to be found in that age (e.g. Epictetus, Seneca, and Marcus Aurelius). The Stoic had often the puritan vices of hardness and self-sufficiency ; but he, and he alone, taught the brotherhood of man, while the rest of the world looked on slaves as mere chattels and all foreigners as barbarians. Moreover, by St. Paul's time Stoicism was beginning to absorb Platonic elements and to lose its " pantheistic materialistic impress " : [1] Seneca shows a longing for the redemption of the soul and Divine help.

Some of these philosophers sneered at St. Paul as a σπερμόλογος (lit. " picker-up of seeds ") : it was a slang word applied to the petty pilferers who lounge about markets, and more loosely as a term of contempt for any one (" bounder "). Others misunderstood him as

---

[1] See Harnack, *History of Dogma*, i. 110, 123. A most interesting study of contemporary Stoicism in contrast with Christianity may be found in E. A. Abbott's novel, *Silanus the Christian*. See especially Chapter IV. (on Epictetus and Paul).

preaching a new god and goddess, Jesus and Anastasis
(Resurrection). They took him before the court of the
Areopagus, which controlled popular lectures and which
probably sat for this purpose somewhere in the Agora.
It does not seem to have been a regular meeting of the
court to try the Apostle, so much as an impromptu gathering to hear his views (17²¹).¹ His speech is of exceptional
interest. He begins by referring to their famous love of
religion ² and their longing to know, as shown by the
inscription, " to an unknown god." This is his text.
He offers them the fuller knowledge which they need.
Many of their own philosophers (notably the Epicureans)
will agree that the Maker of heaven and earth, the giver
of life, is not contained by human temples and handiwork
as if He lacked aught. But at this point he turns rather
to the Stoics : God is not far from us (as the Epicureans
thought), but made us all ; He set His traces in nature,
to make us grope after Him ; as Epimenides said, He is
immanent in us all, " in Him we live and move and have
our being " ³ ; or again, as the Stoic Aratus of Tarsus
wrote in the *Phaenomena*, " we are His own kith and kin."
The Divine, then (note the philosophical word, not
" God "), is not like any graven image. What He *is*
like, He has taught the world at last, by sending to them
a man to declare Him—One whom He raised miraculously
from the dead and will send back shortly to judge the
world. From first to last he tells them, not that they

¹ There has been much discussion whether " the Areopagus " in 17¹⁹
means (*a*) the hill of that name, a low spur which runs out on the west
of the Acropolis, with the market-place lying below to the north ; or
(*b*) the court which took its name from the hill. But everything points
to the latter.

² δεισιδαιμών sometimes means " religious," sometimes " superstitious," according to its context. But here it must mean " religious " :
Paul would never begin by blatant discourtesy.

³ This is probably a hexameter line. He quotes Epimenides again in
Tit. 1¹² (if he wrote that Epistle).

are wrong in all their ideas of God, but that he can show
them where they are in error and lead them on to fuller,
clearer truth. He never hints at what he says in Rom. 1,
where he also is discussing " natural " religion, that human
sin is responsible for distorted notions of God.

It was a wonderful speech, but it failed on the whole
to reach his audience. To begin with, it was based on
the assumption that they yearned for fuller knowledge ;
but most of them prided themselves on their profound
philosophy. What could an ignorant Jew teach them,
with his silly fables about a Jewish peasant who had
been raised from the dead ? It was obvious that St. Paul
could not touch the Greek mind along that line. He tried
a very different method at Corinth, whither he soon went
in discouragement at his poor success at Athens. The
only way to pierce their intellectual pride was to tell them
in effect, " however wise you are in knowledge, you have
no power to follow out your wisdom : you are slaves of
sin, to judge from your lives. I offer you, not an intellectual system, but a practical means of escape from
sin, which is really the most profound wisdom " (see
1 Cor. $1^{18}$–$2^{16}$, especially $2^2$).

Yet he had won over at least two converts of note at
Athens : one was Dionysius, a member of the Areopagus,
in whose name were forged some strange mystic speculations centuries later ; the other was a woman named
Damaris, who was probably a courtesan of some education,
for so her name suggests, as well as the fact that she heard
St. Paul in a city where respectable women lived in close
seclusion.

8. CORINTH (Acts $18^{1-17}$). — Some fifty miles by
road from Athens, and almost due west of it, lay
Corinth, the political and commercial capital of Achæa as
Athens was the intellectual. Its unique position on the

8

isthmus made it the key of the Peloponnese : but its geographical situation gave it a far higher value still ; it was the port of call between the Ægean Sea and the Adriatic. It is important to remember how it lies on the map. Two or three miles to the north of the ancient city, where the isthmus is narrowest, it is pierced by a canal, begun by Nero in A.D. 52 and finished by the Greeks in 1893. This is 3½ miles long. The isthmus widens towards the city : a line drawn from Lechæum, its port on the western Corinthian Gulf, to Cenchreæ on the eastern or Saronic Gulf, is about 7 miles. In St. Paul's day, small ships were hauled over the neck without unloading ; other wise merchandise was transshipped from one port to the other. The voyage round the Peloponnese was not only much longer, but necessitated going round Cape Malea with its dangerous currents and sudden storms. Thus Corinth was a channel of intercourse from east to west and *vice versa*.

Towering above the ancient city on the south is the citadel, the Acro-Corinthus, which rises to a height of 1800 feet. Its extensive summit once held a whole town, where now is nothing but a few sheep and many eagles— except some fortifications and marvellous great cisterns in the ground, constructed by the Republic of Venice, which held it for several centuries against the Turk. Plutarch says it was by nature so strong that it could be held by 400 soldiers, fifty dogs and as many keepers (quoted by C.H. p. 322, n. 4).

Little need be said of the history of Corinth. It had been founded by the Phœnicians, who left there as a bane-ful legacy their hideously immoral worship of Ashtarte. When the Dorian Greeks came in the ninth century B.C., they retained this cult so foreign to their race, but called the goddess Aphrodite. We are told that in her Temple were 1000 sacred prostitutes. In classical times the city spread its colonies east and west along the shores of the Mediterranean, and became a leader of commerce. In due time Rome conquered her, and in 146 B.C. she rebelled. Lucius Mummius, moved as much by commercial jealousy as by political severity, burnt the place to the ground. But in 44 B.C. Julius Cæsar refounded it as the seat of the governor of Achæa, and made it a Roman " colony." It quickly surpassed even its former greatness : the inner city was 5 miles round, the outer city twice as much. The Roman colonists of 44 B.C. and the Government officials must have been largely outnumbered by the Greek populace ; but they jostled in the streets also against men of every nation in the Levant. Like all cosmopolitan places it was a hotbed of vice, fostered here by the sexual worship of the " Love " goddess.

St. Luke is as accurate as usual in describing its governor. For Achæa was under a proconsul from 27 B.C.–A.D. 15, and again after A.D. 44.

Till recently nothing was known of Gallio's proconsulship, except a remark in a letter of his brother Seneca that he had caught a fever in Achæa. But in an inscription lately discovered at Delphi, Gallio is called by the Emperor Claudius his " friend and proconsul of Achæa " ; and the inscription is dated by the Emperor's twenty-sixth *acclamatio imperatoria* (the *acclamatio* was an address of praise from the Senate to the Emperor), which, as we know from other sources,[1] denotes a date shortly before August A.D. 52. It seems clear that Gallio's tenure of office began in the previous July ; so that here we have, what is rare in St. Paul's life, a certain date as landmark.

To return to St. Paul, he must have reached Corinth towards the end of A.D. 51.[2] At first he had no thought of

[1] See D.S., App. I. p. 652.
[2] Acts 18[11] gives the total period of his stay there as eighteen months.

making a long stay there : he was hoping to return soon
to Macedon, but waited for the return of Silas and Timothy
to learn whether that was possible. He preached in the
synagogue every Sabbath (v.[4]), working on weekdays at
his trade of tent-making. This brought him in touch with
a Jew of the same trade, who bore the Latin name of
Aquila and whose family came from Pontus in the north
of Asia Minor. This man had been living at Rome with
his wife Priscilla, which is the diminutive of Prisca, the
name of a leading Roman family (the *gens Servilia*). It
is possible that she herself belonged to that family,[1] for
it is noticeable that in four places out of six where she
and her husband are mentioned together, her name is
placed first.

They had recently come to Corinth owing to the edict of
Claudius which expelled all Jews from Rome owing to some
riots in the Ghetto.[2] St. Luke does not tell us when they
were converted to Christianity ; but the natural inference
is that it was at Corinth under St. Paul's influence.

After a time, Silas arrived from Macedon, accompanied
by some Philippian Christians who brought a gift of money
to Paul (2 Cor. 11[9]) ; and Timothy came back from Thessalonica. They both reported the continuance of fierce
persecution in the north ; obviously the time was not yet
ripe for St. Paul's return there.

He accepted the fact as God's will, with sorrow indeed
for his Macedonian converts, but with joy as far as Corinth
was concerned : for he was already " engrossed in " the
work there (v.[5], note the Imperfect συνείχετο).

Before long the old story repeated itself : the Jews
would have none of him. He had already converted the

---

[1] So Hort. Otherwise she may have been a freedwoman of the family.
St. Luke's habit of putting her name before her husband's may be due
to her greater Christian influence rather than her patrician birth.

[2] Suet. *Claud.* 25. See further on p. 247, § 3.

ruler of their synagogue, Crispus [1]; also a leading God-fearer, a Roman " colonist" named Titus Justus.[2] So the Jews were lashed to fury ; they turned him out of the synagogue.[3] But Titus Justus had a house next door, and here the Christian Church met. Nothing could be better calculated to annoy the Jews further, and it seems at first sight to be a sign of singular lack of tact on St. Paul's part. Perhaps it was the only house available which would hold them all, and it was thought that nothing could make Jewish hostility keener than it already was.

So he went on working for eighteen months, sometimes making tours into the country round Corinth (see 1 Thess. 1[7], 2 Cor. 1[1]). When Timothy came from Thessalonica, he had brought a most cheering report. But it was inevitable that such an infant Church, left perforce to its own devices, should have its difficulties. St. Paul had centred his preaching to them on the certainty that Christ would soon return to judge the world ; and the Thessalonians were, some of them, living in such fervid expectation of an imminent Parousia (Second Advent), that they could not settle down to workaday life. To meet these difficulties and others of a kindred nature, St. Paul wrote his two letters to Thessalonica early in his stay at Corinth.

It was in July 52 that L. Junius Annæus Gallio arrived at Corinth as proconsul. He came of an eminent Latin family from Spain. His younger brother was the able and famous Stoic philosopher Seneca,[4] who after being

[1] There seems to have been only one ἀρχισυνάγωγος at Corinth; see vv.[8, 17]. Contrast the synagogue at Antioch in Pisidia (Acts 13[15]) ; and see Mark 5[22]. The ἀρχισυνάγωγοι were not the governing body (ἄρχοντες), but simply arranged the services : see Schürer, II. 2. 64–5.

[2] The name appears as Tit*i*us in some MSS. and versions (B Vulg. Boh.).

[3] " He shook out his raiment " (v.[6]), a recognised way of disowning any further dealings with them.

[4] Their nephew was Lucan, who wrote the epic poem known as the " Pharsalia," which, in spite of some beautiful passages, is forced and artificial and contains some fulsome flattery of Nero.

in exile from A.D. 41–49 was now high in Court favour, and the tutor of the future Emperor Nero. Seneca was a man of great insight and strong ideals ; though we cannot acquit him of a certain weakness of character, even allowing for the difficulty of controlling a Nero. It is from his pen that we have a description of Gallio (Sen. *Nat. Quaest.* 4 Præfat.) as gentle, courteous, truthful, and lovable.[1]  The Jews of Corinth perhaps mistook his gentleness for weakness ; for they seized the occasion of his coming into office as suitable for bringing a charge against Paul : he " persuades men to worship God contrary to the law." [2]  It was a purely Jewish grievance, as Gallio at once saw ; he would not even hear the prisoner's defence, but dismissed the charge with contempt as a matter of " words and names, and their own law," which they must settle in their own religious court (Acts 18[15]) : and he " drove them out." What happened next is not very clear ; but apparently v.[17] means that the crowd, who never loved the Jews, seized Sosthenes, Crispus' successor as ruler of the synagogue, and thrashed him outside the tribunal ; and the proconsul, thinking that rough justice was done, took no steps to stop it.

In the following spring St. Paul felt a wish to return home. Probably he planned to reach Jerusalem in time

---

[1] Seneca says of him, " quem nemo non in sinum recipit," and " inexpugnabilem virum adversus insidias " (the Stoic ideal).

[2] Why was the case brought before Gallio rather than the " duumviri " ? According to Mommsen (*History of Rome*, vol. iii. p. 50, n.), the Roman Governor exercised superintendence over the criminal jurisdiction in certain (probably the more serious) cases : " the Roman *provincia* was primarily nothing but a ' command,' and all the administrative and judicial functions of the commandant were originally collateral duties and corollaries of his military position." See also vol. iv. p. 545, where, after pointing out that a Roman colony in the new Empire administered its own affairs, Mommsen says : " The more important processes came before the Roman authority . . . as a rule the governor of the province " ; and, in the footnote, that the governor heard them in Corinth.

for the Feast of Passover or of Pentecost, and then go and spend his furlough at Antioch. It has been suggested that he was ill and needed a change.[1] At any rate he went down to Cenchreæ to catch a boat which was sailing for Ephesus and Cæsarea ; and while he was there he shaved his head, in the Jewish manner of performing a vow, perhaps (as Ramsay suggests) as thanks for safe embarkation after all his dangers. It is interesting to find that in this instance he observes a national rite of the Jews, either for his own edification or possibly because there were on board the boat a large number of Jews going to Jerusalem for the feast. In the case of Acts 21[23-24] he is moved by the desire to prove in Jerusalem that he has not abjured all Mosaic rites for himself.

Priscilla and Aquila went with him as far as Ephesus, where they remained for a while as missionary pioneers. They were still there when Paul himself reached the city on his third missionary journey, for he mentions them as joining in his greetings to the Corinthian Church (1 Cor. 16[19]). But soon after this, they went back to Rome (see Rom. 16[3]). Timothy seems to have gone with the Apostle all the way ; at any rate he was with him at Ephesus a year later. Silas drops out of St. Paul's history at this point ; but he is probably the Silvanus who acted as St. Peter's amanuensis in writing 1 Peter (see 5[12])—indeed, the Pauline touches in that Epistle, which are in such strong contrast to the general style that is quite un-Pauline, are perhaps due to Silas, for Peter was probably a poor linguist and required help in writing Greek.

[1] So D.S., p. 189, n. 1. He quotes as evidence Paul's vow at Cenchreæ (Acts 18[18]) ; and the term (προστάτις) " succourer " which he uses of Phœbe, the deaconess of Cenchreæ, in Rom. 16[2] as though she had nursed him through a bad attack on the eve of his voyage. But both these points admit of other explanations. Num. 6 gives directions for those Jews who took the Nazirite vow for a time ; they let the hair grow until the period was completed and then shaved it.

So St. Paul came to Jerusalem once more, though but on a flying visit (18²²).¹ He spent most of his furlough at Antioch, which was really his spiritual home.

He must have thought over his two great missionary journeys with a strange mixture of feelings. In a sense he had succeeded beyond his wildest hopes : humanity was unconsciously hungering for the strength and joy which Christianity offered, and the Gospel was on its way to win the whole world. God had delivered him again and again from the savage cruelty of mob violence. But there was another side to it all : at Pisidian Antioch, Iconium, and Lystra ; at Thessalonica and Berœa, and almost at Corinth, the Jews, his own people, with their unique knowledge of God, had cut short his work and driven him out with unscrupulous violence. Can we wonder at the strength of his language about them in 1 Thess. 2¹⁵⁻¹⁶ ? Yet, fortunately for him, such bitterness could not live in his heart for long. Christ touched it with His spirit ; and in Rom. 9¹⁻³ we find it transformed into a wondering pity for his race who could be so unworthy of their past. He was very human ; that is why he could become, in so real a sense, a Saint.

¹ Pentecost in A.D. 53 fell on 12th May. See Lewin, *Fasti Sacri*.

# CHAPTER VIII.

## THE EPISTLES TO THE THESSALONIANS.

1. DATE AND PLACE OF WRITING: GENUINENESS OF
2 THESSALONIANS.—(a) 1 Thessalonians is indisputably
written from Corinth during the eighteen months which
St. Paul spent there on the second missionary journey.
For it is clear from chaps. 1 and 2 that he had lately gone
to Thessalonica from Philippi, where he had suffered cruel
persecution (see $2^2$). Since then he had visited Athens ($3^1$).
Timothy and Silas (Silvanus) were now with him ($1^1$); and
the former had lately returned from Thessalonica, where
he had been sent to visit the Church ($3^{2-6}$). All these
details harmonise with the time of the Apostles' sojourn
at Corinth as described in the last chapter, and with no
other. Probably a year had elapsed since he left Thessalonica; there had been several deaths among the Thessalonian Christians, see $4^{13-14}$; some commentators infer,
from the language of v.$^{14}$, "those who have fallen asleep
*through* (διά) Jesus," that these had been martyrs for the
faith.

(b) 2 Thessalonians, in the words of Dr. Lake (*Earlier
Epp.* p. 61), "so closely resembles 1 Thessalonians that it is
usually conceded to be indisputable that, if it be genuine,
it must have been written at the same time as, or
immediately after, the former Epistle."

Timothy and Silvanus are still with him ($1^1$).

The only doubt is whether the Epistle be a genuine
letter of St. Paul. It is quoted as such by Polycarp early

in the second century ; and no doubt is felt about it by
any of our early authorities. The chief difficulty in
accepting it is the apparent inconsistency between the
eschatology in this and in the first letter. In 1 Thessalonians the Second Advent is imminent ; in 2 Thessalonians
(see $2^{1-12}$) there is to be a considerable development of the
historical position before the Lord returns (*i.e.* the growth
of the infant Church protected by a sheltering force which
is probably Roman Law : later on, a violent outbreak of
apostasy, led by an Antichrist).

But we question whether the very obviousness of this
difficulty is not an argument for the genuineness of the
letter. Would any forger have ventured on it ? Moreover, a few years of history might witness all the development that he predicts in $2^{1-12}$. In 1 Thess. $5^2$ he uses
language which proves that he felt quite uncertain when
the Parousia would be ; only he looked for it soon. We
are reminded of our Lord's own words as the Synoptic
Gospels record them : in Mark $13^{32}$ He says, " of that
day or that hour knoweth no one . . . not even the Son " ;
and He speaks at times as if He might return quickly, at
times as if He were like one who went away for a long stay
in another country. In 2 Thessalonians St. Paul is damp-
ing down the overhot excitement of the Thessalonians
about the Second Advent : his general attitude is—the
Parousia is a certain thing in no distant future, but it
cannot be yet awhile.

2. RELATIONSHIP BETWEEN THE TWO LETTERS.—There
is a very strong family likeness between the two letters :
they show a remarkable repetition of whole phrases. Yet
in other ways there is an equally marked contrast. The
first letter is warmly affectionate : the second is colder.
The first is addressed to Gentiles who have recently re-
nounced idolatry ($1^9$), and who need an emphatic warning

against the lusts of the flesh ($4^{3-8}$) : it does not contain a single quotation from the Old Testament nor any sign that he has in mind Jewish Christians.  On the other hand, in the second letter there is not a word which hints at a heathen past : the Old Testament is not indeed quoted by name, but the passage in $1^{8-10}$ is almost entirely a string of Old Testament quotations. He appeals to Christian " traditions " ($2^{15}$ $3^6$) ; and the word for the Second Advent is no longer exclusively " Parousia " as in 1 Thessalonians, but also " Apocalypse " ($1^7$, cp. $2^{6-8}$). This contrast has led Professor Harnack to suggest that the two letters were written concurrently to different sections of the Thessalonian Church.  Its members were predominantly Gentile ; to them 1 Thessalonians was written.  But there was a strong Jewish minority, to whom, according to this theory, the second letter was sent.  The emphatic command in 1 Thess. $5^{27}$, that the letter shall be read to " all the brethren " may point to some division between the two sections.  Perhaps Timothy had told him that the Greeks were perplexed chiefly by the death of some of their number, while the Jews had difficulties of a rather different kind, though also connected with the Parousia.

But if so, why should St. Paul address the second letter simply to the Church of the Thessalonians and give no hint that it is meant only for a certain section of them ? It may be that he refused to emphasise or recognise divisions in the Church : he might attain his object by having the second letter delivered to a Jewish Christian.

The whole hypothesis must remain very uncertain.  It is simpler on the whole to suppose that the second letter was dispatched three months after the former, reiterating much of what he had said.  If so, he had received news from Thessalonica in the interval, reporting that unhealthy excitement about the Parousia was still dominant.[1] The colder tone of the second letter is amply explained by his displeasure that the earlier epistle had not produced a greater effect.

### 3. 1 THESSALONIANS. PARAPHRASE AND NOTES.

(a) THE FIRST THREE CHAPTERS tell of his strong affection for them, and of the great anxiety which he had felt on their account when he had to leave them to face bitter persecution with so little guidance from Christians of longer experience in the faith. But all this has turned into joy and gratitude to God since Timothy has returned to tell him of their splendid steadfastness.

One phrase recurs so often in these chapters that it must be significant, namely, " as ye yourselves know " ($1^5$ $2^{1.\ 2.\ 5.\ 11}$ $3^4$ ; cp. $2^{10}$). He appeals to their knowledge about his own life among them, and his unflinching zeal for the gospel in spite of the sufferings he had endured for it at Philippi. Again they *know* he never flattered them nor sought fame or money, though he might have claimed board and lodging from them ($2^{7\text{-}9}$) ; they will *remember* how he worked at his trade late into the night to support himself ($2^9$) ; they are *witnesses* (v.[10]), they *know* (v.[11]) of his unfailing love and yearning that they should live as befits members of God's Kingdom ; they *know* that he had foretold persecution ($3^4$).

All this implies that persecution had brought doubt and despondency to some of them. Could it be true, after all, that Paul, as his Jewish enemies said, was only like one of the Greek Sophists who went round lecturing for no fees in the hope of getting a connexion which would bring fame and a lucrative position ?

$1^1$. " Paul, Silvanus, and Timothy greet the Church at Thessalonica. We thank God for you, constantly remembering you in our prayers, for your *faith, love, and hope.*

---

[1] For details, see the notes in § 3*b* and the beginning of § 4 below.

(v.⁴) God loves you and your ' election ' is certain, for it is
proved by the fact that the gospel message did not end
in pious talk among you, but produced the same miraculous
results and spiritual power and great assurance as, you
know well, were given to me to show in my ministry
among you. (v.⁶) In sore persecution the Holy Spirit gave
you joy and made you an example to all Christians in
Macedon and Achæa : so that because of you the word of
God has sounded a message not only there but in places
far beyond. (v.⁹) People are talking of our coming to you,
and your conversion from the service of idols to that of the
living and only true God, and to eager expectation of His
Son's second coming from heaven—Jesus, who was raised
from the dead and is alive to deliver us from the judgment
to come.

2¹. " I need not tell you of our work among you, how
rich in results it was : you know how, after ill-treatment
at Philippi, we came to Thessalonica and, after all we
had suffered for preaching, we were bold to tell you the
glad tidings and never spared ourselves. We did not
try to mislead you [as Sophists might] : we had no hidden
motive of unclean desire or cunning self-seeking. God
thought us fit to be entrusted with His message, and so
we speak it as trying to please only Him who ' tries men's
hearts.' We never flattered you—you know that—nor
made our work an excuse to gain money ; we did not
seek to establish our reputation with you or any one,
though as Christ's apostles we might have become a
burden to you [i.e. by claiming that you should pay us
for our keep, see v.⁹] : we became like little children
towards you—nay, like a mother suckling her own infants.
(v.⁸) Our longing was not only to impart to you the good
tidings but to enable you to win your own souls, because
we loved you. Remember our toil and moil : we worked
day and night at our trade to keep ourselves, so as not

to be a burden on you while we preached. (v.¹⁰) You
yourselves and God know that towards those that have
Christian faith our conduct was holy, righteous, and
irreproachable—that, like a father with his children, we
tried to comfort and exhort every individual among you,
urging you to make your life worthy of God who ever is
calling you into His Kingdom.

(v.¹³) " That is why we can give thanks for you, because
you received our message as God's word to you, as it is
indeed, and as it is proved to be by its active power in
the lives of you who have faith. For after the example of
the Christian Churches in Judæa, who were persecuted by
the Jews, you endured persecution from those of your
race. Oh, these Jews! they killed the Lord and the
prophets, and persecuted us to the uttermost ; they do not
seek to please God and are hostile to all men ; they try
to stop us speaking the word of salvation to the Gentiles.
But the judgment of God is coming surely and speedily
on them to the utmost."

[*Notes.*—(*a*) In 2⁷ we have followed the reading of
W.H., who read νήπιοι, " babes " (with ℵ B C D Latt.
Boh. etc.). In this case St. Paul inverts his metaphor
in the middle, as so often, see on Gal. 4¹⁹. The inferior
MSS. read ἤπιοι, " gentle," to make the metaphor
homogeneous. However, it is possible that the former
reading, νήπιοι, is an error due to doubling the last letter
of the previous word ἐγενήθημεν.

(*b*) 2¹⁶ᵇ. R.V. reads " is come," a literal rendering of
ἔφθασεν. But probably the Aorist tense is anticipatory
(like the Hebrew *perfect* of prophetic certainty), *i.e.* it
means, " is certain to come." We are told that if a tourist
in a modern Greek café calls impatiently to a waiter, the
latter replies deprecatingly, ἔφθασα, " I am there."]

2¹⁷. " When I was forced to leave Thessalonica for a
time, I felt bereft of my children : but my heart is with

you, and I dearly long to see your faces. On two separate occasions I planned to come and visit you, but Satan hindered me [*i.e.* reports from Thessalonica made it clear that a visit would cause trouble in the place]. For you are our hope and joy, our victor's crown in which we shall glory in the day when we shall face the Lord Jesus at His coming again.

3¹. " So much did we feel our separation from you, that I preferred to be left all alone in Athens and sent Timothy to establish your faith, for fear persecution might weaken you. You yourselves know that opposition is to be our lot ; we ourselves warned you that trouble would come, and it did. So, unable to bear uncertainty, I sent to find out how your faith stood it, fearing that the tempter might have ruined my work. But lately, when Timothy returned with a splendid report of your faith and love, and your desire to see me, I was relieved of my anxiety about your suffering : it means life to me if you stand stedfast in the Lord. What thanks can I give to God for this great joy, though night and day I still yearn beyond measure to see you face to face and to make up whatever your faith still lacks ?

(v.¹¹) " May God make the way clear for us to come to you ! May the Lord give you abounding love for one another and for everybody, such as we bear to you. May He strengthen your hearts and make you above reproach at the coming again of Jesus with His saints."

(*b*) CHAPS. 4–5 give practical advice and instruction. St. Paul must have heard from Timothy that some of the Thessalonians were so full of the nearness of the Parousia as to live in a state of unhealthy excitement. They neglected their business (4¹¹) for emotional ecstasies, and other people had to support them (4¹²). Their revivalist experiences (cp. 5¹⁹⁻²⁰) made them fancy themselves superior to their spiritual leaders (5¹²⁻¹³). But beyond this they were at a loss what to think about some of their number who had recently died. St. Paul had taught them that soon, when Christ should come again on the clouds, all His faithful servants should be caught up to Him in the sky, to reign henceforth with their Lord in eternal bliss ; for his eschatology was still very primitive, being almost the same, in fact, as before his conversion. He had not had time to teach them (or if he had, they had failed to understand him) that Christians who died before the Parousia should also rise again. This is the assurance which he now gives them. It is just possible that the Thessalonian difficulty was somewhat different. They may have been told by their Jewish members that Messiah was to reign *on earth* for a season before the general resurrection of the righteous ; and their sorrow may have been to think that their own dead would miss the joy of the perfect earthly kingdom. However, this interpretation does not accord well with 4[13], where he tells them not to grieve as the heathen who have no hope of a resurrection.

For the rest, he stresses chiefly the duty of chastity (4[3-8]). In Greek cities sins of the flesh were regarded as inevitable ; and Christians living among so much immorality were in danger of insensibly lowering their standards. The Council of Jerusalem had thought it necessary to warn Gentile Christians against fornication.

4[1]. " Finally, my brothers, we beseech you to live as we taught you you ought in the Lord Jesus ; indeed you do, but strive to excel ever more and more. You know what Jesus in His life on earth charged us. [Note the reference to our Lord's teaching : he had taught them *the sayings of Jesus as he knew them*. This implies that something like a written Gospel already existed, cp. v.[15].] God's will is that you should sanctify your lives ; especially that you should keep away from fornication, each one of you knowing how to get the mastery of his own body (vessel) by sanctifying and honouring it; not as the victim of lust, like the Gentiles; impurity means wronging your brother, and as we told you before, God punishes all such sins. (v.⁷) He did not call us to be impure, but to be sanctified: therefore to disregard this is to disregard not man but God, who puts His Holy Spirit into you.

(v.⁹) "As regards brotherly love you have no need that I should write to you: God has taught you that, and you show such to the Christians in the whole of Macedon. But I do beg you to excel in this more and more, and to make it your ambition to be calm and quiet [note the epigram]: let each one of you look after his own affairs and work with his hands, as we told you to do, that you may win respect from those outside the Church and may not lack the necessaries of life."

[*Note on v.⁴.*—St. Paul compares the body to an earthenware vessel, σκεῦος, in 2 Cor. 4⁷. So in 1 Sam. 21⁵ David assures the priest that "the *vessels* of the young men are holy," meaning that their bodies are ceremonially undefiled. The suggestion that in 1 Thess. 4⁴ "vessel" means wife is linguistically improbable and makes St. Paul guilty of very bad taste in using such a word.]

4¹³⁻¹⁸ is particularly interesting as showing St. Paul's eschatological beliefs at this time. They are much the same as those which he learnt as a child of Pharisee parents, except that now he acknowledges Jesus as the Messiah and awaits His second coming. The dead are conceived as rising out of Sheol, the place where the Pharisees placed an intermediate existence between death and resurrection. They are to be snatched up into the air, *i.e.* to meet Christ face to face for the first time. Contrast Phil. 1²³, where death, to St. Paul, means to "depart and be with Christ" immediately.

*(v.¹³) "About those who fall asleep, my brothers, I

9

want you to have knowledge, that you may not grieve at
their deaths as the people who have no hope beyond. We
believe that Jesus died and rose again : just so when men
have fallen asleep with Jesus, will God bring them back
with Him. We have the Lord's own teaching to assure
us that we, who are left alive till His second coming, shall
not precede those who have fallen asleep. For the Lord
will descend from heaven with a loud summons, the voice
of an archangel, and the trumpet of God : then first those
who are dead in Christ shall rise : afterwards we who are
left on earth till that day shall be caught up with them into
the air to meet the Lord, and we shall be for ever with
Him. Comfort one another by this truth."*

[*Note on v.*[14].—τοὺς κοιμηθέντας διὰ τοῦ Ἰησοῦ may
mean " those who have fallen asleep *through* Jesus," *i.e.*
been martyred for His sake. This is the more natural
rendering of the Greek. But it is not likely that St. Paul
would speak only of martyrs ; the phrase probably means
" with Jesus," almost " in Jesus " (as R.V., cp. v.[16b]),
though the use of the preposition is unusual. Lgt. says,
" it was Jesus who transformed their death into a peace-
ful slumber." The suggestion that the words " through
Jesus " are to be taken with the main verb (" will bring ")
is rejected by most commentators, and rightly as I think.]

5[1]. [Notice the semi-prophetic rhythm of vv.[1-3].] " If
men ask when the second coming will be, you know already
that the time of it is unknown [see Mark 13[32]]. The day
is to come like a thief in the night. When men say,
' Peace and safety,' then suddenly destruction is on them
as her travail on a woman with child, and they shall in
no wise escape [see Luke 21[34-36]]. But *you* are not in
darkness that the day should surprise you as if you were
thieves [note the inversion of his metaphor, according
to the W.H. reading : he passes in thought from the un-
expectedness of the second coming or Parousia, ' coming

*[margin handwritten note:]* The time of the second coming unknown

like a thief in the night,' to its joyous and brilliant light
—it is the day]. For you are all sons of light. But
because we are not sons of darkness, let us not fall asleep
spiritually like others, but be watchful and sober. Sleep
and drunkenness belong to the night ; sobriety to the day.
Therefore '*put on the breastplate*' of *faith and love,* and
as '*a helmet*' the *hope* of '*salvation.*' For God appointed
us, not for His judgment, but that we might win salvation
through Jesus who died for us, that whether awake or
asleep we may live with Him. Help and exhort one
another, as I know you do.

(v.[12]) "Your leaders, who work hard for you, and give
you counsel, should be recognised and held in great love.
Be at peace with each other. Counsel the unruly, cheer
the faint-hearted, help the weak, show patience to all.
(v.[15]) Take care that no one pays back evil for evil, but
always aim at doing good to every one. Always be glad,[1]
be unceasing in prayer, give God thanks in everything :
this is God's will for you in Christ. (v.[19]) You must not
quench the Spirit nor despise inspired utterances ; yet
you must test every message (by the teaching of Christ),
hold fast to what is good, avoid every appearance of evil.

(v.[23]) "May the God of peace sanctify you, and make
you complete, and may you be kept, *spirit, soul, and body,*
without loss or blame, till the coming again of Jesus Christ.
God, who always is calling you, is faithful : He will perform it.

(v.[25]) [Probably he writes the last four verses in his own
writing.] "Pray for us : salute all the brethren with a
holy kiss.[2] I adjure you to have this letter read to all.
The grace of our Lord Jesus Christ be with you."

---

[1] Note the emphasis on joy as a positive duty in St. Paul. Cp. Phil. 4[4]
(written in jail). " No literary work has ever so often repeated the word
'joy' as the New Testament " (Renan, *The Apostles,* 5).

[2] See note 1, page 242.

4. 2 THESSALONIANS.—The second letter covers very much the same ground as the first, but with the differences noted above. The difficulties of his readers centre round the Parousia. St. Paul was credited with asserting that "the day of the Lord is now present" (2², see R.V.), for that is the literal translation of ἐνέστηκεν, and it nowhere bears any other meaning. Nevertheless it seems reasonable to suppose that this is a vivid way of saying "is just on the point of coming" (cp. ἔφθασεν, 1 Thess. 2¹⁶). This belief had produced among them intense spiritual excitement, leading them to neglect their daily work and to despise authority and tradition. St. Paul speaks so strongly about it and gives it so much space (in 3⁶⁻¹⁵), that we must believe either that this revivalism had grown since he wrote the first letter, or that it was more marked among the Jewish section at Thessalonica than among the Gentile. In chap. 2 he tells them that the second coming of Christ cannot take place just yet ; for it is to be preceded by certain signs of the end. These signs call for our detailed consideration.

(a) There is to be a great "apostasy," when the "man of lawlessness" shall be "revealed" (ἀποκαλύπτεσθαι, in vv.³· ⁸, is the word which he has used in 1⁷ of Christ's coming). This Antichrist (though he does not use the name) is to set himself against all established religion and to claim to be divine (v.⁴): *his* Parousia (v.⁹) is to be accompanied by miracles worked through the power of Satan. But in the end, when the conflict is at the sorest, the Lord Jesus shall come and "slay him with the breath of His mouth" (v.⁸), and shatter his influence by His own self-manifestation.

(b) The "secret symbol of lawlessness" is already at work (v.⁷). But there is "one that restraineth" (v.⁷), a "restraining force" (v.⁶), which for the present prevents the revelation of the lawless man, but which shall be removed before long.

The first question is where St. Paul got this belief. The myth of the conflict between the good god Bel and the dragon Tiamat comes from the dim dawn of history in Mesopotamia. The Jews did not believe it, as their Assyrian and Babylonian cousins did, to be a true account of the creation of the world. To them the dragon element was not inherent in creation, but came in later with the fall of man. Still they used the myth as we use the story of St. George and the Dragon, to represent the ever-present struggle between good and evil in human life. The dragon (Rahab, Leviathan, etc.), is in the Old Testament a poetic symbol for the ruthless militarist powers of Egypt and Assyria, monsters who came breathing fire across Palestine.

In the age of the Jewish Apocalypses (*i.e.* since about 200 B.C.) the belief had become dominant in the Pharisaic schools, that the conflict between good and evil was to become ever more intense as the world grew older, till in the very climax Jehovah or His Messiah should intervene to take vengeance on the wicked. This climax is the Armageddon of the Christian Apocalypse. St. Paul had been brought up in this belief, and had seen no reason as yet to discard it, though in later years, as we shall see, he changed his mind considerably and looked for the conversion of the whole world rather than for an Armageddon. Probably he had heard certain apocalyptic sayings attributed to our Lord, which on the face of them seem to confirm the Pharisaic eschatology (see Matt. 24^15-27, Mark 13^14-27, Luke 21^10-12. 25-28). But did St. Paul give any *precise* content in his own mind to the " man of lawlessness " and the " restraining force " ? The word " apostasy " shows that he expected the attack to come from the Jews or Jewish Christians (cp. his strong language about Jews in 1 Thess. 2^15-16). The " restraining force " was clearly Roman Law and Government, which up till now in his experience had restrained Jewish violence. He foresees that, sooner or later, Rome will change her attitude to Christianity and unleash Jewish hatred. Naturally he had no clear prevision of details : he simply puts his general convictions into the mould of his Pharisaic belief.

## Paraphrase and Notes.

### 1¹⁻². Address to the Thessalonians.

(v.³) " We have to give thanks always to God for you, my brothers, as you deserve, because your faith and love to each other grow steadily. We tell the other churches of your constancy in persecution. The world will see the proof of God's righteous judgment ; for He is fitting you for His Kingdom, and will bring affliction on those who afflict you and give rest to you who are afflicted now, in the day when Jesus is revealed from heaven with His mighty angels ' *in a blaze of fire, inflicting punishment on those who know not God and do not listen* ' to the glad tidings of our Lord Jesus. For their verdict shall be separation in eternity [1] ' *from the face of the Lord and the glory of His might, when He comes to show His glory among His saints and His wonder* ' among all who have had faith on Him (for our witness to you awoke a response of faith in you). (v.¹¹) I pray continually that it may be so, that God may make you worthy of your calling and fulfil every good resolve and work of faith in you mightily, that the name of Jesus may be glorified in you and you in Him, according to the gracious gift of God and Christ.

2¹. " Now concerning the second coming of the Lord

---

[1] Lit. " eternal destruction," a Jewish phrase which does not imply annihilation ; for in the Jewish Apocalypses it is found side by side with passages which describe the continued sufferings of the wicked after death. We shall see that St. Paul in later years came to hope for the universal salvation of all mankind.

and our gathering unto Him, do not be easily shaken from a sane position : *if any spiritual revelation or speech or letter is repeated to you as coming from me, to the effect that the ' day of the Lord ' is coming immediately, do not be unsettled by it. (v.³) Let no one deceive you : until the apostasy, of which I have told you, has come about, and the lawless man is revealed, who is doomed to destruction, who shall oppose and set himself up as superior to every god or object of worship, seating himself on the very shrine of God and giving out that he is God¹, (the Parousia cannot take place). (v.⁵) I told you these things at Thessalonica. You know what power it is that keeps him back, so that he cannot be revealed till the time is ripe. For the secret power of lawlessness is already at work ; but it cannot be revealed until he who keeps it back is removed out of the way. (v.⁸) Then shall the lawless man be revealed, but the Lord ' *shall slay him with the breath of His mouth* ' and lay him low by the manifestation of His coming. But the coming [Parousia, the word used of Christ] of the lawless man shall be accompanied by the working of Satan with false miracles and wonders to mislead those who are perishing through their refusal to love the truth : because of this God shall make them the victims of lies, and for their delight in unrighteousness.*

(v.¹³) " But we have to thank God always for you, my brothers whom the Lord loves, because God chose you to be a sort of holy first fruits ² to find salvation in consecra-

---

¹ Since the Roman Emperors, even before Domitian, claimed worship for themselves and almost deity, as the incarnation of State-rule, some have argued that they must be meant here. But St. Paul could scarcely call this an " apostasy." However, the *language* of v.⁴ was probably suggested by the attempt of the Emperor Caligula in A.D. 39 or 40 to set up his image in the Temple at Jerusalem. Cp. Herod Agrippa I., in Acts 12²⁰⁻²³.

² Reading ἀπαρχήν with B G Vulg. ἀπ' ἀρχῆς would refer to God's predestination, issuing in their call (v.¹⁴).

tion of spirit and faith in the truth : He called you to this by our preaching that you might win part in Christ's glory. Therefore stand fast and hold by the Christian traditions which we have taught you by speech and letter.

(v.[16]) " And may the Lord Himself and God our Father, who loved us and gave us eternal comfort and good hope in His goodness, comfort your hearts and confirm you in every good work and word.

3[1]. " For the rest, my brothers, do pray for our work, that God's revelation to men may move forward and be honoured ; also that we may be delivered from the enmity of perverted men : for all have not faith.  (v.[3]) The Lord is faithful to guard you from the evil one.  We are confident you will carry out our charge to you.  May the Lord guide you into the love of God and the endurance of Christ.

(v.[6]) " Our charge to you, in the name of Christ, is to avoid any one who is lazy, against the Christian traditions we gave you.  You know that, when we were with you, we did not live a lazy life.  We refused to accept our keep from any one ; we worked for our food, by toil and moil, day and night, so as not to burden any one : not because we have not the right to demand it, but simply to set you an example.  (v.[10]) For we laid down the rule at Thessalonica, that the man who will not work, shall not eat.[1] But we hear that some among you live such lazy lives, not *working* but being *busy*bodies [note the epigram].  We charge them in Christ to set calmly to work and win their daily bread.  (v.[13]) And you must not grow weary of welldoing.  If any one refuses to obey this charge of mine, mark him out and do not associate with him, to make him ashamed of himself : but do not count him as an enemy ; advise him as your brother.  May the Lord of peace give you peace.

---

[1] Some of them were content to live on alms, as if worldly affairs were beneath their notice.

(v.[17]) [*Autograph*].—" I, Paul, salute you in my own writing. You will recognise my writing in future, as a guarantee that you have my real opinions. Christ's grace be with you all ! "

## A. Note on the Expectation of a Speedy Second Coming.[1]

During the earlier part of our Lord's ministry, His Apostles followed Him as a great religious reformer or prophet. But from the time when St. Peter recognised in Him the Messiah who should lift from His chosen people the curse of the Fall (Matt. 16[16]), the little band began to acknowledge Him as the Christ. Yet to some extent this recognition made them misunderstand Him more than before ; because they could not dissociate His work from the preconceived notion which they had of the Messiah, *i.e.* that He should establish a world-wide Davidic Kingdom on earth. Then Calvary came to shatter all their beliefs ; He died the death of the vilest criminal and seemed disowned by God. The Resurrection and Pentecost, followed by the revelation that Christianity was to be a Catholic (world-wide) religion, not a Jewish sect,—these and the daily experience of joy and life and power " in " the risen Christ cleared away most of the misunderstandings from the minds of the Apostles.

But some things of necessity remained dark mysteries to them, because they had as yet no data by which to interpret Christ's teaching ; among the chief of these was the meaning of what He had said about His second coming (Parousia). It was absolutely inevitable that their records of His teaching about it should be confused, as in point of fact we find them. The great eschatological

---

[1] For the position taken in this note, see *The Mind of the Disciples*, by Bishop Neville Talbot, pp. 188 ff.

discourses of the Synoptic Gospels (Mark 13=Matt. 24= Luke 21) seem to combine prophecies about the end of the world with other prophecies about Christ's spiritual revelation to the world and about the Fall of Jerusalem. This confusion, as we have said, was inevitable to men in the position of the Apostles : it is not to be attributed to the Master Himself, but to the minds of His first recorders.

They passionately desired His second Advent. Therefore they concentrated on any of His teaching which seemed to point that way. All the more noteworthy is it that they still faithfully recorded such sayings of Christ as that in which He definitely stated that He did not know when the Parousia should be (Mark 13$^{32}$=Matt. 24$^{36}$) ; or such parables as those of the Wicked Husbandmen, the Talents, the Draw-net, the Mustard-seed, etc., which contemplate the possibility of a remote Advent.

St. Paul began by sharing the common conviction of the early Church in an imminent Parousia. But as time went on, he gradually learnt to regard it as more distant, though he never (as far as we can see) guessed how distant. By the time that St. John wrote, the conception of the Parousia is spiritualised : Christ is always coming to His Church as the Holy Spirit to guide them into truth and inspire them with power. It is not that he disbelieves in an end of this world-order (cp. " in the last day," John 6$^{39, 40, 44, 54}$ 11$^{24}$ 12$^{48}$) ; but the final coming is in a hazy future, while the all-important fact is the daily coming of the Lord in the Spirit.

Now this revolution in thought was effected by the passage of time, which made clear the distinction between the ever-repeated Parousia and the final Advent. And, like the earlier adjustments of Messianic ideas in the minds of the Apostles since the Resurrection, the change was wrought without any convulsion in the Church.

Once more, then, it seems certain that the Lord did not Himself teach a speedy return except in a spiritual sense ; and if we find one or two sayings (such as that recorded in Matt. 16[28]) which seem to prove the opposite, we may reasonably suppose that the confusion in the Apostles' minds has coloured the form of words ; *e.g.* St. Mark's version of Matt. 16[28] (Mark 9[1]) gives a different turn to the words, and makes them refer to the coming of God's Kingdom in the Church.

The publication of Schweitzer's book, *The Quest of the Historical Jesus,* recalled the attention of theologians to the neglected question of Jesus' eschatological teaching. He maintained that Jesus Himself believed and taught the imminence of His external, objective Messianic Kingdom, which was to be established by God's miraculous inter-ference. If this were true, then Jesus' ethical teaching (in the Sermon on the Mount and elsewhere) would only be an " Interim-ethik " ; *i.e.* such commands as " Resist not evil," " Give all you have to the poor," etc., are impossible in the life of a community stretching over centuries, but are practicable and desirable in a church which should only exist for a few short years. Schweitzer's work has been invaluable in making men think out the question it raises ; but his hypothesis neglects half the facts.

## B. Note on Greek Mystery Religions in relation to St. Paul.

1. THEIR ORIGIN AS NATURE-WORSHIP.—The origins of religion are composite and manifold. But, all the world over, primitive man found himself stricken with awe and a sense of weakness in face of the great forces of nature. He made himself deities, now of the heavenly bodies, and now again of the reproductive forces of nature.

Year by year spring brought him the same miracle of life renewed, when the world was clothed once more in wondrous green. But every winter the life of nature seemed to fail. What could be done to ensure the revival of field and woodland, and the productivity of sheep and oxen ? The answer was found in mimetic magic : it could be done by a dramatic representation of the death of the old year and the coming of the new with vigorous life and youth.[1]

This was the origin of the so-called "Mystery" religions. They were essentially systems of religious magic. They were originally cults practised by a clan or a state.

2. THE SPIRITUALISING OF MYSTERY RELIGIONS.—Man cannot feed on bread alone ; his spirit has instinctive needs which clamour for satisfaction. We may perhaps trace two stages in the development of Mystery Religions from mere nature-worship. First, the death of the old year and the coming of spring naturally turn the thoughts of men to their own death and suggest hope of a renewed life in the unknown land to which we must all go. The rites which magically bring new life and vigour to the soil and to animals may also confer on men a new lease of life beyond death. At this stage it becomes doubly important to learn the exact formulæ and practise the correct magic. Plato tells us that the Orphic Mysteries seek " to deliver men from the torments of the other world " ; for Orpheus had been there and knew the passwords. So there arises a class of priests whose business it is to practise and hand on the ritual unchanged : they become the guardians of the gate, the only legitimate

---

[1] In Greece the Mystic at his rites looked up to the sky-father and down to the earth-mother and cried ὕε κύε (" rain, conceive "), as Mr. A. B. Cook tells me. We find precisely the same sort of prayer in the *Rigveda*.

intermediaries in approaching the deity. And, to preserve
the distinction between those within the fold and those
without, the rites become a secret only imparted to
the select initiate, a " mystery " with all the fascination
that secret things always have for human beings. Now
just because these secrets came to be so jealously guarded,
we have little exact information about the details of
Mystery Religions ; and we cannot date the various
stages in their development with any certainty.

Secondly, we know, however, that they gradually acquired
more and more of an ethical element. He who would
attain to a blessed life beyond death, must purify his
soul in this life. Those who came seeking initiation
must first practise purificatory rites : they must die to
the old life, before they could be reborn into the higher
life. Thus, for instance, the Eleusinian Mysteries at
Athens were in early days practised by the State simply
to ensure the fertility of Attica : they were sheer magic.
But as early as the fourth century B.C. purity of life was
required from the initiate, with ceremonial bathing in the
sea at his initiation. This means that they had become
an individual religion.

Much more important and widely spread were the
Mysteries which sprang out of the worship of Dionysus,
who was the offspring of the sky-god and the earth-
goddess, giver of life and god of wine. These Mysteries
were spiritualised, on the one hand by Pythagoras as
early as the sixth century ; on the other, in the form of
the Orphic Mysteries, so called because Orpheus had been
to Hades and knew the way there. In the latter it was
taught that man is doomed to a cycle of births and deaths
(the " cycle of nature," κύκλος or τροχὸς τῆς γενέσεως,
which we find in the New Testament once, Jas. 3⁶) ; from
this he can only win escape by purification and initiation.
They seem to have represented dramatically the death

and revival of the deity under the name of Zagreus,[1] just as in Asia Minor they enacted that of Attis, beloved of Cybele ; and in Egypt, that of Osiris, brother of Isis. For the Hellenistic age, which followed the conquests of Alexander the Great and opened up easier communication between the nations of the Levant, brought a great intermixture of national cults.

The leading characteristics of all these Mystery Religions, as we find them in the second century B.C., may be summarised as follows :

(a) The quest was for $\sigma\omega\tau\eta\rho\iota\alpha$, " salvation,"—not quite in the sense of rescue from sin, but rather deliverance from fate : men sought some guarantee of a happy future beyond death.

(b) The three grades or steps were (1) purification, (2) initiation, (3) enlightenment or the beatific vision ($\epsilon\pi o\pi\tau\epsilon\iota\alpha$ : see 1 Pet. 2[12] 3[2], 2 Pet. 1[16]) : this was the summit of progress.

(c) The initiatory rites were secret : they were handed down by a priestly class who were credited with magic powers.

3. INFLUENCE OF GREEK MYSTERY RELIGIONS ON THE EARLY CHURCH AND ON ST. PAUL.—The Mystery cults, to judge from the scanty evidence which we have, were not widely extended in the Roman Empire before A.D. 100.[2] At the same time, the influences which were at work making them more spiritual and ethical, bear witness to, if they did not actually create, certain spiritual yearnings of the human heart which were becoming articulate in the common language of St. Paul's age. Salvation, rebirth,[3] spiritual, transformation, revelation, knowledge, justi-

[1] Really derived, as Mr. A. B. Cook tells me, from Mount Zagron in Mesopotamia.

[2] The recently discovered basilica at Rome, where neo-Pythagorean Mysteries were celebrated, dates from A.D. 52.

[3] Cp. an inscription of the third century B.C. at Rome, " renatus in vitam æternam." (I owe this reference to Mr. A. B. Cook.)

fication—these are a few of the terms well known to popular speech (see Reitzenstein). Ἐμβατεύω in Col. 2[18] is a word definitely borrowed from the Mystery Religions of Asia. In this *indirect* way the Mystery Religions must have had a real influence on the early Church,[1] though it must still be remembered that in St. Paul's lifetime the Mysteries had not yet attained their fullest sway.

But the suggestion is often made that St. Paul directly borrowed from the Mystery Religions (1) what, for the sake of convenience, we may call a magical view of the Sacraments and therefore presumably of the Christian priesthood ; (2) what we may also call a magical view of the Atonement. In using the word " magical " in this connexion, we do not mean to convey a disparaging meaning. The " Catholic " view of the Sacraments is akin to mimetic magic ; that is, by a dramatic representation of a truth in Baptism or the Eucharist, something *external* to the worshipper is effected, some mystic transaction takes place quite apart from the faith of the believer, objectively or, as the mediæval theologians say, *ex opere operato*. In a somewhat similar sense all " transaction " views of the Atonement may be called magical ; not that there is any mimetic magic, but that the process depends on an outside *act* which unlocks the door. The forensic view of the Atonement formulated by Anselm, which holds that God like a human lawgiver assesses a definite penalty for every sin, and that Christ paid it *instead of* us, may justly be called magical in that it is a mysterious transaction independent of us, a *tertium quid* independent of God and us His sons. The same applies to the early Greek view of the Atonement, that at the Incarnation Jesus Christ metaphysically united the essence of Godhead and

---

[1] Schweitzer (*Paul and his Interpreters*, p. 227) concludes from the evidence available that the Mystery Religions and St. Paul equally found this religious vocabulary *already in existence*.

manhood ; so that, since the birth of Christ, humanity as
such is as different from what it was before as man is
different from his ape-like ancestor. This view may be
called " magical," because again it is not sheerly ethical
and spiritual, but refers us to a mysterious transaction
apart from our common dealings with God.

We have to answer, then, these two questions : (1) Did
St. Paul hold such views either of the Sacraments or of the
Atonement, or is this whole " magical " way of looking at
religion foreign to his teaching ?  (2) If he did hold such
views, did he borrow them from the Greek Mystery Religions, rather than from the early Church ?

The former question cannot be discussed here even
briefly : it is treated in other parts of this book in reference
to passages in his Epistles.  I can only say that, in my
opinion, St. Paul knows nothing of either a magical priesthood and sacraments, or of a magical atonement (cp.
pp. 73-4 above).

But the second question remains : If St. Paul did teach
magical views, is it likely that he borrowed them from the
Greek Mystery Religions ?  Space forbids anything but a
brief and dogmatic assertion of my opinion.

(a) No such figure as a Redeemer-god, in the sense of a
god *incarnate* who died and rose again, is to be found in
any Mystery Religion (see Schweitzer, *Paul and his Interpreters*, p. 193).

(b) The immediate origin of Christian baptism is to be
found in Jewish ceremonial washings ; and of the Eucharist,
in the Jewish Passover.[1]  But this does not exclude the

---

[1] The " breaking of bread " seems to have been unknown among
the Jews.  Our Lord probably originated it and practised it habitually
among His disciples: every Oriental would understand its significance
as a symbol of unity.  At the Last Supper, Jesus combined it with the
loving-cup as drunk at the Passover: His words made them symbolic
of His broken body and poured out blood, which were to be the means
of continued union with Himself and with others through Him.  As to

possibility of magical conceptions *being transferred to these two Sacraments at a later date* by people familiar with the baptismal rites and sacred feasts of Mystery Religions.

(*c*) Such transference is, however, highly improbable in St. Paul himself, however likely in the second century. The Apostle tells us that the Greeks looked on his preaching as folly (1 Cor. 1[23]).   Again, in 1 Cor. 10[21] he may perhaps be warning his converts against partaking of the sacred meals connected with the Eleusinian Mysteries ; but in any case he calls it " the table of demons " and is hardly likely to have borrowed consciously from such a source.

A century later than St. Paul the position is very different. The Christian Church had then become mainly Greek rather than Hebrew ; and the Mystery Religions had attained a much wider influence on the Mediterranean world.   Magical views of the Christian Sacraments and Atonement would almost inevitably be taken by men who were converts from the Mystery Religions.   But the possibility of such a transference at the later date does not make it any easier to believe that we should attribute the same to St. Paul.

[The student, who wishes to pursue this question further, should consult R. Reitzenstein, *Die hellenistischen Mysterienreligionen*; H. A. A. Kennedy, *St. Paul and the Mystery Religions*; L. Patterson, *Mithraism and Christianity*.]

the origin of Baptism, it must be remembered that, among the Jews, ceremonial washing was a frequent act, performed whenever ceremonial defilement was supposed to have been incurred.   But when a proselyte was admitted, he was cleansed once for all by a baptismal rite which purified him from the pollutions of heathenism.   What John the Baptist did was apparently to adopt the latter rite, and to call on the pious Jew to undergo the baptism provided for the unclean Gentile.

# CHAPTER IX.

## THE THIRD MISSIONARY JOURNEY.

1. Ephesus, the Town and Temple.—Three rivers run into the Ægean about the middle of the west coast of Asia Minor. The most northerly is the Hermus, with Smyrna near its mouth. Next towards the south, beyond the range of Mount Tmolus, is the Cayster, with Ephesus at its mouth. Not far to the south again, beyond Mount Messogis, lies the great valley of the Mæander, which after running for many miles due west (*i.e.* straight towards Ephesus) turns south-west as it nears the sea, and has the port of Miletus near its mouth.

The great trade-route from the Euphrates to Ephesus, which we have had occasion to mention several times, followed the course of the Mæander nearly to the sea ; but at its westerly end it ran over a low pass on Mount Messogis to Ephesus. There was, however, a horse-road which left the main route west of Pisidian Antioch, and ran straight across the hills to Ephesus, descending steeply by the short course of the Cayster, and so being shorter by many miles than the main road.[1] This is the way by which St. Paul came to the city, " by the upper country " (Acts 19[1]).

Ephesus lay 3 miles from the sea, with a fine harbour, now completely silted up and lost in marshes. In St. Paul's time, however, it was one of the biggest ports in the world, since the harbour of its rival Miletus was already

---

[1] See Ramsay, art. " Ephesus," in Hast. *D.B.*

spoiled by the sand washed down by the Mæander.[1]
It was the gateway of Asia, the first port of call for ships
from the Farther East. Next to it on the way to Rome lay
Corinth, and the connexion between the two cities was
close and frequent.

Ephesus was now the capital of Asia and the seat of its
proconsul (19[38]). Next to the governor, the town-clerk
(19[35], γραμματεύς) was probably the most influential man
in the city. He was the medium of communication
between the proconsul and the popular Assembly (ἐκκλησία,
19[39]), and he had to arrange the business to be discussed
by the latter. The Assembly was nominally the highest
municipal authority, though at this time their power was
only nominal : it was the Senate which actually held
control and it was the instrument of the Roman Government.[2] Ephesus was also the headquarters of a confederacy of Asian cities, which held common festivals and
games, and which supervised and encouraged the rising
cult of the Roman Emperor. This worship was very
much like that given, till recent years, to the Chinese
Emperor. Law and government alone stand between

---

[1] It must be remembered that, as the Mediterranean is a practically
tideless sea, harbours tend to silt up more rapidly than those on an
ocean. But even round the English coast, the river Dee has been
rendered useless for commerce, and the Mersey would soon be ruined
but for constant dredging.

[2] The Romans did not leave many towns in Asia Minor " free," as
they often did in Greece (e.g. Athens). Such towns " retained, as far as
Roman burgesses were not in question, the full control of justice ; only,
the general enactments as to appeals to the Emperor on the one hand
and to the senatorial authorities on the other [i.e. in imperial and
senatorial provinces respectively] seem to have also included the free
towns. Above all, they retained full self-determination and self-administration. [He quotes the coinage of Athens, which did not bear the
Emperor's head.] . . . As a matter of course the Roman Government
nevertheless exercised continuously a regulative influence over the
constitution even of the freed communities " (Mommsen, Roman
Provinces, i. 262–3).

man and chaos : they are divinely appointed, and the ruler, who represents the State, is God's vice-regent, the embodiment of all stability and civilisation. Not till the time of Domitian did the Emperor claim to be fully divine ; but his statue stood in the State temples, and the cult which centred round him was in the eyes of the Government the most important bulwark of the Empire. It always found favour in Asia, particularly at Pergamus ; well may the Apocalyptic writer say to the "angel" of the church there, "I know where thou dwellest, where is the throne of Satan" (Rev. 2¹³). That was thirty or forty years later than St. Paul's time ; but Ephesus had already one temple to the Emperor. The "Asiarchs" of Acts 19³¹ were probably the officers of the Asian confederacy, charged with the general oversight of the imperial cult, of festivals and games, etc. In the riot of Acts 19 it is noteworthy that they were friendly to St. Paul, and stood aloof from the clique which was interested in the Temple of Artemis.

It was this Temple which was the chief glory of Ephesus ; it was regarded as one of the seven wonders of the world. Artemis was the Greek name given to the goddess (later, the Latin name, Diana) ; but she was anything but the chaste maiden worshipped by those names. She was an old Lydian nature-goddess, akin to Cybele. Her image, as depicted on the Ephesian coins, bears in its upper part the likeness of a woman with many breasts, symbolising fertility and reproduction ; her lower half is simply a pedestal with rude conventional carving. Her hands are outstretched, each resting on what looks like a modern gardener's fork ; it was called a "key" (κληΐς) and connected her with the ground as an earth-goddess. The image was of great antiquity, and, as often in such cases, the legend ran that it had fallen from the sky (διοπετής, 19³⁵, means that, and not "which fell down from Jupiter," as E.V.). Pliny tells us (*Nat. Hist.*, xvi.

79) that it was so black with age that no one could distinguish whether it was made of ebony wood or the vine.

The temple was the fifth which stood on the same spot. Its predecessor had been burnt down on the night when Alexander the Great was born ; the whole of Asia joined to bear the cost of the new building, which took two hundred and twenty years to erect. Its total length, as the excavations have proved, was just under 323 feet, its breadth 151 feet 6 inches.[1] It had 127 columns, each 60 feet high. Its treasury was a sort of bank for the province : its shrine was a sanctuary for criminals. The city's proudest title was νεωκόρος (Acts 19[35]), "Temple-sweeper" (*i.e.* Sacristan) of Artemis, though the temple long represented the old Lydian element as against the Greek culture of the town. It was a mile away from Ephesus ; but it was connected by a long rope, to secure the favour of the goddess for the people. Pilgrims thronged the precincts ; those who could afford it purchased models of the goddess seated in a niche, some to dedicate in the temple, others to carry home or to bury with their dead. These models were made in marble, terra-cotta, and silver [2] (see Acts 19[24-25, 38] : the "craftsmen" are the silversmiths' guild, while "the workmen of like occupation" are probably the workers in terra-cotta, etc.).

Of the temple scarcely anything now remains. But it is different with the theatre, where the riotous meeting was held (19[29]). Its stage is still standing and its auditorium. It was also an enormous building, probably holding as many as 24,000 people.

2. St. Paul at Ephesus (Acts 19).—(*a*) St. Paul

---

[1] See D. G. Hogarth, *Excavations at Ephesus*, 1908.

[2] No silver shrines have been found ; but Ramsay (*Expositor*, IV. ii. 16) points out that they would be melted down. See Furneaux' note *ad. loc.* in his edition of Acts.

probably left Antioch in the summer of A.D. 53,[1] and
travelled through the "Galatian region" (18²³), *i.e.*
probably Lycaonia and Phrygian Galatia, and the rest
of Phrygia, *i.e.* Asian Phrygia. But instead of following
the main trade-route down the valleys of the Lycus and
Mæander, he took the shorter and more hilly horse-road
to the north of it. He was accompanied by Timothy ;
and Gaius of Derbe joined him either in Lycaonia or later
on at Ephesus.

St. Paul had set his heart on raising a substantial
sum of money from his Gentile converts to assist the
poor at Jerusalem. He hoped in this way to make both
Gentile and Jewish Christians realise their essential unity
in Christ, however they might be sundered by differences
of nationality or controversies about the importance of
the Mosaic Law ; and he wished the Gentiles to recognise
their vast indebtedness to the church at Jerusalem as the
source of all their spiritual wealth (see what he says in
Rom. 15²⁶⁻²⁷, and the earnestness with which he asks the
Romans to pray for the success of his project, 15³⁰⁻³¹).
But he would not handle this money himself : it had been
said by his enemies in Corinth and elsewhere that his
refusal to accept his keep from the local church was only
camouflage, concealing a deep-laid design to line his own
pocket in an underhand way. Therefore he asked those
who contributed to elect commissioners of the fund, who
should travel with him to Jerusalem and administer it
(see 1 Cor. 16¹⁻⁴, 2 Cor. 8¹⁸⁻²¹). Probably two were chosen
to represent each province (see above, p. 67).

---

[1] It might be supposed that he would spend a longer time at Antioch,
and not leave till the following spring. But it has been shown that
the details of his voyage from Philippi to Jerusalem at the end of the
third missionary journey are only reconcilable with the date of Passover
A.D. 57, and not A.D. 58 (see Ramsay, *T. and R.C.*, 289–90). Reckoning
backward from this, he must have reached Ephesus not later than the
autumn of A.D. 53.

(b) *Acts* 18²⁴–19⁷.—Shortly before St. Paul reached
Ephesus, a number of disciples of John the Baptist had
come to the city, whether by concerted action or haphazard. Priscilla and Aquila fell in with one of these :
he was a Jew from Alexandria, named Apollos. St. Luke
calls him λόγιος (18²⁴), which may mean either " learned "
or " eloquent." The last clause in the verse (" he was
mighty in the Scriptures ") perhaps points to the former
meaning. He was a clever philosopher, who could talk
attractively (1 Cor. 2¹ 3¹˙ ⁵), and was particularly well
instructed in the Old Testament.

He was an earnest and religious man, who had been
" instructed in the way of the Lord " and could teach
accurately " the things concerning Jesus," but only " knew
the baptism of John." There is some difference of opinion
as to what St. Luke means. Some ¹ understand by " the
things concerning Jesus " Old Testament prophecies of
the Messiah ; but in that case St. Luke must surely have
written " concerning the Christ." The following section
(19¹⁻⁷) seems to make clear what is meant. There we
are told that men baptized with John's baptism " of
repentance " had never heard of the giving of the Holy
Spirit. So probably Apollos : he recognised Jesus as the
Messiah, and knew of His earthly life, and probably of His
Resurrection ; but that was all. To him Jesus may have
been the Christ who had gone away to sit at the right
hand of God—the absentee Christ, as He is to a large
number of modern Sunday-school scholars. He knew
nothing of Pentecost and the gift of the Spirit which brought
inspiration and a sense of invincible power to the Christian
for whom Christ was a daily Presence.

¹ So Lake, *Earlier Epistles*, p. 109, following J. H. Hart in the *Journal
of Theol. Studies* for October 1905. D.S. agrees, and supposes that the
" Way of the Lord " was the name for a handbook of O.T. prophecies
of the Messiah ; but " the Way " is a technical term in the Acts for the
Christian position generally (see 19⁹˙ ²³ 22⁴ 24¹⁴˙ ²²).

Priscilla and Aquila felt that this was the very man to send to the infant church at Corinth : his knowledge of the Old Testament would make him a formidable disputant with the Jews, and his philosophical gifts would give him weight with the Greeks. His success with the latter was all too marked : entirely against his own will, he created a party at Corinth (1 Cor. 1¹²) who contrasted his brilliance with the plain and simple style of preaching about salvation from sin, which St. Paul had adopted of set purpose (1 Cor. 2¹⁻²). When Apollos came to know it, he apparently left Corinth at once and returned to Ephesus (where he was when St. Paul wrote 1 Cor., see 16¹²) ; and he utterly refused for the time being to return to the Achæan capital.

The story of the twelve other disciples of the Baptist (19¹⁻⁷) need not detain us. It is strange to our way of thinking that St. Paul should rebaptize them into the name of Jesus. It shows, not that he attached a magical value to the Name, but that views of baptism were still rather indefinite. Years before, the symbolic washing in Jordan had brought to them the blessed sense of forgiveness : repetition of the symbol now would help them to faith in the real Presence of Jesus and the gift of His Spirit—that faith which alone can create the reality (Heb. 11¹).

(c) St. Paul would reach Ephesus some time in the autumn of A.D. 53. He stayed there over two years (" three months," 19⁸ ; then " two years," 19¹⁰ ; then " for a while " more, 19²². In 20³¹ his total stay is a " space of three years," i.e., in Jewish reckoning, anything between two and three years). He meant to go on to Greece after Pentecost A.D. 56, which fell on 9th May ; the riot was probably early in May if the conjecture be sound that it coincided with the great festival of Artemis.[1]

The Apostle no doubt worked at his tent-making from

[1] For evidence that the Artemisian festival was in May, see Lewin, *Fasti Sacri*, No. 1837, who quotes Boeckh, 2954.

dawn till 11 a.m. every weekday, and again after 4 p.m.
People at Ephesus left off work during the midday hours
of heat. For the first three months he had the synagogue
open to him (v.⁸) : when he could no longer use it, he
borrowed or hired the " school of Tyrannus " ; the Codex
Bezæ states, no doubt with truth, that he taught there
" from the fifth hour to the tenth," that is, when the school
and his own workshop were closed.

(d) *His Dealings with Corinth.*—His relations with the
Corinthian Church at this period are complex and obscure
to us. He wrote 1 Corinthians towards the end of his
stay at Ephesus, when he was intending to cross into
Greece after the next Pentecost (1 Cor. 16⁸), *i.e.* in the
winter of A.D. 55 or early spring of A.D. 56. He wrote
2 Corinthians from Macedon in the following autumn.

Further, it seems clear—

(i) From 1 Cor. 5⁹, that he had written to Corinth a
letter which is lost to us, warning them not
to mix with fornicators ;

(ii) From 2 Cor. 12¹⁴ 13¹⁻² and 2¹, that he had paid
*two* visits to Corinth,¹ and that the second
had been very painful. The Acts makes no
mention of this second visit ; but he must have
gone over by sea from Ephesus and returned
there ;

(iii) From 2 Cor. 2³˙ ⁴˙ ⁹ and 7⁸ᶠᶠ˙, that between
1 and 2 Corinthians he had written a very
severe letter to them demanding the punishment of some Christians who had defied his
authority.

Thus we know of four successive letters : (*a*) one about

¹ Some commentators take 2 Cor. 12¹⁴ to mean, " this is the third
time *I have made plans* to come to Corinth " ; and similarly 13¹. But
2¹ becomes intolerably obscure if it means, " I have resolved that my
second visit to Corinth shall not be painful."

fornicators ; (b) 1 Corinthians ; (c) about January A.D. 56, a severe letter asserting his authority ; (d) 2 Corinthians, about November A.D. 56. Can we date his unpleasant visit from Ephesus to Corinth ? It must obviously be placed *either* before 1 Corinthians, perhaps in connexion with their tolerance of fornicators, *or* in the spring of A.D. 56, in connexion with their defiance of him. The former alternative seems more probable.[1]

Perhaps it was a year after his unpleasant visit to Corinth that he wrote 1 Corinthians ; and the letter was met with defiance in some quarters and an upheaval in the Corinthian Church. In the spring of A.D. 56 St. Paul heard of it, and sent such a peremptory and severe reply that his affectionate heart reproached him afterwards (2 Cor. 7[8ff.]) : he suffered mental torture during all his stay at Troas and after landing in Macedon, and only found relief at last when Titus joined him about September, reporting that the majority at Corinth were loyal to him. Then he wrote 2 Corinthians about November ; and soon afterwards pushed forward himself to Corinth in the late autumn of A.D. 56.

We defer our account of the circumstances which led

---

[1] In 2 Cor. 1[15-22] Paul is defending himself against a charge of caprice in constantly changing his plans. He first wrote from Ephesus that he was coming to Corinth by the land-route through Macedon (1 Cor. 16[5-8]) ; next he wrote to say that he would come straight by sea (2 Cor. 1[15. 16. 23]) ; finally he changed back to his first plan. The reason he gives for his final decision is that he wanted to defer his arrival at Corinth, in the hope that the severe letter (No. (iii) above) might bring them to their senses and spare him the necessity for taking strong measures with the refractory section. But if, in the interval between these letters announcing a change of plan, he actually went to Corinth by sea, then he had *not* changed his plans twice before writing 2 Corinthians. He *had* gone by sea, as in his second plan. Moreover, there is no time between January–November A.D. 56 for all the necessary interchange of letters, *plus* the unpleasant visit. Ships did not sail before February. Lightfoot and Zahn, however, hold that there was only one change of plan (not two), and that he announces this change in 1 Cor. 16[6-8].

him to write 1 Corinthians till we come to deal with the
Epistle ; and must now return to the events which closed
his ministry at Ephesus.

(e) *Acts* 19[11-20].—Paul was about two years teaching
in the School of Tyrannus (19[10]).  He had probably not
gone much outside the city ; for he was still unknown by
face to the Christians of Colossæ at a much later date
(Col. 2[1]).  But Ephesus was the gateway to the populous
valleys of the Mæander and its tributary the Lycus.  Men
like Epaphras the Colossian (Col. 4[12]) had learnt of Christ
in Ephesus, and gone home to be missionaries to their
people (Col. 1[7]).  Doubtless others had done the same for
Smyrna, Pergamus, and all the seven cities of the Apocalypse ; so St. Luke says, with pardonable exaggeration
(19[10]), " all that dwelt in Asia heard the word of the Lord."
The Apostle's ministry was marked by " special miracles "
(19[11]) : both demoniacs and invalids were cured even by
handkerchiefs and linen aprons (v.[12], St. Luke uses Latin
words, *sudaria* and *semicinctia*) which had touched his
body.[1]  His success in casting out spirits was so marked
that a magic influence was attached to the mere name of
Jesus.  For Ephesus was a home of magic : " Ephesian
letters " (*i.e.* particularly potent magical formulæ) were
famous.[2]  Acts 19[13] tells us that there were in the town
some Jews, who went from place to place and made a living
as exorcists : they now began to use as their magic formula
the words, " I adjure you by Jesus whom Paul preaches."
Among them were seven sons of a Jewish " chief priest "
named Sceva.  It is not certain what " chief priest "

---

[1] There is nothing incredible in this.  Thirty years ago similar cures
were effected by a Russian monk, John of Cronstadt, in Petrograd.
It is the power of suggestion working on a strong faith, though there is
the element of superstition in the idea that potency was transferred from
him to the linen.

[2] The cult of Diana survived for the practice of magic throughout
the Middle Ages.

($ἀρχιερεύς$) means here : according to Schürer, it was only used of those who had actually held the office of high priest or were members of the high-priestly families. If so, Sceva must have belonged to a prominent ecclesiastical family in Jerusalem. Two of his seven sons (19[16]) were mauled by a demoniac one day when they used the name of Jesus, with the result that Paul's reputation as possessor of a supreme magic spread through the city and men flocked to him to learn his secret. Some of them made a living as professors of magic, and were led by him to abjure it though it left them without the means of support. They collected all their books on magic and made a public bonfire of them : St. Luke asserts that the marketable value of what was burnt was calculated as 50,000 drachmæ (that is £2000 in our money if we take the drachma as equal to a franc ; a good deal more if we take the drachma as roughly equivalent in purchasing power to the *denarius*, which is a labourer's day-wage in Matt. 20[10]). In this connexion it must be remembered that ancient books, written by hand, were enormously costly.

(*f*) *His Plans for the Future.*—The Apostle had now fulfilled his early dream of planting the Cross in the chief cities of Asia Minor ; and he had been led on by the clear guidance of the Holy Spirit to be the missionary of Greece. He could not stop at this point. His calling and his gifts singled him out for pioneer work : his belief in the imminence of the Parousia summoned him to new lands yet untouched. When he wrote his letters to the Thessalonians, he still held the Jewish belief in which he had been brought up—that the forces of good and evil were working up to a last tremendous struggle, in the crisis of which the Messiah should come to lift the faithful remnant out of the evil world to reign with Him in heaven. But we notice a new note in the Epistles of the Third Missionary Journey—a new hopefulness. The Gentiles were crowding into the Church, hungry for the gospel. Did not it mean that in the end, by God's wondrous mercy, the whole world would kneel before Christ—even the Jewish nation, which seemed then to reject Him with such fierceness ? (cp. 1 Cor. 15²²·²⁵, Rom. 11²⁶·³²). If it was agony to *him* that men, particularly his own nation with their unique religious history, should refuse the gospel, what must it mean to Christ ? Could there ever be a Kingdom of Heaven while most of the world was left to live in a hell ? (This is the *motif* of Rom. 11¹³⁻³⁶.)

With these new thoughts and new hopes within him, he turned longing eyes to the mistress of the world, Imperial Rome (Acts 19²¹). He was ever proud of his own citizenship. Her law and order were wonderful—had they not been a strong protection to the gospel ? Her wise adaptation of her rule to the varying characteristics of many races of men was his admiration—had he not seen it in native state, Roman *colonia*, Greek πόλις ? The catholic Empire was the very type of the Catholic Church, which with infinite adaptation was to combine the many in a supreme unity " in " Christ. There was already a Christian Church in Rome, the centre of the world—so he knew from the many who came or went through Corinth and Ephesus to the capital. He must go there himself ; and then on even to Spain (Rom. 15²⁴).

Meanwhile he must pay a speedy visit to Greece to settle things there, and go once more to Jerusalem to one of the great feasts. So he sent ahead of him Timothy with Erastus, the former treasurer of Corinth city (Rom. 16²³, 2 Tim. 4²⁰), probably on the business of the money collection.

(*g*) *The Riot.*—He had meant to stay at Ephesus over the Feast of Pentecost on 9th May. But his life had been in danger of late from certain elements in the mob (see 1 Cor. 15³¹⁻³², " I die daily. . . . I have fought with beasts at Ephesus " ; cp. 16⁹).

It is a striking fact that the progress of Christianity had brought about a marked diminution in the sale of the model shrines of Artemis. Thus it touched the pockets of the guilds who made them : as at Philippi, it threatened vested interests, but now on a larger scale. Demetrius gathered the silversmiths in his guild, as well as others who made the models in terra-cotta, etc., and roused them to violent action by an appeal, not only to their financial interests, but also to their pride in their goddess. They rushed into the streets crying, " Great is Artemis of the Ephesians ! " (or, according to the reading of D, " Oh, great Artemis of the Ephesians ! " a common liturgical formula, as is proved by local inscriptions).[1] They soon collected a vast mob which thronged into the huge theatre, having managed to seize St. Paul's two Macedonian workers, Gaius and Aristarchus—or, according to a more likely reading given in several manuscripts, the Macedonian Aristarchus and Gaius (of Derbe), both of them administrators of the fund for the Jerusalem poor (see 20[4]). Paul's life was in imminent danger (cp. 2 Cor. 1[8]) ; but he was undaunted, and his first thought was to go in person straight to the theatre ; from this he was only dissuaded by the Asiarchs, who were friendly as the representatives of Roman law and order.

In the theatre confusion reigned. St. Luke, with one of his delightful touches, says that " the majority knew not why they were come together." The Jews were afraid that at any moment the popular fury might vent itself on them ; so they persuaded one of their number, named Alexander, to go up on to the stage and address the mob. In 2 Tim. 4[14], St. Paul warns Timothy at Ephesus against the malicious hatred of a worker in bronze, named Alexander : it is possible that he was the would-be speaker of Acts 19[33] (see, however, note on 1 Tim. 1[20], p. 376). For

[1] See Ramsay, *Church in Roman Empire*, pp. 139-42.

if the latter was a member of the metal-workers' guild, Demetrius and the others might secure him a hearing. It was all in vain ; as soon as they discovered he was a Jew, the mob howled him down by crying, "Great Artemis ! " For two hours they shouted themselves hoarse ; at last the town-clerk secured silence enough to address them, and persuade them to disperse quietly. No one, he said, was ignorant of Ephesus' proud title as " sacristan " of the image which fell from the skies. On what charge could they detain the Christian preachers ? They had not been caught robbing the temple or blaspheming the goddess. If there was any charge against them, it could not be heard in that place : " there are regular assizes and there are proconsuls " to administer justice. Anything beyond such a law-case must go before a lawful [1] meeting of the Assembly. If the crowd refused to disperse after his warning, they might find themselves accused of " riot," and they could not offer any reasonable excuse for such a mob meeting. [2]

St. Paul had, in any case, meant to leave the city soon, and he hastened his departure in view of the danger to his life. He set out for Troas, to sail to Macedon and visit Greece proper.

3. FROM EPHESUS TO CORINTH (Acts 20[1-2]). 2 COR-
INTHIANS AND ROMANS.—The dangers which had sur-
rounded him during the last year at Ephesus, culminating in the riot, had been a terrible strain on his nerves. On top of this came his devouring anxiety about the Corinthian Church : he had dispatched Titus with a very severe letter to them ; who was to return by the overland

---

[1] Ramsay insists that ἐννόμῳ (v.[39]) can only mean " lawful " as opposed to " irregular." " Regular " (R.V.) would be νομιμός.

[2] Reading in v.[40] περὶ οὗ δυνησόμεθα, and omitting the οὐ as obvious dittography, with D and one or two Latins.

route, so as not to miss the Apostle if he should leave
Ephesus in the meantime. The weeks passed and still
Titus did not come to report what effect the letter had.
2 Corinthians, written from somewhere in Macedon in the
ensuing autumn, reflects the strain. In 2¹² he says that
when he reached Troas, " a door was opened unto me in
the Lord " ; but his distracted state prevented him from
taking advantage of it : " I had no relief for my spirit."
In his depressed condition he was feeling as a heavy burden
his " daily anxiety for all the Churches " (11²⁸). Perhaps
it brought on a return of his old malady ; at any rate his
language in 1⁸⁻⁹ implies that he was really very ill physically : " we were weighed down exceedingly, beyond our
power, insomuch that we despaired even of life " ; in
fact, he told himself that it was the " sentence to death "
(v.⁹).

He crossed to Macedon, in his eagerness to meet
Titus, and would naturally push on through Philippi to
Thessalonica. He was still in an overwrought condition ;
in Macedon, " our flesh had no relief, but there was trouble
at every turn with external wrangling and internal fear "
(2 Cor. 7⁵). Yet St. Luke in Acts 20² relates that he " made
a missionary tour through those parts," a phrase which
suggests that he preached in some new places. Now in
Rom. 15¹⁹, written a few months later, he claims to have
carried the gospel from Jerusalem in the east as far west
as Illyricum. The words " as far as " (μέχρι) need not
imply that he had entered Illyricum : they must at least
mean that he had gone close to its borders. The Via
Egnatia ran west from Thessalonica to Dyrrachium (the
modern Durazzo) on the Adriatic ; when it had crossed
the watershed of the (Albanian) mountains, it was still
in the *province* of Macedon, though in the old *country* of
Illyria : the southern border of the *province* of Illyricum
ran some way to the north of the road. The most natural

interpretation of Rom. 15[19] is that the Apostle had made a brief tour along this road ; [1] and if this be true, then it seems easier to date it at this time, rather than on the second missionary journey, and to see a reference to it in the vague words, " those parts " (Acts 20[2]).

Titus came at last, bringing news which was a great relief to St. Paul's anxiety. They met somewhere in North Macedon, perhaps at Thessalonica. The majority of the Corinthian Church had decided on stern measures against some flagrant offender, as the Apostle had demanded, though apparently there was still a recalcitrant minority who defied his authority (2 Cor. 2[5-6] : see further below in the notes on 2 Corinthians). The news brought to him a sense of relief that was well-nigh overwhelming : in his gratitude to God he began to pen the letter which we call 2 Corinthians. The note of joy is dominant in the first nine chapters, though there are touches of self-justification throughout and of warning to his readers.[2] But before he reached the end, his outburst of glad feeling had somewhat spent itself : the victory had been hardly won, and there was still the defiant clique. He ends on a note of greater sternness, of more vehement self-justification, with some passages of pungent irony (chaps. 10–13) ; so much so, that many commentators cannot believe the last four chapters to be part of the same Epistle as the first nine. This theory will be discussed below (pp. 219 ff.) ; but it seems to raise greater difficulties than it solves.

Titus carried the letter, and with him went some other

---

[1] It may mean :

    (a) As far as and including the old country of Illyria.

    (b) As far as the eastern boundary of that country.

    (c) As far as the boundary of the province of Illyricum.

(c) seems most natural, in view of St. Paul's preference for using names in their official sense. If this be accepted, then he had entered the country which lies west of the watershed.

[2] Cp. 1[15-17] 2[17] 3[1] 5[12], etc.

well-known missionary (2 Cor. 8$^{18-19}$), who had been appointed a delegate of the fund, perhaps St. Luke, and a third who is unnamed (v.$^{22}$). Their business was primarily to collect the Corinthian subscriptions to the fund before Paul himself arrived.

It was probably about December 56 that the Apostle went south into " Hellas " (Acts 20$^2$). The name, which occurs only here in the Bible, denotes the ancient Greece, *i.e.* Thessaly and the contemporary province of Achæa.[1] He only stayed in the country for a period of three months, *i.e.* till the sea was open for navigation in February 57 ; most of it was, no doubt, spent at Corinth, where he was the guest of Gaius (Rom. 16$^{23}$, cp. 1 Cor. 1$^{14}$), a wealthy convert.

It was there that he wrote the Epistle to the Romans. His mind was turning eagerly, as we have seen above, to the Imperial City. He was only too conscious that grave danger menaced him on all sides and especially in his forthcoming visit to Jerusalem (see Acts 20$^{22-23}$, Rom. 15$^{30-31}$) ; but if God brought him safe through it, he purposed to go west to Rome in the ensuing summer. Prisca and Aquila, driven from Italy by Claudius' edict some seven years previously, had now returned there ; and Epænetus had gone with them from Ephesus (Rom. 16$^5$). There, too, were men like Andronicus and Junias, Jewish Christians converted before St. Paul himself (16$^7$) ; Urbanus, who had worked with Paul somewhere (v.$^9$), and an old friend, the mother of Rufus, perhaps the wife of Simeon who bore our Lord's Cross (Mark 15$^{21}$, for the Second Gospel was probably written at Rome). These, and others like them, had been the founders of

---

[1] The use of the word in this sense seems incompatible with Ramsay's suggestion that Luke was a Macedonian. For in that case he would not be likely to use a term which implied that Macedon was outside Hellas.

the Roman Church; for it seems clear that hitherto none of the older Apostles had visited the city.[1]

From these old friends St. Paul had an intimate knowledge of the spread of Christianity in the capital. He sends greetings, for instance, to " Mary who has laboured so much for you " (Rom. 16[6]); and to the Christian slaves and freedmen in the great Roman households of Narcissus and Aristobulus (vv.[10, 11]).

Some commentators find it incredible that he should have known so many Christians in the city personally and by repute. But the influx of Syrian traders into the capital was so great that the Roman satirist complains that the " Orontes had flowed into the Tiber " ; and the need for missionary work there would draw many a Christian. (See further on p. 244, § 2.)

The great interest of the Epistle to the Romans is that it was called forth by no special or local circumstances (as all the other Epistles were except " Ephesians "). Dangers were thickening round the Apostle, and his life hung by a thread. He wanted to commit to writing *his* Gospel, his presentation of Christianity as no national creed, but a world-religion for Jew and Gentile alike. He wanted to work out in all its implications the doctrine of free forgiveness and the power to overcome sin " in Christ." There is no controversy here other than the perennial struggle between the legalistic Judaism of the Pharisees or the Antinomianism of the Greeks and the Gospel of Christ. It is St. Paul's message to the Christian world, explaining the Catholic religion. " Ephesians " is its complement, where he works out the relations of the one and the many, the individual and the society,

---

[1] St. Peter went there at a later date. St. Paul says in Rom. 15[22] (διό) that the reason he had not come sooner to Rome was his resolve to preach primarily in places where " Christ was not named " (15[20]). Even now his chief objective was Spain (v.[24]).

and shows how " in Christ " there is realised a great Unity amid Diversity and Diversity in Unity.

4. CORINTH AND MACEDON (Acts 20³⁻⁶).—In the spring of A.D. 57 he apparently meant to sail on the first ship going east, so as to keep in Jerusalem the Passover, which in this year fell on Thursday, 7th April. At the last moment he learnt of a Jewish plot to assassinate him, either in the port of Cenchreæ, or more probably on the voyage ; for the steerage passengers would include many Jews going to the Feast, and it would not be hard to murder him in the dark, and throw his body overboard. So he determined to go by the slower overland route through Macedon and to keep the Passover at Philippi (20³⁻⁶) ; the delegates of the fund meanwhile went on by the ship to Ephesus and then went north to Troas to wait for him.[1] They would not carry the fund in actual cash, but in some form of draft.

5. FROM MACEDON TO JERUSALEM (Acts 20⁷–21¹⁷).— St. Paul was now pressing on with all possible speed, in order to reach Jerusalem before 28th May, the date of the Feast of Pentecost (Acts 20¹⁶). He knew full well that the bitter enmity of the Jews, which had been growing in intensity for years, had reached almost breaking-point ; he anticipated the worst at Jerusalem—" I know that ye shall see my face no more," he said to the Ephesian elders at his farewell to them (20²⁵) ; at Tyre and again at Cæsarea the Christians warned him of his danger in the Holy City. It might have seemed only prudent to arrive

---

[1] This seems to be the meaning of 20⁵. Though προσελθόντες (W.H.) has better manuscript authority, προελθόντες ("going on before") is probably the right reading : for we know that, of the delegates, Gaius and Timothy were with Paul at Corinth, and the two Macedonians also if we may judge from 2 Cor. 9⁴. Luke, on the other hand, went with St. Paul to Philippi (ἡμᾶς, v.⁵) which had become almost his home.

there, granted that he must go at all, at a time when the
city was not thronged with pilgrims to one of the great
Feasts. But that was not his way. It was believed of
him in Jerusalem that he taught the Jews of the Dispersion
to give up the Law of Moses (21[21]) : well, then, he would
show, by his public attendance at a Feast, that he kept
the Law himself ; and as for the danger, it was nothing
compared with the need of teaching men the " Gospel
of the grace of God " (20[24]).

St. Luke, who was now with him, dwells on the details
of the voyage so fully that we can trace from his itinerary
the dates with approximate certainty.

> The days of unleavened bread ended on Thursday,
> April the 14th.
>
> He left Neapolis, the port of Philippi, on Friday, the
> 15th.
>
> He arrived at Troas four days later, on Tuesday,
> the 19th.
>
> He left Troas after six days there ; he walked to
> Assos (20 miles), and picked up the ship about
> midday ; they sailed on to Mitylene in the isle
> of Lesbos in the afternoon, on Monday, the 25th.
>
> They sailed to a point on the mainland, opposite the
> isle of Chios, on Tuesday, the 26th.
>
> They reached Samos and anchored somewhere on the
> south-east of the island (D says off the point
> of Trogyllium, which is the northern promontory
> of the Bay of Miletus), on Wednesday, the 27th.
>
> They crossed the bay of the Mæander to Miletus by
> midday on Thursday, the 28th.
>
> Thence he sent a messenger to Ephesus, who returned
> with the Ephesian elders by midday on Saturday,
> the 30th.
>
> They left Miletus and sailed to the isle of Cos on
> Sunday, May the 1st.

They sailed to the port of Rhodes, in the north of the island, on Monday, the 2nd.

They reached Patara in Lycia and disembarked on Tuesday, the 3rd.

They took a passage on a large ship, sailing from Patara, straight across (by the west of Cyprus) to Tyre, where the ship was to unlade her cargo, probably in four days.

They stayed six days at Tyre, (about) Saturday, May the 7th, to Friday, the 13th.

They went on by the same ship to Ptolemais (25 miles) on the morning of Saturday, the 14th.

They took passage on a coasting vessel to Cæsarea (30 miles) on Sunday, the 15th.

They left Cæsarea on muleback or horseback to ride to Jerusalem on Thursday, the 26th.

They spent the night at the house of Mnason of Cyprus in some village, and reached Jerusalem on Friday, the 27th, the day before Pentecost.[1]

No one can read the Acts without noticing that St. Luke, from chap. 20 to the end of the Book, records the travels of St. Paul and his legal trials in much greater detail than any other part of the history; and clearly this is deliberate on his part, not fortuitous. They are the real climax of the book. Ramsay points out (*T. and R.C.*, pp. 303 ff.) that the historian always dwells with emphasis on the Apostle's relations to the Roman Empire; he concludes that St. Luke, writing during the persecution under Domitian, wished to show that, before the Roman authorities were deceived by a false prejudice against the

---

[1] He cannot have reached Jerusalem earlier, because in 24[11] we learn that the trial at Cæsarea was only " twelve " days (=eleven) after his arrival at the Holy City. He seems purposely to have timed his visit thus, in order that his first public appearance might be as a participant in the Jewish Feast.

Christian Church, they had always been favourable in their treatment of its missionaries. This theory would explain why the Acts gives us such a wealth of detail about the riot at Jerusalem, and St. Paul's speeches to Felix and Festus ; but it scarcely explains why we are told so much about the voyages to Jerusalem and to Italy. Rome is no doubt the climax of the tale : but it seems more likely that the historian had in mind the Church at Rome rather than the Government. He marks how God led the Apostle there by a way far other than he had ever dreamed, through perils of assassination, of judicial murder, and of shipwreck.

But we must return to the incidents of the six weeks before he reached Jerusalem.

*Troas.*—St. Paul must have left Philippi immediately after the days of unleavened bread (20⁶) : for he could not tell how long the voyage might take ; and he was so eager to reach Jerusalem for Pentecost that he even decided to omit a visit to Ephesus (20¹⁶). The language of this verse suggests that he hired a boat at Troas to take him to Patara, from where he could get a big ship sailing straight to Palestine : for from this time forward he seems to have been in circumstances of some affluence ; he could afford at Cæsarea to hire mules for the whole party to ride to Jerusalem ; at Jerusalem to pay the expenses of four men who had taken a vow (21²³) ; and later, at Rome, to hire a lodging and pay for the keep of the soldier who guarded him (28³⁰). We know that sometimes he received gifts from his converts (*e.g.* from the Philippians during his first imprisonment at Rome, Phil. 4¹⁰). Possibly also his father was now dead, and he had inherited a certain amount of money.

But if he hired his own boat at Troas, why did he stay there six days, instead of pressing on ? It seems as if he had to wait for a ship. Perhaps he sailed on a small cargo boat, which would have put in at Ephesus if paid to do so ; but he " decided " against this visit (20¹⁶), and resolved to see the elders of Ephesus while the boat was in Miletus harbour.

At Troas the Christians welcomed him. They were mostly working folk ; for they met for worship up in the third or top storey (Acts 20⁹) of a house, where the cheapest lodgings would be found.¹ The last day of his stay was the first day of the week (20⁷) ; and they crowded the room in the evening (that is, either on Saturday night after sunset, which by Jewish reckoning was Sunday ; or more probably on Sunday night, following the Greek reckoning). He was, of course, to preach to them : after he had finished, they were to take together the Agape or Love-Feast, to which every member contributed some food, ending with the sacred " breaking of bread " or celebration of Holy Communion. It is an illuminating picture of the earliest Christian worship. On the night before He had died, Jesus had eaten a supper with His Apostles, and afterwards instituted the sacrament of the Eucharist : the early Christians met in the evening, when the day's work was done ; and after the meal which marked their unity, they broke the bread and poured out the wine " in memory of Him," confident that He really stood among them, an unseen guest, and gave the elements into their hands just as really as He had done on that sacred Thursday. We find the same form of worship at Corinth (1 Cor. 11¹⁷⁻³²) ; we have it specially brought to our notice in that case only because of the hateful abuses which accompanied it.

On this Sunday night in Troas, the Apostle had much to say to them : it was midnight, and they had not yet begun the feast. Eutychus was crowded on to the window-ledge, and the room was hot with lamps and many people :

¹ Cp. Juvenal, 3. 199 (quoted by D.S.).

he fell so soundly asleep that he tumbled backwards out of the window. St. Luke says briefly that he was dead ; and surely, as a doctor, if he were present, he must have examined the young man. When he records that Paul threw himself upon [1] the boy and embraced him ($20^{10}$), this can only mean that he thought the Apostle had tried to work a miracle ; and the words, " the life is still in him," that the attempt was successful. There can be little doubt that a miracle is intended. On the other hand, it is possible that St. Luke had already left Troas on board the boat ($20^{13}$) before the accident occurred. If so, it is quite probable that Eutychus was not dead, only stunned.

Ramsay tells us that on that coast in summer the wind normally blows from the north all the early part of the day, but dies down in the afternoon, and goes round to the south in the evening. Thus the boat, with St. Paul's companions on board, would start in the early hours of the morning, while he himself lingered on till dawn in the upper room. Then he left and walked 20 miles across the peninsula to Assos, where he was taken on board ; and they probably got on to Mitylene before nightfall.

*Meeting with the Ephesian Elders* ($20^{17\text{-}38}$).—From Miletus he sent a messenger to Ephesus. This meant first a sail of about 10 miles across the Bay of the Mæander ; then a land journey of about 20 miles. Paul did not know what the future had in store for him, but was convinced that the best he could hope for was imprisonment ($20^{22\text{-}23}$). He was nearly sixty years old ; and if he escaped the perils at Jerusalem, he meant to go to the far west of the Mediterranean world. So he was convinced that he would never

---

[1] The word is ἐπέπεσεν : it is not the natural thing to do with some one who has tumbled out of a third-storey window and may have broken many bones !  St. Luke's laconic and almost casual way of recording such an astounding miracle is surprising to our minds : it is surely significant that the miracle did not seem so astounding to him, doctor as he was.

see his converts in Asia Minor again (v.[25]), though in this
he was probably mistaken ; for it seems fairly certain
that he revisited Asia after his first Roman imprisonment :
on this point we may trust the evidence of the Pastoral
Epistles, whether he wrote them or not.

In his speech to the Ephesian Elders he asseverates
most solemnly that he had done his utmost to serve them
honestly and lovingly. In future they must be the chief
human shepherds of the flock of God entrusted to them ;
and they must be very watchful, for terrible " wolves "
would attack the sheepfold, and from within there was
sure to arise a still greater danger in the perversion of true
religion (vv.[28-31]).

It is interesting to note the evidence of this passage as
to the development of the Christian ministry. We have
already seen that St. Paul appointed in every local church
" presbyters " [1] or elders, after the Jewish method. Here
in v.[28] he calls them " bishops " or overseers, using the
Greek equivalent for elders to emphasise their functions.
So at a later time in Phil. 1[1] he refers to *two* orders of a
regular ministry at Philippi, the bishops or elders, and
the deacons (that is, servers).

In the last clause of v.[28] there is some uncertainty as to
whether we should read the " Church of God " ($\Theta\epsilon o\hat{v}$ with
א B) or " the Church of the Lord " (with Irenæus in the
second century, D and the old Latin). If " God " is
adopted, then we must render, " the Church of God which
He won by the blood of His own (Son)."

---

[1] Though Presbyter is the derivation of our word " Priest," it of
course carries none of the sacerdotal implications which the latter word
has acquired in English. The sacrificial priesthood among the Jews
were called $\iota\epsilon\rho\epsilon\hat{\iota}s$, which St. Peter uses when he bids the *whole* Church
remember that they are " an elect race, a royal priesthood ($\iota\epsilon\rho\acute{a}\tau\epsilon\nu\mu a$),
a holy nation, a peculiar people " (1 Pet. 2[9]). All these terms are of
set purpose Jewish ; St. Peter is emphasising the fact that Christians
are the true Israel of God.

St. Paul ends (v.[35]) with repeating a saying of Christ which is not recorded elsewhere : " It is more blessed to give than to receive."

*From Patara to Jerusalem* (21[1-17]).—From Patara communication by ship with the Levant was frequent. Paul would take passage on a large ship, chartered with a cargo for Tyre. They probably sailed first along the coast to Myra (as D adds) ; thence they put out to sea, and headed past the west coast of Cyprus straight for Phœnicia. There was now no hurry, as there was well over a fortnight before Pentecost ; and as the ship was going on along the coast to Ptolemais,[1] after unlading most of her cargo at Tyre, the Apostle decided to wait for her. This meant a stay of six days in the Phœnician port : there were some Christians there, though only a few humble folk, for he had to search them out (v.[4]). They knew [2] of the terrible danger which he would incur at Jerusalem, and begged him, but all in vain, not to go there. After a day at Ptolemais, the modern Acre, he took a coasting vessel to Cæsarea. St. Luke does not say that he went by sea, but the direct road from Ptolemais to Jerusalem by land would not take him anywhere near Cæsarea. By keeping to the coast ports he would be mainly among non-Jews.

At Cæsarea he stayed with Philip the Evangelist,[3] one

[1] This seems to be the natural inference from St. Luke's language. In v.[7] we should translate, " we, having finished our voyage, arrived from Tyre at Ptolemais."

[2] " Through the Spirit " in v.[4] does not, in all probability, imply that their information was supernaturally received, but means that their fears were well founded, and that St. Paul received their warnings as a message from God to prepare himself for violence.

[3] The exact meaning of " Evangelist " is unknown. In Eph. 4[11] (where St. Paul is speaking of spiritual gifts rather than formally defined offices) he mentions four types—(1) Apostles, (2) Prophets, (3) Evangelists, (4) Pastors and Teachers. This suggests that Evangelist was a name given to those who by the power of their sympathy were successful in getting men to confide in them and winning converts. Cp. Philip and the eunuch, Acts 8[26-40].

of the seven original Deacons at Jerusalem, who had four
daughters endowed with the gift of " prophecy " or inspired
utterance. St. Luke's mention of these prophetesses
seems to imply that they warned St. Paul of the peril in
which he stood : and their warnings were made more
specific by Agabus, the prophet who had foretold at Antioch
the famine (Acts 11²⁸) of A.D. 45 or A.D. 46.

This man had just come from Judæa and would know
from first-hand evidence the violence of Jewish animosity
against the Apostle ; by a vivid symbolic act, after the
manner of the Old Testament prophets, he tried to make
him realise the danger (21¹¹) : he assured him that it was
no nervous fancy but the warning of the Holy Spirit.
Even St. Paul's companions now besought him to give up
his visit to Jerusalem, but he was unshakable in his conviction that he must bear his witness there. Their tears
and entreaties tore at his heart, but he could not give way.

So after about a fortnight at Cæsarea they procured
horses or mules (ἐπισκευασάμενοι, 21¹⁵) for the 64-mile
ride. It was too much to do in one day ; but some of the
Christians at Cæsarea knew a man called Mnason, a disciple
of long standing, who had a house at some village on the
road, where the travellers could be put up in more safety
than at Antipatris or at some village inn. For the correct
translation of Acts 21¹⁶ undoubtedly is, " There went with
us some disciples from Cæsarea, *to bring us to the house of
Mnason*, that we might lodge with him." ¹ The next day,
the eve of Pentecost, they reached the city and received
a great welcome from the Church : the following morning
they went at once to the house of St. James, the president
of the local presbyters, who were all assembled to greet
them.

---

¹ D inserts a clause to make it clear that this is the sense. " Taking
with them Mnason that we might stay with him " is the erroneous
rendering of the E.V.

# CHAPTER X.

## 1 CORINTHIANS.

(See above on pp. 153–4.)

1. DATE AND PLACE OF WRITING: INDISPUTABLE GENUINENESS.—We have already seen that the Epistle was written from Ephesus some months before he left, that is, in the winter of A.D. 55 or early spring of A.D. 56.

Its genuineness, as a Pauline letter, is admitted by practically every one. Quite apart from a mass of other evidence, we have the words of Clement of Rome, who wrote to the Church of Corinth about A.D. 95 to upbraid them for their internal quarrels; in chapter 47 he says: "Take up the Epistle of the blessed Paul the Apostle. What did he first write to you in the early days of the Gospel? . . . Concerning himself and Cephas and Apollos, for that even then ye had made parties and divisions" (see 1 Cor. 1$^{12}$).

Thus the Epistle is of paramount importance; and particularly in the account which it gives of our Lord's Resurrection appearances (15$^{1-8}$), and as evidence of St. Paul's Christology.

2. OCCASION AND OUTLINE ANALYSIS.—Corinth was, as the history of the place foreshadowed, a very home of Antinomianism in the Church. "All things are lawful to me" (1 Cor. 6$^{12}$ (twice) 10$^{23}$ (twice)), was their cry. If Christ superseded the Mosaic Law, has He not abolished all law? If all men are sinners and are only accepted by

God through the mediation of Christ, is not the conclusion inevitable that they should cease to worry about
morality and follow all impulses as both natural and
indifferent ? Men brought up in a city where sexual
indulgence reigned supreme, and where (in all probability)
the Greek mystery religions made many people familiar
with magical conceptions of all religion, would easily come
to regard the Christian sacraments in the same light, as
passwords to God's favour.

St. Paul had already, as we have seen above (p. 153),

    (*a*) probably paid a visit from Ephesus to Corinth of
        a very painful nature—they had simply refused
        to recognise his authority ;

    (*b*) certainly written to them a letter, now lost, in
        which he bade them sternly to avoid immoral
        people (1 Cor. $5^9$).

*A.* Shortly before he wrote 1 Corinthians, some " people
of Chloe's household " ($1^{11}$), probably servants, had come
to Ephesus and given him bad news about the Corinthian
Church. He deals with it, certainly in chaps. 1–4, and
probably also in chaps. 5 and 6.

Let us see what this bad news was :

(1) 1 Cor. $1^{10}$–4. Party spirit, which was the bane of
a Greek city, had arisen in the Corinthian Church. Men
had begun to label themselves by names : " I belong
to Paul," " I to Apollos," " I to Cephas," and " I to
Christ " ($1^{12}$).

Can we form any notion of what these various groups
stood for ? It seems clear that Hort is right in saying
(*Judaistic Christianity*, p. 95) that the Epistle is " free
from direct or indirect warnings against Judaistic limitations of the Gospel." And it is quite certain that a
certain section of the Church at Corinth refused to acknowledge St. Paul's apostolic authority (cp. $4^{2-5}$ $9^{1-15}$ ; and
2 Corinthians *passim*) : he was no Apostle, they said ; he

had not known Jesus on earth ; he dared not claim to be maintained by the Church, but sought to make money in doubtful ways ; his teaching was too elementary and lacked philosophical depth, and his preaching lacked rhetoric.

In view of these facts we may reasonably conjecture that :

    (a) the partisans of " Cephas " [1] refused to acknowledge any authority other than that of the older Apostles, who were conveniently far away ;

    (b) those of " Apollos " emphasised philosophy and rhetoric ;

    (c) those of " Christ " were utterly Antinomian.

(2) 1 Cor. 5. There had been a disgusting case of incest by a Corinthian Christian, and the Church had done nothing in the matter. They had simply protested that, in a city like Corinth, St. Paul's command to refuse all intercourse with immoral persons was hopelessly impossible.

(3) 1 Cor. 6$^{1-7}$. There had been an outburst of litigious spirit among them—Christian quarrelling with Christian and taking him into heathen law-courts.

(4) 1 Cor. 6$^{8-20}$. Antinomianism had led them to sexual sins of every sort. They argued that all things were lawful to them ; that it did not matter what they did with the mortal body, as long as the immortal spirit sought after God.

*B.* Shortly afterwards, however, three Corinthian Christians—Stephanas, Fortunatus, and Achaicus—had

---

[1] It is quite likely that St. Peter had paid a visit to Corinth ; Dionysius of Corinth, in the second century, says so definitely. It is usually supposed that he is wrongly inferring it from our present passage. But (1 Cor. 9$^5$) St. Paul mentions the fact that St. Peter used to travel with his wife and accept hospitality from the local churches ; he puts in Cephas at the end, though he has mentioned the rest of the Apostles earlier in the verse, as if he knew that the Corinthians were familiar with St. Peter's customary action.

come to Ephesus with better news of the Church's attitude towards St. Paul, and showing great personal respect to him. They brought with them a letter asking his advice on certain questions of practice ; but they also had to report some further abuses and misunderstandings.

## Questions Answered.

It is probable that his answer to each question is introduced by the words, " Concerning . . . " ($7^{1.\ 25}$ $8^1$ $12^1$ $16^1$ $16^{12}$). So we may summarise them as follows :

(1) 1 Cor. 7. About marriage.

vv.$^{1-2}$. A general statement of his opinion that celibacy is better than marriage, considering the nearness of the Parousia.

vv.$^{3-6}$. Sexual intercourse, so far from being wrong, is a duty for those who are married.

vv.$^{10-24}$. Separation of husband and wife is not right, as a principle ; even if one of them be a heathen, the marriage must stand, unless the latter desires a separation.

vv.$^{25-35}$. About unmarried women ; grounds for his general verdict given in vv.$^{1-2}$.

vv.$^{36-38}$. About those who are betrothed.

vv.$^{39-40}$. About the remarriage of widows.

(2) 1 Cor. 8–10. Is it right to eat food sacrificed to idols ?

Chap. 8. No food can influence for evil the man who is strong, as his readers pride themselves on being. But they must think of the weaker brother, who has only just been emancipated from idolatry.

Chap. 9. The principle that freedom must be limited by brotherly love is illustrated by the writer's own refusal to be maintained by

his converts, which is based on love for others
and the need for self-discipline in himself.

Chap. 10¹⁻¹³. They must not run their heads
into temptation, relying on the Sacraments
as charms to keep them from sin. Hebrew
history proves the danger of that. God
only keeps in hours of temptation those who
are humble and watchful.

Chap. 10¹⁴⁻³³. Summary of the question of eating
food sacrificed to idols. It is at any rate
wrong to go to a sacramental feast in an
idol's temple; not because the idol is a
real God, but because there is a real demon
lurking in the idolatrous conception of God:
a sacramental feast brings them into actual
communion with the demon, just as the
Eucharist brings us into communion with
Christ.

(3) 1 Cor. 12–14. About spiritual gifts.

Chap. 12. The Holy Spirit gives different powers
to individual Christians; but as they all
come from the same Spirit, they are meant
to be used to enrich the corporate life of
the Church, not to gratify the possessor.

Chap. 13. Therefore Love is the supreme gift,
necessary to make the others effective.

Chap. 14. Speaking " in a tongue " is therefore
out of place in public worship unless some one
can interpret; and even then, everything
must be orderly. Prophecy is a higher gift;
but women ought not to speak in public.

(4) 1 Cor. 16¹⁻⁴. About the method of collecting the
und for Jerusalem.

(5) 1 Cor. 16¹². About their request that Apollos should
eturn to Corinth.

*Further Abuses and Misunderstandings at Corinth.*

(1) 1 Cor. 11[1-16]. Their defiance of convention in letting married women pray or preach in public without wearing a veil. A woman ought to cover her head as a sign of dedication to her husband.

(2) 1 Cor. 11[17-34]. The degradation of the Love-Feast (Agape) and Eucharist into a selfish and riotous meal. Its true meaning as expressing the Lord's death requires the utmost reverence from all present.

(3) 1 Cor. 15. Denial of the resurrection of the dead at Corinth, owing to the difficulty of understanding how personal life could go on without any sort of body.

### 3. PARAPHRASE, CHAPS. 1–4.

1[1-9]. *Opening Address to the Christians of Corinth.*— With them he couples " all who call on the name of our Lord Jesus Christ in any place, their Lord as well as ours," in order to remind them that they are too self-assertive and individualistic in following their own opinions and neglecting the common experience of Christendom.

He thanks God (vv.[4-9]) for their rich spiritual endowment, particularly in intellectual insight and clear exposition. Their real communion with the Risen Lord is a guarantee that, whatever their faults, He will lead them on.

1[10]-4. *Their partisan spirit is the result of intellectual arrogance and exaggerated individualism.*

1[10-31]. " All Christians are in personal communion with Christ (v.[9]) : they are at one in Him, whatever their different standpoints. But Chloe's people have told me that the Church at Corinth is in danger of splitting into four parties, with different labels. If each is ' in Christ,' Christ is apparently divided into four ! Christ alone was crucified for you, and therefore you live in Him, the *one* Christ. ' Into ' Him only were you baptized, not into me! Fortunately I, Paul, baptized scarcely any one personally, or you might suppose it meant union with me, not with Christ. My business is to preach the Gospel : and that not in the form of philosophical discourse dazzling the intellect ; but in the sphere of practice, offering men a way of salvation in the crucified Christ, which experience shows to be effective."

[*Note.*—In v.[17] the " Cross of Christ " means primarily the message of a crucified Messiah : to the Jews the fact of crucifixion seemed evidence of utter failure ; to the Greeks the idea of salvation through a martyred Jewish carpenter seemed intellectually contemptible. But the Cross to St. Paul always is the supreme evidence of a God who does not live far off in bliss, but who feels His children's sins and sorrows far more poignantly than they do ; who always bears in Himself the sufferings of the world, and therefore offers us " at-one-ness " with Himself.]

*(v.[18]) " The Cross is folly to the world which rejects God ; yet it brings the power of God in actual life to those who trust. (v.[20]) Greek philosopher ($\sigma o \phi \acute{o} s$) and Jewish scribe ($\gamma \rho a \mu \mu a \tau \epsilon \acute{v} s$) alike have missed the way : for when (v.[21]) God in His wisdom decreed that He would not reveal Himself to the arrogant wisdom of men, He decided to save the world by a method which appeals to faith in Himself—that is, a moral quality, but which to naked reason looks like sheer folly. While the Jews are looking for stupendous miracles as a proof of God's force, and the Greeks are demanding a philosophical scheme, God has sent a crucified Christ, who is recognised, by all who have tried trusting Him, as God's real Power and real Wisdom. . . .

(v.[26]) " That is why among Christians there are so few with philosophical learning and worldly power and noble birth.* (v.[29]) Thus is human arrogance confounded. In union with Christ the believer can recognise the supreme

wisdom of the scheme which brings us the glad sense of a
real righteousness imparted to us (δικαιοσύνη), of power
to progress (ἁγιασμός), and of redemption as from slavery "
(ἀπολύτρωσις).

[*Note.*—St. Paul here is not condemning philosophy as
such, any more than he is in Col. 2⁸.  He was himself the
greatest of Christian philosophers.  What he reprobates
is that superior attitude of so-called intellectualism which
philosophises in the abstract, quite apart from the experience of life.  The true function of philosophy is, as
Hegel said, to explain life, not to construct it.  You can
only criticise a system of belief from within, not from
without.  Spiritual things can only be appraised by
spiritual men (2¹³).]

2–3². " For these reasons I myself deliberately discarded
rhetoric and philosophical argument in presenting to you
the mystery¹ of God : men enslaved to sin cannot be
rescued by intellectual reasoning, but only by the presentation of Jesus Christ as crucified for our salvation.
I preached to you in almost nervous self-distrust, seeking
only to show you God's Spirit and Power. . . . (v.⁶) The
world which crucified Christ has always regarded Christianity as folly ;  but the Christian of ripe experience
[τέλειος, opposed to the ' babe ' in Christ, 3¹] finds in it
the deepest, truest wisdom (v.⁶), surpassing all he has ever
imagined.  *(v.¹⁰) The Holy Spirit has revealed it to
us ;  our spirit illumined by Him can search into even the
deep mysteries of God.  (v.¹¹) Only the human spirit can

---

¹ " Mystery " is one of the words which was probably common in
the religious parlance of that age owing to the increasing prevalence
of the " Mystery " religions.  But in the term " Mystery religion " it
denotes a magic representation of what it was supposed to effect.  In
St. Paul it is always *the secret of eternal life*, concealed from the world
before the Incarnation but *now revealed in Christ* ; except in Eph
5³², where it is used, as in the Apocalypse, for a mystic symbol which
has a deep spiritual significance (cp. 2 Thess. 2⁷).

understand the human heart; so only God's Spirit can make clear the things of God. (v.[13]) We have to interpret spiritual truths by spiritual faculties.[1] The natural man, unenlightened by the Holy Spirit, must regard it all as folly, because only spiritually can it be sifted; but the spiritual man can sift and judge of all life, though others cannot judge of him.* And you Corinthians were so limited by fleshly ideas, such babes in Christ, that I had to give you as it were the food of infants."

[*Note.*—St. Paul in this passage recognises the difference between men in spiritual insight. But it is vital to notice that he does not erect a barrier between the advanced Christian and the babe in Christ (as the Gnostics did, for instance). The latter can always become mature, if he will follow Christ. Limitations of intellectual power or of education cannot stop him: and spiritual faculty is infinite in every one who is " in Christ."]

3³. " You still are dominated by the flesh [σαρκικοί is more qualitative than the σαρκίνοι of v.¹, though E.V. has ' carnal ' in both places]; look at your jealousy and strife; you live like men of the world. One of you says, ' I follow Paul '; another, ' I follow Apollos.' But what are Paul and Apollos except Christ's servants who led you to believe, as Christ empowered each of us ? I set the plant, Apollos watered it : but it was God who made it grow. . . . (v.⁸) Apollos and I are on one level, though God shall give each of us his own appropriate reward according to our work. We are simply fellow-workers with God : you are God's field or His building.

---

[1] The last three words of v.[13] admit of a number of different renderings. But as πνευματικά is Neuter, it is preferable to take πνευματικοῖς as also Neuter. συνκρίνειν is used in the LXX of " interpreting " dreams. So it seems best to translate either as above, or " interpreting spiritual truths by spiritual language." The E.V., in trying to preserve the classical use of συνκρίνειν (" compare "), makes the passage unintelligible.

(v.[10]) "By God's grace I laid the foundation like some skilled master-builder ; another man raised the building on it. But each must take heed how he builds on it. There cannot be any second foundation besides the one that is laid, namely, Jesus Christ ; but the builders may raise on it enduring work in gold, silver, and marble, or less durable work in wood, hay, or straw. The judgment-day will be like a fire testing the work of each builder. (v.[14]) If a man's work stands the fire, he shall have his reward ; if it is burnt up, he will lose his work, but he shall himself be saved, though as a man escaping from a burning building.

(v.[16]) "Do you not know that you are literally God's shrine, where His Spirit dwells ? Him who ruins this shrine, God will bring to ruin : for God's shrine is holy.

(v.[18]) "Do not be deceived. Those who pride themselves on earthly wisdom must become as fools before they can receive the true wisdom. For the world's wisdom is folly in God's eyes. . . . (v.[21]) So let no one brag about earthly leaders : in Christ you win the whole world ; Paul and Apollos and Cephas, life and death, the present and the future, they are all yours and you are Christ's and Christ is God's.

4[1]. "Think of us only as of Christ's ministers and stewards who dispense God's long-hidden secrets. The chief quality needed in a steward is loyalty. To me it matters very little how you or any human tribunal [lit. ' day,' cp. Old English ' daysman.' It is contrasted with ' day of the Lord ' in 3[13]] judges my actions : I cannot even judge my own actions ; I may be conscious of no wrong in myself, yet that does not clear me in the sight of God. Wait for Christ's judgment ; when He comes, He will make clear the secrets of each heart.

(v.[6]) "Now in writing thus I have used ' Paul ' and ، Apollos ' as mere names to drive home my meaning :

I have had in mind other people.[1]  *The lesson I want you
to learn is summed up in the Jewish proverb (?), ' Never
go beyond what Scripture bids ' : that is, do not take up
party cries, when you all belong to God.[2]  (v.[7]) Who is it
that makes you different from your neighbour ?  What
talent have you that you did not receive from God ?  Then
how can you pride yourself on it ?  (v.[8]) [Probably ironical
statements, rather than questions as in W.H.] All your
yearnings are already satisfied, so it seems !  You are so rich
spiritually !  You have already attained the full Kingdom
of God while we struggle to attain it !  Ah, I would that you
had, that we might be enriched by the joy of your triumph.
(v.[9]) We Apostles, it seems, are put last by God, like the
criminals who are executed in public at the end of the
gladiatorial games, while the whole world of angels and men
plays the part of the spectators. . . . (v.[13]) We bear gently
with our persecutors ; we meet slander with conciliation.
We are like the scapegoats offered as sacrifices in the old
heathen world to avert the wrath of their gods."*

[*Note on v.*[13].—" Filth " (pile of garbage) . . . " offscouring." The E.V. is translating literally, *i.e.* we are
treated as the scum of the world. But the sense given
in the paraphrase (" scapegoats ") is a possible rendering
of both words. Suidas tells us that at Athens, in times of
plague, etc., human victims (" Jonahs," so to speak) were
cast into the sea with the words περίψημα ἡμῶν γένου
ἤτοι σωτηρία καὶ ἀπολύτρωσις [3] (" be thou our ' garbage '

---

[1] This is the full force of μετεσχημάτισα. σχῆμα, in its rhetorical
sense, means a veiled allusion.

[2] That these words are a proverb is suggested by the word τό in
introducing them.  The exact meaning is lost to us : perhaps it was used
of people who were too hotly partisan in a good cause.  It is clear
that there was no misunderstanding between Paul and Apollos.  The
latter apparently left Corinth when he found that he was unwittingly
creating a party, and for a time he refused to return there; see 16[12].

[3] Note this proof of the common use of the religious terms " salvation "
and " redemption."

or salvation and redemption "): for the victims were chosen
from the "scum" of society. In the Septuagint of Prov. 21[18]
περικάθαρμα ("offscouring") means "ransom for . . .," and
in Tob. 5[24] περίψημα ("filth") is similarly used. Such human
sacrifices may have been given up in St. Paul's time, but
the words remained in popular speech. Among the early
Christians, ἐγὼ περίψημα σοῦ (" I am your ' offscouring, ' "
i.e. doormat, so to speak) was a term for great affection.]

4[14]. " I am saying this, not to shame you but to give
you counsel as my dear children : you may have countless
tutors in Christ, but I am your only father in Him. Copy
my ideals : I am sending Timothy, whom I love as my
true son in the Lord, to you that he may remind you of my
way of life in Christ as I teach it in every church. (v.[18])
Some of you are swollen-headed, as though I were not
coming to Corinth. But I shall soon come, if Christ allow
it, and shall take account not of what professions you make,
but of the Christian *power* which you show in life. . . . Am
I to use my authority to smite you, or will you let me
show loving meekness ? "

## 4. Chaps. 5–6. The Case of Incest. Their Litigious Spirit. Antinomian Sexual Immorality.

5[1]. " I am actually told of fornication among you, and
of a worse type than is found even among the Gentiles ;
a man has taken his father's wife. And you remain self-
satisfied and take no steps to excommunicate the offender !
My own verdict on him (meeting in spirit with you as
president of your Church Council, and with the power of
Christ among us, though I am absent in body) is that the
man should be excommunicated at once and sent back into
the outer world, the domain of Satan, for the destruction
of his flesh,[1] that his spirit may be saved at the judgment-

---

[1] Cp. 1 Tim. 1[20]. The phrase here may simply mean that unchecked
immorality will cause disease, and so bring him to repentance ; but it is

day. Your self-satisfaction is indeed out of place. Do you not know that a little leaven leavens the whole lump ? Then (as the Jews do at the Feast of Unleavened Bread) get rid of all the old leaven : you are indeed the dough that should have none of the world's leaven.[1] For indeed Christ was killed as our Paschal Lamb : therefore let us keep our feast, not with the old leaven of wickedness, but with the unleavened bread of sincerity and truth.

(v.[9]) " I wrote to you in my last letter that you must not associate with fornicators [and you dismissed my advice as impracticable in a town like Corinth]. I did not mean that you were to avoid entirely all heathen who were immoral or unscrupulous or violent or idolatrous : for that indeed would require you to go quite out of the world ! But as a matter of fact what I meant, in writing to you,[2] was that you were not to associate with any professing *Christian* who is guilty of such sins or of drunkenness ; do not even admit him to your common meal (Agape). It is not for us to judge people outside the Church, whom we leave to God : but it is our duty to judge people inside. Therefore ' *expel the wicked man from your midst.*'

6[1]. " And you *dare*, when one of you has a complaint against his neighbour, to go to law with him in the law-

much more probable that St. Paul believed that physical suffering would inevitably follow the verdict of excommunication ; see below, 11[30]. " The power of the Lord Jesus " strongly suggests something miraculous. This verse was a stand-by to the Spanish Inquisition.

[1] Possibly he was writing about the time of Passover. His thought of Christ as the Paschal Lamb lends some support to St. John's Gospel in dating the Crucifixion on Nisan 14th—the day that they killed the Paschal lamb—as against the Synoptists, who put it a day later and make the Last Supper the Paschal Feast.

[2] It is usual to take ἔγραψα in v.[9] as " I wrote," and in v.[11] as " I now write " (Epistolary Aorist). But it is hardly likely that he would express himself so obscurely. In v.[11] the translation should probably be, " but as a matter of fact (νῦν) I wrote . . ."

courts of the *unjust*!  Why not take the case before your
fellow-Christians ?   Do you not know that at the last day
Christians shall judge the world ? [1]  If so, are you unfit
to decide petty cases in everyday life ?   If we are to judge
angels, surely we can judge matters of everyday life.
Nay, rather, if you must have lawsuits about such matters,
appoint as judges the least-esteemed Christians among
you ! [2]   (v.[5]) Can no one be found among you with enough
wisdom to judge between a man and his brother, but
brother sues brother, in a heathen law-court ?   (v.[7]) To
begin with, it is a serious loss to you that you have litiga-
tion with each other :  better to suffer wrong and depriva-
tion.  But you yourselves are guilty of wrong-doing and
deprive others who are your brothers.  (v.[9]) Remember
that unrighteous men shall not inherit God's kingdom—
fornicators, idolaters,[3] adulterers, victims and workers of
unnatural vice, thieves and profiteers, drunkards, abusive
and violent men.  Some of you were such :  but you asked
God to wash you clean in baptism, you were sanctified
and set right with Him, in the name of Christ and the
Spirit of God.

[1] The Synoptic Gospels appear to interpret literally our Lord's
apocalyptic language about a future judgment-day or final assize :
cp. Matt. 19[28] = Luke 22[30], " ye shall sit on twelve thrones, judging the
twelve tribes of Israel."   St. John's Gospel spiritualises the judgment :
men are, *ipso facto*, judged by their inward disposition ; judgment is
self-inflicted, automatic :  at death our eyes are opened to our own
state.   Christ does not judge us, but His *words* do (John 12[47. 48], etc.).
In this conception of judgment, the Church, which upholds a Christian
standard before men on earth, has a large share in judging each one
of us.   But St. Paul appears here to take the judgment as an external
assize which shall be held at the Parousia.

[2] I have followed A.V., rather than R.V. and W.H.   If, with the
latter, the sentence is interrogative, it means, " Do you set up as your
judges the *heathen* whom you despise ? "   But I cannot think that
St. Paul would use such a term about the heathen.

[3] The constant mention of idolatry among sexual sins should be
noticed.   For sexual immorality in Asia Minor and Syria and at Corinth
was practised as a religious rite.

*(v.¹²) " You argue that ' all things are lawful to a Christian ' : yes, they are, but with limitations ; remember that it is not all things that are a help to us. If liberty becomes licence, it ceases to be liberty : for licence makes us slaves to sin and no longer free men. (v.¹³) You argue that sexual acts are bodily and cannot influence your spirit any more than the food you eat. But there is no real parallel between the cases. The stomach is part of our flesh, a temporary thing that shall perish like the food it takes. But the body is more than a thing of flesh : it is bound up with the inner personality which goes with us into eternal life and belongs to Christ. (v.¹⁴) The spiritual body, which He gives us for eternity, cannot be dissociated from the fleshly body which we now inhabit. (v.¹⁵) Your bodies are limbs of Christ : shall I take away Christ's limbs and make them limbs of a harlot ? For sexual union means real union of the whole personality : on the other hand, he who is united to the Lord becomes one spirit with Him. (v.¹⁸) Sexual sin is unique among sensual sins in its deadly effect on a man's personality. (v.¹⁹) Do you not know that the body of each of you is a shrine of the Holy Spirit ? You are not your own masters, for Christ bought you at great price. Glorify God, therefore, in your body."*

[*Note.*—In 10²³ below he again answers the plea of the Antinomians that " all things are lawful." But there he says we must limit it by the law of love, *i.e.* consideration for others. Here the limiting principle is primarily the effect of licence on ourselves. The Antinomian argued that if circumcision and other outward bodily acts have become matters of indifference to a Christian, so have sexual acts also.

In v.¹⁴ when he says, " God will raise *us* up," he does not mean " will raise up the body of flesh." In v.¹³ᵇ he has already explained that the belly shall perish ; so in 15⁵⁰ he says emphatically, " flesh and blood cannot inherit God's kingdom."]

5. MARRIAGE PROBLEMS RAISED BY THE CORINTHIANS.—
7¹. "You ask me in your letter about marriage. It is a
good thing for a man not to be married ; but because of
sexual temptations some should marry in faithful mono-
gamy. Wife and husband owe it to each other to con-
summate the marriage when wedded. . . . (v.⁵) They may
rightly agree to some separation for a time, to give themselves to prayer ; but not for too long, lest Satan tempt
them to impurity. This, mind you, is not a command but
sympathetic advice. I wish that all men could be unmarried as I am ; however, different men have different
graces given them by God.

(v.⁸) "To unmarried men, whether bachelors or
widowers, and to widows, I give the advice that they had
better remain as I am. But if they lack self-control, let
them marry ; it is better to marry than to be a prey to
the fires of lust. (v.¹⁰) To those who are married, I give
this charge—not I, but the Lord—that in general a woman
ought not to leave her husband ; if she does leave him,
she must remain unmarried or be reconciled to him :
similarly a man must not send away his wife. So much is
Christ's clear teaching.¹ (v.¹²) But in the cases of mixed
marriages between a Christian and a heathen, I can only
give my opinion, not Christ's teaching. A Christian

¹ Note his reference to our Lord's words—again a sign that there was
already some collection, probably in writing, of the sayings of Jesus.
Christ, in answering a question which arose from Herod's divorce of his
wife to marry Herodias, lays down the general principle that divorce is
wrong. In St. Matthew (5³² 19⁹) He is represented as allowing one
exception to the general rule, namely, adultery, which by its very nature
may be held to sever the marriage bond. This exception is probably
inserted by the author of the First Gospel. Among the Jews adultery
was punished by death, and the question of remarriage after divorce
could normally not occur. "Matthew," writing perhaps for Alex-
andrians, among whom the Jewish Law would not hold, gives it as his
opinion that Christ would have allowed this one exception. St. Paul
cannot fairly be quoted on either side.

husband or wife, wedded to an unbeliever, should not seek separation as long as the unbeliever is content with the home. (v.¹⁴) The marriage is consecrated by the religion of the one who views it in God's sight : why, you know your children are holy, and therefore be assured that your wedded life is holy. (v.¹⁵) [a parenthesis] (It is quite a different matter if the unbeliever wants to go ; let him do so. A Christian in such cases is not enslaved ; God intends us for peace and not bickering.) Do not seek separation, I say : it is always possible that a Christian may convert the unbelieving husband or wife.¹ (v.¹⁷) Your own conversion has made a complete change in your inner life : but it ought not, other things being equal, to make any change in your external conditions of life. That is the principle I lay down in all the Churches. If a man was circumcised before his conversion, let him not undo it ; if uncircumcised, let him not seek circumcision : for the only thing that matters is the keeping of God's great commands. I say that each man should continue in the external position in which he formerly was. If you were a slave at conversion, do not be troubled at your lack of outward freedom ; though of course if you *can* win your freedom, you had better do so.² The Christian slave is Christ's freedman, just as the Christian freeman is Christ's slave. He bought you with a great price : therefore do not enslave yourselves in spirit to other men. But to return to my general point, *usually* let each man go on with the life he was living before conversion."

[*Note on St. Paul's Preference for Celibacy as shown in this Chapter.*—We have to remember that he still expected the

¹ v.¹⁶ is sometimes taken in just the opposite sense : *i.e.* let the unbeliever go, if he wants, *for* it is not very likely that you will manage to convert him or her. Such pessimism is wholly unlike St. Paul, and it makes chaos of what he has said in v.¹².

² The object to Χρῆσαι must be τῷ ἐλεύθερον γενέσθαι.

Parousia to happen very soon, as he says in v.[29]. That is the sole reason of his advice to remain unmarried—that the Christian may be more free to do the Lord's work in the short time that remains. In Eph. 5[32] he tells us that the union of two lives in marriage is the same in kind as the union between Christ and the Church. The man who wrote that cannot have regarded married life as a lower way, though permissible. The derogatory view of marriage held in the early Church 150 years later came from the unclean world without.

But how can he have recommended marriage in 1 Cor. 7 only as a safeguard against lust, when he lifts it to such a glorious height in Eph. 5[32] ? We must remember that he was writing to people living in an inconceivably foul society, many of them tainted in their own past life. He is not here recommending marriage without affection, merely as a safeguard to external morality : he presupposes the affection in any case. He says, " If a man and woman love each other, still let them remain unmarried for the sake of God's urgent work, unless it leaves them a prey to sexual passion."

Yet we may doubt whether in A.D. 56 he had realised how Christian marriage reveals to men and women new heights and depths in the love of God for us. He was always progressing and learning. Eph. 5[32] reaches perhaps beyond what he could have written at this time.]

(v.[25]) " But about those who have never married, there is no recorded word of Christ : I can only give you my opinion as one who by the Lord's mercy has been made faithful. Well, then, the present stress of circumstances is such that I think it is better for a man to remain as he is. If you are bound already by the marriage tie, you should not seek release ; if not, you should not seek a wife : but if you do marry, you have not done wrong. . . . But married folk shall have many anxieties [in these days of persecution, etc.], and I would spare you them. I mean,

the opportunity to do Christ's work is short ; so that all
ordinary conditions of life are changed—married people
living away from their wives, those in sorrow forgetting it
and similarly those who are joyous ; those who buy as if
nothing belonged to them and those who use the world
as making little use of it : for the present outward order
is passing away.   (v.[32]) I want to save you care : the unmarried man is free to care only for the service of the Lord ;
the married man must care about helping his wife, and
so he is torn in two directions.[1]   And the woman who
has no husband and the virgin are free to care for the
service of the Lord, seeking to be holy in body and spirit ;
but the married woman must care about the things of this
world, to help her husband.   (v.[35]) My object is not to put
a halter on you,[2] but to help you to live a fine life, waiting
on the Lord without distraction.[3]   (v.[36]) If a man is
betrothed to a girl and his passions are strong, so that
he does not feel that their relations to one another are
right without marriage, let them get married.   But the
man who is master of his passions and agrees that celibacy
is desirable at the present time, will do well to continue unmarried.   So also with the father of the girl : if he gives her
in marriage, he acts well ; if he does not, he acts better." [4]

[1] Following the W.H. reading (the second marginal reading of the
R.V.).   The text is in great confusion here.

[2] *i.e.* to curtail your freedom, probably.

[3] ἀπερισπάστως.   Robertson and Plummer (*Internat. Crit. Comm.*,
*in loc.*) quote a striking parallel from Epictetus (*Dis.* iii. 22), the Stoic
slave of Asia who was St. Paul's younger contemporary.   "In the
present state of things, which is like that of an army placed in battle
order, is it not fit that the philosopher should *without any distraction*
(ἀπερίσπαστον) be employed only on the ministration of God, not
tied down to the common duties of mankind nor entangled in the
ordinary relations of life ? "

[4] Others interpret v.[36] of the father of an unmarried daughter
(as R.V.), translating ὑπέρακμος as " of full age for marriage."   But
v.[37a] seems to have no application to a father.   For the rendering of
ὑπέρακμος as " passionate," see Lake, *Earlier Epistles of St. Paul*, p. 186.

(v.³⁹) A widow is free to remarry if she wishes; but it must be a Christian marriage. And I think she is more blessed if she remains single, and I believe I have the Spirit of God with me in saying this.

6. CHAPS. 8–10 (For the unity of thought in this section, see the outline analysis on p. 176).—[*Note.*—In dealing with the problems connected with food which is part of a beast sacrificed to an idol, St. Paul discusses three concrete cases :

(1) Meat sold in the market was often such. He tells them (10²⁵) that it is absurd over-conscientiousness to bother about that.

(2) At a dinner in a heathen household the meat was often part of a private sacrifice. St. Paul's advice in this case is (10²⁷ᶠᶠ·), " Eat it without scruple, unless some other guest is uneasy in conscience about it and tells you that the meat is part of a sacrifice : in that case, abstain for his sake."

(3) A Christian might be asked to a sacramental feast in a heathen temple, particularly when he belonged to a trade-guild. St. Paul absolutely forbids him to go (10¹⁴⁻²² and 8¹⁰). But before he comes to these concrete cases, he first expounds the larger principle that liberty must always be conditioned by love for your neighbour.]

8¹. " Next as to your questions about meat offered to idols—no doubt we all have superior knowledge and think it weak to consider such food as in any way affected. But knowledge by itself may make men self-sufficient : love is needed to build us up. If a man prides himself on his knowledge, let him remember that his knowledge is very limited as yet. Where knowledge of God fails, love brings us into intimate communion with Him. (v.⁴) Now knowledge truly tells us that there is no God save one, and that there is no real idol-God. It is true that there are

demon powers worshipped as gods, and they exercise real
influence over their worshippers [see 10¹⁹⁻²¹]. But we
know that they are not gods, and we have nothing to do
with any save the one God the Father, who is the source
of all things and our goal, and one Lord, Jesus Christ,
through whom all things were created and by whom alone
our life is sustained. (v.⁷) But it is not all men who have
such clear knowledge. Some, having been used in the
past to think of the idol as a god, eat the meat conscious
that it has been part of a heathen sacrifice, and their conscience being weak suffers defilement. Of course what we
eat will not bring us nearer God : if we abstain, we lose
nothing ; if we eat, we gain nothing. But take care that
this freedom of yours does not become a stumbling-block
to the weak. (v.¹⁰) If you with your superior knowledge
go to a feast in an idol's temple, the weaker brother may
see you and your example may lead him on to eat the
sacrificial meat : so he is led to destruction—he, your
brother, for whom Christ died. By sinning against him,
you are sinning against Christ.[1] I tell you I would rather
give up meat altogether than cause temptation to a
brother.

9¹. " This principle—that Love, not self-assertion, must
be our dominant motive—is the reason why, when I was
at Corinth, I worked for my living and refused to accept
it from you. Some of you saw in that a confession that
I have no apostolic rights. But my apostleship is proved
by two clear signs—I am an eye-witness of the risen Lord ;
and the work I have accomplished—in other words, the
fact that *you* are Christians—is the seal that authenticates
it. This is my answer to inquisitive people. My right
to be kept at the expense of my converts is beyond
question ; moreover, if I were married, I should have the

---

[1] Here again we have an echo of some of our Lord's sayings, *e.g.*
Luke 9⁴⁸.

13

right to bring my wife with me and claim maintenance also for her, as the rest of the Apostles do, and the Lord's brothers, and Cephas himself. Or is it only I and Barnabas who have no right to claim exemption from manual toil ? (v.⁷) A soldier is paid : a vine-grower lives by selling his fruit, and a shepherd the milk of his flock. If you want something more than an analogy from common human life, look at the passage in the Mosaic Law which forbids the muzzling of an ox when he is treading the grain.[1] Is God only thinking of the oxen in this command ? May we not be certain [πάντως = assuredly] that He means us to draw a lesson from it ? The lesson is that the man who ploughs and the man who threshes ought both to work in the hope of sharing in the corn. (v.¹¹) We sowed spiritual grain among you : is it too much that we should expect to reap your worldly possessions ? If any one has the right, it is I. Yet I never claimed it, but I would bear any hardship rather than hinder the spread of the gospel. (v.¹³) In the Jewish law Levites have their tithes and priests their portion. So also the Lord commanded that those who preach the gospel shall live by it.[2] But I have not used my right, I repeat. (v.¹⁵) I have not written this in order to claim it from you in future : *I had rather die than—but no one shall deprive me of my source of pride. Preaching by itself would give me nothing to be proud of : for I am bound to preach or to be condemned to spiritual misery. To preach *willingly* is my reward : if I were unwilling, I should still be like a steward with his duty. My reward, I say, is to preach without pay and forbear to claim my right.*

(v.¹⁹) " Free as I am from all, I have made myself slave to all, in my longing to win over more. To the Jews, I became as a Jew [keeping the Law among them] ; to the Gentiles as a man living without law, acknowledging

---

[1] *i.e.* in threshing.  [2] See Luke 10⁷.

only the law of Christ. . . . I have become all things to
all men that at all costs I may save some. All I aim at
is the furtherance of the gospel, that I may have a share
in it. (v.²⁴) Also this gives me a self-discipline. In your
Isthmian games at Corinth and other great athletic
meetings, many enter for a race, but only one can win
the prize. Therefore, the competitors train hard for
months of self-denial—in order to win the fading crown
of leaves! How much harder must we train for the
crown that never fades. Therefore I run my race with
no wavering aim : I am like the boxer who takes every
care not to hit the empty air. Nay, I hit my own body !
I bruise it sorely, for fear that, after calling others to
compete in the games, I myself may be disqualified."

[*Note.*—In v.²⁷ κηρύξας (R.V. " preached ") has a
double sense : in the games it was used of the herald
announcing a race, in the New Testament it is used of
announcing God's message. So also ἀδόκιμος means, in
the games, " disqualified " (for having broken some rule) ;
in the religious sense, " rejected " by God.]

10¹. [*Note.*—The connexion of thought with chap. 9
is this : " A race is often lost by over-confidence. That
is precisely your danger. You treat the two Sacraments
which our Lord instituted, Baptism and Holy Communion,
as charms which secure to you eternal life : you think
that you have no further need of watchfulness. But
take warning from the story of the Hebrews in the wilderness."]

(v.¹) " Remember that *all* our fathers after the Exodus
were granted spiritual privileges analogous to our two
Sacraments : they were *all* baptized into Moses, when they
ventured into the Red Sea in complete trust in him ;
they were *all* fed with food from heaven, the manna and
the water from the rock ; for the rock, according to tradition, followed them wherever they went, and so is a type

of Christ.[1] *Yet most of them did not please God ;* for '*their bodies were scattered in the wilderness.*' (v.[6]) In all this we have a warning from God not to lust after evil as they did, nor to imitate their idolatry and their fornication, and their presuming on God's goodness, and their discontent. (v.[11]) We have a warning in their fate, and it was recorded in Scripture to teach us who live at the end of history. So the man that is over-confident of his stedfastness must take good heed lest he fall. (v.[13]) Yet do not be over-anxious : all your temptations are such as are common to humanity. God will not allow any temptation to go beyond your power of resistance [if you are humble and watchful], and will in every case provide a way of escape.

(v.[14]) " Therefore [in connexion with the question of sacrificial meat] you must be careful to avoid idolatry. *You yourselves have common sense and can judge what I am saying. At the Christian sacramental feast, the cup brings us into communion with Christ's life-blood which He poured out to give us life, and the bread into communion with His body broken for us (for we, though we are as many as the broken fragments of bread, are yet, in this communion, one loaf, one body, all quickened by the *one* spiritual life of Christ to perform our diverse functions as members of His one body).[2] [Just in the same way remember that a sacramental feast in an idol's temple must involve you in real communion with the

---

[1] This Jewish legend arose from the fact that (in the JE narrative) the water from the rock is recorded at Rephidim, at the beginning of the wanderings ; and (in the P narrative) at Kadesh-Barnea, at the end. Philo allegorises the rock and the manna as denoting Divine wisdom, which sustains all who desire it.

[2] Cp. the *Didaché*, chap. ix., probably the earliest Christian prayer known to us for use at the Eucharist : " as this broken bread was scattered as grain upon the mountains and was gathered together to become one, so may Thy Church . . ."

demon whom they worship.] Everywhere it is true that
men who eat the sacrifices have real communion with
the god they worship. (v.¹⁹) Is this statement inconsistent with what I have said above [8⁴], that an idol is
no true god, and that food offered to it is harmless ? No,
for the mind of the worshipper is in real communion with
demon powers : the food is unchanged, but the man who
partakes is not.¹ You cannot drink the cup of the Lord
and the cup of demons ; you cannot share in the table ²
of the Lord and the table of demons. Or are we ' *intending to provoke the Lord* ' ?*

(v.²³) " You plead again in this connexion that ' all
things are lawful.' Yes, but all things do not help and
strengthen. Our rule must be to seek always what will
help our neighbour rather than please ourselves. [See
note on 6¹².] (v.²⁵) When meat is offered for sale in the
market, buy and eat it and do not think it necessary to
make inquiries about it for conscience' sake : for ' *the whole
earth belongs to the Lord and all in it.*' Again, if you are
invited to dine with an unbeliever, eat of any dish which is
offered to you without making inquiries about it : but if
some one there says to you, ' this meat has been offered in
a temple,' ³ avoid eating of it lest you weaken *his* conscience
(not your own, for no other man can judge how I use my
freedom in God's sight : if I thankfully partake of food
as God's gift, my own conscience is clear). (v.³¹) Make
this your test in all such difficulties, that you are to *do
everything for the glory of God.* Avoid giving offence to

---

¹ The argument implies that there is no change in the *food* in either
case, the heathen feast or the Christian sacrament.

² For the use of the word " table " in connexion with the Mystery
religions, see Lake, *Earlier Epistles of St. Paul*, p. 199, n. 1. We have
the phrase " the table of Serapis."

³ The word is ἱερόθυτον. The change from the opprobrious
ἐιδωλόθυτον (" sacrificed to an idol ") is a clue to the weak brother's
state of mind.

Jew or Greek or Christian, as far as you can ; my own rule
for myself is this—to aim at what is best for the majority,
not simply at what helps myself. In this I am trying to
imitate Christ, and I ask you to follow my example."

7. CHAP. 11. ABUSES CONNECTED WITH (a) THE
EMANCIPATION OF WOMEN (vv.[2-16]) ; (b) THE LORD'S
SUPPER (vv.[17-34]).

11[2]. " You do remember me in everything, I am glad
to say, and try to maintain the Christian traditions as 1
gave them to you. *But as regards the position of women,
I want you to realise that though Christianity regards men
and women as equal in the sight of God, yet women are
meant by God to be dependent on men. God's order is,
first Himself, then Christ, then men, then women. (v.[4])
Your action, in allowing women at Corinth to take part in
public worship unveiled, forgets this fact of their dependence
and is, in the state of your society, a danger to morals.
Women of bad character have their heads shaven as a
symbolic penalty : it is similarly a dishonour to a woman
to unveil her head in public. (v.[7]) To cover your head
denotes that some one else is present on whom you are in
dependence : therefore a man ought not to do so in public
worship and a woman ought. A man is made in God's
image and represents His glorious creative power on earth ;
but the wife is the husband's glory, as the story of her
creation shows [Gen. 2]. (v.[10]) Therefore a woman ought
to wear a veil in public worship because the veil is her
authority and dignity—just as the angels veil their faces
before God."*

[Note.—v.[10] is difficult. In rendering " ought to have
(the veil which is) her authority," we are following Ramsay,
who agrees with Thomson. His comment (Cities of St.
Paul, pp. 204 ff.) elucidates the whole section : " In Oriental
lands the veil is the power and the honour and dignity of

the woman. With the veil on her head she can go anywhere in security and profound respect. . . . She is
supreme in the crowd. . . . But without the veil the
woman is a thing of naught whom any one may insult."

" *Because of the angels* " is very obscure, and there are
innumerable interpretations. That suggested above seems
the simplest. Otherwise it may mean, " because of the
temptations which evil angels suggest to men " ($\dot{\alpha}\gamma\gamma\acute{\epsilon}\lambda o\nu\varsigma$
=the Hebrew and Rabbinic " Shedhim "). We are not
convinced by the suggestion that " the angels " means
" the clergy " !]

(v.[11]) " But husband and wife are complementary to
each other in the Lord. *Though the wife is subordinate,
she is not in any way inferior.* Woman was created from
man, but man is always born of woman : all things, remember, come from God. You can judge for yourselves
what is appropriate for women : is it seemly for a woman
to pray in public with her head unveiled ? Does not
nature itself teach you that it is a glory to a woman to wear
long hair, though a disgrace to a man if he does so ? for
her hair is given her as a covering. Such is my opinion :
if any contentious person refuses it, I can only say that
the custom is unknown to us and to the churches of
God everywhere."

[*Note on St. Paul's Ruling* (11[2-16]).—Most people will
agree that he was right in the general advice which he
gives in this section. For women in a city like Corinth
to claim sudden emancipation and defy all the conventions
of the time would be to court insult and misunderstanding.
I suppose that the nearest parallel to-day would be found
in some Indian city where " purdah " is strictly practised.
Some of his arguments (*e.g.* that it is unnatural for a
woman to wear short hair) may seem to us as quaint as
the statement often heard thirty years ago, that it was
unnatural for a woman to ride a bicycle. That, however,

ought not to blind us to the seriousness of his argument, that a married woman is meant by God from her very nature to be dependent on her husband up to a point, and that dependence does not imply any sort of inferiority. But it is ludicrous in our age to argue from St. Paul's ruling, given to women in Corinth in A.D. 56, that a woman must not appear in a modern church without a hat !]

11[17]. [Another case in which their meetings for public worship were doing harm : *the cliques, even at the Agape.* The Agape or Love-Feast was a common meal, to which each brought some food, and ended with Holy Communion : it was an imitation of the Last Supper.]

(v.[17]) " Again, I cannot approve of another feature of your Church meetings, which is doing harm rather than good : I hear that you are divided into cliques, and I am afraid it is partly true. There must indeed be different opinions among you : they help to bring to the front the most genuine Christians.[1] But I hear that even when you come to a Love-Feast, you do not make it a real Supper of the Lord : each of you devours the food which he has brought without waiting for the others and without sharing it. So the poor man goes hungry, while the rich man even drinks too much. (v.[22]) If you merely want to eat and drink, do so at home, and do not despise the Church of God and shame those who are needy. No, I cannot approve. (v.[23]) I handed on to you what I received by sure authority from Christ Himself,[2] that the Lord Jesus, on the very night He was betrayed, took bread and gave thanks to God and broke it, saying, ' This is My body [given] for you. Do this in remembrance of Me.' And after the supper He took

---

[1] St. Paul probably was often met with the retort, " You all claim personal inspiration by God : but see what a chaos of different opinions is the result." He gives an answer here : he never doubted that truth would prevail in the Church at last, though new developments might be championed by a small minority for a long period.

[2] Probably through the Apostles who were present at the Last Supper.

the cup and said, ' This cup is the new covenant [sealed] in My blood : do this, whenever you drink it, in remembrance of Me.' So, as often as you meet to obey this command of the Lord, you are telling of the Lord's death for you, till He comes again. (v.[27]) Therefore whoever eats the bread or drinks the Lord's cup with unworthy motives, is insulting the [spiritual] body and blood of the Lord. Each man ought to examine his own heart before he eats the bread and drinks of the cup. If you come without discerning its real meaning, you are only bringing judgment on yourselves : indeed many among you have for this reason been punished with sickness and bad health, and some even with death. (v.[31]) God's judgment is avoided by self-judgment : it is sent to correct us and save us from the condemnation which the world incurs. So, my brothers, when you meet for this purpose, wait for the others : if a man merely wants to satisfy his hunger, let him eat at home. Other matters of a like nature I will put in order when I come to Corinth."

[*Notes on* 11[17-34].—(*a*) *The words of administration* as given by St. Paul differ to some extent from the version found in Matthew and Mark. This is most noticeable in the words about the cup :

Matthew⎫ " This is *My* blood of the covenant which is
Mark    ⎭    shed for many."
Paul . . " This cup is the new covenant in My blood."

Both versions clearly go back to the same Aramaic original. Matthew and Mark make the words a reference to God's covenant with Moses at Sinai, where it is said (Ex. 24[8]), " this is the blood of the covenant." It is clear that both versions have much the same meaning : and the turn which St. Paul gives to the words is probably due to his wish to make it plain to the literalistic Western mind that our Lord did not mean " this wine is My (literal) blood."

So he gives the words as, " this cup (*i.e.* act of drinking) represents the new covenant maintained in My spiritual life." We may compare the teaching in John 6[27ff.] with its emphatic declaration in v.[63] that our Lord's words about eating His flesh and drinking His blood are not to be interpreted materially but spiritually, " they are *spirit* and life."

Again, the words " *do this in remembrance of Me* " are not found in the Synoptic Gospels, apart from St. Luke (if Luke 22[19b-20] be genuine). But they are presupposed by the custom of the early Church in Jerusalem ; see Acts 2[46], for the daily Agape and Celebration.

(*b*) *Verse* [26] is sometimes supposed to mean, " You plead Christ's sacrifice by (somehow) re-enacting it." But what St. Paul says is, " You *tell forth* the Lord's death." He, the risen Lord, is always present, there and elsewhere ; but in certain acts and places His presence is more actively realised by us. In repeating the Last Supper, we can see Him by the eye of faith, and share with Him (in the *breaking* of the bread, and the *pouring out* of the wine) His crucifixion and resurrection (cp. Rom. 6[4], where this is said of Baptism). So we receive His spiritual life anew and in fuller measure.

(*c*) *St. Paul's View of the Sacraments.*—It is evident from 10[1-11] that he regarded Baptism and Holy Communion as supreme acts, because instituted for us by Christ ; though he looked on every good thing in life as sacramental (cp. marriage, Eph. 5[32]). The question is, did he regard these two as magically efficacious, *ex opere operato*, as the Mystery religions regarded their sacramental rites ? Does Rom. 6[4] imply that Baptism, as a dramatic representation of death to sin and rising to a new life washed clean, effects in some magical way what it represents ? [1]

---

[1] Of course, in one sense all Christians must believe that sacraments have an objective value : Christ is present, and through the symbolic act we realise His objective presence and partake His objective life. It is a case of the psychological *suggestion* of a real truth.

Does 1 Cor. 11²⁶ mean that in the Eucharist we re-enact the Lord's death, because He is miraculously identified with the consecrated bread and wine, and our reception of them effects our identification with Him ?  If so, he leaves his meaning singularly obscure.  We have pointed out above that the words, " this *cup is the new covenant in My blood*," can scarcely mean " this wine IS My blood." The Aramaic original of the words must have left " this " without a noun ;  St. Paul inserts " cup," not " wine."

Our Epistle proves that the early Church made the Agape and Celebration a replica of the Last Supper, as indeed we find them still in the *Didaché* (early second century probably), in Ignatius (slightly later), and even in Clement of Alexandria (at the end of the second century). They realised that Christ was really present, just as He had been in the upper room at Jerusalem, *i.e.* apart from the bread and wine, not concealed in them (except in so far as He is in all food which we take).  Indeed, there is not a word in the New Testament to show that the bread and wine were ever consecrated.  In connexion with 1 Cor. 11, " Beet points out that private members were able to appropriate beforehand the food designed for the Communion, which implies that they were not in the habit of receiving the bread and wine from the *Church Officers*.  From this we infer with certainty that, when Christ ordained the Supper, He did not direct, and that, when 1 Corinthians was written, the Apostles had not directed, that the sacred rite should be administered by the Church Officers and them alone " (Robertson and Plummer, *Internat. Crit. Comm. on 1 Cor.*, p. 256).  That is perhaps too sweeping a statement, and fails to make any distinction between the common meal and the more sacred rite which probably followed it.  But the chief point holds good ; there is no reference to the authority of the Presbyter.

The terms which St. Paul uses of circumcision in Rom. 4¹¹

(see note on p. 257) help us to understand St. Paul's view of the Sacraments. He says that Abraham received circumcision as a *sign and seal* of his righteousness. If we may venture on an analogy, we might say that demonstrations of affection in home life are a " sign " and " seal " of love ; *i.e.* they are not only a proof of it, but the outward act tends to increase it.

The recurrence of such abuses as St. Paul notices in 1 Cor. 11 in connexion with the Celebration probably tended to separate the Agape from Holy Communion as time went on. Also it was found convenient to have the celebration in the morning before the day's work : thus the communicant would receive before breaking his fast. To ensure reverence, only a Priest was allowed to celebrate. The customs which thus grew up, came in time to be regarded as absolute necessities, especially when a magical import was attached to the Sacraments under the growing influence of the Greek Mystery religions.]

8. CHAPS. 12–14. ABOUT SPIRITUAL GIFTS, ESPECIALLY " PROPHESYING " AND " TONGUES." LOVE AS THE SUPREME GIFT NEEDED TO VITALISE ALL OTHERS.

*Note on " Prophesying " and " Tongues."*—These gifts seem both to be subconscious powers in men, quickened by spiritual emotion. If uncontrolled, they were as dangerous as any other unregulated emotion. At Corinth they had led to excessive individualism : they were not used in the service of the Christian society, but merely to feed the complacency and self-satisfaction of those who possessed them.

The gift of " PROPHECY " means the power to preach with insight into the inner meaning of God's ways ; to understand the spiritual significance of contemporary events and tendencies. But it has this in common with the gift of "tongues," that it contained an element of religious ecstasy: the prophet was held to be possessed by the Divine Spirit.

The gift of " Tongues " has been variously interpreted.

(1) Some understand it of the ecstatic and meaningless cries which are known at revivalist meetings. Men and women become so utterly overpowered by emotion that they utter weird sounds that are not words in any human language.

(2) Others take it to mean utterances in some foreign language which the speaker does not know.[1]

The second view seems the more probable. There is an à priori probability that what happened at Corinth was the same thing in kind as what happened at Jerusalem on the Day of Pentecost. In Acts 2 St. Luke definitely represents the Apostles as speaking in foreign languages which could be understood by men from various countries abroad. He does not say that the Apostles themselves understood what they were saying.[2] In 1 Cor. 14[27] the " tongue " could be interpreted if there was some one present capable of doing so ; but in modern revivals no one, as far as we know, claims to interpret the ecstatic cries. In 14[14] the man who prays with a " tongue " does not intellectually comprehend what he is saying, though his spirit is lifted up to God ; but it is not an uncontrollable impulse, implying loss of calmness (14[27-28]). Granting, then, that foreign languages are meant, can we find parallel instances to the gift ? Every sound, which falls on the ear, is probably stored somewhere in the brain,

[1] It is perhaps scarcely necessary to say that the view of many older commentators, which regards the gift of tongues as a *permanent* and miraculous endowment with the knowledge of foreign languages, is quite indefensible. The Apostles had to learn languages, for missionary work, with the same effort as the rest of us : and some of them never attained much proficiency in Greek (*e.g.* St. Peter).

[2] Let us grant that St. Luke is not such a weighty historical authority in the early chapters of Acts as he is for St. Paul's life. Yet it is clear (a) that he had heard of Pentecost from some who were present : (b) that he had himself been at places like Corinth, where the gift of tongues was known.

though it is not reproducible by the conscious will. In moments of high tension, however (*e.g.* in delirium, as in anæsthesia), people are known to utter things which they could not reproduce in ordinary consciousness : it is an uprush from the " subconscious "[1] or " unconscious " self. But the suggestion that such cases offer a parallel to "tongues " is not altogether convincing. Jerusalem at feast-time and Corinth at all seasons were cosmopolitan centres where many languages could be heard. However, we can scarcely suppose that the Corinthian Church would be edified if some of its members were in a moment of spiritual exultation to repeat what they had heard in a foreign tongue on the streets of Corinth (shall we say ?).

12[1]. " But as regards spiritual influences, I want you to recognise that they are not all to be accepted as good. In your heathen days you were helpless victims of demon spirits. Therefore, we need a criterion and we have one ready : whatever helps us to acknowledge more thoroughly Jesus as Lord,[2] is from the Holy Spirit : whatever leads us to repudiate Him, is not.

(v.[4]) " All good gifts, however diverse, proceed from the same source and are directed to one purpose [the service of the whole Church]. The Holy Spirit communicates different gifts to us ; the Lord Jesus apportions our various spheres of service ; God the Father gives the power to make all these diverse gifts effective. (v.[7]) Each individual has his own particular endowment *to use for the good of all.*

[1] See Wright, *Some New Testament Problems*, pp. 292–4. He quotes the case of an ignorant girl who was servant to a Protestant pastor. She had heard him reading aloud extracts from Scripture in languages of which she could not understand a word. But when she lay ill of fever, she repeated long passages in Hebrew, Greek, and Latin, in her delirium ! The Freudian explanation that the unconscious self is stored with repressed instincts forming a complex, scarcely explains such phenomena.

[2] " Jesus is Lord " was probably the earliest baptismal confession of faith.

(v.⁸) One group of gifts confers the power of putting into speech our insight or experience : a second group includes faith, the power to heal, the power to do mighty works, prophecy, the ability to discriminate between good and evil manifestations : a third group consists of the power of ' tongues ' and the interpretation of them. But all these gifts come from the same Spirit, who gives something to each individual man.

(v.¹²) " The Church is more than an agglomeration of different units, it is a live organism like the human body, which has unity though composed of different limbs. The body of Christ is similar, of which our baptism made us members in the one Spirit—yes, Jews and Gentiles, bond and free alike, were made to drink the one Spirit. (v.¹⁴) Take the human body : if the foot (v.¹⁵) or ear (v.¹⁶) says it does not belong to the same whole as other members, none the less it *is* part of the body. (v.¹⁷) And the different members have different functions, though they form one body. . . . (v.²¹) The eye cannot say to the hand, or the head to the feet, ' I have no need of you ' ; but the members which seem to be weaker are all the more necessary, and those which are held in less honour are clothed all the more carefully and made to look seemly, while the rest that look more seemly have no need. God, then, compounded the body, giving more honour to what needed it most, that there should be no division between the members but that they should care for and aid each other. (v.²⁶) If one member is in pain, all the members share its pain : if one member is glorified,¹ they all are glad with it. (v.²⁷) *You* are Christ's body and severally members of it. God appointed in the Church some as Apostles, some as prophets, some teachers, some workers of mighty deeds, some men who have gifts of healing, of helping, of ruling,

¹ Here, as so often in St. Paul, his metaphor breaks down in language, because he is thinking first of its spiritual application.

of speaking unknown tongues. But *all* men have not all these gifts ; God divides them among different people. Seek eagerly the greater gifts, but, (13¹) above all, the supremely excellent way, that is *Christian love,* [which all can attain and] which vitalises all other gifts.

13². " I may speak all the tongues of men and of angels ; but if I lack love, I am become like a sounding gong or clanging cymbal.¹ I may have the gift of prophecy and know all secrets of the world, all knowledge ; I may have faith enough ' to move mountains ' : but if I lack love, I am naught. I may give away all I have in doles to the poor, I may give my very body to be burned ; ² but if I lack love, it is no help to me. (v.⁴) Love is patient and kind ; love knows no jealousy, does not give herself airs, is not conceited, not bad form ; she seeks not her own advantage, does not allow herself to be provoked, does not let evil dwell in her mind, is not gladdened by unrighteous acts but only when truth prevails. (v.⁷) Love is ever ready to find excuses ³ for others, to believe in them, to hope for them, to endure at their hands. (v.⁸) Love never fails. Prophecy, tongues, knowledge have their day and cease to be : for prophecy and knowledge only reach part of the truth ; and when that which is perfect shall come, all that is partial shall cease to be. Now we are like

¹ Both were used in heathen worship. At Dodona in Greece omens were taken from gongs hung on trees, and a " gong of Dodona " seems to have become a proverb for an empty talker. Cymbals were used in the worship of Cybele, Dionysus, etc.

² Reading καυθήσωμαι with E.V. W.H. read καυχήσωμαι, with א A B Egyptt. and Origen. But " boast " seems out of place, as such a motive would at once imply that love was lacking. If " burnt " be right, St. Paul may have heard at Athens how a few years earlier a Buddhist had burnt himself alive in their market-place to show his devotion to his religion.

³ στέγει may mean " beareth " as E.V. : it has that sense elsewhere in N.T. But then there is little difference between it and the last word of the four (ὑπομένει). So it probably means " covers up."

children in our speaking, thinking, reasoning; but the
child grows up and puts away childish things. Now we
see truth dimly [1] as if reflected in a [metal] mirror; then
we shall see face to face. Now I know only in part; then
I shall know as fully as God knows me. (v.13) Faith, hope,
and love shall abide when all other gifts merge away in
perfect vision; but love is the greatest of the three.

14[1]. " Therefore make love your supreme quest; and
then you may safely desire spiritual gifts, especially
prophecy. The man who speaks in a tongue, speaks not
to man but to God, for no one understands him and what
he means is hidden in his spirit: but the man who
prophesies, helps and inspires and cheers others. The
one helps only himself, the other the Church. I would
like you all to have the gift of tongues, but I would prefer
for you the gift of prophecy. The latter is the greater gift,
except where the man who speaks in a tongue can interpret
his meaning to help the Church. (v.6) Granted that I can
speak to you in tongues, how will it help you, unless I
can make clear some revelation or new bit of knowledge
or prophecy or teaching? Inanimate instruments like
the flute or harp are no use if there is no variation in their
notes; unless a trumpet gives a clear note, no one will
prepare for battle. So you do not help unless your utterance conveys meaning; you are wasting your breath.
(v.10) Every sound in the world has some significance;
but if I do not know it and any one talks to me, he and I
will regard each other as barbarians. (v.12) You are keen
for spiritual gifts: try to increase those which help the
Church. Let the man with the gift of tongues pray for the
power of interpreting them. (v.14) It is better to pray

---

[1] Ἐν αἰνίγματι is literally " (as) in a riddle." In Num. 12[8] the Septuagint has, " I will speak to him mouth to mouth, with sight of him, and
not by riddles " (δι' αἰνιγμάτων). The " riddles " are dark sayings
covering a reality.

14

both with mind and spirit than with spirit only.  If you worship only in spirit, how can the man who is uninstructed say ' Amen ' to your thanksgiving ?  He does not know what you are saying. . . . (v.[18]) Thank God I have the gift of tongues more than you all : but in a Church meeting I had rather utter five words with my mind to instruct others than ten thousand in a tongue.

(v.[20]) " Brothers, do not be childish in thought, only in wickedness :  in thought be grown-up.  Isaiah foretells that even when God spoke to His people through men of foreign tongue, they would not listen :  such tongues then are a sign only to those who do not believe, not to those who do believe.  (v.[23]) If uninstructed men or unbelievers enter a Church meeting where every one is speaking with tongues, will they not say you are mad ?   But if they come in when everybody is prophesying, their sins are brought home to them, their conscience is searched, things hidden in their hearts are made clear, and falling on their faces they will worship God, proclaiming that ' God is really among you.'

(v.[26]) " When you meet, some one has a hymn to sing, some one a teaching or revelation to give, some one a gift of a tongue or the power to interpret it :  very well, let it all be done in a way to help others.  Never let more than two or at most three people give utterance in a tongue at any meeting, and then it must be by turns, not all at once, and only when some one is present to interpret :  otherwise let the speaker keep silence and speak only to himself and God.  (v.[29]) Similarly let two or three prophets speak one after the other, and the rest think about what is said. If a man sitting by has a sudden revelation, let the first man stop.  You *can* prophesy one at a time, for the teaching and inspiration of all ;  prophets have control over the spirit which moves them ;  for God loves not disorder but peace.  This is the custom in all Christian Churches.

(v.³⁴) " Women should not be allowed to speak publicly in Church meetings : they must take a subordinate place, as also the Mosaic Law commands. If they want to ask any question, let them ask their husbands at home. Remember that you are not the only Christians in the world !

(v.³⁷) " If any one prides himself on superior spiritual knowledge, let him show it by recognising that what I have said accords with Christ's law of love. If he disregards that, he will himself be disregarded.[1] To sum up : be eager for the gift of prophecy ; do not suppress the gift of tongues : but let everything be done decently and in order."

## 9. Chap. 15. Difficulties felt by the Corinthians about the Resurrection.

[*Note on the Nature of these Difficulties.*—The belief in a resurrection for the righteous was by this time held by most Jews except the Sadducees. It seems clear that the difficulties at Corinth were raised, not by Jewish, but by Gentile Christians. The position was probably as follows. These men had been brought up, not to the belief in a full personal survival after death which the Mystery religions were beginning to spread ; but to the old Greek conception of existence after death as a sort of half-life in a bodiless state. St. Paul has this conception in view when he writes 2 Cor. 5³⁻⁴, where he insists that death will not leave us " naked," unclothed, but clothed with a more glorious and complete body. The main reason for the Christian emphasis on the resurrection of the " body " was to safeguard against the notion that life after death is a dim half-existence ; and to emphasise the truth that it is a full personal life, with larger and quickened powers.

These Greeks at Corinth doubted how that could be. They could not believe that the mortal body which decayed

---

[1] ἀγνοεῖται, the reading of א A D. Otherwise read ἀγνοείτω with B, *i.e.* " Let him disregard it (I will not argue further)."

in the tomb should be given back to man ; and St. Paul agrees that they are right—"flesh and blood cannot inherit the Kingdom of God, nor doth mortality inherit immortality " (15⁵⁰). But if so, the Corinthians could not see how there could be a full personal life after death. They disbelieved in our resurrection ; possibly they denied the survival of any personal consciousness.

*St. Paul's Solution.*—The conception of a "spiritual body " is not original. Some of the Jewish Apocalypses had already taught that the body at the resurrection of the righteous shall be transfigured into a " garment of glory." But the term "spiritual body " apparently was coined by the Apostle. It seems to be a contradiction in terms to speak of a body made of spirit ; but he means by it some outward expression of the personality such as is needful to the fulness of individual life. We cannot visualise it, because it lies beyond our experience, though not contrary to our experience.

We may ask how this fits in with the belief that our Lord rose from the tomb with His earthly body (however much it was transfigured). It seems clear that St. Paul believed in the story of the empty tomb : there is no point in his saying that Christ rose again *on the third day* (15⁴), if the resurrection appearances were merely spiritual and His mortal body decayed in the tomb. He probably thought that our Lord's body was semi-earthly, semi-spiritual, in the forty days after the Resurrection ; and that this was a special miracle, with no counterpart in our future experience ; a miracle wrought by God to convince mankind that the Resurrection was no hallucination.]

[*Note on* 15¹⁻⁸.—This list of Resurrection appearances of our Lord is probably the earliest *written* record which we have. It is penned some twenty-five years after the events. The appearance to " over five hundred brethren at once " (probably not recorded in the Gospels) is particularly interesting because it can scarcely be considered a hallucination. That St. Paul really believed in the empty tomb of our Lord is clear from his mention of the Resurrection " *on the third day* " : if he had considered the Resurrection merely spiritual and not bodily, why not place it at the moment of Jesus' death ? He had clearly talked to Peter (v.[5]) and James (v.[7]) about it, as well as to some of the five hundred, " of whom the greater part remain until now." In v.[5] " the twelve " is used loosely for all the Apostles : in reality Judas was absent.]

15[1]. " I must call to your memory again the good news of the Lord's Resurrection which was told you ; it is your strength, your salvation, if you hold it fast— that is, unless you have believed in vain. First and foremost I told you the facts of it as I received them [from the eye-witnesses], that Christ died for our sins as the Old Testament foretold ; that He was buried and raised the third day, as was again foretold. He appeared to Cephas, to the twelve, to over five hundred brethren at the same time, of whom most are still alive, to James, to all the Apostles. His last appearance was to me, as to some babe suddenly and prematurely born. I am the least of the Apostles, not worthy to be called an Apostle, because I persecuted God's Church. But God's grace has made me such as I am now, and His grace was not without its effects, for my work of toil for Christ has been wider than that of all the others—but it was all God's grace, not my own power. But let us leave the personal element : they and I alike preach the same Resurrection message, and you believed it.

(v.[12]) " So I cannot think how some of you now maintain that there is no resurrection of the dead. If that is true, then Christ has not been raised ; then our preaching is all unreal and so is our faith ; we have been telling lies about God ! . . . If the dead are not raised, Christ has not been raised ; then your faith is an empty, useless thing, you are still in your sins : also our dead Christian friends have perished in their sins. (v.[19]) If our union with the risen Lord is a delusion, goodness becomes an impossible and a torturing dream.

(v.[20]) " But Christ *has* been raised, the first-fruits of the dead. Man brought in death ; it needed man to bring resurrection. Adam transmitted death to all men, Christ will give life to all. But in Christ's army there are different companies : first He Himself rose ; those who are Christ's at His coming shall rise next ; then shall be the end, when He hands over the Kingdom to God the Father, after destroying every hostile power. (v.[26]) Death shall be the last enemy to be destroyed : for we read, ' *He has put all things under His feet*,'—' all things,' that is, with the exception of Himself : but at the last He also shall subject Himself to the Father, that God may be all things in all men."

[*Note on v.*[24-28].—The Jewish Apocalypses distinguished between the Messiah's Kingdom and the final Kingdom of God : St. Paul still finds a meaning in the distinction. Now we reach God only " in Christ " ; at the end we shall have a more perfect and direct union with Him. Again the Kingdom of Christ has always on it the sign of the Cross—that is, suffering in love for the sinful world, a suffering borne both by Christ and all His saints. But in the final Kingdom of God all suffering shall vanish, for God shall be " all in all." It seems clear that by this time St. Paul, having seen how men everywhere offered an eager welcome to the Gospel, had come to hope for the ultimate salvation of all the world (cp. Rom. 11[25, 32]). The bitterest enemy of all, the Jews, shall be converted (Rom. 9–11). Indeed, the whole argument of Rom. 11 turns on the fact that there could be no imaginable heaven for St. Paul as long as his own race were excluded.]

(v.²⁹) " If all this faith is a delusion, how is it that some of you are baptized on behalf of dead friends ? [1] Why, again, do we run into danger for the Gospel every hour ? Brethren, I assure you by the pride I have in you in Christ, I am in daily peril of death. At Ephesus, I have been like one in the arena fighting with wild beasts. Why ? If the dead are not raised, life in Christ is a delusion, goodness an impossible dream ; then it is more rational to adopt the old cry, ' *Let us enjoy the good things of earth while we can* ' (Isa. 22¹³). (v.³³) Do not be deceived : [as Menander writes] ' bad company corrupts good character.' Awake to your sober senses : for some of you, to your shame, do not know God.

(v.³⁵) " One of you may object, ' How can we conceive of a resurrection body for the dead ? ' Consider a seed cast into the earth : it dies, yet out of it rises a beautiful growth, whether it be corn or other plant. What grows is quite different from the seed which dies, yet it is intimately connected with it : God gives to every kind of seed its appropriate growth. (v.³⁹) Take mortal bodies— God has given them different forms in human beings, animals, birds, and fishes. There are heavenly bodies and earthly bodies, quite different from each other. Sun, moon, and stars have each their particular beauty, and one star differs from another. (v.⁴²) So God makes the risen body different from the material body. The one suffers corruption, the other knows no corruption : the one is inglorious, the other beauteous : the one weak, the

---

[1] We do not know what this custom was (thirty-six different explanations have been suggested !). Apparently some of the Corinthians were baptized vicariously for their dead heathen friends : Tertullian (c. A.D. 200) mentions this practice as existing in his own day. It is argued that St. Paul would have disapproved of such an act as superstitious. But if it be not superstitious to pray for dead friends, why should it be considered so if you put your prayer into symbolic act and are baptized for them ?

other strong : the one a body of this material world, the other of spirit alone. The Scripture says, ' *the (first) man (Adam) became a living soul* ' : the last Adam (Christ) has become a life-giving spirit. In God's order the earthly life precedes the spiritual : the first man was made from the ground ; the second man is from heaven, and He gives His heavenly nature to His followers. (v.[49]) The spiritual form which He Himself has, He can give to us.

(v.[50]) " Understand me : *human flesh and blood cannot be carried into God's Kingdom beyond death* ; nothing subject to corruption can dwell where all is incorruptible. I tell you Christ's secret : we shall not all die before His coming ; but all of us shall be changed.[1] When the last trumpet sounds, the dead shall appear all in a moment, in the spiritual, incorruptible form which they have already taken, and we who are on earth shall be changed into the same. (v.[53]) Our mortal and corruptible bodies must become immortal, incorruptible. Then at last shall the words of the prophet be fulfilled, ' *Death is swallowed up in victory. O death, where is thy victory ? O death, where is thy sting ? ' The ' sting ' of death is sin which is quickened by the law : but thanks be to God who always gives us the ' victory ' through Christ. Therefore go forward in unshakeable confidence in the work of the Lord, knowing that your efforts are not futile in the Lord."

[*Note on St. Paul's Change in Belief about an Intermediate Existence after Death.*—For long after his conversion (as we have seen in our discussion of 1 Thessalonians, p. 129) he retained much of his Pharisaic eschatology, such as his belief in an intermediate existence. But when he wrote 2 Corinthians, he had clearly given it up : in 2 Cor. 5[1-10] he teaches that the spiritual body is given us at the

---

[1] The Greek text is in great confusion here. The E.V. (following B Jerome, etc.) seems to give the best sense : so W.H.

moment of death, or else that it is then set free from the mortal body which conceals it. Death means to go and be with Christ immediately (2 Cor. 5⁷⁻⁸ ; Phil. 1²³). There is no intermediate existence, and judgment comes in full at the moment of death. In 1 Cor. 15 this particular point is not so clear ; but in v.⁵² it is said that the dead will appear with Christ in a state of incorruption, *i.e.* clothed in the spiritual body.]

### 10. CHAP. 16. NEWS OF HIMSELF AND HIS PLANS : GREETINGS.

No paraphrase of this chapter is needed.

vv.¹⁻⁴ give directions for the fund which he was raising among the Gentile Churches to assist the poor Christians at Jerusalem. v.³ announces his intention of asking them to appoint delegates to take the money to Palestine ; and promises that, if it seems worth while, he himself will go with them.

vv.⁵⁻⁹ concern his plans for the coming months. He will stay at Ephesus till Pentecost : then travel through Macedon to Corinth, where he may spend the winter.

vv.¹⁰⁻¹² are about Timothy's reception at Corinth and Apollos' unwillingness to return there as yet.

vv.¹³⁻¹⁴. General encouragement to watchfulness and endurance.

vv.¹⁵⁻²⁰. Personal messages.

vv.²¹⁻²⁴. His autograph message at the end.

[*Note on* " *Mārān 'āthā,*" *v.*²².—It is an Aramaic phrase, probably a commonplace in the early Church : it means, " Our Lord is coming," or possibly, " O Lord, come." It is found in the *Didaché*, x. 6 (probably to be dated about A.D. 105), as part of the invitation to Holy Communion : " If any one is holy, let him come : if any one is not, let him repent. Maran 'atha."]

# CHAPTER XI.

## 2 CORINTHIANS.

1. DATE AND PLACE OF WRITING.—The situation implied in the Epistle has been sufficiently described above (see pp. 153-4, 159 ff.). It must suffice to say here that—

(a) the letter was written from Macedon towards the close of A.D. 56, when the return of Titus with news from Corinth had relieved St. Paul of an overwhelming anxiety which had seriously undermined his health :

(b) the Apostle had paid a second visit to Corinth since the second missionary journey, and had found there a situation which had caused him much pain. Very possibly he had crossed by sea from Ephesus, and returned in the same way, some time before 1 Corinthians was written :

(c) after sending the letter which we call 1 Corinthians, he had written again to the Corinthians in very severe terms, demanding the punishment of certain refractory members of their Church. This letter was couched in such stern language that he afterwards almost regretted writing it. Titus had lately brought him word to Macedon of its effects on the Corinthians, and his report was on the whole favourable.

We can date the writing of 2 Corinthians within narrow limits. In $8^{10}$ and $9^2$ we learn that the Corinthians have begun to collect money for the Jerusalem fund " last year," in accordance with his instructions given in 1 Cor. $16^{1.\ 2}$. Now the new year, according to both the Macedonian and Jewish reckoning, began in September.[1] Therefore, this

---

[1] To be exact, the civil year among the Jews began in September. But the Hebrews, like the Babylonians, seem to have dated the sacred

letter is probably to be dated after that month. But we know that St. Paul spent three months in Greece proper and left Corinth as soon as the sea was safe for navigation in A.D. 57—that is, in early February. Therefore he left Macedon in November.[1]

The *genuineness* of 2 Corinthians is not denied by any sober critic, though the letter was apparently unknown to Clement of Rome.

2. UNITY OF THE EPISTLE.—The first nine chapters are full of thanksgiving and joy at the good news which Titus has brought (see 7[4-7, 11]). If there are touches of self-justification and of censure of his readers, they are (as has been well said) " the rumblings of a departing storm." He assumes that the great majority of his readers are with him. It is rather startling therefore to find a great change of tone in the last four chapters (10–13). His brightness and confidence are gone : in their place we find fierce polemic. For sustained irony and self-justification these chapters have no parallel in his letters. The difficulty is real and needs explanation.

Some go so far as to say that the last four chapters absolutely stultify the first nine ; and to the suggestion that he may have received bad news from Corinth after writing chap. 9, they retort that, if so, he would inevitably have torn up the earlier portions of his letter.[2] The suggestion, now widely adopted, is that we have in 2 Cor-

year from March, and this way of reckoning became increasingly popular among the Jews after the Exile (see Abrahams in Hast. *D.B.*, art. " Time," vol. iv. p. 764).

[1] Lgt. (note on 1 Cor. 5[8]) infers from 5[1] that 2 Corinthians was written about the time of the Feast of Tabernacles, which in A.D. 56 fell on 13th September. During the Feast the Jews live in temporary booths or wooden shelters.

[2] See J. H. Kennedy, *The Second and Third Epistles of St. Paul to the Corinthians* (1900), and G. H. Rendall, *The Epistles of St. Paul to the Corinthians* (1909).

inthians *two different letters* ; and that chaps. 10–13 are a part of the severe letter mentioned above (see 1 c. : and 2 Cor. 2³· ⁴· ⁹ and 7⁸ᶠᶠ·) But further, there is one section in the first nine chapters which is thought by many to interrupt the sequence of thought more violently than any other digression in St. Paul's writings, namely, 6¹⁴–7¹. This also, it is said, must be an extract from the severe letter ! We shall deal with the latter passage below in the paraphrase of the Epistle. It has been shown, I think, that there is a real connexion of thought between 6¹¹⁻¹³ and 6¹⁴–7¹, which sufficiently explains the digression. And it is almost impossible to believe that any one would cut out one such section from a letter and dump it in the middle of another Epistle.

But the theory of a separate origin for the last four chapters is more plausible. According to it, the original ending of 2 Corinthians and the original beginning of the severe letter are both lost. Some one deliberately fitted the two Epistles into one whole.

But all this adds enormously to the difficulty of the theory. It is hard to conceive any reason why any one should suppress part of either letter. There is no possible parallel between such a book as that of Isaiah, which is probably a collection of addresses on similar subjects from several different prophets, and a *letter* of St. Paul on a definite topic. In the former case (Isaiah) nothing is excised : the editors of the book simply had in their hands a number of prophetic utterances delivered on various occasions.[1]

Is there no less desperate explanation of the difficulty in 2 Corinthians ? St. Paul had received from Titus news

---

[1] See what is said below on Romans (p. 245). The theory as to the Pastoral Epistles, which supposes that they are genuine letters of St. Paul edited by a later hand, offers no real parallel to the theory we are discussing in 2 Corinthians, where both letters are *ex hypothesi* genuine.

which brought him huge relief ; the majority of the Church at Corinth had done their duty. But there was an impenitent minority ; and though he begs for their lenient treatment now that victory is certain, they are clearly inclined to defy him still and to put sinister and malignant interpretations on all his actions. The undertone of self-justification and censure in the first nine chapters is thus explained. He wrote these in the first flush of joy and relief. But as he went on and the first impulsive feeling moderated, he may well have wished to make it clear to his obdurate adversaries that they must not take his leniency for weakness. We shall see below how foul their slanders were. Can we wonder that a sensitive and affectionate man like St. Paul felt deeply the cruelty and danger of such unchristian behaviour ? Though he held his hand, he spoke out with biting irony and unfaltering authority. If passages in chaps. 10–13 seem more savage than what we have learnt to expect from him, we must remember what he had been through during the previous months. Even a saint lapses from meekness at times. Moreover, the sinless Master Himself had spoken very sternly and uncompromisingly to the hypocrites, though He was always very tender to the victims of passion.

3. The Nature of the Opposition at Corinth.— Clearly, whoever they were, his enemies in the Corinthian Church launched unscrupulous attacks on his personal character and motives. They accuse him of capricious whims in changing his mind ($1^{17-20}$ ; cp. $10^1$). They say that he is no true apostle and he knows it ; therefore he dare not claim pay for his work ($11^{7-9}$ $12^{11-18}$) : yet all the time he is seeking to make money in underhand ways ($2^{17}$), if not guilty of actual embezzlement ($12^{16-18}$) : he whittles down the word of God to please his hearers ($4^2$) ; he cringes when he is present, being a mean-looking little

Jew and a poor preacher (10¹⁰), but tries to bully them and lord it over them when he is absent (10⁸⁻⁹ 13¹⁰ 1²⁴) : in a word, his religion is self-centred, not Christ-centred (1¹² 5¹⁶ 10²).

In 7¹² we have mention of an unnamed offender and of the person injured by him. St. Paul states that he wrote his stern letter, not for the sake of these two, but " *in order to let you realise how seriously you do care for me* " (Moffatt). This language does not suggest a glaring sin against God : clearly he has in view a wrong done to himself, and he is the injured man.[1] So in 2⁵ he tells them that the pain inflicted falls on them more than on himself. Throughout he is thinking of the malicious attack on his character by a party at Corinth led by one outstanding figure (7¹²).

What then was the motive of this savage attack ? It is clear that it was led by some Hebrew-speaking Jewish Christians (11²²) ; but equally clear that they did not openly challenge the non-obligatory nature of circumcision. They hated St. Paul as the man who had overthrown the Law : they obviously were urging the permanent value of much in the Mosaic Code—so much may be inferred from the emphatic language about its inferiority and temporary nature in 3⁴⁻4⁶. They had come, probably from Jerusalem, with " letters of commendation " (3¹) ; and in some way, we do not know how, they challenged his presentation of Christianity (11⁴). Probably they appealed from him to the authority of the older apostles, whom they called " the super-apostles " [2] (οἱ ὑπερλίαν ἀπόστολοι, 11⁵ 12¹¹). In their arrogant opposition to him, he calls them " men who masquerade as apostles of Christ . . . false apostles " (11¹³). This is perhaps a bitter reference to their claim to represent apostolic authority. But the language seems to

---

[1] Beyschlag and Pfleiderer suggest that Timothy was " the man who was wronged " (see Findlay in Hast. *D.B.*, art. " Paul ").

[2] Unless by this term he means his opponents themselves.

suggest that their leader really could claim the title of apostle in its wider sense, that is, as applied to men like James the Lord's brother, Andronicus, Junias, and Barnabas (Acts 14[14], Rom. 16[7])—not, of course, that he was one of the Twelve.

### 4. PARAPHRASE OF THE EPISTLE.

1[1-2]. THE SALUTATION.—Its form is noteworthy : " to the Church at Corinth, *together with all Christians in the whole of Achaea.*" The trouble seems to have spread from Corinth to some neighbouring churches.

1[3-11]. THANKSGIVING FOR THE RELIEF GRANTED HIM IN TITUS' REPORT.

(v.[3]) " Blessed be God the Father of our Lord, the God of mercy and all comfort. Trouble does this for us, that when we have experienced God's marvellous comfort, it teaches us to comfort others in trouble. (v.[5]) If we have an abundant share in Christ's sufferings, we also have in His comfort. Our troubles are borne for you, to bring you in the end comfort and salvation ;[1] and when we win comfort, it enables us to comfort you in similar troubles. We have a sure hope for you, knowing that you share our troubles and will share our comfort. (v.[8]) I will not hide from you the great trouble which came to me in Asia.[2] I was weighed down till I could scarcely bear it and utterly despaired of my life. When I asked myself what was going to happen to me, the answer was ' death.' So God taught me not to rely on myself but on Him who can raise the dead. He rescued me out of this bitter death and will rescue me still,—I know He will,—if you work to help me with your prayers, that a chorus of thanskgiving for His grace to me may rise from many in unison."

1[12]-2[17]. ASSERTION OF HIS UTTER HONESTY IN DEALING

---

[1] *i.e.* human suffering, borne for Christ's sake, is in the end redemptive, as Christ's own suffering was in infinitely higher degree.

[2] *i.e.* his persecution at Ephesus, his inward anxiety about other churches (11[28]), and his nervous prostration (see 2[13]).

WITH THEM. ANY CHANGE IN HIS PLANS HAS NOT BEEN
DUE TO CAPRICE. THE SEVERE. LETTER.

(v.¹²) " My great boast is that I have a clear conscience
about my treatment of others and especially of you : I
have heard God's call to holiness and sincerity ; I have
lived in God's grace, not satisfaction of self.  (v.¹³) *Believe
me, what I write to you is sincere : it has no other meaning than what you read or can readily recognise : ¹ and I
hope you will realise the full meaning of my letters as you
have largely realised that of my life,² namely, that we are
your boast as you are ours in the judgment-day of Jesus.*

(v.¹⁵) " Having this confidence in you, I wanted to
come straight to Corinth, thence to Macedon and from
there back to Corinth on my way to Judæa, so as to give
you the joy of two visits.³  Did I show caprice in giving
up this scheme ?  *Do I consult my own whims in making
a plan, as if it rested with me myself to say ' yes ' and
' no ' ?  God is my faithful witness that my word to you
is not a capricious change of ' yes ' to ' no.'  (v.¹⁹) For
His Son Jesus Christ, whom Timothy, Silvanus, and I
preached among you, has always a positive purpose,
directed to one real end, a constant ' yes ' : in Him is
' yes ' to all the promises of God.  Therefore our human
part is but to say ' Amen ' to God through Him for the
greater glory of God.*  It is God who makes you and us
alike stedfastly loyal to the anointed Christ and who
anointed us, who set His seal on our work and has put
in our hearts the first payment ⁴ of the Spirit.

(1²³) " My decision not to sail straight to Corinth, but
to travel overland through Macedon, was due to my wish
to spare you pain.  Not that we wish to dominate your
faith as some of you think : we are only aiming to give

---

¹ There is a verbal play in these two verbs, ἀναγινώσκετε, ἐπιγινώσκετε.
² This phrase I have borrowed from Moffatt.  ³ See n. on p. 154 above.
⁴ On ἀρραβών as a business word, see on Eph. 1¹⁴ (p. 332, n. 2).

you joy ; for your own faith must be your support. (2¹)
No, but I made up my mind not to pay another
painful visit to Corinth. I have none to comfort me
if I cause you pain ! It was in order to avoid this that I
wrote you of my change of plan, being confident that
when I am glad, you are glad too. My letter was written
with many tears from a very heavy heart, written not to
pain you but to convince you of my special love for you.

(v.⁵) "If any one at Corinth has brought sorrow, it is
not so much to me as to practically all of you (I speak
charitably).¹ The majority of you have decreed a punishment for him which is more than enough : show him your
loving forgiveness now lest he be driven to reckless despair.
(v.⁹) My great object in writing was to test your loyalty
to me. I forgive any one whom you forgive : I do so for
your sakes in the light of Christ's face [see 4⁶], that Satan
by his wiles may not get advantage over us.

(v.¹²) "My anxiety was such that when I got to Troas
and began to preach, though I had a splendid opening,
I could not rest because I did not find Titus there : so I
bade them farewell and left for Macedon. But thanks
be to God who always brings us triumph in Christ and
helps us to spread in every place the fragrance ² that
comes from knowledge of Him. (v.¹⁵) In our lives all
men smell the sweet fragrance of Christ rising up to God ;
to those who are perishing it is a deadly scent making for
surer death, to those who find rescue it is a sweet savour
leading from life to fuller life. Ah, who is sufficient ³
for such responsibility ? For we do not, as the majority
of them, adulterate ⁴ the word of God : we have a single
eye to God's truth in what we say."

¹ v.⁵ is difficult, but the R.V. rendering is almost certainly right.
² The words for "fragrance " in vv.¹⁴⁻¹⁶ have a special connexion with
Jewish sacrifice, and suggest the sacrifice of Christ and of our lives in
His service.        ³ The answer is in 3⁶.        ⁴ Trade metaphor.

3¹⁻⁶. THE EXISTENCE OF THE CORINTHIAN CHURCH IS THE BEST PROOF OF HIS HONEST WORK.

(v.¹) " Do you think that in speaking of the vital importance of my message, I am ' again commending myself ' ? Do you think I need letters of commendation to you, such as my opponents brought ? I tell you, *you* are my letter of commendation which can be recognised and read by all : you are clearly a letter of Christ, written through my agency, not in ink but, in spirit ; not in stone tables like the Law given to Moses, but in tables of the heart.   (v.⁴) Christ gives me such confidence towards God.   Not that of myself I am sufficient to achieve anything : all our sufficiency comes from God, who has made us capable of ministering His new covenant, which is no longer of the written code that kills, but of the spirit that gives life."

3⁷⁻¹⁸. CONTRAST OF THE OLD COVENANT, IMPOSED FROM WITHOUT AND TEMPORARY, WITH THE NEW COVENANT, INWARD AND ABIDING.

(v.⁷) " The contrast between the Old Covenant and the New, is the contrast between the temporary light on Moses' face when he came down from the Mount and the radiant glory on Christ's face.   The glory on Moses' face was a real, if transient, glimpse of God's glory, though the Law accentuated sin and brought death to men : much more then must the new ministry of the spirit, which brings life, excel in glory.   (v.¹⁰) *The Old was indeed made glorious, but not in respect of permanence, because there was a much more glorious ministry to come.

(v.¹²) " Our confident hope gives us great boldness : we have no need to copy Moses when he put a veil on his face to prevent the Israelites seeing the fading of the glory.   (v.¹⁴) And the veil denotes *their* blindness [1] to

---

[1] Ἐπωρώθη strictly means " were hardened." But it looks as if St. Paul, and perhaps Hellenistic Greek, confused it with ἐπηρώθη, " were blinded."   See 4⁴ " he *blinded* their minds " (ἐτύφλωσεν).

God's true glory ; for up to the present time the same veil
blinds them, remaining unlifted when the Old Covenant
is read : this veil is only done away in Christ. We read
[Ex. 34³⁴] ' *Whenever Moses turned to the Lord, he took
away the veil* ' : that is, he had an open vision of God's
glory for the moment. (The Lord in this passage means
the Spirit, for wherever the Lord's Spirit is, there is
freedom.) (v.¹⁸) But we Christians all of us have an unveiled face towards God : we behold for ourselves as in a
mirror ¹ [that is, in Christ's face, 4⁶] God's glory : and so
we are always being transfigured into the image of God,
rising from glory to glory, because we have the Spirit of
the Lord."*

[*Note on the Allegory of Moses' Face.*—Most characteristi-
cally he changes the significance of the veil on Moses'
face midway. In v.¹³ Moses puts it on because he does
not wish the Israelites to see that the light on his face
is fading. But in vv.¹⁴⁻¹⁵ the veil denotes the blindness
of Israel to the glory of God.]

4¹⁻⁶. SUCH A MINISTRY OF GLORY DEMANDS UTTER
TRUTH : WE HAVE TO SHOW MEN THE GLORY ON CHRIST'S
FACE.

(v.¹) " God in His mercy entrusted to us this surpassing
ministry. We may not play the coward ; but we have to
renounce all secret and shameful motives, all self-seeking
and cunning manipulation of God's revelation. (v.³) If
there are some from whom the Gospel light is hidden, it
is because they have allowed the sham god of this world
[Satan] to blind their minds, to shut out from them the
light of Christ *who is the image of God*.² It is not ourselves

---

¹ Philo uses κατοπτρίζεσθαι in this sense. Probably the R.V. text
is a mistranslation.
² See on Col. 1¹⁵. Christianity rests on the fact that Christ is found
to be in experience the "image" of God : when we see Christ, we
instinctively say, " God is just like that."

that we proclaim but the lordship of Christ Jesus : we are your slaves for His sake. Because the same God who said ' *let there be light* ' [Gen. 1] is He who shed on our hearts the bright light of His glory in the face [1] of Christ."

4[7]–5[10]. BODILY WEAKNESS IS LITTLE TO MEN WHO HAVE THE SURE HOPE OF THE GLORIOUS SPIRITUAL BODY.—[One of the greatest passages in all St. Paul's writings. We must remember that he wrote it after recovery from a serious illness.]

(v.[7]) " Our body which enshrines this treasure is but an earthenware vessel.[2] So much the more does God's surpassing power stand magnified. (v.[8]) We have to bear many a tribulation, but He never allows it to overwhelm us. (v.[10]) We share the cross that we may share the risen life of Jesus even here on earth. (v.[12]) We endure suffering because by it we secure your redemption into life.[3] We have the same sort of faith as the Psalmist who cries, ' *I had faith : therefore I spoke.*' We know that He who raised Jesus, will raise us and you. So we suffer for your sake, in order that God's grace may touch you and create gratitude to Him in many hearts.

*(v.[16]) " Therefore we do not lose courage. Our bodily frame comes ever nearer to dissolution ; yet our inner self is renewed day by day. When affliction comes, it is a *light* and temporary burden, because we know that it is working out for us a *weight of glory* beyond all words, if we fix our eyes on the eternal and unseen which alone endure.

5[1]. " When the material body is broken up, like some temporary booth,[4] we know that we have an eternal home in heaven, our spiritual body. (v.[2]) Our spirits know no

---

[1] πρόσωπον is primarily " face " here, because the reference is to Moses' face ; but the word carries the bigger meaning of " person."

[2] Cp. 1 Thess. 4[4].

[3] For the thought of all Christian suffering as redemptive, see 2 Cor. 1[6], Col. 1[24].

[4] See p. 219, n. 1

rest, in yearning to put on the heavenly habitation over and above our poor mortal selves ; we are sure that so covered we shall not feel naked [1] and shivering. (v.[4]) We are weighed down by the longing, not to put off our human vesture, but rather to put on an ampler covering, to feel our mortality swallowed up by life [the finite expanding, as it were, into the super-finite]. And this yearning is what God created in us : it is the word of His Spirit, of which He has given us a first payment. (v.[6]) Therefore we are always of a good courage. While we dwell in this body, we are to some extent absent from the Lord, because we do not see Him now but hold to Him by faith. So we are content to leave this body and go to Him. Whichever be our present lot, to stay or go, our ambition is always to please Him who is judge of each man's deeds in this life."*

[On this section see note on p. 211 about the nature of their difficulties, and note on p. 216 about St. Paul's belief in an intermediate existence. Here it is clear (1) that death means to St. Paul to " depart and be with Christ " (Phil. 1[23]), see v.[8]. Death means seeing Him at once with open vision, v.[7] ; (2) that the spiritual body is conceived as a larger, freer " clothing " than the material body which is dissolved in the grave. It is not clear whether he thinks of the spiritual body as growing in the Christian during life on earth, or as assumed at death (5[1-4]).]

5[11-19]. FURTHER SELF-JUSTIFICATION AGAINST THEIR CHARGES.

(v.[11]) " Therefore when we seek to persuade men, we always have the fear of Christ before our eyes, as God knows and I hope you know. I am *not* ' again commending myself.' I am showing you how to answer those who cannot see beyond a man's external dignity. *(v.[13])

---

[1] " *Naked*," *i.e.* condemned to a half-life like some ghost (cp. the Hades of the Greeks) ; reft of the fulness and zest of personal life.

They say I am mad : I am only mad for God's glory,
I am sane enough in my service of you. I am constrained
always by the love of Christ, with whom we all died that
we might live only to Him. (v.[16]) Therefore I cannot
estimate men by external appearances. I once so estimated Christ Himself [before my conversion], but now I
know Him.* Every one who is in Christ has become a
' new creation ' [Rabbinic term for a proselyte]. (v.[18])
God made this change in us by reconciling us to Himself
through Christ ; therefore we are entrusted with this
message of reconciliation to others."

[*Notes.*—v.[16] is difficult and open to many interpretations. But in this Epistle " according to the flesh " occurs
several times elsewhere and always meaning " actuated by
worldly motives or appearances." It seems best to take it
so here. He probably refers to the time when he regarded
Jesus as a crucified criminal disowned by God.

(v.[18]) It is noteworthy that the New Testament writers
never speak of God as reconciled to us.]

5[20]–6[10]. THE GUIDING AIM OF HIS LIFE IS TO BE A TRUE
AMBASSADOR OF CHRIST.

(v.[20]) " Therefore we are Christ's ambassadors to you,
imploring you to be reconciled to God. Think of it :
Christ the sinless was made the personification of sin for
us, in order that in union with Him we might become the
very righteousness of God. (6[1]) As workers with Christ we
beseech you not to reject God's grace in this day when
He offers it. (v.[3]) I try not to offend any one's scruples,
for the sake of my ministry. I have not spared myself :
I have persevered in spite of persecution, privation,
scourging, imprisonment, rioting ; I have persevered with
toil and lack of sleep, with fasting and self-consecration,
with knowledge and patience and kindness, with holiness
of spirit, maintaining my love of men and truthful speech
by God's power ; making righteousness my armour on the

right hand and the left, throughout praise or censure;
(v.⁹) accounted a deceiver, I have been true; ignored,
I have still been recognised; '*dying, I have found life*';
'*punished, but never put to death*'; loaded with sorrow,
yet always glad; poor, but making many rich; having
nothing, but possessing the whole world."

6¹¹–7¹. He begs for their Generous Love; but
in v.¹⁴ goes off on a Digression on the Limits of
Toleration.

[*Note.*—In v.¹¹ he uses a phrase from Deut. 11¹⁶ (Septuagint) to express his *large* love for them and beg them to be
equally large-hearted, namely, " (our) heart is enlarged."
But in its original context the phrase occurs in a warning [1]
against a large-heartedness which leads to a false toleration of heathen gods; and St. Paul remembers that. And
the same warning was sorely needed by the Corinthians,
who tended to be tolerant of any or every wickedness.
So off he flies at a tangent in v.¹⁴: " When I say, ' do be
large-hearted,' I do not mean that you should compromise
with idolatry and uncleanness." (So Bishop Chase.).]

(v.¹¹) " I am speaking out my inmost thoughts to you:
'*my heart is wide open*' to you in love: restraint comes
from you, not me. Give me back like for like, you who are
my children: I beseech you to give me a large-hearted
affection.

(v.¹⁴) " But remember the restriction which the Scripture places on the '*open heart.*' You are too ready to
open your hearts to unbelievers with all their idolatrous
abominations. What is there in common between light
and darkness, Christ and Beliar,[2] God and idols? (v.¹⁶)
We are the shrine of the living God. Remember that in

---

[1] " Take heed lest *thy heart be enlarged* [Heb. be deceived], and ye
turn aside and serve other gods . . ."

[2] " Beliar " (W.H. text) is probably the Syriac form of " Belial," the
term used to describe Satan in the Book of Jubilees, etc.

the Scriptures God promised to dwell in Israel, only on condition that they refused to touch the unclean thing. (7[1]) These promises should stir you to cleanse yourselves from every pollution of flesh or spirit."

7[2-16]. HE RETURNS TO HIS PLEA FOR THEIR AFFECTION. HIS TORTURING ANXIETY ABOUT THEIR RECEPTION OF THE SEVERE LETTER TILL TITUS CAME.

(v.[2]) " Open your hearts in love to us, I say. There is not one of you whom we wronged or corrupted. I am not saying this bitterly, but with a love that makes me spiritually die and rise again with you. (v.[4]) I am very confident, very proud of you : you have been a wonderful comfort and joy after my trouble. (v.[5]) When I came to Macedon, I could not rest, between external conflict and internal worry. But God, who comforts those that are brought low, gave me comfort when Titus came : he told me of your sorrow for what had happened, of your zeal for me. (v.[8]) After I sent that stern letter, I was almost sorry I had written it, because I knew it would give you pain if only for a time ; but now I am glad I wrote, not because it gave you pain, but because your pain led you to real godly penitence. (v.[10]) God sanctions pain which leads to penitence and so to a salvation which knows no regret : but the world, alas ! through pain only finds death. See in your own case how your pain in the light of God has produced in you eagerness, fear of God, longing to punish the offence. (v.[12]) Well then, my letter was written, not so much for the sake of him who did the wrong nor of him who was wronged, as for your sake, that I might make clear to you your real keenness for us in God's sight. Therefore I am comforted. (v.[13]) And my comfort was increased by seeing how much joy and reassurance Titus felt about you : sometimes I may have boasted to him about you, but he found it no exaggeration. And his affection for you is warm, when he remembers how

loyally and respectfully you received him. I am so glad
that I can feel confidence in you."

8–9. CONCERNING THE COLLECTION OF MONEY FOR THE
CHRISTIANS AT JERUSALEM.

(v.[1]) " I want to tell you of the practical results of
God's grace in the Churches of Macedon. They were
suffering persecution and were themselves much im-
poverished ; yet their abounding joy was seen in the
wealth of their generosity. Of their own accord they
earnestly besought me to let them contribute money
towards the task of ministering to the saints, giving even
more than they could afford : (v.[5]) they surpassed all
my expectations, because they had first dedicated themselves so wholly to the Lord. So I am encouraged to
ask Titus to continue the collection of this generous
gift which he has already begun at Corinth. You are
richly dowered with faith and the power of expression and
knowledge, with zeal and love for us : [1] I want you to show
that you excel also in generous giving. (v.[8]) This is not a
command, mind you : I only quote the keenness of others
to test the genuineness of your love. You know our
Lord's rich gift to us, how *being rich He became poor for our
sake*, that we might gain riches through His poverty. My
opinion is that this collection is good for you ; last year
you not only started to contribute but expressed your
willingness to give more. (v.[11]) And now carry that out :
you have the wish to do it ; give as you can afford. The
will to give is what God values, the amount of the gift
must vary according to each man's means. (v.[13]) We do
not want to burden you while others are relieved ; let
there be give and take in the matter : at the present time
you have money to spare to meet their need ; we hope that
what they have to spare may be given to meet your need ; [2]

---

[1] Reading ἐξ ὑμῶν ἐν ἡμῖν ; with ℵ C D Latt.

[2] Probably he means *spiritual* wealth.

just as in the giving of manna in the wilderness [Ex. 16¹⁸] we read, ' *he who got much had nothing left over, and he who got little had not too little.*'

(v.¹⁶) " Thanks be to God that Titus is just as keen about you as I am : when I urged him to go, I found he was quite eager apart from my request.[1]  I am sending with him the brother whose missionary work is praised in all the Churches, and who also has been appointed by the Churches [2] to travel with me as an administrator of this fund. . . . (v.²⁰) I asked for the appointment of administrators because I am careful to give no one any chance of slandering me in the distribution of this lavish gift ; for we have to make our honesty above suspicion not only in God's sight but also men's.  (v.²²) With him I am sending another brother, whose keenness I have often tested and who now is even keener because he believes in you.  Remember about Titus, he shares my work ; about the brethren, they are ambassadors of the Churches [in the matter of the fund], the glory of Christ.  Here is an opportunity to show your love and vindicate my boasts about you."

9¹. " About the service you are doing to the saints at Jerusalem, I need write no more.  I know your keenness : I have told the Macedonians that Achæa was ready last year, and stirred up the majority of them to emulate you.  But the reason I am sending on the brethren is that you may not fail to come up to my boast !  Think if the Macedonian delegates come to Corinth with me and find you unprepared—how we should be let down, not to say you !  So I thought it necessary to send them on in front

---

[1] ἐξῆλθεν is Epistolary Aorist probably : not " went forth " (R.V.) but " is going forth."

[2] See p. 67 for the delegates.  " The brother " in this verse is very likely St. Luke (though " gospel " in v.¹⁸ of course does not mean " written gospel ").

that your promised gift may be ready, as a gift and not something extorted from you.

(v.⁶) " Mark this : the man who sows with niggardly hand will reap a niggardly harvest ; and he who sows generously will reap a generous harvest. I want each of you to give what he has made up his mind he can afford, and not as though he were forced to it, for ' *God loves a cheerful giver.*' God can make His gifts to you abundant, that always having a sufficiency of everything you may yourselves abound in forwarding good work, imitating the man mentioned in the Scriptures who ' *scattered his goods in gifts to the poor ; his righteousness abides for ever.*' God, who gives a bountiful store of ' *seed to the sower and bread for food,*' will give you a rich [spiritual] harvest : making you rich in your bounties, for which men will give thanks to God. For this money which you are offering to God is not only supplying the needs of the saints but making many grateful to God, proving to them your whole-hearted adhesion to Christ's Gospel : (v.¹⁴) they will pray for you and feel warmly towards you, because God has given you such abounding grace. I thank God for His unspeakable gift."

**10–13. STRONG ASSERTION OF HIS APOSTOLIC AUTHORITY.** —The word to " boast " or " glory " (καυχάομαι) occurs oftener in these chapters than in all the rest of his writings put together.

**10. HIS ADVERSARIES JUDGE SIMPLY BY APPEARANCES, AND BOAST OF THEIR SUPERIORITY.**

(v.¹) " I Paul appeal to you myself by the meekness and reasonableness of Christ : you say that when I am with you I am humble, but when I am away I am self-confident : do not, I beseech you, force me when I come to show ' self-confidence ' or to tackle those who assign to me mean motives of the flesh. We ¹ live in the flesh, of course, but

---

¹ The plural here, as so often in St. Paul, is due to his wish to avoid egotism.

our warfare does not obey its dictates : our weapons are divinely strong [1] to demolish the enemy's strongholds and all that exalts itself against the knowledge of God ; we subjugate every thought to Christ. (v.[6]) We are ready to punish any disobedience when the majority of you have come back to loyalty. But you judge simply by what meets the eye. Remember that if any of my opponents is sure that he has Christ on his side, we also are Christ's as well as he. (v.[8]) If I boast freely of our authority which Christ Himself gave us—to build you up, not to overthrow you—you must not think that I am simply trying ' to frighten you by letter ' : ' his letters,' *he* says, ' are authoritative and strong, but his bodily appearance is weak and his speech contemptible.' *Let that man be assured that, when I come, I will act according to the tenor of my letters. (v.[12]) I confess I am not bold enough to compete with them in their self-commendation : they compare themselves only with one another in a mutual admiration society. They have no standard measure set by God : hence their lack of perception. (v.[13]) If we are forced to boast openly, we shall at least keep in view the standard which God sets to measure by, which marks for us in our sphere of preaching your city of Corinth. (v.[14]) We are not stretching beyond our province as though it did not reach you : we were the first to bring you the gospel of Christ. (v.[15]) We may be allowed to boast of our own labours, but never of anything that is not ours : we hope that as your faith grows, our allotted sphere may be enlarged to include lands beyond Achæa ; never to pride ourselves [as our opponents do] on what some one else has achieved in his allotted sphere. (v.[17]) But all self-glorification is wrong : '*if a man glories, let it be in the Lord.*' That man is accepted whom the Lord commends, not he who commends himself."*

[1] Cp. Acts 7[20], Moses was " divinely beautiful " (lit. " beautiful to God ").

11. His Opponents claim to follow [or, perhaps, to
be] Super-Apostles. Have they done for the
Corinthians all he has done, or borne such Sufferings anywhere as his ?

(v.[1]) " I have been foolish enough to glorify myself :
but do bear with me a little, for my aim is not myself but
you.  For I wedded you to Christ like a pure maiden to her
husband.[1]  I am afraid that somehow your minds may be
corrupted from simple devotion to Christ, as Eve was
utterly taken in by the serpent.  (v.[4]) Your courtesy is
perfect towards a stranger who comes in and preaches
another Jesus, a different Spirit and a different gospel !
(v.[5]) I hold I am not inferior in any way to your ' super-
Apostles.'  I may be ' unpolished in speech,' but my insight
into Christianity is proved to the world by the Church I
have built up at Corinth.  (v.[7]) Or did I do wrong in
abasing myself for your sake ?  I worked for my living
and refused to accept any money while I preached to you :
I robbed other Churches, accepting their gifts while ministering to you :  when I was in need at Corinth, I refused to
paralyse any of you by letting you keep me :  but some
Macedonian Christians [2] supplied my need.  For my
determination was not to make myself a burden to you,
and I never will.  (v.[10]) As Christ's truth is in me, this
shall always be my boast in Achæa.  Is it because I do *not*
love you ?  God knows the truth.  *(v.[12]) My opponents
accuse me of self-seeking : but it is they who exact pay
from you and glory in doing so,—not I !  Therefore I
shall always refuse pay at Corinth ; that I may shame
them into practising similar self-denial.[3] *  (v.[13]) For

---

[1] The famous Old Testament metaphor of Hosea.  Frequent also in
N.T. (cp. " *adulterous* generation ").

[2] Cp. Phil. 4[15-16].

[3] v.[12] is very obscure.  But we know from v.[20] that his opponents
accepted money.

they are really *false* Apostles, cunning to fill their own pockets, decking themselves out as Apostles of Christ : and no wonder, for Satan decks himself out as an angel of light ! It is not strange therefore if his ministers deck themselves as ministers of righteousness : but their end shall be worthy of their deeds.

(v.[16]) "Again I say, do not think me a fool, boasting for my own glory. If you do, still allow me my little boast. Boasting is folly and is not in Christ's way : but since they boast their worldly position, I will meet them on their own ground. (v.[19]) You seem to find pleasure in bearing with fools, I suppose because you feel so wise. You bear with a man who bullies and robs you, who captures you [1] and is arrogant and treats you outrageously. To my own discredit I admit that I was ' too weak ' to treat you like that ! Yet, to imitate their foolish boasts, I have the same grounds for confidence as they. Like them, I was brought up to speak Hebrew, a member of the privileged race of Abraham. I have more claim to be Christ's minister (though I am crazy to boast like this) than they : they cannot boast such toils, imprisonments, floggings, dangers to life itself. The Jews gave me thirty-nine [2] lashes on five occasions ; the Romans scourged me three times,[3] I was stoned once [at Lystra], shipwrecked three times, spent a night and a day in the sea : think of my long travels, in danger from swollen rivers and from brigands, from my own race and from Gentiles, in city and wilderness and sea and among false brethren, in toil and moil and watchful nights, in hunger and thirst and lack of food, in cold and nakedness. (v.[28]) Beside external dangers, I

---

[1] λαμβάνει, see 12[16].

[2] The Law forbade more than forty ; so they gave thirty-nine, for fear of a miscount.

[3] This can only have happened in a Roman colony. We know of it at Philippi : the other two were probably Pisidian Antioch and Lystra.

have to carry every day the weight of anxiety for all the Churches : I bear in my heart the weaknesses and failures of any member. (v.[30]) My opponents point to my weak and scarred body : it is my pride. I assure you before God that I have not exaggerated. At the very outset of my Christian ministry, when I was in Damascus, I only escaped with my life by being let down from a window over the town-wall in a large basket ; for Aretas' ethnarch [1] was watching the town to seize me."

12[1-10]. HIS VISIONS.

[He passes on in his " boasting " to speak of mystic visions. He tells of one which he had fourteen years earlier : so it seems clear that such visions were not frequent, and that he was not wont to seek a state of trance. He speaks of himself in the third person (v.[2]), and at first sight v.[5] reads as if he were referring to some one else : but v.[7] proves that this is not so. It is characteristic of such visions, whether of Christian or non-Christian mystics, that *the sense of personal identity* is merged for the time being : the mystic seems to be in the presence of a stupendous glory, so absorbing that everything else is blotted out of his consciousness. So St. Paul says (v.[5]) that he can claim no credit for his vision ; it came from without, unsought : he will only " boast " in his physical weaknesses. He only mentions the vision to show that God has not withheld from him a great privilege.

But the vision was followed (v.[7]) by an attack of his old physical weakness of which he had never been cured. We have already discussed his " thorn in the flesh " (see p. 9). He regards it as the work of the devil ; but in its continuance he sees the loving purpose of God, who allows it that he may be kept from pride and made conscious, in his weakest hours, of the sufficiency of God's grace.]

[1] See p. 27 ff.

(v.[1]) " You force me to boast, though it is not good for men. So I will come to visions and revelations of the Lord. I know a man who, fourteen years ago, was snatched in Christ right up to the third heaven : [1] whether he was in the body or out of it, I know not. There he heard words which no man may utter. For *him* I will boast of the privilege, but for my true self I will only boast of my own weaknesses. (v.[6]) I could tell of more such experiences ; but I forbear for two reasons—first that I want you to estimate me by your own experience of me, and secondly because the revelations were so transcendent. Therefore, to keep me humble there was given me a thorn in the flesh, a messenger of Satan to buffet me. Three times I besought the Lord to remove it, but His answer is, ' My grace is enough for you ; My strength is made perfect in human weakness.' That is why I gladly make boast of my physical weakness, because it means that the power of the Lord rests on me. I welcome weakness, insult, difficulties, persecutions, afflictions for Christ's cause ; for when I am weak in myself, then I am most conscious of the strength of God in me."

12[11-18]. ABOUT HIS MOTIVES IN REFUSING PAY.

(v.[11]) " What a fool I am to write this ! But you forced me into it. You ought to have vouched for me yourselves. I am in no way inferior to your ' super-Apostles,' though I be nothing in myself. I worked among you all the signs of an Apostle, miracles and miraculous changes. No other Church had more done for it than you, except that I refused to paralyse you by claiming pay. Forgive me this wrong !

[1] The " third heaven " = " paradise " in v.[4]. The Jews at this time sometimes spoke of seven heavens (as the Persians did), sometimes of three. In the *Secrets of Enoch* and elsewhere, " paradise " is placed in the third of seven heavens, as the intermediate abode of the righteous after death. But St. Paul's language here, " as far as . . ." suggests that he means the highest heaven, the very abode of God.

(v.[14]) " I am preparing to pay a third visit to Corinth, and again I will take no pay. I do not want your money, but you. Children do not support their parents, but parents their children. I will most gladly spend anything and be myself spent to the uttermost to help you. Apparently the more I love you, the less do you love me. (v.[16]) ' Yes,' you say, ' quite true that you have refused pay. It was only a cunning ruse to capture us more effectually in your own selfish interests.' Can you say that any of my messengers to you, Titus or the brother I sent with him, ever extorted money from you ? Did not we all show the same spirit, adopt the same principles ? "

12[19]–13[10]. HE IMPLORES THEM TO RENOUNCE HIS OPPONENTS AND SPARE HIM THE NECESSITY FOR STERN MEASURES.

(v.[19]) " ' Again defending yourself,' do you say ? We are speaking in God's sight in union with Christ. I love you, and do everything with an eye simply to build you up. I am afraid that when I come I may find you other than I wish and you may force me to be other than you wish ; afraid of your strife, jealousy, temper, factiousness, backbiting, gossip, conceit, and disorder ; afraid that, when I again visit you, God may humble me, because I may have to take stern measures with men who are secretly leading unclean lives.

13[1]. " This is my third visit to you. I shall hold an inquiry, calling for witnesses as the old law of Moses directs. I warn you, as I did at my second visit, that when I next come, I shall spare no one. (v.[3]) You seek proof that Christ speaks in me : you have evidence in the Christian strength which He gave you through my preaching. Christ was crucified in weakness and lives in power : we share both with Him, and will prove His power, if need be, on those who oppose.[1] (v.[5]) It is

---

[1] He has in mind " the supernatural infliction of suffering " (Plummer) ; cp. 1 Cor. 5[5].

*yourselves* you must test, not I. Or do you accept the verdict of others about yourselves, not realising that Christ is in you (as indeed He is, unless you fail in this vital test) ? I hope you will realise that Christ is also in us : we can stand the test. I pray God that you may not do anything evil ; not that we want to prove our own success, but that we want you to do right however much we seem to fail. (v.[8]) We can only act for the truth, not against it. We are glad when you are strong in the time of our weakness : we pray but for your progress. I am writing this in order that, when I come, I may not be forced into a severe use of the power which the Lord gave me, *to build you up, not to overthrow you.*"

13[11-13]. AUTOGRAPH MESSAGE.

v.[11]. " Finally, my brothers, farewell . . . agree with one another, and the God of love and peace shall be with you. Greet one another with a holy kiss.[1] All the Christians here salute you.

v.[14]. " May the grace of Jesus, the love of God, and the fellowship of the Holy Spirit be with you all."

[*Note.*—v.[14] forms the clearest statement in St. Paul's writings of his belief in the Trinity : but cp. 1 Cor. 12[4-6]. We must beware of supposing that the Apostle had any hard-and-fast doctrine about the Trinity : see note on Rom. 8[9-11].]

---

[1] The kiss of peace was an integral part of early Christian worship. See 1 Pet. 5[14], Justin Martyr ; cp. 1 Thess. 5[26].

# CHAPTER XII.

## THE EPISTLE TO THE ROMANS.

See general remarks on pp. 156–7 (*f*) and pp. 162–3.]

1. TIME AND PLACE OF WRITING.—(*a*) Rom. 15 was certainly written to the Church at Rome towards the close of the third missionary journey. For years he has been longing to see them (v.[24]); but his principle has always been in planning a missionary tour to seek new ground where Christ's name is unknown (v.[20]), and this has been his reason (διό, v.[22]) for not visiting Rome. But he is planning a journey to Spain (v.[24]); so they lie on his route to the West and he can achieve his desire. He hopes to come quite soon. First he must take to Jerusalem the money given by the Gentile Churches for her poor (v.[26]). Yet he knows that this visit is fraught with dire peril to his life and liberty (vv. [30-32]): he beseeches them urgently to pray for him. All these data presuppose that he is writing from Corinth in the winter of A.D. 56–57.

(*b*) Rom. 16 was clearly written from Corinth, after the Apostle left Ephesus on the third missionary journey. For (1) the letter is entrusted to Phœbe, deaconess of Cenchreæ, the eastern port of Corinth, to convey (16[1]); (2) St. Paul is now staying with Gaius, the Corinthian mentioned in 1 Cor. 1[14], and the local Church meets in his house (Rom. 16[23]); (3) St. Paul sends greeting from Erastus, the city treasurer (Rom. 16[23]). In 2 Tim. 4[20] we find Erastus at Corinth. Therefore it is certain that

whether chap. 16 is an original part of the Epistle to the
Romans or not, it was written about the same time and
from the same place as Rom. 1–15.

2. UNITY OF THE EPISTLE.—*A.* Many recent commentators regard chap. 16 as a fragment of a letter to Ephesus,
which somehow got bound up with the Epistle to the
Romans.  They argue that it is incredible that the Apostle
can have had so many friends at Rome as he mentions in
chap. 16.  They point out that several of these people had
some connexion with Ephesus : Prisca and Aquila had been
there when 1 Corinthians was written, and were there again
later according to 2 Tim. $4^{19}$ ; Epænetus ($16^5$) is " the first-
fruits of Asia " ; Phœbe ($16^1$) came from Cenchreæ, the
easterly port of Corinth, from which there were boats
sailing to Ephesus almost every day.

But though this theory has found some eminent advocates, it is in our judgment incredible.  Think, to begin
with, of the enormous improbability that two letters
sent about the same time from the same place to Rome
and Ephesus should happen by some mysterious coincidence
to be joined together at some later time : the common
date and common birthplace of Rom. 1–15 and Rom. 16 are
an overwhelming argument for the traditional view, that
they belong to one letter.  Again, among the names in
Rom. 16, there are at least as many links with Rome as with
Ephesus.  " The household of Narcissus " (v.[11]) suggests
Christian slaves belonging to Claudius' famous freedman
of that name who had been lately executed by Nero's gentle
mother Agrippina.  " The household of Aristobulus "
(v.[10]), taken in connexion with the subsequent greetings to
" Herodion," inevitably suggests Aristobulus the younger,
grandson of Herod the Great, who lived and died in a
private station at Rome.  Prisca and Aquila had been at
Ephesus nine months earlier, but they had come there from

Rome six years before and are likely to have revisited the Imperial City as soon as the opportunity offered.[1] The very existence of a Christian Church at Rome is sufficient proof that many Eastern Christians visited her, and this explains the number of St. Paul's greetings.

It is the fashion of the moment to adopt theories of multiple-letters in St. Paul ; but we feel that their advocates do not sufficiently weigh the difficulties involved. Surely it is a very different thing to admit manifold sources in a book such as Isaiah, where compilers had in their hands a mass of undated prophecies. But in the case we are considering we are asked to suppose that a complete letter from the Apostle existed at Ephesus with a definite salutation, and that it was mutilated and its opening verses suppressed in order to make it appear as part of a letter written to the Western capital. Surely local pride would have rebelled, even if no worthier motive was involved.

*B.* There is, however, some documentary evidence for omitting both the last two chapters (15 and 16). Marcion, the second-century Christian Gnostic, edited a New Testament of his own, and in Romans he cut out these two chapters ; but his object is sufficiently explained by the fact that 15[4, 8] speak in high terms of the Old Testament, which he regarded as anti-Christian.

There is other evidence of the omission of 15 and 16 in sources which cannot well have been influenced by Marcion.

(1) Two manuscripts of the Vulgate seem to leave them out of reckoning in their chapter-numbers (or sections).

(2) There is widespread confusion as to the position of

---

[1] After all, the voyage to or from Rome was not regarded as a terrible undertaking in St. Paul's time. At Hierapolis in Phrygia there has been found the tomb of a merchant who records that he had done the voyage between Asia and Rome *seventy-two* times (Mommsen, *Prov. of Rom. Empire*, i. 360).

the Doxology in $16^{25\text{-}27}$. Many authorities insert it after chap. 14, as if they knew of a version of the Epistle which concluded there.[1]

What are we to make of these facts ? There is a general agreement that chap. 15 is an original part of the Epistle to the Romans, because it continues the subject of chap. 14. The solution is probably to be found in the suggestion that there were in circulation *two* versions of the Epistle : [2] an edition containing the whole letter as we have it in our Bible, and a shorter edition for general reading, with the topical allusions cut out. We are confirmed in this view by the fact that some authorities [3] omit the words " in Rome " in the opening salutation ($1^7$), just as the words " in Ephesus " are omitted in Eph. $1^1$ because that letter was an encyclical. The reader in each place would fill in the name of the city where he took the letter. But in " Ephesians " the omission in the salutation seems to be original and is supported by the best manuscripts : here it has little support. If St. Paul himself had published two editions of " Romans," it is difficult to suppose that he would have omitted from the shorter or encyclical version $15^{1\text{-}13}$, which (as noticed above) continues the subject of chap. 14. The choice of $14^{23}$ as a conclusion can best be explained either as due to Marcion's influence, or (more probably) to the clumsy chapter-numbering which put a break there : in either case, it is late, and not due to St. Paul himself.

3. THE CHRISTIAN CHURCH IN ROME.—At the end of the third century there was a tradition current that St. Peter was Bishop of Rome for twenty-five years (about

---

[1] L and more than 200 minuscules, as well as some of the Fathers (*e.g.* the Latin Version of Origen). Others insert the Doxology both after chaps. 14 and 16.

[2] This view is adopted, in one form or another, by Lightfoot, Gifford, Lake, etc.

[3] God and the commentary of Origen.

A.D. 42–67). This is given by Eusebius of Cæsarea and Jerome.

There can be little question that St. Peter was in Rome at the end of his life and was martyred there. We have evidence of it in 1 Peter, which was clearly written in the Imperial City (5¹³, where " Babylon " must mean Rome). And we have ample testimony in the early Fathers : his connexion with the city is mentioned as early as Clement of Rome (A.D. 95). But the earlier traditions mention nothing of his supposed episcopate of twenty-five years : he was in Jerusalem at the Church Council of A.D. 50 ; and the silence of Romans and of Acts 28 about him seems to show that he was not in Rome in A.D. 57 or in A.D. 61.

" Romans " witnesses to the existence of a fairly large number of Christians in the city, mainly Gentile ; but the language of the Roman Jews as reported in Acts 28²² indicates that the Church was composed of people in a humble way of life, who were only known by hearsay, not by personal contact, to the Jews of the ghetto across the Tiber. It is true that Suetonius, in recording how Claudius expelled the Jews from Rome in A.D. 50, gives as its reason certain riots in the ghetto " at the instigation of one Chrestus " (" Chresto impulsore," Suet. *Claud.* 25). Now in all probability " Chrestus " is a Latin rendering of Christus ; but it does not follow that the Christian Christ is meant. It is more in harmony with Acts 28²² to suppose that some other Messianic claim led to the disturbance.

How then did the Roman Church come into existence ? We are driven to suppose that the constant influx of Eastern Christians into the capital had brought it to the birth. Indeed no further explanation is needed, when we remember that Christians in those days were mostly missionaries at heart. This supposition is confirmed by, and in turn confirms, the large number of Christian friends in Rome to whom St. Paul sends greeting in Rom. 16.

4. OBJECT OF THE EPISTLE.—This has already been discussed briefly above (pp. 162–4). Two points there mentioned must be borne in mind : (a) That the Imperial City of Rome stood in St. Paul's eyes as the type of the Catholic Church, and he yearned to bring her to the world-wide faith ; (b) that in the Epistles of the third missionary journey we can trace a larger hope and broader religious outlook that had come to him—the hope that all mankind would accept the Gospel at the last.

The Apostle was now on his way to Jerusalem, with his eyes fully open to the extreme peril involved for himself. He could not overlook the probability that he would never be allowed to go to Rome ; and he wanted to put down on paper " his " gospel, i.e. all the need of sinful humanity and the salvation which God offered freely " in Christ " to all men, however steeped in sin. He wanted to explain his new hope of universal redemption, showing how even the bitterly hostile Jews might be won to Christ through the Gentiles whom they despised. The Epistle is not a complete compendium of Christian doctrine. But it is a powerful exposition of the catholicity of the gospel through " justification by faith " and " sanctification."

It must be always remembered that " justification " is a law-court metaphor denoting a verdict of " not guilty," i.e. exempt from paying the penalty of transgression. Like all metaphors, it cannot cover the whole ground : it gives no counterpart to religious " sanctification " or growth in holiness. But in the Christian life, as St. Paul lived and taught it, justification and sanctification are practically inseparable : they are both reached through " faith," i.e. trust in God's love, through daily experience of Christ's presence and comradeship. Justification is the result of the first step in turning to the heavenly Father ; it is the sense of relief, the peace found in a realisation of forgiveness : sanctification is the progressive strength found in the inspiration of the Lord ; it is the result of the life which He pours into His followers ; it is positive, active, quickening.

The doctrinal portion of the Epistle falls into three main divisions :

(a) Justification, $1^{18}$–5.

(b) Sanctification, 6–8.

(c) The rejection of Christ by the chosen people of Irsael, pointing to the hope of their conversion through the Gentiles, 9–11.

Finally, it should be remembered that in this Epistle (as in 1 and 2 Corinthians and Galatians) we have a work of which the Pauline authorship has never been doubted by any sane critic.

5. PARAPHRASE OF THE EPISTLE.—A. INTRODUCTION ($1^{1-17}$).

(v.[1]) " To the Christians at Rome, greeting from Paul, Christ's slave, destined before his birth to preach the glad tidings which God promised in the Old Testament prophets ; that is, the message of His Son, born of David's house according to the flesh, marked as Son of God according to His holiness of spirit by being raised from the dead. Through Him we received divine grace as Apostles, to preach loyalty to Him and faith among the Gentiles, among whom you also are called to belong to Christ.

(v.[8]) " I thank God for your faith, the report of which has spread everywhere. God is my witness how unremittingly I pray for you and ask that my way may be made clear now at last to come to Rome. (v.[11]) I long to see you that I may impart some spiritual gift to strengthen you—nay, that you and I may comfort each other by our common faith. I have often planned to come to Rome, but have been prevented hitherto ; for I wish to reap a harvest in your city, as elsewhere among the

Gentiles. (v.[14]) To Greeks and non-Greeks, to wise and uninstructed, I owe this debt : so, as far as it rests with me to settle anything,[1] I feel eagerness to preach in Rome also. I am not ashamed of the gospel message : for it brings God's *power* in life to every one who has faith, Jew or Greek. It reveals God's righteousness [2] to men who rise from faith to fuller faith, as it is said in the Scripture, ' *the righteous man shall find life through faith.*' "

B. JUSTIFICATION BY FAITH ($1^{18}$–5).

$1^{18}$–2. GOD'S JUDGMENT ON SIN. THE UNIVERSALITY OF SIN AMONG MEN.—" The first thing revealed is the sternness of God's judgment on all impiety and unrighteousness on the part of men who hold [3] the truth and yet live unrighteously. Yes, they hold the truth, for God Himself gave them such knowledge of Himself as is attainable without more direct revelation. (v.[20]) His unseen attributes of might and other divine qualities may be clearly seen in the universe which He has created : so that they have no excuse to plead for their failure to worship Him as God. Why were their minds so darkened and their thoughts of Him made so futile ? It was through their own conceit : they thought themselves wise in their utter folly and changed the glory of the incorruptible God into idols in the image of corruptible man and birds and quadrupeds and reptiles. It was for this reason that God gave them up to follow their own lusts : they dishonoured their bodies in unclean practices, because they chose to worship the creature rather than the Creator, a lie rather than the truth. (v.[26]) They adopted all manner of unnatural

---

[1] The clumsiness of the words, "that which rests with me is eager to preach," is due to his wish to avoid saying, "I am eager," as if he were arbiter of his own acts.

[2] God's *righteousness* is far more than His justice : it includes all His Divine qualities, *i.e.* forgiveness amongst others : see 1 John 1[8].

[3] So Lightfoot with A.V. It seems more forcible than the R.V. " hold down the truth," *i.e.* refuse to admit.

vices, females lusting for females and males for males :
and they received full punishment in their own bodies.
(v.²⁸) They did not see fit to keep God in their view, so
He gave them up to an unfit mind ; they were filled with
unrighteousness, wickedness, covetousness, malice ; they
were swayed by jealousy, murderous feeling, strife,
cunning, ill-nature ; they became gossips, slanderers,
hating God, outrageous, proud, boastful, inventors of
evil, disobedient to parents, without respect for common
sense or for their plighted word, without affection or pity.
(v.³²) They know well enough God's decree that such
crimes deserve death : yet they not only do them in
passion, but scheme in cold blood to help others in them."

[*Note on v.*³².—The manuscripts give various readings in
the last clause, probably because commentators found it
hard to believe that consent to evil is as bad as personal
wrong-doing. But the text of W.H. (paraphrased above)
is strongly confirmed by the repetition of the phrase in
St. Paul's disciple, Clement of Rome, xxxv. 5.]

[CHAP. 2.—He turns on the Jew, who is delighted by the
unsparing condemnation of Gentile sins, much as Nathan
turned on David after the story of the poor man's stolen
lamb.]

2¹. "*They* are without excuse [1²] : but have *you* any
more excuse, any of you who sit in judgment on them ?
In judging your neighbour, you condemn yourself, for you
are guilty of the same practices. God judges by deeds, not
words : do you who judge though you are equally guilty—
do you reckon that *you* will escape His judgment ? Or
do you despise His loving-kindness and forbearance, not
knowing that He spares you only because He would bring
you to repentance ? (v.⁵) Your hard impenitent heart is
storing up for you punishment, in the day when God
will punish and show His righteous judgment : '*He will
reward every man according to his deeds*' ; those who are

stedfast in good and seek glory and incorruptibility, shall win the life of eternity ; those who are factious and yield to unrighteousness rather than righteousness shall find anger and affliction, yes, every man who works out evil ends, Jew first but also Greek ; while glory and peace shall be his who works good, Jew first but also Greek. God shows no respect of persons. (v.[12]) All who knowing no law have sinned, shall perish apart from law ; and all who have sinned under Law, shall be judged by Law. For it is not hearing law but doing it that puts us right with God.[1]    Sometimes Gentiles who know not law act as it commands ; they are then a law to themselves, showing that they have the law written in their hearts : and their conscience [2] bears its witness in them ; their inward thoughts accuse them, or it may be excuse them, in mental debate.    So shall it be, I say, on the day when God judges the secrets of the human heart by Christ, as we preach.

(v.[17]) " If you are a Jew and rely on the Law and pride yourself on God and know His will and approve only what is excellent, with the Law to instruct you, and are confident that you are a leader of the blind, a light of those in darkness, an instructor of fools, a teacher of babes, having a model sketch of knowledge and truth in the Law [3]—why, I say, do you who teach others not teach yourself ?    You tell them not to steal, but you steal ; not to commit adultery, but you commit adultery.    You loathe idols, but you rob temples !    You pride yourself on the Law,

---

[1] This sounds like St. James.  To St. Paul faith necessarily produces some works, but they are poor enough in God's holy sight : it is not they, but the faith which actuates them, which put a man right with his God.  Faith is the driving power :  a man necessarily becomes like what he loves.

[2] συνείδησις is not as wide as our word " conscience."  It is properly " consciousness " of what one has done or is doing.

[3] vv.[17-20] give, in inimitable touches, the pride of the Jew.

but you dishonour God by breaking it : indeed, as the Scripture says, ' *The name of God is blasphemed because of you among the Gentiles.*' Circumcision is only of use if you carry out the Law : if not, it is become like uncircumcision. If an uncircumcised man keeps the requirements of the Law, shall not he be counted as circumcised ? And if he keeps the Law, he will judge you who, in spite of having the written Law, transgress it. The true Jew and the truly circumcised are not those who are such on the surface, but those who have their heart circumcised : their ' praise ' [1] is from God, not men. "

3[1-8]. ANSWER TO THE OBJECTION THAT, IF THE JEWS ARE AS GREAT SINNERS AS THE GENTILES, THE OLD COVENANT AND MOSAIC LAW HAVE BEEN USELESS.

*(v.[1]) " What use then has Judaism served ? It has brought many blessings. First, the intimate revelation of God [2] was entrusted to the Jews. (v.[3]) God promised a fuller revelation yet, and we cannot think that He would break His word though some were unfaithful to Him. God must prove to be true though ' *every man be found a liar* ' : as the Psalmist says, ' *That Thou mayest be vindicated in Thy words, and prove Thy case when Thou pleadest it with men.*' [3] (v.[5]) But, you may ask, would it not be immoral for God (if I dare use such language of Him) to carry out His promises to a faithless race ? If He still does so, does it not follow that the more unrighteous men are, the more it shows up God's righteous-

---

[1] " Judah " in Hebrew means " praise." He plays on the word " Jew."

[2] " The oracles of God " in 3[1] include all His ways of speaking to men, whether by direct inspiration or by the events of history which He taught them to understand.

[3] κρίνεσθαι is probably Middle and means this : so Lightfoot. The thought of God deigning to plead His case with men is familiar in the Old Testament. (In this passage the Hebrew means " when Thou judgest.")

ness in keeping His promises ?   This last inference *must*
be wrong somewhere :  we know that the Judge of the
world must do right.   (v.[7]) If it is true that the more false
I am, the more clearly does God's true dealing stand out
to His glory, then does it follow that it is right to do wrong
that good may come (as people, who misunderstand justification by works, falsely maintain that I teach) ?    Such
casuistry is self-condemned and incurs God's righteous
judgment."*

[*Note on vv.*[3-8].—Chaps. 9–11 prove that St. Paul himself
had felt acutely the difficulty which he here mentions—
*i.e.* How could God rightly fulfil His promises to the
Israelites, seeing that they had become faithless ?   If God
is bound by unconditional promises, might it not logically
be argued that human sin only makes for the glory of God ?
He refuses to be driven by casuistic logic into denying a
clear truth.]

3[9-20]. ARE THE JEWS ANY BETTER THAN THE GENTILES ?

(v.[9]) " But are we Jews any better than the Gentiles ? [1]
Not a whit : as I have already stated, Jews and Greeks
are all alike under the yoke of sin.   The Old Testament
Scriptures  prove  it . . . [Here  follows  a  medley  of
quotations, vv.[10-18], which state the universality of human
sinfulness] . . . (v.[19]) You cannot argue that these
passages [2] are addressed to *Gentiles* !   Nay, the very use
and object of the Law was to make men conscious of sin.

3[21-31]. THE WAY OF REDEMPTION.

[The problem is this—see end of v.[26]—How is the
righteous God, who cannot compromise with sin, to
" justify " the sinful man whom He loves inalienably ?]

*(v.[21]) " God has shown a way to reconcile His anger
and His love and show His righteousness undimmed :

---

[1] προεχόμεθα is probably Middle, in spite of the lack of any literary
parallel.   This sense is demanded by his answer.

[2] " The Law " here=the Old Testament.

and this way is partly foreseen in the Law and the Prophets. It is this : God's righteousness is communicated to all without distinction, through faith in Christ. (v.²³) All men have sinned and are conscious of their shortcoming : but they are offered free justification in His loving-kindness *through the freedom which they win in union with Christ Jesus.* God has publicly proclaimed Him to be our *propitiation* through faith, in our union with His blood [*i.e.* His life offered up to God]. In this way God shows His righteousness, though He has hitherto passed over human sin in His forbearance ; He has shown His own righteousness now through Christ : so that He is at once righteous, and yet can accept and justify sinful men if they put faith in Jesus.*

(v.²⁷) "Therefore no man can boast of his own excellencë,¹ as if he earned salvation. Men are justified, made right with God, by faith alone, quite apart from their excellence. Monotheism implies that God is God of Gentiles as well as Jews. This is not to make the Mosaic Law of no effect, but rather to commend the Law as making men more conscious of sin and eager for redemption."

[*Notes on* 3²¹⁻²⁶.—This passage is vital for understanding St. Paul's conception of Christ's work for men, which he bases not on any theory of Atonement, but directly on his own religious experience.

It is important to realise the exact "nuance" of two words in v.²⁴.

(1) "*Redemption*" (ἀπολύτρωσις) simply is a metaphor of buying the freedom of a slave. The Septuagint speaks of God "redeeming" (ἀπολυτροῦσθαι) Israel out of Egypt : *i.e.* He freed them from slavery at the cost of His own mighty works. So He frees us " in Christ," at the

---

¹ " Works " cover both moral excellence and observance of ritual. The Jews classed the two together.

cost of His own suffering. If we insist on asking to whom the price was paid, the only possible answer is " to us men."

(2) " *Propitiatory* " ($i\lambda\alpha\sigma\tau\acute{\eta}\rho\iota\sigma\nu$, an adjective). Heathen writers speak of " propitiating a god " ; and the Old Testament is not free from similar phrases of God. But the whole conception is utterly alien to the New Testament, where the words " propitiate God " never occur. See the uses of the word in 1 John 2[2] and Heb. 2[17]. As Westcott points out, " The propitiation acts on that which alienates God, and not on God whose love is unchanged throughout." In other words, it is *our* hard and sinful hearts which are " propitiated," not God. Thus the New Testament never speaks of God being reconciled to us ; always of us being reconciled to God : cp. Rom. 5[10] (see Westcott on 1 John 2[2]).

Next we must note St. Paul's exact words as to the way of redemption (vv.[24-25]) : it is " *in* Christ Jesus," " *in* His life-blood," *i.e.* in union with Him and His life-force, in that union which may be realised in His daily presence in our lives. There is no sort of theory here : it is simply experience.

Finally, the suffering of the Cross is only part of the suffering which God Himself endures as long as mankind is in the world. The essence of it lies in the perpetual clash between His perfect holiness and His love for us the unholy. Being what He is, He cannot abate either. It is true that St. Paul never directly speaks of God Himself suffering : but the idea is implicit throughout his writings, and He does speak of the Holy Spirit suffering (Rom. 8[26]), and says in the following verse that in this the Spirit is in absolute union with God.]

4. THE CASE OF ABRAHAM. WHY WAS ABRAHAM SELECTED TO RECEIVE THE REVELATION AND PROMISE : WAS IT FOR HIS OWN EXCELLENCE, OR BECAUSE HE TRUSTED GOD ? [See note on Gal. 3[6-22], on p. 80.]

(v.[1]) " What shall we say of Abraham, the ancestor of
the Jews ? If works were the reason of his justification,
he has something of which to boast : but he had nothing
to boast of towards God, for we read ' *he* HAD FAITH *in*
*God and it was counted to him for righteousness.*' When
a man works, his wages are not reckoned as a gift, but as
a debt to him. But [returning to the religious parallel]
here we have the case of a man not performing works,
but simply putting faith in God, who justifies even the
impious : it is his faith which is counted as righteousness.
David in the Psalm has such a case in view when he says,
' *Blessed are those whose lawless deeds are forgiven, and*
*whose sins are covered up, blessed is the man whose sin the*
*Lord will not reckon.*' (v.[9]) Now, was Abraham circumcised or uncircumcised when the blessing was pronounced
on him ? . . . He was uncircumcised. He received circumcision later as a ' *sign,*' as we are told, that is, a seal
of his previous righteousness through faith in God : [1]
in this way he is the father both of all the uncircumcised
who have faith, so that righteousness is reckoned to them,[2]
and of those Jews who, besides being circumcised, also
show similar faith. (v.[13]) It was not because he kept
the Law that Abraham or his seed received the promise
of inheriting the world, but because he had the righteousness of faith. If the Law was his claim, his faith is superfluous and the promise is void.[3] For the Law brings only

---

[1] St. Paul regarded Christian sacraments as essentially " signs " and
" seals," just as words are a sign of thought, and " seal " it by giving
it clear, outward expression : see above, pp. 202 ff. So " seal " became
a term for baptism in the second century.

[2] The word " reckoned " needs care. St. Paul never teaches that
righteousness is imputed to men by a fiction on the part of God. God
gives us the sense of His forgiveness when we have humble faith, because
then we are in such a state that we can receive His Spirit and His
strength.

[3] Because the promise was unconditional on anything like circumcision
cp. Gal. 3[18] for the mutual exclusiveness of a free gift and a bargain.

condemnation, by creating definite transgression. (v.[16])
God asks of us faith, that He may bestow His loving grace ;
so that God's promise stands to all the spiritual seed of
Abraham—that is, all who have his faith ; (note the verse
of Scripture which says, ' *I have made thee the father of*
MANY NATIONS ') : he trusted in God's power to quicken
the dead [1] and to call into being what does not exist.[2]
Abraham's faith hoped against hope, and in this way he
became the spiritual ' *father of many nations.*' He was
not weak in faith : therefore though he clearly saw [3] that
his own body was as good as dead and that Sarah was too
old to bear a child in the course of nature, he fixed his
eyes on God's promise and never admitted unloyal doubts,
but was made strong in faith : he gave God glory and
was fully persuaded that what He had promised, He was
able to perform. (v.[23]) All this story stands as a lesson
to us about faith in Him who raised Jesus from the dead."

5[1-11]. OUR GROUND FOR SERENE CONFIDENCE IN GOD'S
SURPASSING LOVE.

(v.[1]) " Think what peace this justification by faith
offers us towards God. Christ has led us into God's
gracious love and we triumph in hope of attaining God's
glory : nay more, we triumph also in our very afflictions,
knowing that they create in us stedfastness, depth of
character, and hope which ' *does not betray us.*' God's
Holy Spirit pours forth love for Him into our hearts ;

---

[1] Alluding to the birth of Isaac when Abraham's body was " as good
as dead " (v.[19]).

[2] Literally " calleth the things that are not *as though they were.*" The
form of expression is due to its application to justification by faith,
" summons up things non-existent in us."

[3] The Western text (D G Lat. vet.) inserts οὐ before κατενόησεν, " he
did *not* see that . . ." This is an excellent example of the tendency in
copyists of the text to alter a reading into something *apparently* easier.
The insertion of the " not " actually ruins the force of the passage, which
consists in the antithesis, " he clearly saw that he was too old . . . yet
he never doubted."

(v.⁶) since when we were weak Christ died in suitable time for the ungodly. How often will you find any one dying for the merely upright man ? Perhaps for a really good man [1] some might dare to die. But think of God's love which led Christ to die for us when we were rebels against Him. (v.⁹) Much more then, if He has brought us justification by our union with His life-blood, will He save us from the judgment to come. If His death reconciled us to God while we were His enemies, much more will His life in us save us now that we are reconciled. We can go further still and glory in God through Christ who brought us the reconciliation."

5¹²⁻²¹. THE FIRST ADAM AND THE SECOND ADAM : THE NATURAL MAN AND THE SPIRITUAL MAN (BOTH *HUMAN*).

*(v.¹²) " Therefore as by one man sin first came into the world and so introduced death, and death extended its sway over all his descendants because they all were sinners [so by the second Adam life came into the world, see vv.¹⁵⁻²¹] : between Adam and Moses it is true that men did not as a whole sin deliberately against God's Law as Adam did ; for there was no Law and therefore they sinned unconsciously, without incurring guilt ; yet death had sway over them, because they were committing acts of sin, though not guilty as Adam was, who is the type of the coming second Adam." *

[*Note on* vv.¹²⁻¹⁴.—Death was, as we know now, in the world for ages before mankind appeared : but St. Paul accepts the early stories of Genesis as historically true. In any case, the sting of death is sin ; and but for human errancy, God might have ordained some other door than death into the fuller life beyond.

v.¹²ᵇ has given rise to endless discussion since the days of Augustine and Pelagius, who represent the different schools which emphasise respectively predestination and freewill.

[1] " Good " is probably in this passage more than " righteous."

St. Paul seems simply to state that " death passed to all men *because all men did (actually) sin.*" He suggests no theory as to the *cause* of this universality of sin, whether it be mainly due to heredity or to early environment in infancy. He simply believes that the first man started the entail of sin in the world and all men grow up with a certain predisposition to sin. Christ exactly reversed the process : He started the entail of " life " and so is the " second Adam."

With our modern knowledge we feel certain that primitive men never started with such a clean slate as Paul attributes to Adam : they inherited the instincts of the tiger and the ape. But the root fact of Christianity remains, apart from any variety in explanation, that *all men are sinful and need a Redeemer* : St. Paul adds that this Redeemer must be a man like ourselves. It is also unquestionably true that we are too much dependent on our environment to make it possible for the individual to be perfected in the present state of the society to which he belongs. Individual redemption in Christ is, thank God, a fact : but it is always conditioned in part by our environment, particularly our Church. All men are linked together by indissoluble ties.]

(v.[15]) " Contrast the first Adam and the second : the sin of the one brought death to the many : much more did the grace of the one *man* Jesus Christ bring God's gracious gift to the many. (v.[16]) The result in the case of the first Adam was that judgment issued in condemnation : in the case of the second Adam that, in spite of many trespasses, the issue is acquittal. (v.[17]) If the result of the one man's sin could be such widespread death, much more must it be true [1] that Christ's righteousness will bring to

---

[1] Notice his glorious optimism. Good is much more infectious than evil, God much more powerful than the devil, even in men who have freewill. Note also that he expresses a hope of the ultimate salvation of all men (*e.g.* in v.[19]).

men life in the Kingdom of God. (v.[18]) The one man's fall brought condemnation to all men : so Christ through one act of supreme righteousness offers all men the right relation with God which means life. (v.[19]) The one man's disobedience made the many sinful, the other man's obedience shall make the many righteous. (v.[20]) The object of the Law between the first Adam and the second was to quicken the sense of guilt in man. But grace is always more effective than sin."

*C.* Rom. 6–8. Sanctification or Growth in Christlikeness.

6. Is the Doctrine of Free Forgiveness Immoral ? Does it mean Licence to Sin ? On the Contrary, it is conditioned by the Words " in Christ " : Union with Him makes Sin lose its Power over us.

(v.[1]) " Does it follow that we may remain in sin, to make God's grace more effective ? Never. Justification implies a real death to sin : [it breaks down the barriers which keep God out of the soul :] it floods our springs of action with the clean waters of His Spirit. Immersion in baptism is a real union with Christ's death on Calvary ; coming out of the water of baptism clean means a real union with His risen life. (v.[5]) We must share in a real sense His crucifixion, if we would share His Resurrection : it is a real death to our old self and sin. (v.[6]) He who has died with Christ is acquitted of sin, just as in human law death clears all scores. To have died with Christ is the guarantee that we shall live with Him ; for Christ being raised is alive for ever. (v.[10]) His death carries with it death to sin, and His life life to God. So reckon yourselves dead to sin and alive to God in your union with Christ.

(v.[12]) " The slavery of sin is a tyranny ; do not constantly present your limbs to sin to be weapons of unrighteousness, but once for all present yourselves to God and your limbs as His weapons of righteousness. Sin shall not be tyrant over you, since you are no longer under Law but under grace.

(v.[15]) " Once more, does this freedom from Law imply licence to sin ? Never. You have only a choice between two slaveries—the slavery to sin which brings death, or the slavery to obedience which brings righteousness. (v.[17]) Thank God that though you were slaves of sin, yet with your whole heart you turned to obey the teaching into which you were delivered as slaves ; [1] so now you are set free from sin and made slaves to righteousness. ' Slavery ' to righteousness, do I say ? In reality it is the only true freedom ; but I am using a feeble human metaphor to make you understand that this freedom can only be found *in God's service*. Do not keep veering between two masters. (v.[20]) When you were slaves of sin, you paid no allegiance to righteousness ; what was the result of that life of which you are now ashamed ? The end of such a life is death. (v.[22]) But now that you have been made free from sin and made slaves to God, you have as the result progressive holiness, and the end is life eternal. For the wages [2] of sin is death, but the gift of God is eternal life in Christ Jesus our Lord."

7. FREEDOM IN CHRIST (*continued*).

[*Note on vv.*[1-6].—Hosea's metaphor of Israel as Jehovah's faithless bride became a commonplace among the Jews and is frequently found in the New Testament, *e.g.* Eph. 5[25. 26. 32]. St. Paul here illustrates Christian freedom by the marriage laws : the soul is likened to a bride wedded to sin ; but her first husband dies, and she is then wedded to Christ. She may not serve both lords at the same time.]

(v.[1]) " You know something of human law, and that it only has authority over a man as long as he is alive. Law binds a wife to her husband as long as he lives ; if he has

---

[1] We should expect, " which was delivered to you " : he purposely inverts the phrase to mark the need of " slavery to God."

[2] Military metaphor, as " weapons " in v.[13].

died, she is freed. Well, then, she is called an adulteress if she becomes another man's while her husband is alive. But if her husband is dead, she is free to belong to another man. (v.⁴) Just so you were put to death to the law [1] through the crucifixion of Christ, that you should belong to a new lord—Him who was raised from the dead that our union may be fruitful [2] toward God. (v.⁵) When we were under the sway of the flesh, sinful passions quickened by the Law worked in our bodies, bringing forth fruit unto death : but now we have had the Law annulled to us, we have died to our old bondage so that we can be God's slaves in a new spirit, not under the old letter of the Law."

7⁷⁻¹⁴. THE FUNCTION OF THE LAW IN MAKING MEN CONSCIOUS OF SIN.

(v.⁷) " We spoke of passions quickened by the Law : is this to make the Law equivalent to sin ? Never : but I only came to recognise sin as such through the Law ; for instance, I did not know lust [3] as such except through the Law, which said, ' *Thou shalt not lust.*' Sin found a basis of attack in the commandment, and worked out in me all manner of lusting : apart from the command ' do not,' sin has no life. (v.⁹) The first stage in my life was before I realised the Law [when I was non-moral, not immoral]. Then when the Law became a reality to my consciousness, sin sprang into life, and the command which was meant to bring life brought me death. (v.¹¹) Sin found its point of attack in the commandment and deluded me.[4] So the

[1] His metaphor strictly would require, " the law was put to death to you." But he inverts the words, because he is thinking of the spiritual antitype. In baptism we were symbolically " put to death to the law," with all that it meant of the sway of sin. See v.⁶.

[2] Continuing the marriage metaphor.

[3] Includes much more than sexual lust.

[4] The psychological insight which he shows in this passage is amazing. To focus the attention on negative rules (" do not do this or that ") is a sure way to keep the forbidden sin before the mind and so strengthen its attraction. See on Gal 5¹⁶.

Law and its commandments are holy and good in themselves, not sinful. (v.[13]) But how could a thing good in itself become deadly to me ? It did not : it was sin that was deadly ; the Law served to show it up for what it is, something that produces death, so that sin might become loathsome in my eyes. The Law is spiritual, but I by myself am swayed by flesh, sold to be the slave of sin."

7[15-25]. THE TYRANNY OF SIN REALISED AS AN ALIEN INTRUDER.

(v.[15]) In this state I do not give conscious assent to what I am doing. What I will is not what I practise, but I do things I hate. My real self assents to the beauty of the Law ; but sin dwelling in me forces me, and it is not my real self which acts. (v.[18]) In the fleshly side of my nature when dominated by sin, there dwells nothing good. I can will what is good, but not carry it out. For I do not do the good that I will, but I practise the evil which I do not will. (v.[20]) So it is not my real self that is acting, but an alien intruder, sin. This, then, is the rule in life, that when I will to do good, evil besets me : in my inmost self I assent to the law of God, but a different law fights in my body against the law of my mind, and makes me a prisoner of sin. (v.[24]) Oh, wretched man that I am ! Who shall deliver me from this death-ridden body ? Thanks be to God, I am delivered by Jesus Christ our Lord. But the gist of the matter is this : by myself, without Christ, I serve the law of God in my inner mind, but the law of sin in my flesh."

8[1-17]. HOW WE TRIUMPH OVER SIN IN CHRIST.

(v.[1]) " But there is another conclusion to the whole matter : those who are in Christ have no condemnation, because spiritual life is found in union with Christ and has set them free from the sway of sin and death. *(v.[3]) For as regards redemption which the Law could not give— that redemption wherein it was weak because human flesh is weak—God accomplished it by sending His own Son in the likeness of sinful flesh and as a sacrifice for sin ;[1] thus He condemned sin in human nature and rescued the sinner, in order that the requirements of the Law might be fulfilled in us who follow the spirit, not the flesh.* (v.[5]) Those who follow the flesh have their minds set on fleshly things ; and those who follow the spirit, their minds set on the things of the spirit : but the fleshly mind means death, the spiritual means life and peace. The former means enmity towards God . . . and men swayed by the flesh cannot please God. (v.[9]) But you are swayed by the spirit, since *God's Spirit* dwells in you. Any man who has not *Christ's Spirit* is not His ; but if *Christ* [2] is in you, though your body is doomed to die for sin, your spirit is alive because of righteousness. (v.[11]) If the Spirit of God, who raised Jesus, dwells in you, God will quicken your spiritual body within you through the Spirit. (v.[12]) It follows that we are debtors, not to live according to our lower nature, which means death, but by the Spirit to kill the evil deeds of the body, which means life. All who are led by God's Spirit are God's sons. For you did not receive the spirit of slavery to be afraid of God, but the spirit of His adopted sons, which makes us cry to Him in our hearts, ' Abba, Father ! ' [3] (v.[16]) We are conscious of the Divine Spirit moving in our spirit, to assure us that

[1] Probably St. Paul means these words to have a sacrificial sense. In the Jewish sin-offering the victim had to be perfect without blemish. Its cleanness was a symbol of what the offerer prayed to become. There was no thought of transferring his guilt to the victim, except in the case of the scapegoat on the Day of Atonement ; and the latter was *not* sacrificed : it was unclean and therefore was driven out for the wild beasts to eat.

[2] Note the equivalence of the three phrases in italics. Throughout this passage it is hard to know when to write " spirit " with a capital S and when not. St. Paul regards the human spirit as only alive when quickened by God's Spirit.

[3] For this bilingual phrase, see note on Gal. 4[6] (p. 84).

we are children of God,[1] heirs of God and fellow-heirs with Christ if we have part in His sufferings that we may share His glory."

8[18-30]. THE PAIN WHICH COMES TO ALL LIVING CREATURES (NOT ONLY MEN) IS AN EARNEST OF THE FREEDOM AND GLORY WHICH AWAIT THEM HEREAFTER.

[*Note*.—This is the most wonderful passage ever written on pain. St. Paul says (*a*) vv.[18-25], that the suffering is insignificant compared with the glory which it brings to all living creatures ; (*b*) vv.[26-30], that the Holy Spirit shares in all our suffering ; and if God Himself thus bears it, we can bear it too, assured that it has its good purpose.]

(v.[18]) " For I reckon that the sufferings of this present time vanish into insignificance against the glory which shall be revealed as ours. With tense expectation the whole creation waits eagerly for the revealing of the sons of God.[2] The animal world was subjected to pain not by its own doing, but by man's ; there is sure hope therefore that all creation will share in man's new freedom from corruption and the glory of the children of God. (v.[22]) We know that all creation suffers pain together until now ; and we human beings, because we have the first-fruits of the Spirit, have an added anguish in our earnest longing for the spiritual redemption of the body as part of our adoption by God. (v.[24]) Hope rescued us from sin and despair : and hope is a necessary part of man's education on earth, creating in him the quality of endurance.

[1] For the appeal to religious experience, cp. 1 John 2[20, 27] 3[24] 4[16].

[2] No doubt St. Paul accepted literally the story in Genesis that the result of man's fall in Eden brought death and war into the whole animal world : so all living creatures are waiting to regain their Eden, when again " the wolf shall dwell with the lamb . . ." (Isa. 11[6-9], a picture of the Messianic age). We must again repeat that scientifically it is not true that animals were first brought under pain by man's sin : but the whole plan of creation is surely adapted to educate a sinful world.

(v.²⁶) " In suffering we must remember that God's Spirit shares it all with us. We do not know what prayer to offer in our hours of pain : but the Spirit knows and prays for us aright with groanings inexpressible. *And God has exactly the same mind about it all as the Spirit* : the Spirit pleads in fullest harmony with the Father. (v.²⁸) And we know that all things (including pain) work out for good to those who love God.[1] Remember, too, that God's call to us has been no sudden thing : before He called us, He must have taken thought of us and marked us out to become essentially like His Son. Since He has called us, He has justified and glorified us. Therefore we are in His hands throughout, and no evil can touch us."

8³¹⁻³⁹. THE FINALE OF SUFFERING : A TRIUMPHANT PÆAN OF JOY AND GRATITUDE TO GOD.

(v.³¹) " If God is on our side, who can harm us ? If He spared not His own Son in His love for us, will He not give us everything else good ? Who will accuse God's chosen people ? It is God who makes us right with Himself—who shall condemn us ? (v.³⁴) It is Christ who died, or, rather, was raised again, to sit on God's right hand and plead for us. Who shall separate us from His love ? Shall affliction or difficulty or persecution ? Shall hunger or lack of clothing or danger or the sword ? We are like the men in the Psalm who cry, ' *For Thy sake we are killed all the day, accounted as sheep for the slaughter* ' ; but in all these things we are more than conquerors through Him who loved us. Neither death nor life, neither angels nor spiritual powers, neither things present nor future, neither height nor depth nor any created thing, shall be able to separate us from the love of God in Christ Jesus our Lord."

*D.* CHAPS. 9–11. THE PROBLEM OF THE JEWISH RACE :

---

[1] A sublime expression of Christian optimism : not, " all things are for the best in the best of possible worlds," but, " all things, however evil in themselves, combine to work for good to men who love God."

WHY, WITH THEIR UNIQUE RELIGIOUS HISTORY, HAVE THEY
REJECTED CHRIST ? GOD'S PROMISES TO THEM ARE
IRREVOCABLE : HE CAN BRING GOOD OUT OF EVIL, AND HE
WILL ASSUREDLY AT THE LAST CONVERT THE JEWS THROUGH
THOSE VERY GENTILES WHOM IT HAS BEEN THEIR SIN
TO DESPISE.

[*Note.*—These chapters present many difficulties to a
modern reader, and, at first sight, seem to teach in places
an intolerable predestinarianism. In my opinion most of
the difficulties disappear if we keep in mind the following
points throughout (though it is only fair to say that many
commentators would deny them).

(*a*) The main thought is of *privilege to believe*, whether
for nations or individuals, but primarily for nations. The
root question with St. Paul is, " Why has God given me this
incalculable joy and privilege on earth, while my nation
remains out in the cold ? " He is thinking of privilege
in this world, not the next.

(*b*) He states that no one is worthy of such privilege
or has earned it ; but God of His mercy *chooses some in
order* (*not* to give them eternal life, but) *to make them His
messengers to mankind*.

(*c*) God's will is that *all men shall be saved in the end*.
It is vital to the proper perspective of the whole passage
to remember that St. Paul now believed in the ultimate
salvation of all men, even his bitterest opponents the Jews.]

9¹⁻⁵. HIS GRIEF FOR ISRAEL : THE PROBLEM STATED.

(v.¹) " I tell you solemnly in Christ, the Holy Spirit
within me making me conscious of the need for utter
sincerity, that the unbelief of my own race, the Jews, gives
me a never-ceasing pain of heart. I could pray that I
myself might be accursed and banned [1] from Christ if I
could win them thereby. (v.⁴) They are of the chosen race

---

[1] " Anathema "=the Hebrew ḥerem in the sense of something devoted
to destruction (*e.g.* the spoils of Jericho in the Book of Joshua).

of Israel; they received adoption from God and His glorious presence [1] and the worship of the Temple and the promises; they are of the race of the great Old Testament leaders, and from their stock was the Christ born : I thank God, who ordains all things, for His inestimable gifts to them." [2]

9⁶⁻¹³. GOD'S GIFTS WERE NEVER GRANTED TO ALL THE FLESHLY DESCENDANTS OF ABRAHAM, BUT TO CERTAIN GROUPS CHOSEN FOR NO MERIT OF THEIR OWN.

(v.⁶) " It is not as though God's promises to Israel have failed. It was never true that all Israel's descendants were the real Israel : thus God said to Abraham, ' *In Isaac* [not in Ishmael] *shall thy seed be called* ' : that is, his seed who inherit the promises does not comprise all his descendants. Sarah bore a special son who was marked as a child of God's promise. (v.¹⁰) But Isaac and Ishmael had different mothers ; let us take the later case of Jacob's two sons born of the same mother : before they were born— that is, before they had done anything good or evil to *merit* God's choice—it was said to Rebecca, ' *The older shall serve the younger,*' making it clear that God's call does not depend on human deserts. So the prophet [' Malachi '] writes, ' *Jacob I loved, but Esau I hated.* ' " [3]

9¹⁴⁻²⁹. IS SUCH DIVINE CHOICE UNJUST ? NO ONE

---

[1] " The glory " was a Hebrew name for the Shekinah, *i.e.* the cloud which was said to rest upon the Ark at the Exodus : this was interpreted as an outward and visible sign of God's abiding presence, and so it became to the later Jews a symbol of the Messiah.

[2] The R.V. text makes " God blessed for ever " an epithet of Christ, following the punctuation of the oldest Greek manuscripts. But punctuation only dates back to the third century A.D., an age of little critical insight. It is not St. Paul's way to use " God " absolutely of Christ, though St. John does it.

[3] In Malachi " Jacob " and " Esau " stand for peoples, not individuals. '' Hated " means " treated as hostile." Still St. Paul chooses extreme terms to throw his meaning into high relief—Why was Israel favoured *in this world* above Edom, so that the latter became God's enemy ?

DESERVES GOD'S GRACE; BUT HE CHOOSES OUT SOME TO
WORK OUT HIS PURPOSE OF MERCY TO THE WHOLE WORLD.
IF HE HARDENS THE HEART OF OTHERS, IT IS BECAUSE
THEY HAVE UNFITTED THEMSELVES FOR HIS PURPOSE:
AND BY THEIR VERY WICKEDNESS HE ACHIEVES HIS
PURPOSE OF MERCY TO THE WORLD.

(v.[14]) "This may seem at first sight unjust: but we
know there can be no injustice with God: He says to
Moses, '*I will have mercy on whomsoever I will*': this
shows that *no man earns His mercy by a good life*; but He
extends His undeserved mercy to some. (v.[17]) In the
Scripture it is said to Pharaoh, '*For this very reason I
saved thee from the plague, to show men My power*'; but
He hardened Pharaoh's heart.[1]

(v.[19]) "You will object that, if God acts so, He cannot
blame us for opposing His will when in reality we are
working out His purpose [since God uses even man's sin
to achieve His ends]. But, O man, who are you to answer
back to God [whose ways are above our ken]? '*Shall
the pot say to the potter*,' why did You make me so? The
potter, with his own purpose in view, makes out of the same
lump of clay one vessel for an honourable use and another
for a menial use. (v.[22]) Can you accuse God of injustice
because, *though* He wishes to prove His abhorrence of sin,
He yet tolerated men fitted by their own acts for destruction, with the one object of showing His mercy to others,
whom He [in spite of their sin] has fitted to receive it,
and whom He has called to His service, Gentiles as well
as Jews?

(v.[25]) "The Hebrew prophets will prove to you that God
has always shown amazing mercy, which men have never

---

[1] In Jewish thought, when God is said to *harden* a man's heart, it is
always regarded as a penalty for his own sins. "The reward of a
precept is another precept [to be kept], the reward of a transgression is
another transgression," said the Jews.

deserved, and of which only a minority have availed themselves. Hosea speaks of the call of those who were not God's chosen people, to be His sons. Isaiah proclaims that it is only a remnant of the Jews that shall be saved, in two passages."

9³⁰–10. ISRAEL HAS SOUGHT RIGHTEOUSNESS ON THE WRONG LINES—THAT IS, BY CONFORMITY TO EXTERNAL RULES INSTEAD OF THE DEVOTION OF THE HEART. THEY CANNOT PLEAD THAT THE MESSAGE WAS NOT PREACHED TO THEM OR THAT IT WAS TOO HARD FOR THEM TO GRASP.

(v.³⁰) " So the Gentiles, who were not pursuing after righteousness, found the righteousness which comes by faith ; and Israel, though pursuing after the Law of righteousness, failed to achieve it ! That was because Israel set out on the wrong principle of external standards instead of internal faith : they tripped over ' *the stone of stumbling* ' which Isaiah says is laid on Zion and of which he says, ' *he that hath* FAITH *in Him shall not be put to shame.*'

10¹. " I yearn in prayer to God for their salvation. For they have a real zeal for God, but not a clear knowledge of His way. They always are trying to establish their own righteousness, not His : for Christ is the goal to which the Law is directed, bringing righteousness to the man of faith. (v.⁵) In Leviticus Moses declares the principle of the Law where he writes, ' *The man who carries it out shall win life thereby.*' But in Moses we have also hints of the righteousness which comes of faith : for in Deuteronomy it is written, ' *Say not, who shall ascend into heaven* '—(that is, ' How shall we men of earth storm heaven as if we had to bring Christ down to earth ') ? Or, ' *who shall descend into the depths* ' (as if we men had to bring Christ up from the grave) ? But it says, ' *The word is nigh thee in thy mouth and in thy heart* ' : that is, ' If you can confess the simple creed, " Jesus is Lord," and believe in your heart in His Resurrection, you are safe to achieve.' (v.[10]) Righteousness comes by faith in the heart, and salvation by outward confession with the lips. And this simple act is open to *all* mankind; as the Scripture says, ' *No one who has faith in Him shall be put to shame.*' There is no distinction between Jew and Greek; Christ's wealth is poured on *all* who call on Him: for ' *Every one who calls on the name of the Lord shall be saved.*'

*(vv.[14-15]) " [Faith is easy because the human heart recognises and responds to the message.] The only conditions necessary for faith are, first, that men should have been sent by God as His intermediaries : then that they should preach and the message be heard : this hearing awakens their faith and so they call on Him and are saved. [So Israel cannot plead its lack of opportunity.]*

(v.[16]) " But it was always the case that God's messengers have been unheeded, though their good news has penetrated everywhere; yet they have always awakened a response in the most unlikely quarters. Isaiah says, ' *Lord, who hath hearkened to our message?* ' (This implies that the message is inspired by Christ, and that those who heed it are inspired to accept it.) (v.[18]) Can they say they had no chance to hear it ? No, for ' *their sound hath gone forth into all the earth. . . .*' (v.[19]) Can it be that Israel had no chance to understand it ? No : they were the same as early as Moses' time, for he says that God will stir them to jealousy by a foreign nation. Isaiah goes so far as to say, ' *I was found by those who seek Me not . . .*'; and to Israel he says, ' *All the day I stretched out My hands to a disobedient and gainsaying people.*' [So if, then as now, foreign nations with so little insight could understand and accept the message, it cannot be that Israel had, or has, not the chance to understand.]"

11. CAN WE BELIEVE THAT ISRAEL, WHO HAVE LED THE

WORLD IN RELIGION, SHALL TO THE END REJECT CHRIST?
RATHER WE MUST BELIEVE THAT GOD WILL FULFIL ALL
HIS PROMISES TO THEM. THEIR SIN HAS BEEN PRIDE:
SURELY GOD WILL USE THE DESPISED GENTILES TO BRING
THEM BACK AND AT THE SAME TIME DESTROY THEIR PRIDE.
FOR GOD'S SCHEME IS THE ULTIMATE SALVATION OF ALL
MEN.

(v.[1]) " Can it really be that God has finally rejected
His people? I cannot believe it: for I myself am an
Israelite, of the tribe of Benjamin [*i.e.* of unmixed Jewish
blood]. There is now, as in the narrative of Elijah,[1] a
far larger number of the faithful in the Jewish race than
in our despair we are apt to think. He thought he was
the only faithful worshipper left to God: (v.[4]) but God's
oracle said to Him, ' *I have left seven thousand who have
not bowed knee to Baal.*' So now again there is a faithful
remnant: they have faith by God's grace, not their own
merits, for ' grace ' and ' merit ' are mutually exclusive.
(v.[7]) Israel seeks God indeed, but it has failed to find;
all except God's chosen ones have been blinded,[2] as
happened of old and as we see in several Scriptures. . . .
(v.[11]) The people of Israel have stumbled: but can it be
a complete fall?[3] Not so. God's plan cannot be fulfilled without their conversion. And if their rejection of
Christ has been the means of bringing such a blessing to
the Gentile world, think what their full ingathering would
mean!

(v.[13]) " And from this I wish to warn those of you who
are Gentiles against pride in your spiritual privileges.
I am sent to the Gentiles and I lay great stress on my

---

[1] " *Of* Elijah " (R.V.) is a mistranslation.

[2] For ἐπωρώθησαν, see note on 2 Cor. 3[14] (p. 226).

[3] v.[11] should be translated, " stumbled *so as to* fall," *i.e.* the ἵνα, as
often in the N.T., gives the result, not the purpose. Men do not usually
trip up with the *purpose* of falling (as R.V. translates this phrase)!

18

ministry if somehow I may stir up the Jews to emulation.
For, as I said, if their rejection has meant the reconciliation of the world to God, their acceptance will be nothing
else than life from the dead. If the first-fruits of corn
are consecrated to God, all the bread made from the corn
is consecrated : if the root is consecrated, so are the
branches. (v.[17]) God's Church is like some garden-olive
tree from which some of the branches have been broken
off, and in their place branches of a wild olive have been
grafted in [1] : you Gentiles are these wild olive branches ;
you have been allowed to draw your life from the rich oil
of the olive root. Then you must not boast your superiority to its branches ! Remember it is not you who bear
the root, but the root you. (v.[19]) You say, ' Its branches
were broken off that I might be grafted in.' True, but
it was just their lack of faith which caused them to be
broken off, and it is your faith, not your merits, which
gives you your firm position. Do not be presumptuous,
but show a reverent fear. If God spared not the natural
branches of the tree, much less will He spare you [if you
are guilty of similar pride]. (v.[22]) Look at God's kindness
to yourself and severity to them : if you cling to humble
recognition of His kindness, well ; if not, you too will be
cut off. Similarly they, if they do not cling to their
unbelief, will be grafted back ; for God is able to do it.
Against your nature you were cut out of a wild olive and
grafted into a garden-olive : much more easily can the
natural branches of the garden-olive be grafted on it.

(v.[25]) " As I read God's mysterious purpose, it is this—
and it will keep you from pride to remember it. The race

---

[1] St. Paul was probably quite aware that in an orchard such a proceeding is unthinkable. He is trying to bring out the extraordinary
nature of what has happened : if God has made wild-olive grafts bear
garden-olives, all the more easily can He again graft in the branches of
the garden-olive.

of Israel has been to some extent blinded, to open the door
for the Gentiles to come in.   Then at last shall all Israel
be saved. . . . (v.²⁸) They are enemies in respect of the
gospel message, for your gain :  but in respect of God's first
choice of them, He loves them for the sake of their ancestors.
For He never changes His mind about His gifts and calling.
(v.³⁰) Formerly you showed unbelief in God :  now the
way to extend His mercy to you has been made through
the fact of the Jews' unbelief.   They have now lapsed
into unbelief because God has had mercy on you ;  their
pride is their downfall.   But when they have learnt
humility they again will receive mercy.   God has allowed
all men to fall into unbelief, simply in order that His mercy
may be set free to embrace all men.

(v.³³) " O the depth of God's wealth and wisdom and
knowledge !   His ways are too wonderful for us to search
out. . . . (v.³⁶) All things have Him as their source, their
driving power, their goal.   His is the glory for ever: Amen."

[*Further Note on* 9–11.—The relation of God's Providence
to man's freedom, of fate or predestination to freewill, is
an ultimate mystery to the human mind.   But St. Paul
refuses to ignore the hand of God in using all that happens
or can happen to us in this life, in order to carry out His
loving purpose to the world.   He takes a firm stand on this,
that " all things work together for good to men that love
God."

Here, as in 1 Cor. 15²⁸, etc., he shows that he has moved
a long way since he wrote Thessalonians.   We hear no
more of a minority of mankind sharing in the Resurrection
to life :  there is a far grander hope, the ultimate salvation
of all the world.   If he, Paul, can agonise over Israel's
unbelief, Christ and His saints, nay, God Himself, must
agonise infinitely more over it.   The world is God's family :
can there be an ultimate heaven if some of the family
are left out ?]

*D.* CHAPS. 12–15¹³.—PRACTICAL ADVICE.

[A very brief outline of these chapters will suffice, as there is little of difficulty in them.]

12¹. " I beseech you to present your *bodies* to God as a living sacrifice : this is the service natural to mankind.¹ (v.²) Do not adopt the fleeting fashion of this world, but be transfigured into God's unchanging reality.

(v.³) " Be humble and sober-minded : God has given to each individual faith to fit him for a special function in the body of Christ. (vv.⁶⁻⁸) These varying gifts must be developed in His service. (v.⁹) Let your Christian love be unfeigned . . . : show brotherly love to God's family, not pushing yourselves forward nor being half-hearted. . . . (v.¹²) Show endurance under affliction, in prayer, in relieving the needs of other Christians. . . . (v.¹⁴) Bless your persecutors [Matt. 5⁴⁴] : share men's joys and griefs alike. (v.¹⁶) Be united, not proud but putting yourselves on a level with the lowly. (v.¹⁸) As far as possible, be at peace with all men : do not avenge your wrongs but be kind to your enemies. Conquer evil by good.

13¹. " The civil powers are ordained by God (v.³) to restrain evil. (v.⁴) Thus far they are God's ministers to help you. (v.⁵) Be obedient to them [as far as you may consistently with your allegiance to Christ], not only because they have power to punish you, but for conscience' sake. Pay up your taxes and capitation fees.

(v.⁸) " Your only debt to any one must be the debt of love which you owe all men. For [as Christ says], all the Laws of Moses are summed up and transcended in the one rule to ' *Love your neighbour as yourself.*'

---

¹ No English word quite renders λογικήν. The Stoics defined man as a " reasoning " animal (λογικὸν ζῷον). Philo speaks of our faculty of " reason " (τὸ λογικὸν ἐν ἡμῖν) as the *distinctly human control of passion and appetite*, which animals do not possess in like degree. That is St. Paul's meaning here. Cp. 1 Pet. 2².

(v.[11]) " The time of His coming is near : watch for the dawn and put away the habits of darkness."

14–15[13]. DISCUSSION OF THE SCRUPLES WHICH SOME CHRISTIANS FEEL ABOUT VEGETARIANISM OR KEEPING CERTAIN DAYS AS HOLY. THESE THINGS AND OTHERS LIKE THEM ARE NOT VITAL, BUT REALLY OF NO MOMENT. YET NO ONE SHOULD DESPISE THOSE WHO HAVE SUCH SCRUPLES ; ALL SHOULD BE CAREFUL NOT TO GIVE OFFENCE TO THE " WEAKER BROTHER."

14[23] lays down the important principle, that if a man does anything which he is not convinced is right, it is sin. " Whatever does not proceed from faith in God is [for a Christian] sin."

E. 15[14]–16. HIS PLANS FOR THE FUTURE. FIRST, HIS VISIT TO JERUSALEM TO CONVEY THE FUND HE IS COLLECTING : THEN HIS PROJECTED TOUR IN SPAIN, WHICH WILL, HE HOPES, ENABLE HIM TO VISIT THEM IN ROME AS HE PASSES. PERSONAL MESSAGES.

For 15[19-21], see pp. 160–1, and note 1 to p. 163.

15[30-31] are important as showing (a) his natural human dread of violence in Jerusalem ; (b) his steadfast determination to go there, because he hoped that it would make so much for the unity of Jewish with Gentile Christians, if he brought the fund subscribed by the Gentiles and at the same time publicly observed a Jewish Feast.

# CHAPTER XIII.

## FROM THE RIOT AT JERUSALEM TO THE FIRST ROMAN IMPRISONMENT.

1. THE RIOT AT JERUSALEM (Acts $21^{17}$–$22^{29}$).—St. Paul, as we have seen, reached Jerusalem on Friday, 27th May, A.D. 57, when the city was crowded with pilgrims who had come to keep the Feast of Pentecost next day. On the morning of the Feast, the presbyters of the Church met at the house of their leader and president, St. James, to welcome Paul and the delegates of the fund, and to hear the thrilling story of the Third Missionary Journey. But they were very anxious about the danger which he incurred. There was no more inflammable material in the world than the mob crowded at feast-time into the Holy City; and the story had been spread among them that St. Paul had gone about telling Jews abroad that they need not keep the Mosaic Law. It was a lie, but it was believed. Once he was recognised in Jerusalem, an outbreak was certain, unless something could be done to show in act the utter falseness of the story. Four poor Jewish Christians had taken a vow a few days previously : four of the six days of their "separation" were already past [1]—the days

---

[1] It is usually assumed (e.g. by Page) that the "seven" (=six) days were spent by St. Paul with the four men in performing the customary rites, i.e. that they were the last six days of the vow. But Acts $24^{11}$ allows only eleven days between his arrival at Jerusalem and his trial at Cæsarea : it is clear therefore that he cannot have spent more than two days over the vow. The rules for a *temporary* Nazirite vow are given in Num. 6 : it is clear from $6^9$ that the normal period of the vow was six ("seven") days ; and from $6^{10}$ that the offerings were made on the day after.

during which they had practised abstinence. On the next day but one (Monday, 30th May) the "seven" (*i.e.* six) days would be up, and the votaries must present a peace-offering in the Temple and have their hair cut off, to be burned in the fire (see Num. 6¹⁻²¹; cp. Acts 18¹⁸). The proposal was that St. Paul should go with them to the Temple on the Sunday to give notice of their ceremonies of purification on the next day and to pay their expenses, thus publicly identifying himself with a Mosaic ordinance.

Unfortunately some Jews from Asia recognised him walking in the streets with Trophimus of Ephesus. When he entered the Temple on the Monday with the four votaries, the same people saw him in the courts. They jumped to the conclusion that he had brought in the uncircumcised Trophimus with him, an act of sacrilege which meant death. The cry was raised at once : "Here is the man who teaches every man everywhere to despise God's people and the Law and this place ; yes, and he has brought Greeks into the Temple and defiled this holy place." The crowd went wild : they dragged him outside the gates of the inner Temple,¹ which were locked at once, and then turned to wreak their vengeance on him.

But the time taken in hustling him out of the courtyard saved his life. There was a Roman cohort in the Castle of Antonia, a barracks which overlooked the north side of the Temple area and was entered by a large double flight of steps opposite the north-west angle of the outer courtyard. These were troublous times in Jerusalem, and feast-days

---

¹ Round the shrine itself were three inner courts—(*a*) that of the Priests; (*b*) that of Israel; (*c*) on a lower level, that of the Women. Outside the latter were fourteen steps leading down through a low balustrade of stone, inside which no Gentile might penetrate on pain of death. The women's court was surrounded by a wall of its own with gates on each side : the eastern gate was "of brass and very strong, shut at nightfall with difficulty by twenty men" (Josephus, *War*, vi. 5. 3). It was probably this gate that St. Luke means.

above all. Quite lately an Egyptian Jew,[1] infuriated by
the cruel excesses of Felix, the Roman procurator, had
come forward as a prophet calling his nation to arm against
the oppressor : the outbreak was savagely repressed but
its leader escaped. On feast-days Claudius Lysias, the
Tribune in command of the troops, would have all his
men confined to barracks and a strict watch kept in the
Temple area itself.[2]

On this occasion, as soon as the trouble began, word was
instantly carried to the Commander, " All Jerusalem is in
an uproar " ; he turned out his men and his centurions,
and rushed down to the outer Temple court where the mob
were beating Paul to death. The soldiers seized him, and
bound his hands behind him : the Tribune asked who he
was and what he had done. He was greeted with a chorus
of contradictory accusations, and decided to take his
prisoner inside the castle. The infuriated mob surged
round the soldiers as they were on the steps, crying, " Kill
him ! " and the prisoner had literally to be carried into
safety. As they set him down again at the top of the
stairway, Paul turned to the Tribune and said in Greek,
" May I ask you something ? " He was astounded that
his prisoner knew Greek ; for he had made up his mind that
he was the Egyptian Jew [3] who had so lately escaped from

---

[1] See Josephus, *Antiq.* xx. 8. 6, *War*, ii. 13. 5.

[2] See Josephus, *Antiq.* xx. 5. 3 : " When that feast, which is called the
Passover, was at hand . . ., Cumanus ordered that one regiment of
the army should take their arms, and stand *in the temple cloisters*, to
repress any attempts of innovation, if perchance any such should begin ;
and this was no more than what the former procurators of Judæa did
at such festivals " (Whiston's translation). In xx. 8. 11 he tells us
that at the festivals the Roman guard was stationed in the western
cloisters of the outer court of the Temple.

[3] The " sicarii " or assassins of 21[38] are mentioned in Josephus as a
society which became active in the days of Felix. They were fanatical
nationalists who stuck at nothing. They used to assassinate people in
broad daylight.

justice. "No," said Paul; "I am a Jew from Tarsus in Cilicia, and have the franchise of that famous city." So the Commander let him speak from the steps to the mob below in the street: he probably thought it could do no harm, though, as the speech was in the Aramaic dialect, he himself would not understand a word of it.

St. Paul's speech to the crowd was very simple and utterly fearless. He told them how he had been brought up as a strict observer of the Mosaic Law and had received his later education in Jerusalem from the revered Gamaliel: he recounted how his zeal for God had led him to persecute the Christians, with the authority of the High Priest and all the presbytery behind him, and how on the outskirts of Damascus Jesus of Nazareth had appeared to him: then, with more honesty than tact, he referred to his vision of the Lord in the Temple at Jerusalem, when he was bidden to leave the city, " because they will not receive thy witness about Me." So he began to speak of his commission, " I will send thee afar to the Gentiles "; and then the popular fury broke loose: they " shouted and tore their robes and threw dust into the air " (v.²³). The Tribune ordered his men to remove the prisoner instantly into the castle and to scourge him in order to extract the truth from him. It was illegal to scourge or torture any prisoner unless he had proved contumacious under examination; obviously Lysias was suspicious that Paul had not told the truth about himself. But it was illegal under any circumstances to scourge a Roman citizen. So when the men had stripped him and stretched him on a pillar to receive the awful " thongs " ¹ of the scourge, he managed to appeal to the centurion who was in charge: " Is it lawful," he said, " to scourge a Roman citizen, especially

---

¹ Possibly ἱμᾶσιν in v.²⁵ refers to the straps with which they bound him; but it more naturally denotes the leather thongs of the scourge, which were loaded with pieces of metal or bones.

before hearing his case ? " The centurion fetched his
superior officer, who would scarcely believe that he was
a Roman citizen : " I bought the citizenship for a large
sum of money," he said.   " But I was born a Roman," said
Paul.   The Tribune knew he was speaking the truth ;  he
would not dare to claim the position falsely :  and Lysias
was alarmed because he had bound him.

2. His Appearance before the Sanhedrin and
Removal to Cæsarea ($22^{30}$–23).—The Tribune decided
to sift the whole matter as best he could :  but the legal
position was complicated.   The Sanhedrin had jurisdiction
over Jews in religious matters ;  but a Jew who was also
a Roman citizen could claim exemption.   Apparently
Lysias decided to hold an investigation himself in the
presence of the Jewish Court.   So he sent to the High
Priest, asking that they should be convened on the Tuesday
morning.   They habitually met in the hall of Polished
Stone (Gazith) which was in the Court of Israel in the inner
Temple area.   But as no Gentile might enter there, and as
Claudius Lysias wished to be present, they must have used
some other building in the great Court.

So St. Paul faced the Assembly of which he had once
been an ardent member : as he looked round, he must have
recognised the faces of men who had been associated with
him either on the Council or in the school of Gamaliel.
He gazed straight at them (ἀτενίσας, v.[1]) and addressed
them as equals (vv.[1, 5]), not adding the term " fathers "
which he had used to the crowd  the day before ($22^1$).
They regarded him as a traitor to his God :  he asserts that
he has a clear conscience towards Him.   At that Ananias
the High Priest lost his temper and bade those standing
near Paul to strike him on the mouth—it is clear that the
Roman soldiers stood apart at the other end of the hall.
Paul in hot anger at such injustice turned on him, " God

shall smite thee, thou whited wall!" (a proverbial phrase for a hypocrite whose show of piety covers malice). In horror the bystanders exclaimed, "Dost thou rail at God's high priest?" In quick penitence the Apostle apologised: "I did not know, brethren, that he was High Priest," and he tactfully added a command out of the Mosaic Law. The meaning of his words is not quite clear. To take them, with many commentators, as sarcastic (*i.e.* "Who could have supposed that this ruffian was High Priest?") leaves the following quotation singularly inapposite. Perhaps, as the trial was not an ordinary meeting of the Sanhedrin, the High Priest's chair was not raised above those surrounding it, and St. Paul, who had scarcely been in Jerusalem for twenty years, did not recognise Ananias: or perhaps the Apostle had heard the order given, and did not know who had given it, except that it came from one of his judges. If it is true that he was short-sighted (cp. Gal. $4^{15}$), the incident is explained at once.

His outburst of anger is often contrasted with our Lord's calmness under similar provocation at His trial (John $18^{22}$, etc.), and the contrast is just: but his apology to the High Priest was noble. His conduct in the immediate sequel has been more strongly criticised. Verse 6 tells us that he perceived that the Council contained a number of both Pharisees and Sadducees, the latter of whom, recognising no Scriptures but the Pentateuch, had never admitted the belief in a Resurrection beyond death: and he effectually divided the two parties against each other by crying out, "I am a Pharisee and come of a Pharisaic family: it is for the hope of the resurrection of the dead that I am being tried."

Put baldly in this way, it sounds like a dishonest ruse on St. Paul's part; and many commentators suppose that his subsequent words to Felix (Acts $24^{21}$) show that he was conscious of having sinned in this utterance.[1] But the words to Felix only mean, " I did no *legal* wrong unless it was *a legal offence* to say what caused an uproar in the Council." For when he appears before Agrippa, he repeats his plea that his belief in the resurrection of the dead is the kernel of the accusation against him (26[6-8]). He would scarcely have done this if he had felt that his action in the Sanhedrin was sinful.

Now St. Luke omits the speech which the Apostle delivered before the Sanhedrin (23[1]), no doubt because it followed similar lines to those of his speech to the crowd on the previous day : that is to say, he gave them an account of his conversion and the appearance of the Risen Christ. The Sadducees at this point would sneer openly and provoke a certain amount of sympathy with the story among the Pharisees (see v.[9]). It was this that showed him (v.[6]) that the two parties were divided in the Council. He appealed impulsively to the Pharisees : were they not far closer to his beliefs than to those of the Sadducees ? Was not Catholic Christianity a development along the lines of the most spiritual Pharisaic teaching ?

It was a fair plea to make, but it was shirking the question at issue. The Jewish Christians at Jerusalem were tolerated because they kept the Law : Paul was arraigned on a charge of teaching Jews not to keep the Law. No doubt he was convinced that he had already proved his innocence of the charge ; but he had not been acquitted, nor, as a matter of fact, had he convinced the Court. He spoke in sincerity ; his repetition of the same plea before Agrippa shows it. It was not a dishonest ruse, but it was a mistake in judgment, because his adversaries were certain to interpret it later as a diplomatic trick.[2]

[1] " Let them say what fault they found in me when I stood before the Sanhedrin, unless it be with the single sentence I uttered when I stood and cried, ' It is for the resurrection of the dead that I am on my trial to-day before you.' "

[2] This explanation is much the same as that adopted by Rendall, Rackham, and Furneaux in their several editions of the Acts.

The uproar which ensued in the Council chamber was such that he was in danger of being torn in pieces. The Tribune promptly closed his troops round the prisoner and marched him back to the castle. That night in prison St. Paul's fears for the future were set at rest by a vision of the Lord, who bade him take courage (v.[11]) : he had borne his witness like a man at Jerusalem ; he should do the same at Rome. But his adversaries did not mean to let him escape so easily. Assassination had recently become a common resort among the extreme Jewish nationalists, the Zealots. Next morning (Tuesday, 1st June) more than forty men took an oath to abstain from all food and drink till they had killed him. They avowed their plot to some of the chief priests and elders, and through them persuaded the Sanhedrin (who were not as a whole privy to the conspiracy) to approach the Roman tribune with a request that the investigation, interrupted on the previous day, might be resumed ; they meant to attack the guard on their way across the outer court of the Temple.[1]

Paul's nephew, son of his sister, was in Jerusalem : he probably was in close touch with the Pharisaic party ; at any rate he heard of the plot and was able to warn his uncle, who sent him off to have a private interview with the Tribune (vv.[17-22]). Lysias saw at once that the matter was now serious : it did not only concern the prisoner but threatened a grave outbreak which might lead to the loss of many lives. The only thing was to send the Christian down to Cæsarea and hand him over to the Procurator of Judæa and Samaria, who held his Court there in the

---

[1] We may wonder what the conspirators did about their vow when they failed to achieve their purpose. But in a society where vows are frequently taken, it is easy to obtain absolution later, at any rate if the failure to carry out the intention is involuntary (cp. quotation in D.S. p. 485, n. 1).

Prætorium or palace built by Herod the Great. He would take no risks : the escort should be strong enough to preclude any chance of a sudden attack. So he detailed seventy ordinary cavalry and two hundred mounted lancers,[1] under the command of two centurions.

They started at nine o'clock that night, putting Paul on a mule and taking a spare mount for him ($\kappa\tau\acute{\eta}\nu\eta$, v.[24]), for the whole distance was 64 miles. The letter which Claudius Lysias sent to the Governor (vv.[26-30]) is a diplomatic statement : " I rescued the prisoner, having learnt that he was a Roman citizen ! " But he put the case in a light favourable to St. Paul (v.[29]).

They reached Antipatris, at the foot of the Judæan hills (about 12 miles E.N.E. of Joppa and about half-way from Jerusalem to Cæsarea), on Wednesday morning ; and there dismissing the lancers, they rode forward to Cæsarea.

3. St. Paul and Felix (Acts 23[34]-24[27]).—Antonius Felix, procurator of Judæa and Samaria, was not an estimable person. He and his more famous brother Pallas were originally Greek slaves, belonging probably to the mother of the Emperor Claudius, from whom they had received their freedom. Pallas had been a great favourite of the Emperor, and for years was all-powerful ; but after Nero's accession he lost his influence (A.D. 55), and was removed from office. Through him Felix was appointed to his governorship, the first freedman ever to hold such an office with control of military forces. It was

---

[1] It seems clear that we should omit the first $\delta\iota\alpha\kappa\sigma\acute{\iota}ovs$ ("two hundred ") in v.[23], though the manuscript authority for the omission is very slight (only h and a few minuscules). It is most improbable that the force would include any infantry, as the Tribune clearly wished them to move fast enough to get to Antipatris under cover of darkness, as they actually did. Lysias' order should be translated, " Get ready soldiers, namely, seventy cavalry and two hundred lancers." The last word ($\delta\epsilon\xi\iota\sigma\lambda\acute{\alpha}\beta\sigma vs$) may possibly mean " slingers " (Meyer).

perhaps not unnatural that, " with all manner of cruelty and lust he exercised the power of a king in the temper of a slave," as Tacitus says of him (*Hist.* v. 9), even though we must allow something for the prejudice of the Roman historian. His tyranny drove the Zealots into wild excesses, which he ruthlessly suppressed. According to Josephus he was appointed in A.D. 52, though Tacitus places it earlier. Sometime between A.D. 57 and A.D. 60 the riots between the Jews and Syrians in Cæsarea (where St. Paul was then in prison) became so serious that Felix was recalled and impeached ; but he escaped through the intervention of his brother Pallas, who retained some influence with Nero until the Jewess Empress, Poppæa, procured his murder in A.D. 62.

Suetonius says that he married three princesses (*Claud.* xxviii.) : the third, who afterwards perished in the eruption of Mount Vesuvius, was Drusilla, sister to Herod Agrippa II., through whom he perhaps hoped to win popularity with the Jews. This woman had deserted her former husband to marry him.

Such was the man to whom St. Paul was handed over, probably on Wednesday, 2nd June A.D. 57 ; and who held him a prisoner long after he was convinced of his innocence, for something under two years, hoping to receive a bribe from him (Acts 24[26]), and at the end wishing to curry favour with the Jews, who were preferring an indictment against the departing Governor (24[27]).

At their first interview Felix merely asked him of what province he was, and then remanded him till the Jews arrived from Jerusalem. On the following Sunday came Ananias and certain presbyters, with a hired Latin lawyer named Tertullus to conduct their case. This man opened with words of gross flattery, which he thought might be acceptable to the ex-slave. Felix had indeed put down a rebellion, but had driven half the nation into disaffection.

" We thankfully acknowledge, your Excellency, the great peace which we enjoy through you, and the improvement in the state of this nation in every way and everywhere owing to your wise care." He then proceeded to indict the prisoner as a " perfect pest " (v.[5]), accusing him of stirring up sedition among the Jews all over the world as a ringleader of the Nazarene sect, and in particular of sacrilege in the Temple (vv.[5-6]).

In his reply, St. Paul first acknowledged his good fortune in being tried by a man who had been long enough in the country to understand the questions involved. This was Monday, 7th June, and he had only arrived in Jerusalem after an absence of many years on the previous Friday week, to keep Pentecost (v.[11]) and to bring alms for the poor of the place (v.[17]).

He defied his accusers to prove the charge of sacrilege or of promoting sedition in the city ; they had not seen him even talking to any one in the Temple, nor collecting a crowd in a synagogue or in the streets. He acknowledged that he belonged to what they called a " sect " ; but he believed in the Law and the Prophets ; he looked forward, as they did, to a resurrection of the righteous and unrighteous (24[15])[1] ; all he had done in the Temple was to offer certain sacrifices quietly (vv.[17-18]).[2] They

---

[1] This statement raises a serious difficulty. The Pharisees did not teach a resurrection *for the unrighteous* but only for the righteous, so far as we know. And the New Testament consistently takes the same line from beginning to end, except in John 5[28-29] and this passage, Acts 24[15]. Contrast Luke 20[35] (" those who are accounted worthy to attain to the resurrection from the dead "). It would be out of place here to discuss the difficulty at length : it must suffice to say that St. Paul here is probably speaking loosely, to convey to a heathen the belief which Christians shared with Pharisees, that good and evil men alike survive death. (I may be pardoned for referring to a fuller discussion of the point in pp. 50–56 of my book, *Death and Beyond*, Longmans, 1920).

[2] He speaks in v.[17] as if his object in visiting Jerusalem was to bring the fund for the poor and also to offer sacrifices on his own behalf in the

could prove no legal wrong against him, unless indeed what they called stirring up sedition referred to his statement before the Sanhedrin, which had been the cause of a violent split in the Council (v.[21]).

Felix, who already knew something of the Christian teaching (v.[22]), was satisfied that in general it did not involve any legal offence. But in this particular case the whole question hinged on the disturbance at Jerusalem ; and the Governor seized the pretext of wishing to question Claudius Lysias about it as an excuse for remanding the prisoner. It seems intolerable to us that he should have left him nearly two years in prison, without giving a decision one way or the other. His official reason, no doubt, was that to give him his liberty would be to endanger the public peace. St. Luke says that he used to grant St. Paul frequent interviews in the hope of getting a bribe out of him (v.[26]). The first of these was quite shortly after the trial ; Drusilla, his Jewish wife, was curious to see the man. Paul talked to them both about the Christian faith ; his earnestness in speaking of God's future judgment, of God's demand for righteousness and self-control, made Felix uneasy. In their subsequent interviews, the Apostle tried to follow up the impression he had made ; but in vain, for Felix was merely playing with him.

Of the conditions of the Apostle's life in prison we know nothing more than is recorded in Acts 24[23]. Roman Law at this time recognised three grades of imprisonment or custody : [1] first, confinement in the public gaol ; secondly, " military custody," in which the prisoner was kept in the barracks or in a room outside hired by himself

---

Temple. Probably this is literally true : he meant to offer sacrifice ; the suggestion made to him, and which he adopted, was that his sacrifice should take the form of sharing in the vow of the four men.

[1] See C.H. p. 612.

in the care of soldiers, to one of whom he was perpetually chained ; thirdly, " free custody," allowed only in cases of men of high rank, in which some magistrate guaranteed at his own risk that the prisoner should come up for trial at the proper time.

St. Paul, both at Cæsarea and in Rome, was committed to the second grade, *custodia militaris* : at Cæsarea he was confined in the *praetorium* of Herod, at Rome in a hired lodging ; in both cases his friends were allowed free access to him.

Whatever letters he wrote during the two years have perished. He probably read much ; he certainly gained in depth of spiritual insight, as the Epistles of the Roman Captivity prove. St. Luke must have spent a good deal of time with him, and it is more than probable that they were engaged together in collecting material which he after-wards embodied in his Gospel and Acts (cp. 26²⁴).

*Note on the Composition of St. Luke's Writings.*—St. Luke must have intended to write three books. In Acts 1¹ he refers to his Gospel as " the *first* treatise " (not " the former "), and he is too careful a Greek writer to have used a superlative for a comparative, whatever other New Testament writers may have done (*e.g.* St. Paul in 1 Cor. 13¹³). This conclusion is supported by the obviously unfinished conclusion to the Acts, which ends abruptly and without peroration. Therefore Acts 1¹ must have been written some years at least after A.D. 62, *i.e.* when material for a third book was already in his head.

This argument, however, would only affect the final form of the book. St. Luke probably committed to writing most of his account of St. Paul during one of the Apostle's imprisonments : and he probably collected material for the parts of his Gospel which are peculiar to him, *i.e.* especially the Peræan section, or " travel document " (Luke 9⁵¹–18¹⁴), during the two years spent at Cæsarea, probably much of it from Philip the Evangelist (see Milligan, *The New Testament Documents*, p. 138).

Even those who accept the Lucan authorship of the Gospel and Acts differ widely in the dates which they assign to the composition. Harnack (in *The Date of the Acts and of the Synoptic Gospels*) would put the Gospel about A.D. 60, and Acts about A.D. 62. Burkitt (in *The Gospel History and its Transmission*, pp. 106–120) says that the two books " can hardly be earlier than A.D. 100," because he argues that St. Luke shows signs of having read the *Antiquities* of Josephus, published in A.D. 94 ; but the proofs which he offers of this dependence on Josephus are very slight. We have noticed frequent references in St. Paul's Epistles to what he taught his converts about the sayings of Christ : St. Luke, who had shared his missionary work for so long, must by now have felt the need of a full and systematic account of Jesus' life. The two years of enforced cessation from mission work at Cæsarea gave him just the opportunity for collecting material for it.

4. St. Paul before Festus and Agrippa (Acts 24²⁷–26³²).—It was probably in A.D. 59 that Porcius Festus succeeded Felix. In St. Luke's opinion, the only reason why the departing Governor did not release Paul was that he dared not do anything to increase the animosity of the Jews against himself, for they were accusing him formally of maladministration.

Of Festus we know little except what is recorded in the Acts. He came into a regular hornets' nest, and his death after two or three years in office was perhaps brought on by perpetual worry. He seems to have had some sense of justice ; but he was in a very difficult position and allowed his desire to get on good terms at the outset with the Jewish leaders to lead him into injustice against St. Paul.

Two days after his first arrival at Cæsarea, he left for Jerusalem to meet the leaders of the nation. They begged him to bring Paul up to the capital for trial[1] as a notorious offender against all that they held sacred, and a fomenter of sedition. Festus was quite ignorant of Jewish law and religion, and might be expected to grant their request. Some of them had determined that, if he did, his prisoner should never reach Jerusalem alive. The Governor seems to have been without suspicion of this plan ; but, after all, he must maintain his dignity, however anxious he was to placate them : he was only in Jerusalem for little more than a week, and had to hurry back to receive a State visit from his neighbour, King Agrippa II. On this ground he refused to do what they asked, and told them to detail some of their leading men to accompany him to Cæsarea and lay a regular indictment against Paul.

He lost no time. The trial took place the day after his return ; St. Luke gives no details of it, no doubt because it followed much the same lines as two years earlier. The Governor soon saw that the prisoner was innocent of treason against the State (25²⁵) ; but he was most unwilling to offend the Jews at the start of his office. He could not judge how far the Apostle had really imperilled the public peace by a wanton outrage against the national religion. It might be well, after all, to try the man in Jerusalem in the presence of the Jewish Council.

But there was a difficulty. A Roman citizen could claim exemption from their jurisdiction ;[2] it might legalise the trial if he in person were the judge. Yet if it were known to the Roman authorities that he had compelled a

---

[1] Festus, in his account of this to Agrippa (Acts 25¹⁵⁻¹⁶), makes out that they had asked him to hand over the prisoner to them without trial, and that he had peremptorily refused such an unjust request. But this is possibly a deliberate perversion of the facts, designed to impress the wily Herod.

[2] See Burrows in Hast. *D.B.*, art. "Appeal."

citizen to plead his case before the Jewish court, it might
easily be represented as an illegal and tyrannous act.  So
he thought it wise to give the prisoner his choice : " Will
you go up to Jerusalem and stand your trial before me on
these charges ? "  The alternative implied is that of
indefinite detention in the Cæsarean prison.

St. Paul was deeply incensed at the injustice : was he
always to be a mere pawn in the Governor's game with
the Jews ?  " I stand (now) at the bar of Cæsar, where
I ought to be judged. . . . To the Jews I have done no
wrong, as you very well know. . . . I appeal to Cæsar
himself."  So he took a course which perhaps he would
have taken long before but for his unwillingness to em-
bitter Jewish feeling against himself by an appeal to the
hated foreigner (cp. Acts 28[19], " I was *compelled* to appeal ").
Apparently at this time a provincial governor could refuse
to allow an appeal to the Emperor if he were convinced of
the prisoner's guilt,[1] but he did so at some risk to himself.
Felix consulted with his legal assessors (vv.[12. 25]) : they
agreed that no major crime had been proved against him,
and so the appeal was allowed.

Festus was not out of the wood yet.  He had no clear
idea how he should formulate the charges in forwarding the
prisoner to Rome (25[26. 27]) ; it was all " questions about
their own religion, and about a certain Jesus as being dead,
whom Paul asserted to be alive " (v.[19]).  However, in a
few days King Agrippa was due to arrive with his sister
Bernice : they would understand the matter if he referred
it to them.

Agrippa II. was great-grandson of Herod the Great, the
Edomite who by unscrupulous cunning and determination
had won such worldly splendour.  Caligula had granted
to his father, Agrippa I., the title of King.  He was only

[1] So Burrows in Hast. *D.B.*, art. " Appeal," relying on Suetonius,
*Galba,* 9.

seventeen years old when his father died ; and Claudius, thinking him too young to succeed, kept him at the Imperial Court in Rome. The wily Herod soon worked his way into the Emperor's favour, and was given various principalities in the north of Palestine. Before long he managed to extend his rule over all the territory north of a line drawn westward from the Sea of Galilee to the borders of Phœnicia, as well as the country east and south-east of that lake. Clever, indolent, and dissolute, he pursued a pro-Roman policy all through the Jewish rebellion of A.D. 66–70, and lived on at Rome for nearly thirty years after the fall of Jerusalem.

His sister Bernice had all the beauty and more than all the profligacy of the women of her house. She had deserted her second husband, the king of native or western Cilicia, and was now living with Agrippa. Afterwards, when Titus came to Palestine in the Jewish rebellion he became enamoured of her.[1]

Such was the pair before whom the great Apostle was now to appear. Agrippa had for some time wished to see and hear him (Acts 25²²), and welcomed the chance. The trial was a scene of brilliant pageantry, attended by the Roman military chiefs as well as by the prominent civilians of the town. St. Paul had a great opening and took it ; with moderation and courtesy unmixed with flattery he made his defence. After expressing his sense of good fortune in being able to plead before a king who knew the Jewish religion, he maintained that all he taught and believed was a direct fulfilment of the promises and hopes held out to their forefathers in the Old Testament (26⁶⁻⁷. ²²⁻²³). He told again the story of his conversion, when the " heavenly vision " opened his eyes and sent him to preach among the Gentiles (vv.¹⁷⁻¹⁹).

Festus listened in growing perplexity : this Jew, who

[1] See Suetonius, *Titus*, 7.

had spent much time in prison poring over books, who seemed to a Roman soldier to have a terrible store of " learning," was calmly telling them of an incredible vision, and finally of a man raised from the dead ! He called out loudly, " Paul, you are mad ; your long study is driving you to madness." Paul appealed to the King ; *he* must have heard the story of Jesus when it happened ; he knew the prophets who had foretold it : " You believe the prophets, King Agrippa ? I know you do." But the Herod turned it off with an ironical jest : " You think you can make me a Christian all in a minute,[1] as you tell us you became one."

When it was over, Agrippa advised the Governor privately that the Jewish accusations would not hold water and the prisoner deserved his release. But it was too late now to make this tardy reparation : Paul had appealed to Cæsar, and to Cæsar he must go.[2]

5. THE VOYAGE TO ROME (Acts 27–28[14]).—We are fortunate in having a modern book on St. Paul's voyage and shipwreck by a man who was both an authority on naval matters and knew the Mediterranean thoroughly.

---

[1] ἐν ὀλίγῳ may mean (1) " in a short time," or (2) " by a short argument." In St. Paul's answer ἐν μεγάλῳ can scarcely mean " in a long time," but may denote, " by a long argument." However, he may be playing upon Agrippa's words : " I would to God that both in little and in great . . ."—*i.e.* in all respects. So Thayer, who compares ὀλίγον καὶ μέγα in Plato to express totality. The text of Agrippa's words is in confusion : ποιῆσαι (א A B) has much stronger MSS evidence than γενέσθαι (the Latin versions with the later Greek MSS) : but if we accept it, we are bound to give up πείθεις and read πείθῃ (" you are confident of making ") with A.

[2] Canon Gray makes the interesting suggestion that St. Paul would not accept his release. " He had firmly resolved to obtain the verdict of the Supreme Court. He was confident that it must be in his favour, and be final for him and probably other Christian preachers. He was so convinced of the result and so sure of its importance, that he grudged neither time nor money in the prosecution of this appeal."

James Smith of Jordanhill published his *Voyage and Shipwreck of St. Paul* as long ago as 1856, but it is still the classical work on the subject. He has shown not only that St. Luke's account conforms to all we know of ancient ships, but that it considerably extends our knowledge.[1]

It was probably in August, A.D. 59, that the Apostle was handed over to a Roman centurion who was sailing from Cæsarea to Italy with a number of prisoners. The latter were in all likelihood criminals condemned to death, who were often sent to amuse the populace at Rome by being exposed to wild beasts in the arena (cp. 1 Cor. 4[9]).

The centurion Julius belonged to the "Augustan" or "Imperial" cohort (27[1]).[2] This name has raised a difficulty, because cohorts of a Roman legion did not receive names. Mommsen, however, has perhaps supplied the solution : the later Emperors organised a service of officer-couriers, with their headquarters on the Cælian Hill in Rome ; they were on detached duty, and were sent to and fro between the Emperor and his legions on foreign service : they acted as messengers for all manner of purposes ; in particular it was their duty to superintend the regular supply of corn for the Imperial City, which was as entirely dependent on foreign sources as England is to-day ; they also fulfilled police duties, such as were assigned to Julius. They were known as "frumentarii" (corn officers) or "peregrini" (officers for foreign service) ; but they may

[1] It should be noticed that subsequent references in this chapter are to the fourth edition published in 1880.

[2] Josephus, in *Antiq.*, xx. 6. 1, speaks of Cumanus as taking with him a military force consisting of τὴν τῶν Σεβαστηνῶν εἴλην. At this time "cohortes alariæ" was a name given to the foreign troops serving along with the Roman armies, while Sebaste was Herod's name for Samaria. Is it possible that here in Acts we ought to translate the words as "cohort of Sebaste" ? On the other hand, Thayer takes "Augustan" as a title of honour given to certain legions or cohorts, on the strength of an Inscription (*Corpus inscrr. Lat.*, vii. n. 340, 341, 344), "ala augusta ob virtutem appellata."

also have been called the " Imperial cohort." Mommsen maintains that they had been organised by Augustus and therefore were in existence at this date.

Julius embarked on a boat sailing for Adramyttium, near Troas ; she was to call at the seaports of Asia, at one of which he hoped to find a ship sailing for Italy. St. Paul was allowed to take with him Luke and Aristarchus. Now we know from Pliny [1] that even a man's wife was not allowed to accompany him in such circumstances. Therefore if this rule was universal, Luke and Aristarchus must have passed as the Apostle's slaves, unless indeed Luke shipped as doctor. [2]

In the summer the west wind blows persistently in the Levant. An ancient ship had only one large mast amidships, with one large square sail (though a small storm-sail or ἀρτέμων was often rigged up in the bows, as may be seen from the illustrations of ancient ships in Smith) ; therefore it could not sail close to the wind. In going from Cæsarea to Asia at this time of year it was usual to head north-north-west, under the lee of the east coast of Cyprus ; and so they did in this case (27[4]). When they reached the Cilician coast, they would find land breezes to help them and a current that sets westward (*i.e.* a backwash). So they hugged the coast along past Pamphylia to the port of Myra (taking a fortnight from the time they reached the Cilician coast, according to some manuscripts). [3]

In the harbour at Myra was a large vessel bound from Alexandria to Italy (27[6]). It was one of the Imperial corn-fleet [4] and therefore Julius could demand a passage.

---

[1] Pliny, *Epist.* iii. 16 (quoted by Ramsay, *T. and R.C.* p. 316).

[2] So Harnack, *Luke*, 148 and 181. Harnack quotes Acts 27[3] as proof that St. Paul was in bad health : he was allowed to land at Sidon to " obtain attention " (ἐπιμέλεια, which is the technical word for medical attention).

[3] Chiefly the old Latin h and the Harclean Syriac.

[4] This is confirmed by the authority which Julius had over the captain (27[11]).

Grain is a dangerous cargo in rough weather because of its liability to shift : but the size of the boat, which could take two hundred and seventy-six persons on board (v.[37]), made her tolerably safe.[1] She had followed the usual course in heading due north from Alexandria to Myra because of the prevalent west wind. She was now turned due west, hoping for a straight run across the Ægean and past the south coast of the Peloponnese.

But the headwind still held.[2] She found difficulty in making Cnidus (about 140 miles) ; but there she had to leave the shelter of the land and put out to sea. She could not sail in the teeth of it ; so they set her course for Cape Salmone, the eastern promontory of Crete, which lay south-west by south. The Cretan mountains are high, and the south coast of the island trends a little south of west as far as Cape Matala, which is almost in the middle of it. Even so, they found some difficulty in making a port called then (as now) Fair Havens, 6 miles to the east of Cape Matala (27[8]). Here the centurion and the captain held a council to decide what should be done ; it was already early October,[3] the equinoctial gales made sailing dangerous ; and there was scarcely a month to the recognised date for laying up all ships for the winter (11th

---

[1] W.H. read 76, but this number seems too small. Lucian, in *The Ship or Wishes*, tells a story of one of the Alexandrian wheat ships which in Commodus' reign was driven by stress of weather into the Piræus, and of the amazement of the Athenians at her size. It is calculated that this ship of Lucian's was probably between 1000 and 1300 tons, from the dimensions which he gives. Similarly the ship on which Josephus was wrecked, had 600 people on board. See J. Smith, pp. 181–2, 187–190.

[2] In the Ægean Sea the north-west is the prevailing wind in summer, and specially after the beginning of August. See J. Smith, pp. 76, 80. He quotes Pliny, *Lib.* ii. cap. 4, and Sir James Saumarez writing in 1798.

[3] See v.[9]. The Fast (Day of Atonement) in 59 fell on 5th October. Tabernacles fell on 10th October ; so presumably we should date the Council between 5th and 10th October.

November). They could no longer hope to reach Italy that season ; the question was where they should winter.

St. Paul was admitted to their council. His position would secure him very different treatment to that of the criminals on board ; and he had already won the confidence of Julius to some extent. Perhaps his experience of the Levantine seas led him to apprehend danger.[1] At any rate, he urged the wisdom of staying where they were. But Fair Havens was not a secure port in all winds (v.[12]) ; and 40 miles to the west lay Phœnix, the modern Lutro,[2] which faces east and has an island across its mouth. " Lutro," says Captain Spratt (in James Smith, p. 92 note), " is the only bay to the westward of Fair Havens in which a vessel of any size could find shelter during the winter months " : inside its harbour " a vessel is nearly land-locked." If they could only round Cape Matala and negotiate the open bay beyond, they could lie snugly in this port all winter. It was natural that Julius should be guided by the pilot and captain.[3] The majority of those present concurred in his decision.

Fortune seemed to favour them, for the wind went round

---

[1] St. Luke seems to regard his warning as supernaturally given to him.

[2] St. Luke in v.[12] describes Phœnix as a port " looking south-west and north-west " ; for that is the only possible meaning of his words (in spite of the R.V.). Luke never went there, and is only speaking by report. Wordsworth has shown that, just west of Lutro, there is a harbour actually facing south-west and north-west, and it is to-day marked Phenika on the Admiralty chart : he would suggest that this is really the port which St. Luke means. But competent modern observers seem to agree that Lutro is the only really safe harbour on that part of the coast. See Ramsay, Hast. D.B., art. " Phœnix."

[3] ναύκληρος sometimes means " owner of a ship." But if it means that here, the ship did not belong to the Government ; in that case, it is hard to see why the centurion rather than the owner should decide the question where they were to winter. The captain was sometimes called ναύκληρος (see Liddell and Scott's Dictionary, and Ramsay, T. and R.C., p. 324, with the Inscription he quotes in Note 2).

to the south. So they set sail and hugged the coast as far as Cape Matala. On the western side of it the coast-line runs to the north of west : here in the bay of Messaria, with the peaks of Ida towering 7000 feet above them, a fierce hurricane came rushing down on them from the mountains without warning. These dangerous gusts are familiar to any one who has sailed along a mountainous shore ; and in these waters we are told that the wind usually veers from the south round to the north, bringing a gale. St. Luke's language reflects the excitement, " down rushed a typhonic wind called Euraquilo " (north-easter, or, in this case, north-north-easter), " and caught the ship." They were driven out to sea before it, till they reached the Isle of Cauda (now Gavdo), 23 miles to the south-west. As soon as they got into smoother water, under the lee of the island, some of them were told off to haul in the ship's boat which had been towed astern : it was half full of water and it was no easy matter to hoist it on board. But a more serious danger than even the loss of their one boat revealed itself : the ship's timbers had sprung a leak under the strain on the main-mast. Their next task was to " frap " her, by passing ropes transversely round the hull.[1]  After that, they had to consider their future course. If they ran before the wind, it would take them straight on to the famous and deadly quicksands called Syrtis, which lay on the African coast at a distance of between 300 and 400 miles. So they furled the main-sail (" lowered the gear," v.[17]) : this would bring the head of the ship round to the north-west. Next they hoisted a small foresail ($\dot{a}\rho\tau\acute{\epsilon}\mu\omega\nu$, v.[40]) either on the

---

[1] As they did in the case of the *Royal George*. It can be done without lowering a boat. So James Smith understands the words in 27[17]. Others speak of ropes passed round her horizontally near the water-line, but this is incredible. The word $\beta o\eta\theta\epsilon\iota a\iota\varsigma$ for the ropes is perhaps a medical term (see Furneaux, *Acts*, p. 397) ; but some editors adopt Naber's emendation $\beta o\epsilon\iota a\iota\varsigma$, " ropes."

main-mast itself or more probably on some jury-mast in the bows (cp. Juvenal, 12. 68, and see illustrations in Smith), which would keep her drifting west-north-west, that is, on the starboard tack (with the wind on her right). This left them broadside on to the waves, but it gave them the course which they wanted.

The ship was terribly battered (v.[18]), and there was imminent danger of the corn in her hold shifting. So next day they threw overboard a good deal of the cargo : twenty-four hours later they jettisoned " with their own hands " (*i.e.* in spite of their reluctance) all the fittings which they could possibly spare.[1]

But day after day the gale held. They had to be constantly baling her out, and the strain told heavily on them. Everything was soaked, and they could not cook proper meals. So despair and apathy began to prevail. But nothing of this sort could daunt the great Apostle : God sustained him by the conviction that he would bear his witness at Rome ; and if his life was safe, then all on board were surely safe too.[2] In the night he dreamed that an angel came to assure him it would be so. Next morning he told the crew and bade them cheer up ; and they felt that the brave little Jew with the bright face had indeed received a divine oracle.

They had no notion where they were. It was many days since they had seen the sun or stars to take a reckoning (v.[20]). They seemed to be drifting helplessly about (v.[27]) at the mercy of shifting winds in the " sea of Adria " [3] :

[1] Probably the " top-hamper," *i.e.* fittings above the water-line, the weight of which would make her roll. I owe this suggestion and others in this section to Lieutenant Pakenham, R.N.

[2] Luke adds in v.[26] that Paul foretold the shipwreck on an island : this may be a *post-factum* addition.

[3] This use of the name Adriatic has occasioned some difficulty. But the geographer Ptolemy distinguishes the " gulf of Adria," which is the modern Adriatic Sea, from " the Adriatic Sea " which in his time was the name given to that part of the Mediterranean lying between Sicily and Crete (Ramsay, *T. and R.C.*, 334).

as a matter of fact they must have followed a fairly straight
course just north of west. It is 480 miles from Cauda to
Malta, and they struck the Maltese coast on the thirteenth
evening out from Crete ; that is to say, they drifted about
40 miles a day, or one and a half knots an hour, which is
just about what a ship would do in a high wind on this tack.

St. Paul's Bay, the traditional scene of the shipwreck,
fits in with every detail given by St. Luke, except that
there is *now* no sandy beach visible on its west side (v.[39]).
It lies on the north side of Malta and runs into the land in a
south-westerly direction. On the east of it (the side from
which they would approach) is a rocky promontory called
Kaura Point : opposite on the west side lies the small isle
of Salmonetta, with a narrow channel separating it from
the shore.

It was about midnight when the sailors " suspected
land was near " (v.[27]) ; probably they heard the breakers
dashing on Kaura (cp. " the rocks," v.[29]). They took
sounding, and found bottom, first at twenty fathoms, then
at fifteen. The same depths are found in St. Paul's Bay
to-day, going west from Kaura Point. They were clearly
approaching some unknown shore ; so they resolved
to anchor till daylight. They dropped four anchors over
the stern, so that her bow in that wind would swing round
straight for the beach to the west.[1]

Times of crisis test human nature to the bottom.
Paul's greatness, based on unswerving faith in God,

---

[1] In ancient, as in modern, times ships were usually anchored by the
bow (see James Smith, p. 133), because it is much easier to arrest
a ship's way by the bow than by the stern. But if the vessel had been
so anchored on this occasion, she would have swung round with her
head out to sea. On p. 135, James Smith gives an interesting illustration of an ancient ship anchored by the stern. It must be remembered
that in that age the bow and stern were much the same shape. In
St. Paul's Bay, we are told, " the anchors will never start " (*Sailing
Directions*, quoted by Smith, p. 132).

stands out in vivid contrast to the behaviour of the sailors and soldiers. First the crew, well knowing that if it came to a wreck, the solitary boat on board could hold very few, launched it on the pretext of laying out anchors from the bow : the Apostle saw that they meant to save their own lives and desert the rest ; so he told the centurion and his soldiers. They at once cut the boat adrift before the sailors could embark : it says much for the ascendancy which he had won over Julius and his men, that they unhesitatingly believed his assurance of safety for all and sacrificed the boat. Indeed he took the lead in everything : just before dawn, when human vitality is lowest and men are inclined to despair, he made them all take food to cheer them, protesting again that " not a hair of your heads will perish."

Their best hope, now that they had lost the boat, was to beach the ship in as shallow water as possible; so they spent their time in throwing the rest of the wheat into the sea.

When day broke, they noticed what looked like a creek with a sandy beach, probably the narrow passage between the isle of Salmonetta and the Maltese shore. They resolved to drive her ashore there. Ancient rudders were not slung like ours, but consisted of two broad paddles fixed through a hole in the bulwarks, one on each side of the stern, which were hoisted on board when at anchor [1] : they now let them down to steer by. They cut the cables and raised the foresail, and headed her for the seeming creek. She struck on a bank (" place where two seas meet "), probably the reef between Salmonetta and the shore. There is thick tenacious clay near shore in the traditional spot. It was now a question of *sauve qui peut* ; but the soldiers were answerable with their lives for the safe custody of the prisoners, and with the instinct of self-preservation resolved to kill them all forthwith. Julius,

[1] Similar rudders were used down to the middle of the thirteenth century, and may be seen on the Bayeux tapestry (Smith, p. 186).

however, was made of finer stuff : though he would forfeit his life if any escaped, he was determined at all costs to save Paul. True he might let them kill the others, who were condemned criminals ; but they were in no mood to listen to orders, and they might murder Paul if they once began the slaughter. With quick presence of mind, he shouted to every one to jump overboard and get to land as best he could. In one way or another they all came safe ashore.[1]

The island of Malta, on which they found themselves, lies 80 miles south of Sicily : it had an ancient civilisation ; for it was colonised first by the Phœnicians, and then came under Greek and Roman rule successively. When St. Luke calls the inhabitants " barbarians," he is only using the Greek term for any foreigners ; it answers to our word " natives." They spoke Greek ; so intercourse was easy.

St. Paul's Bay was not near any town : the Maltese who had gathered on the shore were cottage folk. It was cold November weather and pelting with rain ; but they did all they could for the strangers. They lit a big bonfire to dry their clothes. The Apostle had helped to gather sticks and was putting them on the fire, when a viper, which was hibernating among them, was roused by the heat and fastened on his hand.[2]

But there are no vipers on Malta to-day, and in any case vipers do not fasten on a man's hand before biting, as we are told this snake did (v.[4]). Therefore, Ramsay has suggested that it was not a viper, but a small species of constrictor (*Coronella austriaca*) which is still found on the island ; it does fasten on the human arm, but its bite is harmless as it has no poison-fangs.

[1] Furneaux (p. 401) points out that the gale had apparently abated ; see vv.[30, 40] ; also the rain (28[2]) shows that the wind had gone down.

[2] However, Harnack shows that καθῆψεν is a medical word for poison taking effect, and he argues that it ought not to be translated " fastened on," but " bit." For the whole subject, see Ramsay, *Luke the Physician*, pp. 63–65.

This suggestion, though adopted by several modern editors, only increases the difficulty. For if there were no poisonous snakes on Malta, the *natives* could not have mistaken this one for a viper. St. Luke indeed might have made the mistake ; but in that case we are driven to the incredible supposition that all he records in vv.[4-6] is a figment of his imagination ! He was himself present : he overheard the natives saying, " This man certainly must be a murderer who has escaped from the sea but whom justice will not allow to live " : he saw them watch the Apostle, expecting him to swell up or to drop down dead at once : he listened to their cries of astonishment when nothing happened and they hailed him as a god. All this bears the stamp of authenticity. There must have been vipers on Malta 1900 years ago ; it is natural that they should have been exterminated now, when all woods on the island have been cleared away. And though a viper may not wrap itself round a man's arm when it is on the ground, it is a very different case when the animal tumbles on to his arm out of some sticks which he is holding.[1]

The shipwrecked mariners were quartered for the night in the farmsteads about. But Julius was offered hospitality in a large house belonging to a man called Publius,[2] whom St. Luke styles the " primate " of the island, a title which a Maltese inscription proves to be correct. The centurion took Paul with him and they stayed there a couple of days while they arranged for a permanent billet all through the winter months. The primate's father was ill with " low fever and dysentery " (the words are technically correct) and Paul healed him. The result was that

---

[1] I consulted on this point Professor Stanley Gardiner, Professor of Zoology at Cambridge, and he confirms the statements made in the last two sentences of the paragraph.

[2] A magistrate would not be known by his praenomen except by his familiar friends : so some suppose that his name was Popilius : but if so, we must *read* Ποπίλιος. Πόπλιος can only mean Publius.

during the three months of their stay on the island (November to February) many sick folk were brought to him and St. Luke; and in their gratitude they made the Christians many presents of things they needed, for they had probably lost all their belongings in the wreck.

Another large corn-ship from Alexandria was wintering at the island: she was called the *Dioscuri*, that is, the Twins, Castor and Pollux. They were the patron deities of sailors; for the blue electric incandescence, which in thundery weather is sometimes seen playing round the masthead at sea, was interpreted as a proof of their protection. This ship was sailing for Puteoli, where at this time the corn-fleet probably discharged their cargoes (rather than at Ostia); and she was large enough to accommodate Julius with his soldiers and prisoners. They sailed on her north to Syracuse in the south-east of Sicily, where they stayed for two days. There is a crypt under the Church of St. John there, dating from the fourth century, and tradition says that St. Paul preached in it. Setting sail again, they had to tack up against the wind [1] to reach Rhegium on the Italian side of the Strait of Messina. But the next day a southerly breeze was blowing, and they ran before it up through the narrowest part of the strait with its dangerous current between the rocks of Scylla and Charybdis, and all the way to Puteoli, 182 miles in one day. The latter is a town situated on the Bay of Naples, west of the city, and was now the chief port of Rome though it was 130 miles away.

When they landed, Julius apparently decided to remain there for six days. St. Paul discovered a small Christian community in the place who invited him to stay with them; and the centurion had such confidence in his prisoner that he gave his consent.

[1] Reading περιελθόντες in 28¹², with the mass of ancient authorities. περιελόντες (א B) means " casting off."

At the end of this time he marshalled all the prisoners and set out for the capital. For a few miles their way lay inland to Capua ; there they struck the great Appian Way from Brindisi to Rome. Meanwhile the Christians in the city had learnt of his approach, and in their enthusiasm they walked out to meet him—one party to Appii Forum, 40 miles from Rome, and another to the Three Taverns, 33 miles away. St. Paul's spirits were overclouded by a natural anxiety about the future : but his meeting with these warm-hearted friends made him forget his fears ; " he thanked God and took courage." " So we came to Rome," [1] the great climax of his life and of St. Luke's history.

The later Greek manuscripts borrowed from the old Latin Version an addition to v.[16], which has no claim to be genuine, but which no doubt records a fact : they state that Julius handed over his prisoners to the στρατοπεδάρχης (military commander). This term is usually interpreted as denoting the prefect of the prætorian guard, who were stationed in barracks outside the city, on the Viminal Hill, and were now commanded by the celebrated Burrus,[2] famous for his integrity. Early in the second century Trajan, in his famous rescript to Pliny, governor of Bithynia, orders him to send condemned Christians in chains to Rome, and hand them over " to the prefects of my prætorian guard." [3]

Mommsen, however, pointed out that one old Latin

[1] These words are put in v.[14], anticipating the meeting at Appii Forum, etc. It is as if St. Luke could not contain his sense of the climax. Rome brings to his mind the incident of the local Christians, and he adds the latter as an afterthought.

[2] After A.D. 62 there were two prefects. The Emperor usually deputed to them (or one of them) the duty of hearing appeal cases ; very probably Burrus tried St. Paul.

[3] Pliny, *Epist.* x. 65 (quoted by Page). This rescript gives very strong support to the usual view.

version (Codex Gigas) in Acts 28[16] gives "princeps peregrinorum"—that is, the commander of the officers for foreign service (see p. 296) to whom Julius perhaps belonged, and whose barracks were on the Cælian Hill in the city.

6. THE FIRST ROMAN IMPRISONMENT.—St. Paul was allowed to live in a hired lodging, where he was free to receive any visitors he liked, though bound day and night to a soldier. He lost no time in inviting the leaders of the Jewish community at Rome to come and see him. He told them that he was driven against his will to appeal to Cæsar (v.[19]), but made it clear that he had no charge to bring against his own nation. He affirmed again to them that his imprisonment was due to his belief in the Messianic hope of Israel. Their reply was non-committal : the Christian " sect " was spoken against on all hands, but they knew nothing against the Apostle personally. So they agreed to meet at his quarters on a fixed day and hear what he had to say about Jesus fulfilling the Messianic prophecies. In the end some of them were convinced by his message ; but the majority refused it, and so once more at Rome he felt free to preach mainly to the Gentiles.

Timothy soon came to join him in the work (Phil. 2[19]), and Mark (Col. 4[10]), and Tychicus the Ephesian.

It was perhaps a year later that St. Paul sent three letters to Asia by the hand of Tychicus. At Colossæ, a place on the great Asian trade-route in the valley of the Lycus, which is a tributary of the Mæander, lived a Christian named Philemon, who had been converted by the Apostle at Ephesus. He had a slave, Onesimus, who ran away and found his way to Rome, and there by a strange guidance found his way to the Apostle's prison and was himself converted. Paul persuaded the man to return to his master, sending with him a private letter to

Philemon, in which he urges him to receive the runaway with gentle forgiveness as a Christian brother.

But news had come from the same town of Colossæ of a new and dangerous superstition which had sprung up there. One of the miseries of heathenism lay in the multiplicity of gods and demons who thronged the daily life of men, demanding each his own due veneration. Every activity had its appropriate demi-god who alone could bring success : every pleasure attracted some jealous demon who would ruin it unless he were appeased. It was an atmosphere of fear, as superstition always is. Apparently the converts at Colossæ had taken over many of these cults into their Christianity, only calling the demons angels. Religion was loaded with a terrible mass of holy days and taboos ; all material things seemed to be inherently evil, and asceticism was enjoined.

So Paul sent a letter to the Colossian Church by Tychicus, bidding them look up only to Jesus Christ. The Lord has the fulness of deity ; Christians have nothing to do with any lesser spirits, good or evil ; there is only one Lord for them.

Still a third letter he sent by Tychicus. This was a general Epistle addressed to the Churches of Asia, though it has come down to us bearing the title " to the Ephesians." In it he refers in several places to the heresy which was prevalent at Colossæ and which no doubt affected other Churches to some extent. But in the main it has a grander theme, and is the complement to the Epistle to the Romans. He sets himself to work out, in labouring sentences which can scarcely express the spiritual grandeur of his thought, the subject of unity in Christ. Like the Roman Empire with its many differing peoples and its varied modes of government adapted to each people, the Christian Church is composed of divers members, with their manifold traditions and temperamental gifts : but all are one in Christ, who sums them all up in Himself : the very diversity of the parts brings a richer life to the unity of the whole.

Some time later, the Christians of Philippi, who had heard of the Apostle's plight, sent one of their number, called Epaphroditus, to convey to him a gift in money which was timely. Epaphroditus stayed on in Rome for a while, but ultimately fell seriously ill, perhaps with Roman fever. Paul sent him back home with a warm letter of thanks to the Philippians, the most joyous, affectionate, and warm-hearted of his extant Epistles, though the note of joy is dominant in all the letters of the first Roman imprisonment. He makes no mention of Luke and Aristarchus ; so they had probably gone off on some mission ; perhaps it was they who, passing through Philippi, had told of the Apostle's fate.

But the Apostle in his Roman prison did not confine himself to writing letters. Day in, day out, he was bound to a Roman soldier, and to many of them he must have told his message.[1] Nor was his influence confined to them. Many outsiders, from a variety of motives, found their way to his prison lodging ; and his inspiration gave a new enthusiasm to the Roman Christians (Phil. 1[13-14]). Christianity even won some ardent adherents in the house of Cæsar himself (Phil. 4[22]).

St. Luke ends his history by telling us that St. Paul remained in confinement a full two years (Acts 28[30]), but

---

[1] Perhaps Phil. 1[13] is direct evidence of this, if the old rendering be right, " My bonds have become notorious in Christ in all the prætorian guard." But we have mentioned, on p. 307 above, the doubt as to whether he was handed over to the prætorian guard or to the foreign corps. Mommsen and Ramsay take " prætorium " in Phil. 1[13] to mean the supreme assize-court of the Emperor, which was presided over by the prefect or prefects of the prætorian guard. In that case St. Paul is referring to a preliminary trial before the court.

always preaching the Kingdom of God and the message
of Christ without hindrance. Those were years of dark
disappointment to the Roman world without. Nero, who
had come to the throne in A.D. 54 at the age of seventeen,
had given great promise at first. His tutor Seneca,
Gallio's brother, was the most enlightened heathen of his
age ; and though he had something of the practical weakness which is apt to beset a philosopher, he dominated the
young Emperor for five years more, and it was the golden
age of the Empire. But, a year before St. Paul came to
Rome, Nero began his career of crime by murdering his
vicious mother. He was already engaged in a love intrigue
with Poppæa, a Jewess by religion, whom he married in
A.D. 62. And though Seneca retained some power till
A.D. 63, his master's vileness and cruel caprices were
already the despair of the Imperial City. St. Paul, however, as we shall see, was probably acquitted and set free
by the beginning of A.D. 62, two years before Nero's ghastly
persecution of the Christians which has made his name the
symbol of lasting infamy.

# CHAPTER XIV.

## THE EPISTLE TO THE COLOSSIANS.

[See general remarks on p. 309.]

1. GENUINENESS.—In post-Apostolic literature there is no clear reference to the Epistle before the middle of the second century (Marcion). This is entirely natural, for the letter is addressed to a small Church in an insignificant town. The whole style is Pauline : there can be no doubt on that score. The whole tone is utterly unlike that of a second-century forger, who would have indulged in fierce invective. The number of individual Christians, mentioned in chap. 4 with circumstantial details, is a strong sign of genuineness. Nor would a forger have selected such a little-known Church as that of Colossæ. Moreover, the Epistle hangs closely together with that " to the Ephesians," the Pauline authorship of which is strongly attested in early post-Apostolic literature. Phrases and even whole verses are found common to the two Epistles, and these fit so naturally into their context that they can scarcely be due, in either Epistle, to a forger plagiarising from a genuine letter of St. Paul. Both letters presuppose a common date and similar circumstances. We must add a third, the letter to Philemon, where St. Paul is also in prison and has the same companions, notably Epaphras, the founder of the Churches in Colossæ and the neighbouring towns. " Philemon " was clearly carried by Tychicus to the province of Asia along with the other two letters in which he is mentioned as messenger (Col. 4[7], Eph. 6[21]).

The Christology of Colossians is advanced (see $1^{18-20}$) : but it is closely paralleled in Phil. $2^{6-11}$, and by many phrases in the Epistles of the second group (especially Corinthians).

Those who question the Pauline authorship of Colossians rest their case mainly on two suppositions—first, that it is directed against Gnostic speculations, and secondly that such theories did not exist before the second century. But the Colossian speculations were not Gnostic, though they had elements in common with Gnosticism (see below, § 3) : indeed Marcion, the great Christian Gnostic of the second century, accepted this Epistle though he ruled out of his Bible anything which made against his own views. And even if Gnosticism were attacked in the letter, it would not prove a second-century date : Gnostic tendencies were no sudden growth, but have their roots in Oriental speculations of much more ancient origin (cp. Acts $8^{10}$).

2. DATE AND PLACE OF WRITING.—Everything points to the first Roman imprisonment. St. Paul is in confinement ($4^{3.\ 18}$ $1^{24}$) but is free to receive his friends and to preach ($1^{28-29}$ $4^3$ $4^{10-15}$). This points to Rome rather than Cæsarea, for :

> (a) Onesimus, the runaway Colossian slave, is with him ($4^9$) : now a runaway would naturally make for Rome on board some vessel, much as our fugitives from justice try to hide themselves in London. It is highly improbable that he would go from Asia to Cæsarea :

> (b) the large number of St. Paul's companions, who nevertheless included only two Jewish Christians ($4^{11}$), suggests Rome rather than Cæsarea. And in the latter place it is doubtful whether the Apostle was free to preach.

Therefore everything points to the first Roman imprisonment, and to the second year of it rather than the first ; for St. Paul had been joined by a number of friends from the East (chap. 4) ; and he is looking forward with some confidence to a speedy release (Philem. v.[22]).

3. OCCASION AND SUBJECT-MATTER.—News of the Colossian Church had been brought to Rome by Epaphras, its founder (1[7]). He reported that many of the local Christians felt dissatisfied with the Pauline gospel : it was too simple and elementary for their taste. How could Paul, rushing on from one place to another without waiting to consolidate his work, give advanced instruction to his converts ? This seems to have been their criticism of Epaphras' teaching (see 1[25-29] 2[4-5]). So they sought to graft various Oriental beliefs and speculations on to the Gospel.

The characteristics of this " deeper " teaching are as follows :

(a) It lays claim to a philosophical basis. Its exponents pride themselves on being an " intellectual oligarchy " (Lgt.), professing to have a fuller insight into truth. Against them St. Paul insists on the *fulness* ($\pi\lambda\acute{\eta}\rho\omega\mu\alpha$) of his Gospel " in Christ." Their philosophy (2[8]) was clearly *dualistic, i.e.* based on the old Eastern belief that matter is essentially evil, and the body with all its feelings thoroughly bad. Ethically, therefore, they upheld asceticism.

(b) Secondly, they pursued an elaborate *cult of angels* (2[18]). A considerable difference of opinion exists as to the origin and exact nature of this. It is surely obvious that St. Paul did not regard this cult as idolatrous, or he would have written against it in far more severe terms. He treats it as a silly superstition, distracting men from the weighty things of true religion, and leading them to squander time and attention on propitiating a host of supernatural beings. It ruined the Christian atmosphere of peace and trust in Christ ; it introduced an element of fear (see p. 309).

There can be little doubt that they gave Jewish names to their hierarchy of angels ; for among their elaborate list of holy days we find mention of the Sabbath and the new moon feast ($2^{16}$). But the question is this : have we here a *Jewish* system, akin to that in vogue among the Essenes of Palestine and transplanted into Colossæ ? or is it an old *heathen* cult surviving in a Jewish dress ?

The latter is surely the convincing view. Again and again in the Christian Church we find heathen deities and demons either emerging as Christian saints and angels or merely surviving as fairies. St. Bridget is the old goddess of the Brigantes : St. George who fought the dragon is the Semitic Bel. The heathen feared [1] a host of demons who swarmed in the air round him, some with power over one act and some over another, so that the appropriate spirit must be invoked at every turn. In many cases these demons are the direct ancestors of Christian saints as invoked (shall we say ?) in South Italy to-day : they would seem also to have been the originals of the Colossian angels. Men do not readily give up all their former beliefs and practices when they become Christians.[2] Three hundred years later the Church Council of Laodicea, near Colossæ, forbade Christians to " abandon the Church of God and go away to invoke angels," on the ground that this is " secret idolatry." Half a century later Theodoret speaks of the

[1] " The animistic heathen is the slave of fear. Christianity is for the animist first and foremost, by universal testimony of converts and missionaries, a *deliverance*, a deliverance from the bondage of fear, fear of a multitude of evil spirits " (Rouse and Miller, *Christian Experience and Psychological Processes*, p. 90).

[2] Let me give two interesting parallels : (*a*) We have an early Hellenistic papyrus which contains a prayer to " Zeus Iao (=Jehovah) and the angel Michael and the archangel Gabriel "—a Catholic mixture ! (I owe this reference to Mr. A. B. Cook). (*b*) According to the *Dialogues* of Gregory the Great (pope, 590–604 A.D.), " one must always be on one's guard against demons. A woman once nearly swallowed one who was sitting on a lettuce-leaf " (Thorndike, *Mediaeval Europe*, p. 152).

prevalent cult of St. Michael in the same neighbourhood.[1]

St. Paul writes against these silly and cruel superstitions. He does not deny the existence of demonic powers of the air, in whom he had been taught to believe as a Jew : but he tells his readers that, however much in heathen days they may have been used to propitiate demons and spirits, they are all done with that now. In Christ there is freedom : Christ has the *fulness* of Godhead which no angel has ; we live in Him and in His *fulness* and may neglect all lesser supernatural beings. In the famous Christological passage (Col. 1[18-20]) there is not a superfluous phrase : every word is written to assure them that we have to deal with Christ alone because He is sufficient and is supreme.

4. COLOSSÆ AND ITS NEIGHBOURHOOD. — We have several times had occasion to mention the great trade-route which traversed Asia Minor from Ephesus to the Far East.[2] Crossing the mountain-pass from Ephesus it followed the northern bank of the river Mæander for some distance, running due east. After a time the upper course of the river tends to the north-east ; but where the Mæander changes its direction, the great road continued to run due east up a lateral valley watered by the river Lycus. It crossed the main river below the junction and continued on the south bank of the tributary. First it passed through the large town of Laodicea, built on the hillside which rises from the Lycus. Nine miles farther east it came to Colossæ, which stood on both banks of the stream, where it flows through a gorge. Away from the road, six miles north of

[1] Legend said that St. Michael the archangel " had saved the people of the Lycus valley from inundation, by clearing the gorge outside Colossæ." In the seventh century the Church at Colossæ became known as the Church of St. Michael of Khonai (Barns in Hastings' *Dictionary of Religion and Ethics*, art. " Michaelmas ").

[2] See p. 146.

Laodicea, stood a third town of importance, the health resort of Hierapolis, high up on the northern slope.

The valley of the Lycus was remarkable in several ways. It is very rich in mineral deposits. The mountain streams, especially at Hierapolis, are impregnated with calcareous matter which leaves a beautiful white layer over the rocks. Precious mineral dyes were obtained from these waters—scarlet, purple, and a rich, glossy black. The whole valley was most fertile, and it produced a breed of sheep with thick wool which was dyed on the spot. North and south rise lofty ranges of mountains which break the piercing winds.

It was one of nature's favoured spots : but it has always been famous for its devastating earthquakes. In A.D. 60,[1] shortly before St. Paul wrote this letter to the Colossians, Laodicea had been wrecked. The wealthy city was offered State grants for her rebuilding, but in her pride she refused all help (see Apoc. 3¹⁷). She owed her wealth to her trade and was now the metropolis of the district.

Hierapolis was a health resort, for her white waters have valuable medicinal properties. Lightfoot (in his Introduction to *Colossians*) gives a striking account of her beauty : over her terraces tumble " cascades of pure white stone " ; in her rocks, says Strabo, are " self-made baths." The local streams were sometimes hot at their rising-point and cooled as they ran ; hence the allusion in Apoc. 3¹⁵. Hierapolis means " sacred city," for she had many temples. Prominent in the district was the *mystery worship* of the Phrygian moon-god, Mên ; so that St. Paul's word ἐμβατεύω (Col. 2¹⁸), used in the Mystery religions, would be readily understood at Colossæ. It is interesting to remember that in A.D. 62 Epictetus, most lovable of all Stoic philosophers, born a slave and crippled by ill-usage in his youth, was a young man at Hierapolis. The many resemblances

---

[1] So Tacitus : but Eusebius puts it in A.D. 64.

between his language and St. Paul's (see footnote 3 on
p. 191 for an example) may be due to direct borrowing on
his part—who knows ?

Colossæ stands in contrast to Laodicea and Hierapolis.
She had known a great past but was now fallen into decay
(so Strabo, A.D. 19). Her coins came to an end soon after
A.D. 200, and by A.D. 400 she no longer existed. So, as
Lightfoot says, the Colossian Church was the least
important to which any of St. Paul's extant letters is
addressed.

The population of the valley was mainly Phrygian by
descent, sharing in the passionate and shifty temperament
of their race. But it was much mixed with Greek blood
and had a veneer of Greek civilisation ; not to mention
that Jews abounded there, as we know from Cicero.

5. PARAPHRASE AND NOTES.

$1^{1-2}$. SALUTATION FROM PAUL AND TIMOTHY.

$1^{3-13}$. HIS THANKFULNESS FOR THEIR PROGRESS IN
CHRIST : HIS PRAYERS FOR THEIR FUTURE.

[Note that St. Paul's way is to praise before he blames.
The emphatic phrases are : " the truth which you have "
$(v.^5)$ ; " you came to a full knowledge of God's grace in
*truth* " $(v.^6)$ ; " that you may be filled with a *full knowledge
of His will* in *spiritual* wisdom " $(v.^9,$ and much the same in
$v.^{10})$ ; " God delivered you from darkness into His Son's
kingdom " $(v.^{13})$.]

$1^{14-23}$. CHRIST'S WORK FOR US. HE HAS THE FULNESS
OF GODHEAD, AND HAS FILLED US WITH HIS LIFE ; SO THAT
WE HAVE IMMEDIATE TOUCH WITH HIM AND WITH NO ONE
LESS.

*$(v.^{14})$ " In Christ we have redemption, that is the
forgiveness of sins [a phrase which covers both justification
and sanctification]. For He is *the image of the invisible
God*, the firstborn of all creation inasmuch as all things

in heaven or earth owe their creation to His indwelling, yes, including all spiritual rulers and hierarchies : He brought them into being and He is the final end to which they move. (v.[17]) He Himself exists before all things, and it is His indwelling which keeps everything functioning [moment by moment] : He is in particular the head of His body the Church. He is *the* ruler ; He is the first-born to lead the way from among the dead, that in every-thing He might have the primacy : (v.[19]) because it was God's pleasure that all the fulness of deity should reside in Him and through Christ to reconcile all things to Him-self, making peace by Christ's blood offered up on the cross—all things, I say, in heaven as well as on earth.* (v.[21]) And so *you*, who once were hostile to God because of your evil deeds, God has now reconciled to Himself by the death of Christ's earthly body ; His will is to present you holy and spotless and irreproachable before Himself, if indeed you cling stedfastly to your faith and refuse to be moved from the hope which came to you through my preaching."

[*Notes.*—It is vital to remember throughout this im-portant passage that every word has its direct bearing on the Colossian superstition. Christ is (1) " *the image of the invisible God* "—the same phrase which he uses in 2 Cor. 4[4]. This is the experiential basis of all Paul's Christology. Christ stands to us for God living under limitations of time and space : as we see Him incarnate, we can only say, " God is like that." Colossian specula-tions are futile compared with this inexhaustible source of knowledge of God. (2) " *Firstborn of all creation.*" Isolated from the context and divorced from Jewish usage, these words would imply that Christ Himself is represented as created. But not only does the context (v.[16]) make the opposite clear : the history of the term is still more decisive. " Firstborn " was applied by the Rabbis to the Messiah, and the Alexandrian Jews used similar terms of the Logos. Rabbi Bechai actually calls God Himself "the firstborn of the world." St. Paul means to convey to the Colossians that Christ is God's firstborn Son, to whom all other sons are subordinate. (3) He is the *Creator and Sustainer of the universe, including all spiritual or angelic beings* : He is not only the Alpha and Omega of creation (16[b]), the starting-point and the final goal ; but by His immanence (" in Him ") all things cohere. Science tells us *how* the world works ; Christ's indwelling is *why* it works just so.

This whole thought is what lies at the back of the Logos teaching of St. John and of Greek and Græco-Jewish philosophy, though St. Paul never uses the word " Logos " of Christ. The " Logos " means not only the side of God which is reflected in creation, which touches the finite world : it is the ultimate *reason* which explains all existence, the eternal principle that underlies phenomena. Therefore angels owe as much to the Logos as does this universe of ours. So St. Paul reminds the Colossians that their angels depend utterly on Christ.

In v.[18] the E.V. renders $\dot{\eta}$ $\dot{\alpha}\rho\chi\dot{\eta}$ as " the beginning " ; but in v.[16] the word meant " rulers " ; therefore here it surely means " *the* ruler."

In v.[19] St. Paul insists that in the incarnate Christ dwelt " *all the fulness* " of God. We share Christ's life, and He can therefore fill us with *His fulness*.

In v.[20] angelic beings are said to be reconciled to God in Christ. Possibly the reference is to fallen angels, who, according to Pharisaic belief, are the agents of human sin.

*St. Paul's Christology.*—It is worth noting that the basis of it rests on his religious experience : (1) he knew the daily presence of the Risen Lord as his redeemer ; (2) Christ's redemptive power rests on the fact that He is the " image " of God. So much is verifiable in experience.

But he goes beyond experience when he teaches our Lord's pre-existence and agency in creation. We know that the early Church as a whole did the same. If we may take St. John's Gospel as a trustworthy record of the teaching (not the actual words) of Jesus, then the Master Himself proclaimed His own pre-existence (" Before Abraham was, I am," etc.). But whether Christ ever explicitly taught this or not, the form of the belief in the early Church owes something to Greek speculations about the Logos and Græco-Jewish theories of the Messiah as the archetypal man existing in *idea* already in heaven (see further below on p. 394).]

$1^{24-29}$. THE SUFFERINGS WHICH ST. PAUL HAS ENDURED IN PREACHING GOD'S SECRET TO " EVERY ONE " WITHOUT DISTINCTION PROVE THAT HE IS REALLY BEARING THE CROSS OF CHRIST.

(v.$^{24}$) " I can rejoice in the sufferings which I bear for the sake of you Gentiles, because I know that all such suffering is redemptive and the only way of redeeming the world, just as Christ's own sufferings were in infinitely greater degree. We have to carry on the cross of Christ to its completed work. (v.$^{25}$) God has given me the wondrous privilege of completing the work of His revelation among you *to the full,* by telling the secret of the world, hidden for so long and now revealed to His saints, showing the wealth of His glory to be realised among the Gentiles : *Christ in you* is this secret, Christ the hope of glory. (v.$^{28}$) We urge it on *every* man (not a select few) ; we teach them the *whole* of this wisdom, straining every nerve to make *every one* an *advanced* disciple ' in Christ,' under God's mighty working."

[*Notes.*—In v.$^{24}$ he says, " *I make up to fulness in my flesh what is lacking in the sufferings of Christ for the Church.*" This is not to deny that Christ's sufferings are complete for the redemption of man ; but the message of redemption must be mediated by Christ's followers, and they have to tread the same path that He trod, the way of the Cross. Experience must have shown St. Paul that persecution won him a sympathy and an attention which he could gain in no other way. "Fulness" (πλήρωμα) and "to fill" or "fulfil" (πληρόω) are keynotes of this Epistle, as they are, in a slightly different context, of "Ephesians."]

2¹⁻⁵. PART OF HIS SUFFERINGS IS HIS POIGNANT ANXIETY FOR THE CHURCHES IN THE LYCUS VALLEY.

(v.¹) "Do realise that I strive hard in prayer and mental solicitude for you and the Laodiceans and others who have never seen me in the flesh. I long that you may be welded together by love and may advance into the wealth of fuller understanding and completer knowledge [you are right in seeking these]. But remember that Christ alone is God's revealed secret ; *all* wisdom and knowledge are hidden in Him. (v.⁴) Therefore beware of plausible theories which may mislead you. I am far from you in body, but I am with you in spirit ; and it is sheer joy to me to see the firmness of your faith in Christ."

[v.³. Cp. Enoch 46³ (in the "Similitudes," which were written about a century before this time) ; "the Son of Man who reveals all the treasures of that which is hidden."]

2⁶⁻¹⁹. WARNING AGAINST SPECIOUS AND DECEPTIVE PHILOSOPHY WHICH, UNDER A GREAT SHOW OF PIETY (ASCETICISM, THE CULT OF ANGELS, AND ESOTERIC VISIONS), BREEDS CONCEIT. GOD, WHEN HE REDEEMED US IN CHRIST, FINALLY DISPENSED WITH ALL ANGELIC INTER-MEDIARIES.—[A very important and difficult passage.]

(v.⁶) "Live in Christ as you were taught about Him at your conversion, firm in faith as you were instructed, and with abundant gratitude to God.

(v.⁸) "Do not be despoiled of truth by some man who

parades as philosophy what is empty deceit,[1] following the traditions of men [2] rather than Christ. (v.[9]) In Him incarnate, I say, resides *the fulness* of deity, and in union with Him you can attain your *full development*. (v.[10]) He is above every supernatural power ; in Him you received the spiritual circumcision, which consists in putting off the fleshly body [3] ; in baptism you were brought into real union with His death and resurrection. (v.[13]) *When you were dead through sin and all uncircumcised, God gave you life with Christ ; God forgave you all your sins ; He wiped off the slate all the reckoning against you for your breach of His ordinances ; He took it out of the way and nailed it to the Cross. (v.[15]) God dispensed with all angelic powers and showed it openly to the world, leading them in Christ's triumphal train.

(v.[16]) " Therefore let no one criticise you for not observing food taboos or holy days (such as feasts, new moons, and sabbaths) ; for all these things are but a shadow of future realities, and you have the substance in Christ Himself. (v.[18]) Let no one rule you out because he takes a fanatical joy in asceticism [4] and the cult of angels, claiming a special initiation into visions ; swollen-headed while he loses touch with Christ, who is head of the Church His body, through whom alone it grows with the wonderful compactness and equipment of ligaments that God has lavished on it." *

[*Notes.*—(*a*) 2[15] is one of the most difficult verses in the

[1] " His philosophy which is vain deceit," does not imply that all philosophy is such.

[2] For the meaning of " according to the rudiments of the world," see note on Gal. 4[3] (p. 83).

[3] " The body of the flesh " means the corrupt affections of the body. The phrase is worded to suggest the cutting off of flesh in outward circumcision.

[4] ταπεινοφροσύνη is literally " humility " ; but in the second-century Christian Fathers it means asceticism, and the verb ταπεινοῦσθαι is used in the Septuagint for the practice of asceticism.

New Testament. There is no space to discuss it adequately
here. It seems to me clear (1) that God is the subject
of the verb, as He has been all through v.[14]. Lightfoot
believed that the subject changed in v.[14] from " God "
to " Christ," because otherwise he could give no satisfactory sense to v.[15]. But it is a desperate expedient
to assume such a change of subject when there is nothing
in the Greek to indicate it. (2) That " *having put
off from Himself*" must govern the following accusatives
" *principalities and powers* " ; we find an exact parallel
just below in 3[9] (ἀπεκδυσάμενοι τὸν παλαιὸν ἄνθρωπον).
Thus the R.V. seems to give the right translation. But
what is the meaning of " God put off from Himself angelic
powers and made a show of them openly, leading them
in triumph in Christ " (or " in the cross ") ? Apparently
it means that, though God in days of old surrounded
Himself with angelic ministers, He dispensed with them
all when He sent His Son ; He stripped off the robe which
veiled Him from human eyes ; He led the angels as it
were behind Christ's triumphal car, as His subordinates
now sharing in His triumph. Cp. the use of θριαμβεύω in
2 Cor. 2[14] where it means " leads us to triumph " in Christ.

(*b*) v.[18] again is difficult. θέλων ἐν ταπεινοφροσύνῃ is
probably a strong Hebraism, found often in the Septuagint
but not elsewhere in the New Testament, and meaning
" taking pleasure in asceticism . . ." Lightfoot and
Abbott, however, regard this as too violent a distortion
of Greek usage to be possible in St. Paul : they render
(with R.V. marg.) " of his own mere will, by humility . . ."
ἃ ἑώρακεν ἐμβατεύων is rendered by the E.V. " dwelling
in the things which he hath seen "—a desperate attempt
to get some sense. But an unexpected light has been
shed on the meaning by the recent discovery of some
inscriptions not far from Ephesus. Ramsay [1] has shown

---

[1] See the *Annual of the British School at Athens* for 1911–12, xviii. 46.

from these that ἐμβατεύω (" to enter in ") was a technical
term in the ritual of the local Mystery religions.  Thus it
is said of initiates that μυηθέντες ἐνεβάτευσαν, " having
been initiated *they entered in*."  In the ceremony of
initiation to the mysteries of the Phrygian god Mên at
Pisidian Antioch (and we have noted above that this
worship was also popular at Hierapolis) it seems that
the opening ceremony was performed in a side-chapel,
and the initiate " *entered in* " from there to the main hall,
to the scene of the mysteries, where the god himself was
somehow represented as present.  Thus the word ἐμβατεύω
probably denotes " entering in to inner knowledge."

For 2¹⁹ see the note on Eph. 4¹⁶ (p. 338, n. 3).  " Supplied " probably means " lavishly equipped by God."
" *Joints* " (R.V.), as in Ephesians, should probably be
rendered " ligaments."]

2²⁰-3⁴. THEIR ASCETIC RULES SOUND WELL, BUT ARE
PETTIFOGGING AND OF NO REAL HELP IN RESISTING PASSION.

(v.²⁰) " You are dead with Christ to the principles
which govern the world of men.  Why then do you adopt
elaborate rules against handling or tasting things which
are merely transitory and perish when they have served
their use ?  (v.²³) Such things have a show of wisdom
with their emphasis on pious worship and bodily self-
denial, but are of no value in resisting the lust of the flesh.

(3¹) " Remember that you have been raised up from
death with Christ : seek higher things, heavenly things
such as surround Christ, with whom your life is bound
up."

[*Notes.*—v.²² should probably be translated " do not
handle *things which* are decomposed with the using " :
cp. 1 Cor. 6¹³.  In v.²³ᵇ the R.V. is probably right, though
the word " value " (τιμή) strictly means " estimated
value " rather than " real value."]

3⁵-4¹. PRACTICAL ADVICE ABOUT SINS OF THE FLESH

AND BAD TEMPER, THE NEED OF A FORGIVING SPIRIT, THE GLADNESS OF THE CHRISTIAN LIFE, THE RELATIONS OF HUSBANDS AND WIVES AND CHILDREN, OF SLAVES AND MASTERS.

[This section has much in common with Eph. 5¹⁵–6⁹. Most striking in both passages is his emphasis on joy, when we consider the writer's position as an old man at the end of a long imprisonment.

> "I think this is the authentic sign and seal
> Of Godship, that it ever waxes glad
> And more glad, until gladness blossoms, bursts
> Into a rage to suffer for mankind" (R. Browning).]

(v.⁵) "Therefore you must put to death with Christ all unclean passions and that greed of possession which is really idolatry. These things bring God's anger on men ; you once lived in them, but now you too must put away all of them, including bad temper and malice, ill-natured gossip and foul speech : (v.⁹) do not tell lies ; put off like some garment your old self and put on the new self which is renewed day by day into *fuller knowledge* as it takes the likeness of its creator. (v.¹¹) This growth is open to every man : there cannot be ¹ any distinction between Greek, Jew, barbarian or nomad Scythian, slave or free ; but Christ is all things in them all.

(v.¹²) " [They are all your brothers.] Therefore as God has shown His love to you, you must put on a heart of pity, kindness, humility, meekness, long-suffering ; bear with one another and freely forgive any one against whom you have a complaint, just as the Lord [God] freely forgave you : and above all put on love, which is the link of the higher life.² (v.¹⁵) And let the peace of Christ hold sway in your hearts, the peace which He designed for you in the one body of believers. And you must be thankful : let

---

¹ So R.V. rightly, against A.V.
² τελειότης, " full development," was the boast of the Colossians.

Christ's revelation dwell in you ; it contains a wealth of the 'wisdom' which you seek. Help one another by glad songs to God with thanksgiving,[1] and sing in your hearts as well. Let your every word and act be in the name [=spirit] of Jesus."

[The rest of the Epistle needs no paraphrase.]

4[2-6]. THE IMPORTANCE OF PRAYER : HE ASKS THEM NOT TO FORGET TO PRAY FOR HIS WORK. TOWARDS THOSE OUTSIDE THE CHURCH THEY MUST SHOW REAL CHRISTIAN WISDOM : LET THEIR SPEECH, PARTICULARLY IN EXPLAINING THEIR OWN POSITION, HAVE THE SALT OF GOD'S GRACE IN IT.

[*Note on* 4[5].—" Redeeming the time " means " making the best possible use of each occasion." The phrase occurs in the Septuagint of Dan. 2[8] : " I know that you are *seeking to gain time* (by making excuses)." [2] It is probably proverbial. " To buy up time " perhaps denotes getting it into your own control.]

4[7-18]. PERSONAL MESSAGES AND GREETINGS.

[*Notes.*—v.[9] We learn here that Onesimus, the runaway slave, came from Colossæ.

v.[11]. Mark and Jesus Justus are mentioned as the only loyal Jewish Christians with him. It is the first mention of St. Mark since the separation at the beginning of the second missionary journey.

v.[14] (combined with v.[11]) proves that St. Luke was not a Jew.

v.[15]. W.H. read " at *her* house " (with B) interpreting $N\acute{\nu}\mu\phi\alpha\nu$ as Nympha, a woman.

v.[16]. " The letter at Laodicea " is perhaps the Epistle " to the Ephesians."]

---

[1] For this sense of $\chi\acute{\alpha}\rho\iota\tau\iota$, cp. 1 Cor. 10[30]. It is the "grace" of gratitude created by the " grace " of God's kindness.

[2] I owe this reference to Professor Kennett.

# CHAPTER XV.

## THE EPISTLE TO THE EPHESIANS.

[See general remarks on p. 309 ; cp. p. 246.]

1. GENUINENESS.—The close linguistic connexion between
"Colossians" and "Ephesians" has already been noticed.
In spite of the difference in the subject-matter of the two
Epistles the number of phrases and even verses which
they have in common is large. Tychicus carried both.
The obvious inference is that they were written and dispatched to Asia at the same time. Failing this, we are
bound to conclude either that one of them is a forgery [1]
in which the writer borrows largely from the other, the
genuine, letter of St. Paul : or that both are forgeries.

No one could maintain that "Ephesians" reads like a
forgery. It is not a polemic against something deemed
heresy—the usual *motif* of the forger : here is nothing
even controversial, but the letter is full of serene joy. It
reaches a wonderfully high spiritual outlook. Moreover,
the Pauline authorship is strongly supported by external
evidence : it is well attested in the early Fathers. Therefore it would need the convergence of a number of difficulties to make us doubt that St. Paul wrote it. Yet this
is doubted by many (*e.g.* Moffatt).

[1] " Forgery " is perhaps too hard a word. The Christians who composed a number of books in the second century in the name of St. Peter,
perhaps did not intend to deceive any one : they adopted a *nom de
plume*, as the Jewish writers of the Apocalypses had done. " Pseudepi-
graphic " is a fairer description because it does not prejudge the intention
of the composer as " forged " does. But it is too clumsy a word.

*Arguments adduced against its Genuineness.*—(*a*) Its style.
It is written in long involved sentences, especially the earlier
chapters : *e.g.* the sections 1³⁻¹⁴ and 1¹⁵⁻²³ each consist of one
huge sentence, with, at the most, colons in the punctuation.
It has not the " torrent-force " of most Pauline Epistles.

But this is scarcely a valid reason for doubting the
genuineness. The phrases and words are admittedly
Pauline throughout.[1] The Epistle does not deal with controversial matters which tend to short sentences : on the
other hand, it is probing very deep spiritual truths which
defy concise or exact expression. The author wrestles with
human language in the effort to express his meaning. He
is moving in the realm of abstract ideas which he twists
round and round to find a balanced statement.[2]

(*b*) Its eschatology is spiritualised : *i.e.* the second
coming of the Lord is viewed, not so much as an external
event, as in the light of His spiritual advent to each man.
Similarly, the view of marriage taken in Eph. 5²⁹⁻³², where
it is likened to the mystic union between Christ and His
Church, is something very different to the view expressed
in 1 Cor. 7.

But it is hard to be patient with such criticism. Are
we really to believe that the great Apostle never progressed
in his insight or changed his views ? Was St. Paul alone
refused the privilege of growth ? Such " inconsistencies "
are the hall-mark of great men, whether they be saints or

[1] Moreover, in some points the style markedly resembles that of
Philippians as well as Colossians (*e.g.* the emphatic and repeated emphasis
on the " wealth of God's glory," as in Eph. 1¹⁸, Col. 1²⁷, Phil. 4¹⁹. This
feature, common to the Epistles of the first Roman imprisonment, is a
strong hall-mark of their genuineness).

[2] It may be felt that this argument fails to explain entirely the
annoying conglomeration of synonyms, *e.g.* in 1¹⁹, " according to the
working of the strength of His might." But this scarcely goes beyond
what we find in Colossians, *e.g.* 1¹¹, or the repetitions in Col. 1⁶⁻¹⁰.
St. Paul's life in prison was more leisurely and meditative than during
his years of rush.

only politicians. Or must we take such a rigid view of
inspiration as to suppose that Paul could not modify his
views, lest we endanger the reality of his central message ?
We have already seen that in the Epistles of the third
missionary journey, where the Pauline authorship is un-
doubted (1 and 2 Corinthians, Romans), he had already
changed his views about the spread of the gospel and
come to believe in the conversion of the whole world.

(c) Its lack of personal greetings is deemed suspicious.
It is in fact *noteworthy*. But it only confirms, what we
have other evidence to show (see § 3), that the Epistle was
not written to any one Church but as an encyclical letter
to all the Churches in Asia.

2. DATE AND PLACE OF WRITING.—St. Paul writes from
prison ($3^1$ $6^{20}$) : and both date and place are clearly the
same as those of Colossians and Philemon, *i.e.* Rome, in the
second year of the first Roman imprisonment (see p. 313).

3. DESTINATION.—In two of the best and earliest Greek
manuscripts, ℵ and B, the words " *in Ephesus* " are lacking
in the first verse of the Epistle. Origen (*c.* 200), the most
scholarly investigator of the New Testament text in the
early Church, did not know these words, and was hard
put to it to explain " the saints who are." Two centuries
later, Jerome cites the reading " *in Ephesus* " as the conjecture of some scholars who wished to make sense of the
verse. Basil says that the most ancient manuscripts
known to him omit the words. Finally, as far back as
the middle of the second century, Marcion gave to the
Epistle the title " *to the Laodiceans*," obviously a conjecture based on Col. $4^{16}$ ; but proving that his text
mentioned no place in Eph. $1^1$.

Thus it is highly probable that St. Paul in the original
letter left a blank after " *the saints who are* . . .," because
the letter was an encyclical sent to several or all of the

Churches in the province of Asia. Tychicus, in reading
it at each place he visited, would verbally insert the
appropriate name, " in Ephesus," " in Laodicea," etc.

A strong confirmation of this conclusion is found in
the lack of topical allusions and personal greetings in the
letter.   In fact, it is a treatise rather than a letter.


4. THEME.—The subject-matter of the Epistle has been
summarised above on p. 309.   The Roman Empire was
a unique example of a unity achièved on a basis of
diversity :  it allowed scope for different national temperaments by its variety of organisation, yet it welded the
peoples in one vast whole.   St. Paul's problem for years
had been just this—to achieve a real unity in the Catholic
Church between Jew and Gentile, not to mention Asiatic
and European.   We may compare the problem of Christian
reunion in our own day, so urgent yet so difficult to solve.
Uniformity is obviously as impossible as it is undesirable :
but a vital unity is not only of the first importance, but
is also possible of achievement because Christ is the living
Lord of all Christians and Christ Himself is one.   The
Lord came, says St. Paul, " to sum up " in Himself
(ἀνακεφαλαιώσασθαι, Eph. 1¹⁰) all the partial revelations
of the past made to all the varying nations of the world :
whatever truth about God any race had apprehended,
was " fulfilled " in Christ.   All temperaments of mankind,
in East and West, old and young, slave and freeman
(cp. Col. 3¹¹), all find their satisfaction, their " fulfilment,"
in Him and their bond of union with each other.   So He
" fulfils " all the past, all human efforts and longings ;
He is the " fulness " (πλήρωμα) of every man, see Eph. 1²³
4¹⁰· ¹³, etc.   The many are scattered fragments apart
from Him :  and the whole body, the one, would lose its
rich complexity if all the units were forced into one mould ;
as it is, He gives to each member a distinct gift—one note,

as it were, to contribute to the great harmony of God's music. So we have unity in diversity, and diversity in unity through Christ : neither the one nor the many alone, but both in a Divine combination.

5. PARAPHRASE AND NOTES.

1¹⁻². SALUTATION.

1³⁻¹⁴. PRAISE TO GOD THE FATHER (vv.³⁻⁶) FOR THE GRACE GIVEN US IN CHRIST, AND TO THE DIVINE SON (vv.⁷⁻¹⁴) FOR HIS REDEMPTION OF JEW (v.⁸) AND GENTILE (v.¹³). GOD'S PLAN WAS REVEALED IN CHRIST THE CONSUMMATOR.

(v.³) " Thanks be to God the Father for giving us every *spiritual* blessing in Christ. (v.⁴) Before ever He laid down the world, He chose us out to become His saints in love, adopted as His sons through Jesus Christ according to *the purpose of His will*, that we should praise Him for the grace which He bestowed on us in His beloved Son. (v.⁷) Through the life-blood of His Son we have our redemption and forgiveness. Such was the wealth of God's grace which He lavished on us, making us understand the secret of *His will* in all wisdom and understanding : (v.¹⁰) for His plan was worked out when the time was ripe ; He *summed up* all things in Christ, heavenly as well as earthly things. (v.¹¹) In Christ we Jews were ' made God's possession,' ¹ for this was the plan of Him who works out everything *according to His will, that His glory should be made known* in us who had long before set our hope in the Messiah. (v.¹³) In Christ you Gentiles too heard the word of truth, the glad tidings of your salvation ; and because you had faith in Him you were sealed with the Holy Spirit as He promised, which is the first instalment ² of our inheritance, assuring us of our

---

¹ An echo of O.T. language where Israel is God's κλῆρος. Cp. LXX of Deut. 9²⁹.

² ἀρραβών was a Phœnician commercial term, denoting a part-payment in advance of delivery of the goods.

redemption and that God claims us as His own people, *making known His glory.*"

[*Note on v.*<sup>14</sup>.—" Unto the redemption of (God's) own possession," means " which consists in God claiming us as His peculiar possession."]

1<sup>15</sup>–2<sup>10</sup>. HE PRAYS THAT GOD MAY GIVE THEM A VISION OF THE GRANDEUR OF THIS INHERITANCE AND ITS UN-LIMITED POSSIBILITIES. GOD WHO RAISED CHRIST (v.<sup>20</sup>), HAS RAISED THEM UP FROM DEATH WITH CHRIST (2<sup>6</sup>). HIS GRACE AND GOODNESS ARE INFINITE.

(1<sup>15</sup>) " Therefore I, hearing of the faith you have in union with Jesus and the love [1] you show to all the saints, never cease to thank God for you. In my prayers I remember you and ask the Father *of glory* to give you wisdom and revelation in clear knowledge of Himself ; to enlighten the eyes of your heart, that you may under-stand what is the hope involved in His calling, what a rich and glorious inheritance you have among the saints, and what is *the surpassing greatness of His power* towards us who have faith, as seen in *the working of the strength of His might.* (v.<sup>20</sup>) By His might He raised Christ from the dead and " *set Him on His own right hand* " in the heavenly sphere far above every spiritual power [2] and above every name that is named not only in this world but in the eternal : and " *He subdued all things under His feet,*" making Him head of the Church which is His body [in *organic* union with Him] and which is the fulfilment of Him who fulfils all things in all men [3] [Christ the Consummator ; see v.<sup>10</sup>].

---

[1] The best manuscripts omit " love " : but " the *faith* which you show *to all the saints* " is not a Pauline phrase.

[2] Here we have an echo of the Colossian question, as above in v.<sup>10</sup>.

[3] Following the E.V., which gives an excellent sense *strongly confirmed by* 4<sup>10</sup>. πληροῦσθαι is then a Middle voice, though there is no exact parallel for its use in this sense. It is used in the Middle, meaning " to get a ship filled," *i.e.* to man it ; and that is fairly close to the sense here, " gets all things filled up in all men."

(2¹) " And you He has raised with Christ and set with Him on His own right hand (v.⁶) : you, I say, who were dead through your sins in which you once lived, following the way of the world, following the prince who holds sway over the air,¹ the spirit who works now in the sons of disobedience. We all of us were among their number, living in the lusts of the flesh, following its impulses ; and we were under God's wrath as much as the rest of the world. (v.⁴) But God was so rich in mercy, He loved us so greatly, that though we were dead through sin, He gave us new life with Christ (it is only His grace which rescued us), He raised us with Him and set us on His own right hand in the heavenly sphere in Christ. (v.⁷) Thus He will show forth in ages to come the surpassing wealth of His grace and goodness to us : for it was by His grace that you were rescued through faith, and your faith itself was God's gift ; it was not for any meritorious acts of your own. (v.¹⁰) For He created us anew in Christ to perform good actions which He Himself prepared for us to do."

2¹¹⁻²². CHRIST RESCUED THEM FROM MISERY AND BROUGHT THEM NEAR TO GOD. HE BROKE DOWN ALSO THE PARTITION BETWEEN JEW AND GENTILE. BOTH ARE EQUALLY MEMBERS OF GOD'S HOUSE, HIS SHRINE WHICH HE IS BUILDING WITH CHRIST AS CORNER-STONE.

(v.¹¹) " Once you Gentiles, despised by the Jews as uncircumcised, were without Christ, you were aliens to the commonwealth ² of Israel, and had no part in the promises ; you had no hope, you were without God. (v.¹³) But now in Christ, in His life-blood, you have been

---

¹ Eph. 6¹², John 12³¹. The Jews peopled the air with evil spirits, hardly less than the heathen did.

² In the Epistles of the first Roman imprisonment we find these metaphors drawn from the Roman Empire : cp. v.¹⁹ and Phil. 1²⁷. This is again a sign of genuineness.

brought inside. (v.¹⁵) He broke down the wall of partition ¹ which kept out the Gentiles, and He abolished by
His incarnation the Law which made you enemies of the
Jews,² recreating us both in Himself into *one* new man ;
*(v.¹⁶) He reconciled us both *in one body* to God by His
cross and killed our enmity to each other. (v.¹⁷) He
came and ' *preached peace to those far off as well as to those
near,*' because through Him we both have access to the
Father *in one spirit.* (v.¹⁹) So you are no longer foreigners
and aliens ; you are fellow-citizens of the saints and
members of God's household. (v.²⁰) You are part of
God's shrine which is built on the foundation of the
Apostles and [Christian] prophets, held together by Christ
as corner-stone : ³ in Him each course of the building is
united as the shrine of God grows, in Him you too are
built up to become the dwelling of God spiritually."*

3¹⁻¹³. God's Wondrous Mercy to St. Paul, to entrust
Him with such a Work and to give Him Power to do it.

(v.¹) " For this reason I, Paul, Christ's prisoner for the
sake of the Gentiles "—[he breaks off his sentence and
does not resume it till v.¹⁴], " for you know, I think, that
God made me steward of His grace to the Gentiles : (v.³)
He revealed to me His secret, which I have been trying
to explain to you briefly, and you can judge my insight
into its meaning by reading what I have written. (v.⁵)
This secret was not made known to men in past genera-

¹ Probably thinking of the wall in the Temple at Jerusalem between
the outer and inner courts : for a Gentile to pass this barrier meant
death, even under Roman rule.

² W.H. take the phrase to mean " the enmity which resided in His
flesh . . ." Our paraphrase follows the E.V., which is probably right,
for (1) it thus forms a close parallel to 16ᵇ, " having slain by the cross
the enmity." (2) The main thought throughout is the enmity between
Jew and Gentile, rather than the enmity of our passions within us.

³ " *Chief* corner-stone " is a mistranslation. In the south wall of the
Temple area at Jerusalem there is a corner-stone nearly 39 feet long,
a huge, straight block of stone where the two walls meet.

tions as it has now been revealed spiritually to His holy apostles and prophets, the truth that the Gentiles as members of one body with the Jews share the inheritance of the promise in Christ through the preaching of His good news. (v.[7]) This is the task of which I have been made a minister by God's gracious gift. Such is the working of His power, that, though I am less than the least of all the saints, it is given to me to preach the unsearchable wealth of Christ and to throw light on God's dispensation of the secret which was hidden in Himself, the Creator of all, for all ages past. (v.[10]) For now He wills that His manifold [1] wisdom shall be revealed even to supernatural powers in heavenly places by the Church, this being the eternal purpose which He carried out [2] in Christ Jesus, in whom we can approach God boldly, through faith in Him. Therefore, I pray that I may never lose heart in the afflictions which I am bearing on your behalf, because they are your glory."

3[14-21]. His Prayer for them that they may be taught to see the Bigness of the Gospel, and realise that their Call is nothing less than to grow into all the *Fulness* of God.

(v.[14]) " For this reason I kneel down [3] in urgent prayer that the Father from whom every family in heaven and earth draws its name,[4] may grant you mighty inward strength through His Spirit according to *the wealth of His glory*; so that Christ may dwell in your hearts in love,

---

[1] *i.e.* " Richly-varied, complex," but all tending to His *one* great purpose, like many colours in a cloth making one design.

[2] " *Purposed* " (E.V.) by Greek rule would require the Middle (ἐποιήσατο).

[3] The Jews stood to pray. To kneel expresses urgent supplication. This verse goes back to 3[1] and finishes what he began to say there.

[4] Rabbinic writers spoke of " the family above " (angels) and " the family below." Bonds of family and race are a copy of the life of God whose essence is Fatherhood.

through faith : that you may strike deep roots and dig firm foundations to enable you to apprehend, in the unity of all believers, the breadth and length and height and depth of Christ's love which transcends knowledge, in order that you may attain full growth into *the fulness of God.* (v.[20]) To Him who can do far, far beyond all we ask or conceive by His power which works in us, to Him belongs the glory in the Church and in Christ for ever and ever, Amen."

4[1-16]. THEY MUST KEEP THE UNITY OF THE SPIRIT (vv.[1-6]). EVERY INDIVIDUAL HAS HIS OWN DISTINCTIVE GIFT FROM CHRIST TO CONTRIBUTE TO THE GROWTH OF THE WHOLE BODY INTO CHRISTLIKENESS. HE IS THE HEAD WHICH GIVES PURPOSE AND LIFE TO IT ALL.

(v.[1]) " I beseech you then, I who am the Lord's prisoner, to live in a way worthy of this great call ; in humility and meekness and in long-suffering love bear with one another ; be eager to keep *the unity* of the Spirit in the bond of peace. (v.[4]) Remember there is *one* body and *one Spirit,* just as there is *one* hope in your call ; *one Lord, one* faith, *one* baptism ; *one God and Father* of all, who rules all and pervades all and is immanent in all.

*(v.[7]) " But to each of us individually God's grace was given in different measure according to Christ's gift. Just as in the Psalm [68[19]] the conquering king ' *ascended on high* [to the Temple mount] *in triumph, leading his train of captives behind him, and gave gifts to his men,* ' [1] so did Christ. (v.[9]) His triumphant ascension is only possible because He too has been down in the fierce struggle of the battlefield : Christ descended to this lower earth [2] and

---

[1] This does not follow the Hebrew text (which reads " received gifts from men ") but a later reading.

[2] Some interpret the phrase τὰ κατώτερα μέρη τῆς γῆς as meaning Sheol, the grave or underworld : the Septuagint in Ps. 63[10] has " the *lowest* (κατώτατα) parts of the earth " in this sense. So a reference is found to Christ's supposed descent to the underworld and preaching

22

shared human travail. And He who descended is the
same as He who ascended above all the heavens in order
that He might impart His fulness to all things.[1]*

*(v.[11]) "And He it is who has made some to be apostles,
some prophets, some missioners, some pastors and
teachers [2]; to fit His saints for the work of the ministry,
in order that the whole body of Christ may be built up
until we reach, *all of us together, the unity* which is found
in faith on Him and in clear knowledge of the Son of God,
till we become as it were *one full-grown man*, grown into
the stature of *His fulness*. (v.[14]) For He would have us no
longer infants who are tossed about and carried hither and
thither on the sea by every wind of human teaching, through
the crafty cunning of men who are skilled in the ways of
deceit; He would have us keep to the truth and grow in
love into Himself in everything. For Christ is the head
of the body : it is joined and knit together by every liga-
ment with which God has lavishly equipped it,[3] and so, each
several part performing its proper function, the whole body
grows and is built up through Christ its head in love."*

to pre-Christian generations from Good Friday to Easter Sunday—a
strange, naïve belief found in 1 Pet. 3[19] 4[6]. But this interpretation is
out of place here : for (*a*) in this verse St. Paul is probably trying to
show that the quotation applies to the Incarnate Christ, not to the transcendent God (see Thayer, *Lexicon, κατώτερος*); (*b*) to take the phrase
as denoting Sheol is to destroy the analogy with the king of Psalm 68,
who *went down* from Jerusalem to battle.

[1] See 1[23] 3[19] 4[13]. Christ has been through the worst that human life
can offer and has won. We share His victory.

[2] Here these are not different institutional orders of ministry : they
simply denote men who have various gifts for service.

[3] See parallel in Col. 2[19]. "Through that which *every joint supplieth* "
(E.V.) makes rubbish. The " supply " is clearly God's equipment of
the body ; see note in Armitage Robinson, *in loc.*, who quotes from
Aristotle *τῷ σώματι . . . κάλλιστα πεφυκότι καὶ κεχορηγημένῳ. ἀφαί*
are defined by Galen in his lexicon of medical terms as *τὰ ἅμματα παρὰ τὸ*
*ἅψαι* (" ligaments, from the verb ' to bind ' "). *ἀφή* is not found in the
sense of a " joint," though it often means " contact " (from the Middle
*ἅπτομαι*, to touch).

4[17]–5[5]. THEREFORE THEY MUST AVOID HEATHEN DEEDS
OF DARKNESS, ESPECIALLY ALL FILTHINESS OF LIFE OR
SPEECH.

(v.[17]) " This therefore I tell you and I adjure you in the
Lord, not any longer to live, as the Gentiles do, in mental
images which only lead to disappointment, with their minds
darkened and strangers to the life of God. It is because
of their ignorance, and the blindness [1] of their hearts :
with their conscience deadened [2] they gave themselves up
to wantonness and all manner of unclean deeds in their
lust of possession. (v.[20]) That is not how you have understood Christ, if you have heard His voice and been taught
in Him (as indeed the very truth [3] is revealed in Jesus) to
put away the old self that was perishing in its former
life when it followed deceitful lusts ; and to find constant
renewal in the spirit of your minds, putting on the new
self which has been created in God's image in the righteousness and holiness of truth.

(v.[25]) " Put away lying and ' *speak the truth to each other*,'
for we are members one of another [Rom. 12[5]]. ' *Be angry
and sin not* ' [*i.e.* if angry, beware of sinning] ; do not let
the sunset find you still nursing provocation : make a rule
of giving the devil no chance. (v.[28]) The thief must give
up thieving and toil with his own hands at some good work,
that he may have something to give to the man in need.
Let no rotten speech pass your lips, but only such as
edifies in the need of the moment, such as may give grace
to the hearers. (v.[30]) Do not grieve God's Holy Spirit,[4]
in which you were sealed for the day of redemption.
(v.[31]) Drop all bitterness and anger and wrath and clamour-

[1] See p. 226, n. 1.

[2] Reading ἀπηλγηκότες with W.H. (not ἀπηλπικότες, " having lost
hope," which is found in " Western " authorities).

[3] Note the emphasis on *truth* in this passage : cp. vv.[15. 24. 25] and 5[9].

[4] Thus the Holy Spirit always " bears the sins " of the world : cp.
Rom. 8[26-27] and Heb. 6[6].

ing and ill-natured gossip with all maliciousness.   (v.³²) Be
kind and forgiving, as God in Christ forgave you.

5¹. " Imitate God Himself because you are His dear
children, and live in love just as Christ loved you and gave
Himself ' as a sweet-smelling sacrifice ' on your behalf.
(v.³) Do not even speak of fornication and other uncleanness
or lust of possession, as befits those who are saints ; ¹ nor
of disgraceful things and foolish tales and low jests, which
are improper :  rather let your speech be full of true grace.²
Remember this for certain, that the fornicator and the
man with a reckless lust for possession which is idolatry,
has no inheritance in the Kingdom of Christ and of God.
(v.⁶) Let no one deceive you with specious arguments :
for it is these things which bring God's wrath on the sons
of disobedience.  Have no share in them.  Once indeed
you were a part of darkness :  but now you are light itself
in the Lord.  Live as children of light ;  for light produces fruit which is goodness, righteousness, truth.  *Examine what is pleasing to the Lord.  Have no share with
the deeds of darkness in which no fruit can grow :  expose
them with the beams of light, for it is disgraceful even to
mention their secret deeds : ³  for everything that is exposed
by light, becomes illuminated ;  everything that is illuminated, becomes full of light.*  As the familiar words say :

> "Awake, O sleeper ;
> Arise from the dead ;
> And Christ shall illumine thee." ⁴

---

¹ ἁγίοις =" separated from all that defiles."

² εὐχαριστία ought to bear its ordinary N.T. sense of " thanksgiving."
But that seems out of place here.  And it is not impossible linguistically
that it means " grace of speech," as the context suggests.

³ i.e. do not talk about them and investigate them needlessly.  If you
yourselves are like beams of light, that is everything, for they will
scatter the darkness.

⁴ Possibly three lines of an early Christian hymn.  It has a swinging,
trochaic rhythm in Greek.

[*Note on v.*[13].—φανερούμενον cannot be a Middle voice (as A.V.), coming so near as it does to the Passive φανεροῦται. The R.V. translation is almost certainly right, though it is an unintelligible sentence in English. St. Paul in his unquenchable optimism says, " As surely as, when you unshutter a dark room, the darkness vanishes and the sweet light floods in, so surely if you show a man light, it will scatter his darkness. Light shows up a thing in its true colours " (cp. 1 John 3[2]).]

5[15-33]. PRACTICAL ADVICE ABOUT MAKING THE BEST OF SPIRITUAL OPPORTUNITIES ; AVOIDING THE EXCITEMENT OF DRUNKENNESS ; REMEMBERING THE TRUE RELATION OF HUSBAND TO WIFE WHICH IS COMPARABLE WITH THAT OF CHRIST TO HIS CHURCH.

[The section as a whole needs no paraphrase.

vv.[15-16]. See note on Col. 4[5] (p. 327).

v.[18]. " If you want zest in life, do not seek it in drink but in the inspiration of the Holy Spirit."

vv.[19-20]. See Col. 3[16].

v.[23]. See paraphrase of 1 Cor. 11[3. 11].

v.[26]. " By cleansing her in the bath of baptism, as she utters her confession " (Moffatt's translation).

v.[32]. In St. Paul, as we have seen, " mystery " usually means the secret of the world revealed in Christ. In the " Mystery " Religions, the word denotes an outward form or ritual which effects a mystic inward process. In the Johannine Apocalypse, " mystery " often has a *somewhat* similar significance, " symbol with a hidden meaning," and we must give it this last sense here. " Earthly marriage," says St. Paul, " has a deep spiritual meaning : and I think in this connexion of the union between Christ and His Church." No higher valuation of marriage is conceivable.]

6¹⁻⁴. ON THE RELATIONS OF FATHERS AND CHILDREN.

6⁵⁻⁹. ON THE RELATIONS OF MASTERS AND SLAVES.

6¹⁰⁻²⁰. THE SPIRITUAL WARFARE AND ITS WEAPONS. It is interesting to note that St. Paul, writing with a Roman soldier beside him, mentions the parts of armour in the order in which the man would put them on.

6²¹⁻²⁴. FAREWELL, AUTOGRAPH MESSAGE.

[*Notes on chap.* 6.

v.²ᵇ means "this commandment is the first in the Scriptures which has a definite promise of reward attached to it."

v.¹⁶. "*Fiery*" is to be taken literally, *i.e.* with their points dipped in some liquid and set on fire.

v.²⁴. "*Uncorruptness.*" ἀφθαρσία usually means "immortality," and ἀφθορία is used for moral incorruptibility. But in Rom. 2⁷ ἀφθαρσία seems to have the moral sense; and so here.]

# CHAPTER XVI.

## THE EPISTLE TO PHILEMON.

1. DATE AND PLACE OF WRITING.—This delightful letter
to a private friend is closely associated with "Colossians"
and "Ephesians." It shows a greater affinity in language
with them and with "Philippians" than with the earlier
Epistles. It sends greetings from the same group of the
Apostle's companions as does Col. 4. Like "Colossians"
it is sent to Asia by the hands of Tychicus and Onesimus
(see Col. 4⁷⁻⁹, Eph. 6²¹). The writer is in prison when he
writes each of the three letters. Thus there can be little
doubt that they form a group, written by Paul in the
latter half of his imprisonment at Rome and sent to Asia
all at the same time and by the same hands.

2. SUBJECT-MATTER. — Philemon was a prosperous
citizen of Colossæ (Col. 4⁹), who had been converted by
St. Paul, probably in Ephesus (Philem. v.¹⁹). He was a
generous benefactor to the local Christians (see vv.⁵· ⁷);
and he had taken a lead in doing evangelistic work
("Philemon our fellow-worker," v.¹): certain church
services used to be held at his house (v.²ᵦ).¹ Apphia (a
name rarely found outside Phrygia) was probably his
wife, and Archippus his son. The latter had apparently
faced danger in preaching the gospel, for he is mentioned
by the Apostle as "my fellow-soldier." He had now
some sort of definite office in the Colossian Church; for

¹ Cp. Col. 4¹⁵.

St. Paul tells the Colossians to keep him up to the full performance of his ministry in Christ (Col. 4[17]).

Onesimus was a slave of Philemon, and " a Phrygian slave was one of the lowest types to be found in the Roman world." [1] Onesimus had stolen money (v.[18]) and decamped with it to Rome, where he would not easily be found. The hand of Gŏd had brought him somehow to the Apostle's prison, and there he had learnt Christ ; and the miracle, which is the irrefragable proof of Christianity in all ages, had taken place in him : the " worthless " Oriental slave (v.[11]) had become St. Paul's faithful minister (v.[13]), his " dear brother " (v.[16]), to part with whom was like parting with his own heart (v.[12]).

St. Paul would have liked to keep him in Rome ; but for the man's own sake it was necessary to send him back to the master whom he had wronged. He sends this letter with him ; and he includes in the address the " Church that meets at thy house," because he is commending Onesimus to them as a trustworthy Christian. " As an expression of simple dignity," says Lightfoot, " of refined courtesy, of large sympathy, and of warm personal affection, the Epistle to Philemon stands unrivalled."

It is interesting to note that " Jerome, Chrysostom, and Theodore of Mopsuestia found it necessary to defend the Epistle against the charge of secular triviality, unworthy of St. Paul, and unbefitting . . . a work to be included in the sacred Canon of the N.T." (J. H. Bernard in Hast. *D.B.*, art. " Philemon ").

3. [The Epistle needs no analysis. The following notes will suffice.]

v.[6]. " *The communication of thy faith . . .* " Light-

---

[1] Marcus Dods, *N.T. Introduction* (quoted by Weymouth). The Latin Comedians offer ample evidence of this.

foot renders, " Your charitable deeds which
spring from your faith. . . ." Vincent
(*Intern. Crit. Comm.*) explains, "He prays
that the love and faith which so greatly
aid and comfort all the saints may likewise
communicate their blessing to Onesimus "
(taking πίστεως as Objective Genitive).

v.⁹. " *Paul the aged.*" Lightfoot, however, renders
it " an ambassador," making πρεσβύτης =
πρεσβευτής and comparing Eph. 6²⁰. The
two forms of the Greek word are used interchangeably in the Septuagint.

v.¹⁶. " *Both in the flesh and in the Lord* " means
both in the outward service of his earthly
master and in his spiritual relationship.

v.²⁰. " *Let me have profit from thee.*" The verb
ὀναίμην is punning on the name Onesimus
(=" profitable ").

v.²². " *Prepare me a lodging,*" *i.e.* in your own
house.

# CHAPTER XVII.

## THE EPISTLE TO THE PHILIPPIANS.

1. GENUINENESS, DATE AND PLACE OF WRITING.—The great majority of sober critics unhesitatingly accept the Pauline authorship of Philippians. There is everything to be said in its favour, and nothing against it more substantial than the suggestion that the mention of bishops and deacons in 1[1] is an anachronism in the Apostle's lifetime. Polycarp, in his letter to the Philippians about the middle of the second century, twice refers to the letter.[1]

St. Paul is in prison (1[14], etc.). He has already been put on his trial (1[7, 16]),[2] but the verdict has not been given. He is certain that he will be acquitted (1[25]); yet in spite of the strength of this conviction, he can still consider the possibility of condemnation (1[20] 2[17]). He sends a greeting from the Christian servants in the Emperor's Palace (4[22]); and reports with joy how the knowledge of the Christian message has been spread among the "prætorian court" (or "prætorian guard," see below), 1[12]. All this proves that he wrote the letter from Rome, near the end of his first imprisonment there.

---

[1] Chaps. 3 and 11. In the former place he speaks of "epistles" written by St. Paul to them, but it is safe to say that he only knew of the one epistle. Lgt. says (*Phil.*, p. 142): "The plural ἐπιστολαί . . . whenever it occurs in prose of a single epistle, seems to denote a missive of importance. . . . It would fitly describe the communications of the blessed Apostle Paul."

[2] So it seems best to interpret ἀπολογία, with Zahn (*Introduction to the N.T.*, i. p. 540), etc. *Contra* Lgt.

2. OCCASION.—His relations with the Christians of Philippi had always been affectionate and untroubled, partly, no doubt, because there were so few Jewish converts there, and partly because of St. Luke's ministry. After his first visit, when he had gone on to Thessalonica, the Philippians had more than once sent him gifts of money (Phil. 4$^{16}$); and again when he was at Corinth (2 Cor. 11$^9$). It may at first sight seem strange that he was willing to accept them, when we remember how strenuously he had refused to take money from the local Church at Corinth (2 Cor. 11); but there is a world of difference between accepting a gift as a pledge of affection and taking pay as a right due to oneself.

For some time before the writing of our Epistle he had received nothing from them, not because (as he says in 4$^{10}$) they had ceased to think of him but because they "lacked the opportunity." Now communication between Philippi and Rome was easy and frequent; for the Macedonian city lay on the Via Egnatia, the great overland road from the Hellespont to the Adriatic. So it was that, as soon as the Philippian Christians heard where he was to be found in Rome, they sent Epaphroditus with another gift and many affectionate messages. Apparently St. Paul had already written to express his gratitude; in this earlier letter he had mentioned two other things— first, a warning against certain embittered Jewish Christians who had made their way to Philippi (see 3$^{1b}$); and secondly, a serious illness, perhaps Roman fever, from which Epaphroditus was suffering (2$^{26·\ 27}$). The Philippians had written back in great anxiety: they wanted news of their messenger: they were agitated to learn that the Apostle's trial had at last come on; it was a crisis for him whom they loved devotedly, and for the Church in Rome: as for their gift to him, it was miserably small in comparison with what they would have liked to send; and there had been such a long time in which they could send nothing at all.

St. Paul's reply is our extant Epistle, the brightest and most affectionate of all his letters. Joy and gladness are the dominant note, and warm-hearted gratitude for their care of him. They must not be depressed. Epaphroditus has quite recovered and will carry this letter ; as for the hearing of his own appeal-case by the Imperial Court, he feels certain of acquittal now ; as for the weary length of his imprisonment, it is incredible how it has served to spread the knowledge of the Christian gospel in Rome. It is true that a clique of Jewish Christians at Rome are not friendly and are preaching in direct rivalry with him ($1^{15-17}$) : but their party-spirit is a small thing : in the enormous population of Rome there is room for them ; the great thing is that Christ should be preached at all.

He speaks in very different terms, however, of other Jewish Christians who, as Epaphroditus had told him, were trying to make trouble at Philippi. Apparently they were like his unscrupulous opponents of 2 Corinthians, men who stuck at nothing in vilifying him, men of whom he does not hesitate to say that they have no true religion but are moved solely by mercenary and selfish motives (Phil. $3^{19}$). They must have been much more extreme than the similar party at Rome : Philippi was a smaller place with a more parochial atmosphere, and the hostile party were likely to upset a keen Christian community who had a singularly untroubled history. As far as they had a positive message of their own, both parties (at Rome and at Philippi) probably urged the great help of the Mosaic ritual with its impressive ritual and the glamour of antiquity.

In chap. 3 St. Paul's sudden outburst against the party in Philippi comes most unexpectedly. The first two chapters are all sunshine and it is clear throughout that the Judaisers had little success. Phil. $3^{1a}$ reads as if he were minded to end his letter—"finally, my brethren, fare well in the Lord." Then without warning comes an outburst of denunciation. Lightfoot suggests that some bad news from Philippi had reached him at this point; but 3[1b] implies that the Apostle had already in his last letter sounded the warning, and it suddenly occurs to him to repeat it more vehemently. Epaphroditus was probably with him as he wrote, perhaps was his amanuensis; in 4[3] he seems to address him directly as " my true yoke-fellow." Perhaps it was he who suggested at this point the need of an emphatic warning against the Judaisers.

In any case, the suddenness of St. Paul's outburst is utterly inadequate to support the contention of some disruptive commentators that there we have yet another fragment of a different letter !

For the Philippian Church itself St. Paul has little but warm commendation. But it is clear, from several hints in the letter, that they were not free from jealousy and quarrels among their members (see 2[1-4. 14]), particularly among the women (4[2-3]). We have already noticed the freedom enjoyed by the sex in Macedon generally and the lead taken by them in the foundation of the Philippian Church (Acts 16[13-14]).

3. TIME RELATION TO COLOSSIANS, EPHESIANS, AND PHILEMON.—It is impossible for us to say with any certainty whether "Philippians" was written before or after the group of three. Lightfoot assigns to it the priority, pleading the resemblance between it and Romans, and finding evidence of advance in the general outlook of the three letters as compared with this.

But such arguments are not convincing if we remember that, at the most, there can only have been an interval of a few months between the dates. The majority of commentators take the other view. In Philem. v.[22] St. Paul "hopes" to be released from prison: in Phil. 1[19, 25] he "knows" that he will (yet cp. 2[17]). This suggests a later stage in the imprisonment. This argument is greatly strengthened if we accept the view that in Phil. 1[7, 16] the word "defence" refers to his trial which had already begun, as seems probable.

It is still further strengthened if we accept as probable the interpretation which Mommsen and Ramsay give to the word "prætorium" in v.[13] (see p. 310, n. 1): *i.e.* that it means the appeal-court, which heard his case, presided over by the prefect of the prætorian guard; but it remains uncertain whether this can be maintained. The old view is that it means the soldiers of the prætorian guard who were responsible for him in prison. Be this as it may, the balance of probability seems to remain on the side of those who put the group of three some months before the end of the imprisonment, and "Philippians" in the last month or two.

### 4. Paraphrase and Notes.

1[1-2]. Salutation from Paul and Timothy to the Philippian Christians and their Bishops and Deacons.

[*Note on "Bishops and Deacons."*—In Acts 14[23] St. Luke tells us that on the first missionary journey Paul and Barnabas appointed [1] presbyters in every church, to act as a governing body as in Jewish synagogues. It is certain therefore that there was such a body of "presbyters" (the Jewish name) or "bishops" (overseers, the Greek name for the same officers),[2] entrusted with the general discipline and care of the various churches. And it is clear that they were dedicated to their office with something in the nature of an ordination (Acts 14[23]).

---

[1] Or "asked the Churches to elect by vote." St. Luke mentions the presbyters of the Christian Church at Jerusalem in 11[30] 21[18], etc.

[2] This name for presbyters was naturally used in Gentile churches, see p. 170.

But if the office of presbyter or bishop was copied from Jewish custom, that of deacon seems to have been entirely original in the Christian Church. Probably for that reason St. Luke gives us an account (Acts 6) of the appointment of the first seven deacons and its intention (though he never calls them " deacons "). They were elected by the Church (6[5-6]) and the Apostles consecrated them. Their work was essentially the care of the poor. Reference is made to it in the " helps " of 1 Cor. 12[28] and the " ministration " (διακονία) of Rom. 12[7] ; and in Rom. 16[1] we hear of a " deaconess " at Cenchreæ, who was no doubt appointed to look after the womenfolk.

Now in 1 Cor. 12[28] and later, in Eph. 4[11], St. Paul speaks, not of bishops and deacons, but of several classes of men with special gifts for the service of the Church : and the whole tone of 1 Cor. 11[17-32] and 14 shows that the presbyters had no special function in conducting public worship. The two orders did not form a clerical caste ; they were only the germ from which, fifty years after this time, the Christian ministry was fully evolved.[1] But it is ridiculous to find any anachronism in their mention in Phil. 1[1].]

1[3-11]. THANKSGIVING FOR THEIR ACTIVE PARTICIPATION IN HIS WORK, AND PRAYER FOR THEM.

(v.[3]) " I thank God for you whenever I pray for you. It is a joy to me that from the very first you have taken an active share in promoting the spread of the gospel. I am confident that God who began this good work in you will make it grow till the day of Christ. It is only right that I should think of you in this way, because I hold you in great affection as men who share God's grace with me even when I am in prison or am making my defence [2] of the gospel and establishing it.    (v.[8]) God knows how I

---

[1] See further below, pp. 364–6.
[2] Probably referring to his trial before the appeal-court (so also v.[16]). Lgt., however, takes the reference as general.

long for you all. And my prayer is that your love may ever increase in fuller knowledge and all perception, so that you may approve in judgment the better course : that you may be absolutely sincere and filled with the fruit of righteousness which grows through Christ to God's glory."

1[12-30]. NEWS OF HIMSELF. HIS IMPRISONMENT HAS ONLY SERVED TO SPREAD THE GOSPEL. IF SOME CHRISTIANS ARE OPPOSED TO HIM, STILL THEY PREACH THE GOSPEL, AND THIS IS A JOY TO HIM. HE SOMETIMES HOPES TO BE CONDEMNED TO DEATH BECAUSE IT WOULD MEAN GOING TO CHRIST : BUT HE WILL NOT DIE YET AWHILE BECAUSE HIS LIFE HELPS THEM. IN ANY CASE THEY MUST BE WORTHY CITIZENS OF CHRIST'S COMMUNITY.

(v.[12]) "I want you to be reassured about my imprisonment, that it has turned out a help and not a hindrance in the spread of the gospel. I have been enabled to make clear what life in Christ means to the whole prætorian court [1] and other circles : and most of our brethren in the Lord have been emboldened thereby to speak the Word of God more fearlessly. (v.[15]) Some of the brethren preach Christ in factious rivalry with us, others in good will. The latter know that I am here to defend the gospel [not through any fault of my own] ; but the others who are possessed by a spirit of factiousness are driven on by mixed motives (οὐχ ἁγνῶς) because they think their freedom to preach will make me chafe against my imprisonment. (v.[18]) Never mind ; it only means that Christ is preached the more, whatever the motives, and at this I rejoice. Yes, and I will rejoice [in my lot], for I know that my position ' *will bring me ultimate salvation* ' [whether I live or die ; see end of v.[20]] because you are praying for me, and Christ is giving me the Spirit in rich measure : I have an earnest expectation and hope that in no possible way shall I be put to shame, but that Christ,

---

[1] Or " to the whole prætorian guard."

now as always, shall be magnified in my person by fearless speech, whether I live or die.

*(v.²¹) " For to me to live means Christ and to die means gain.  If it be my lot to live in the flesh, this will bring real fruit to my labour, and so I do not know which I should prefer.¹  I am drawn in two directions, between my longing to break up my camp and go home to be with Christ,² for that is much, much better for me ; and my desire to remain on in the flesh, which is more necessary for your sakes.  (v.²⁵) Indeed I am quite confident that I shall remain and be beside you all, that you may advance and rejoice in faith, that your pride in me may increase in Christ through my coming again to Philippi.  (v.²⁷) Only do your duty as good citizens [Lgt.]³ of Christ's gospel that, whether I am with you or absent, I may hear that you are standing firm in a united spirit, with one heart fighting alongside of faith in the gospel.  Do not be scared in any way by our opponents ; for their opposition is a proof of their ruin and your own salvation at the hands of God, since you have been allowed the privilege not only of believing in Christ but of suffering for Him : you are only sharing in the fight which I have to wage as once you saw at Philippi and now hear of me."*

2¹⁻¹¹. HE BEGS THEM BY ALL THEIR CHRISTIAN EX-PERIENCE TO LIVE IN UNITY AND LOVE WITH EACH OTHER. THEY MUST TRY TO WIN THE MIND OF CHRIST JESUS, WHO HUMBLED HIMSELF TO COME DOWN TO EARTH FOR THE SAKE OF MEN, AND SO WON THE HIGHEST GLORY AND THE WORSHIP OF ALL BEINGS.

¹ This seems better sense than the R.V. translation ; and it is hard to believe that " then " is a legitimate translation of καί.

² Swete calls this " the one contribution which St. Paul makes to our knowledge of life after death " (*Life of the World to come*, p. 32).  It is noteworthy that there is no hint of an " intermediate " existence.

³ It must be borne in mind that Philippi was a Roman colony and proud of Roman citizenship.

2 3

(v.[1]) " I beseech you by the comfort you have found in Christ, by the cheer which love has brought you, by the fellowship of spirit, by all the loving-kindness you have known, complete my joy by showing unity among yourselves, by brotherly love and sympathy and harmony : keep down the spirit of factiousness and vainglory : be humble and think of others as better than yourselves : do not each set of you consider their own advantage but that of the others. *(v.[5]) Have in you the mind of Christ Jesus, who though He pre-existed in God's own Divine nature,[1] yet did not regard this equality with God as a treasure which He must retain at any price : nay, *He emptied Himself* and took the full nature of a slave ; He came in human form ; and appearing to men as a man, He bore the utmost of human pain, the cross. * (v.[9]) Therefore God exalted Him to the height and bestowed on Him the name which is above every other ; that in the light which the name of Jesus brings,[2] all beings in heaven and earth and under the earth should bow low in worship of Him, and ' *every tongue confess* ' that ' Jesus Christ is Lord ' to the glory of God the Father."

[*Note on* 2[6-8].—St. Paul has already written the same thing more briefly in 2 Cor. 8[9], " for your sakes *He became poor* when He was rich, that you by His poverty might become rich." But here the Apostle introduces the interesting words ἐκένωσεν ἑαυτόν, " emptied Himself." The deduction usually made from this language is that he regarded the Divine nature as wholly different in essence from the human nature, so that at the Incarnation our Lord became absolutely different to what He was before.

---

[1] μορφή (which we have translated " nature " above, vv.[6, 7]) expresses the abiding essence, the inner reality. σχῆμα (rendered above by " form ") denotes something more external and changeable.

[2] The Hebrew attached permanent significance to all names, as indicating character and destiny. So " the name of the Lord " bears the meaning of His revealed qualities.

But his point is simply that Christ *was* very God and *became* very man, and we have no right to press it any further. Experience taught him that the Lord was the "image" of God, and therefore essentially Divine : experience also taught him that He was very man and thus the Saviour of men.

If we are to extract from the language any view of the relations between the Divine and human natures, we might point out that "emptied Himself" suggests limiting the infinite rather than joining together two utterly disparate natures.]

$2^{12-18}$. THEY NEED REVERENCE IN WORKING OUT THEIR SALVATION WITH GOD'S HELP. QUARRELS MUST BE PUT ASIDE. THEY THEMSELVES ARE CALLED TO BE THE LIGHT OF THE WORLD.

(v.$^{12}$) " Obey me now as you have always done, and all the more loyally in my absence. Work out your own salvation with fear and trembling, for it is God who is working in you, to give you both the will and the power to do His pleasure. [Therefore be humble and reverent and on your guard.] (v.$^{14}$) Do away with grumbling and disputes, that you may be ' *blameless children of God in the middle of a crooked generation,*' among whom you are set to shine as stars in the world [Matt. $5^{14}$], holding up the word of life : thus you will be my glory in the day of Christ, the proof that I have not run in vain. (v.$^{17}$) Even if my blood is poured as a libation on the sacrifice of faith which you are offering, I am glad and share your gladness. I ask you in turn to be glad and share my gladness."

$2^{19}$-$3^{1a}$. HE HOPES TO SEND TIMOTHY TO PHILIPPI AS SOON AS HE KNOWS THE ISSUE OF HIS OWN CASE, AND TO FOLLOW HIM BEFORE VERY LONG. HE IS SENDING EPAPHRODITUS AT ONCE, AS HE HAS BEEN VERY ILL AND LONGS TO VISIT HIS HOME. FAREWELL GREETING ($3^{1a}$).

[This section needs no paraphrase. It seems best to

put the paragraph division between the first and second halves of 3¹, rather than after 3¹ (as Lgt. W.H.). For 3¹ᵇ seems to refer to what follows, the warning against the Judaisers.]

3¹ᵇ⁻²¹. WARNING AGAINST JUDAISTIC CHRISTIAN INTRUDERS AT PHILIPPI. HE INSISTS THAT HE HIMSELF, IF ANY ONE, HAD ALL THE ADVANTAGES OF BIRTH AND EDUCATION ON WHICH HE MIGHT BASE A PRETENSION TO RELIGIOUS EXCLUSIVENESS. BUT HE HAD THROWN THESE AS DIRT BENEATH HIS FEET FOR CHRIST'S SAKE : NOT, OF COURSE, THAT HE CLAIMS PERFECTION, BUT THAT HE IS AIMING AT IT STRENUOUSLY AND PROGRESSING.

(v.¹ ) " To write the same things as in my last letter is not a trouble to me and it is advisable for your sake. I repeat—beware of those dogs,¹ those doers of evil, the party of *concision*.² (v.³) We Christians are the real people of circumcision, we who serve God's Spirit and glory in Christ Jesus. We put no confidence in mere fleshly claims—though, indeed, I might do so if any man can. (v.⁵) When I was eight days old, I was circumcised : I came of the race of Israel [the people of promise], of the [pure-blooded] tribe of Benjamin, a Hebrew [in language and customs] descended from Hebrews ; of the Pharisaic school of the Law, and so zealous that I persecuted the Church, and so scrupulous in keeping the Law that in that respect I was blameless. (v.⁷) Yet these things which were in the eyes of the world my advantages, I have counted as mere loss for Christ's sake: nay, rather, I count all earthly things as loss in comparison with the surpassing wonder of the knowledge of Christ, for whose sake I suffered

¹ The same term of abuse which they arrogantly applied to the Gentiles—ownerless pariah dogs, living on street garbage and ever ready to fight.

² A play on " circumcision." " Concision " is a contemptuous word, implying that it is no better than heathen self-mutilation.

gladly the loss of them : I count them as dung, in order to
gain Christ and be found in Him, with righteousness based
simply on faith, not on law : (v.[10]) I seek only to know Him
and the power of His resurrection life [1] and to share His
sufferings : *I try to be conformed to His death in the hope
that I may attain to the resurrection from the dead.[2]
(v.[12]) [They may vaunt their fancied perfection] : I know
too well that I am not yet perfected, but I run a strenuous
race in the hope of acquiring the prize for which Christ
acquired me as His competitor.  (v.[13]) Brothers, I know
*I have not yet* acquired the prize.  My one thought is this :
like some runner for whom it is fatal to look back, I fix
my eyes on the finish and press on towards the prize.
(v.[17]) If any of you thinks that he is indeed ' perfect,'
let him remember what I have said and take the same
attitude : and then if you are mistaken on any point,
trust God to reveal it to you.  But whatever insight we
have already gained, let us be sure that we live up to it.*

(v.[17]) " Imitate me in this attitude, I say, and watch
those who live by this ideal.  For there are many in the
Church, as I have often told you, and now tell you with
grief, who in their lives are enemies of *the cross* of Christ ; [3]
their end is destruction, their god is their belly, and they
glory in their shame ;  their whole outlook is occupied
with earthly things.  (v.[20]) *Our citizenship is in heaven* ; we
wait for a Saviour to come from heaven, Jesus Christ,
and to change the appearance of this lowly body that it

[1] Note that power comes from the *risen* Lord, rather than simply
from the crucified.

[2] The resurrection is of the righteous only, not the wicked.  See Luke
20[35] and note 1 on p. 288.

[3] Lgt. thinks that he is no longer speaking of the Judaisers, but of
the Antinomian section who were common in Greek churches.  But
he has given no indication of a change of subject : probably the Jewish
Christians in question not only took a superior attitude of perfection,
but claimed pay for their teaching ;  thus " their god is their belly."

may take on the real nature [1] of His glorified body in the power of Him who can subject all things to Himself."

4[1-9]. RENEWED EXHORTATION TO BANISH ALL DISSENSIONS. THEY MUST ALWAYS BE GLAD AND LET GOD'S PEACE REIGN IN THEIR HEARTS. THEIR MINDS ARE TO BE FULL OF NOBLE THOUGHTS WHICH ARE CHRISTIAN, OR EVEN OF THE BEST HEATHEN IDEALS.

(v.[1]) " You are my joy and crown ; oh, stand firm in the Lord, my beloved. I beseech Euodia and Syntyche [two Philippian women] to make up their differences in the Lord's strength : yes, and I beg you, my true yokefellow,[2] to help them ; for they have taken a real part in the struggle for the gospel cause with Clement and my other helpers whose names are ' *in the book of life.*'

(v.[4]) " *Always be glad in the Lord* ; I say again, be glad. Let your sweet reasonableness be known to all men : the Lord is near us, so do not be anxious, but in prayer make all your wants known to God with *thanksgiving* : and the peace of God, which surpasses any conception we have, shall guard your hearts and thoughts as sentinel [3] in Christ. (v.[8]) Finally, fill your minds with thoughts of all that is true, is solemn, is righteous, is pure, is lovable, is our ideal —nay, even with all that is good in the old heathen ideals of ' virtue ' and ' merit.' [4] (v.[9]) You have been told by me these ideals, you have seen me strive after them : then practise them ; and *the God of peace* shall be with you."

4[10-20]. THANKS FOR THEIR KINDLY FINANCIAL HELP TO HIM.

---

[1] For σχῆμα and μορφή, see note 1, p. 354.

[2] Possibly addressed to Epaphroditus, to whom he was dictating the letter. To write this appeal in the letter would strengthen the position of Epaphroditus as a peacemaker at Philippi.

[3] Language suggested by his own soldier-guards.

[4] " Virtue " is not a Christian word : it is never found in St. Paul. But it and " merit " were commonplaces of Greek philosophy (*e.g.* Aristotle).

(v.[10]) " I am so glad, in the spirit of Christ, that you
have now at last been able to renew your kind thoughts of
me : you never ceased to think of me, I know, but you
lacked opportunity to show it. Please realise that my
gratitude is not simply due to my own outward need ;
for I have learnt to be satisfied in whatever circumstances
I am placed. I know want and affluence ; I have been
taught the secret of life in all these changes. *I can do all
things in the power of Him who strengthens me.* (v.[14]) All
the same, I thank you for your kindly assistance in my need.
I have no need to remind you that in the early days of my
missionary tours, when I first left Macedon, there was no
Church which felt it owed me a debt and discharged it in
money,[1] except you alone. (v.[16]) When I was at Thessalonica you sent me money on two separate occasions :
not that I am seeking such a gift, but what I do seek is the
spiritual fruit which grows in this way to your credit.
I have plenty and more than plenty : for Epaphroditus'
news of you has more than satisfied me ; he told me of all
your self-sacrifice, so welcome to God. (v.[19]) And my
God shall supply every need of yours in His great and
glorious wealth in Christ. To God our Father belongs all
glory for ever and ever ; Amen."

4[21-23]. AUTOGRAPH FAREWELL.[2]

[*Note.*—" Those who are of Cæsar's household," is of
great interest to us. Lgt. says (*Phil.* p. 171) : " In Rome
itself the ' domus Augusta ' must have formed no incon-
siderable fraction of the whole population " ; and he shows
that the names of several Christians greeted in Rom. 16
are actually found in connexion with the imperial household, *e.g.* Amplias, Urbanus, Stachys, Apelles.]

---

[1] Literally " in the matter of giving and receiving—debit and credit."
He makes his meaning clear in v.[17], where he says that their reward is
*spiritual* enrichment.

[2] Unless, indeed, St. Paul took up his pen at 3[1] and wrote all the last
two chapters.

# CHAPTER XVIII.

## THE PASTORAL EPISTLES, AND THE CLOSING YEARS OF HIS LIFE.

1. THE PASTORAL EPISTLES: GENERAL.—The Epistles known as 1 Timothy, Titus, and 2 Timothy are personal letters—two addressed to Timothy at Ephesus, and the other to Titus in Crete. They are mainly concerned with (1) warnings against a dangerous type of Jewish teaching; (2) regulations for ecclesiastical organisation, particularly for the appointment of bishops and deacons. Timothy and Titus are regarded as St. Paul's delegates to Asia and Crete, exercising an apostolic authority as his representatives: they hold a position which is roughly identical with that held in later times by a bishop.

In 1 Timothy and Titus, St. Paul is travelling about in the East, while in 2 Timothy he is in prison at Rome, and expecting speedy condemnation and execution.

The peculiar vocabulary and style of the three Epistles, together with the similarity of their topics and of the Judaistic teaching which the author condemns, show conclusively that in their present form all three were written or at least edited by the same man about the same time.

2. HISTORICAL POSITION IMPLIED IN THE EPISTLES.—In 1 Timothy St. Paul has lately left Ephesus to go to Macedon (1³), but intends to return to Ephesus shortly (3¹⁴). This apparently cannot be placed in the third

missionary journey, because at that time Timothy had gone to Macedon before the Apostle left Ephesus (Acts 19²²).

In Titus, St. Paul has recently sailed from Crete, where he has left Titus (1⁵), apparently to go to the Greek mainland : for he hopes to spend the winter at Nicopolis in Epirus (3¹²), on the south-eastern coast of the Adriatic Sea.  Once more it is difficult to see where we can find room in the narrative of the Acts for any such visit to Crete.  It is just possible that he went there during the earlier part of his " three " years at Ephesus : but the style of the Epistle to Titus and the ecclesiastical position implied in Crete (see further below) are inconsistent with any such early date for the letter.

In 2 Timothy the Apostle has recently been engaged on missionary work in the East (4¹³. ²⁰) : he is now in prison, calmly facing martyrdom but without any doubt that he will be condemned (4⁷⁻⁸).  Trophimus, who on the third missionary journey accompanied him to Jerusalem (Acts 21²⁹), has been left behind at Miletus ill.   Here, too, it is obviously impossible to harmonise the position with either the imprisonment at Cæsarea or the first imprisonment in Rome.   It is just conceivable that either 1 Timothy or Titus taken alone might be fitted into the third missionary journey : but it is generally agreed that no place can be found for the three Pastoral Epistles, taken together, within the time covered by the narrative of the Acts.   The conclusion then seems inevitable, that if these letters were either written by St. Paul *or record authentic history of his later life*, we must suppose that he was acquitted on his first trial at Rome and liberated from prison.

*Have we any other Reasons for supposing that he was liberated ?*—(a) The Epistles of the first Roman imprisonment prove that he was confident of acquittal and release

(Phil. 2²⁴, Philem. v.²²). And indeed he had every reason
to be so. Christians were not yet persecuted as such.
The Roman tribunals were usually just, and would not
condemn any man, particularly a Roman citizen, unless a
criminal offence were clearly proved against him. They
had hitherto always proved favourable to St. Paul: and
in all probability he would on this occasion be tried by
Burrus, the justest of men.[1]

(b) In August A.D. 64 a large part of Rome was burnt,
and it was popularly believed to be the work of incendiaries
prompted by the Emperor Nero himself. He promptly
sought for a scapegoat, whose punishment might appease
the populace, particularly if it were carried out in scenes of
pageantry such as they loved. So he selected the Christians who had no influential friends : his wife Poppæa
was a Jewess by religion and probably suggested the
appropriate victims.

There is no reason to doubt the tradition that both St.
Paul and St. Peter were martyred at Rome at the end of
Nero's reign. Eusebius of Cæsarea dates St. Paul's death
in A.D. 67, Jerome at the beginning of A.D. 68. But
whether we accept their evidence or no, it remains highly
probable that he was executed between August A.D. 64–
January A.D. 68, either actually in the Reign of Terror
or after it had brought the Christians into bad odour with
the Court at Rome. But the " two years " of imprisonment of Acts 28³⁰ will not carry us beyond A.D. 61 or A.D. 62.
Thus we have to fill a gap in St. Paul's life of at least two,
and more probably four or five years, after the end of Acts.

---

[1] Of course it is possible that some untoward influence led the unscrupulous Emperor to condemn him ; e.g. Poppæa, who was now his
mistress and shortly afterwards his Empress, professed the Jewish faith.
In itself it is not unlikely that St. Paul's Jewish foes would pull the strings
through her. But the question of St. Paul's acquittal cannot be decided
on any one argument : we must be guided (in our present lack of direct
information) by a convergence of probabilities.

(c) Clement of Rome, writing to the Corinthians about A.D. 95, reminds them (§ 5) how the Apostle had " reached the furthest limit (τὸ τέρμα) of the West." It is unlikely that any Roman would designate the Imperial City by such a term ; it most naturally in his mouth would denote the Atlantic coast (see Lightfoot, *St. Clement of Rome*, ii. 30). And this harmonises with St. Paul's definite intention (Rom. 15²³⁻²⁴) to visit Spain after leaving Italy.

(d) The catalogue of New Testament books called the Muratorian fragment, which was written in Latin about A.D. 200, speaks of " profectionem Pauli ab urbe ad Spaniam proficiscentis " (" the departure of Paul from the city on his journey to Spain ").

## 3. RECONSTRUCTION OF THE APOSTLE'S CLOSING YEARS AND MARTYRDOM.

—It seems highly probable from this evidence that after two full years in prison at Rome (Acts 28³⁰) the Apostle's appeal was tried in the Imperial Court and he was acquitted. He probably started soon after his liberation for a missionary tour in Spain, and perhaps the Rhone Valley : for at his age (he must have been about sixty-five years old) and after a long imprisonment, it is hardly likely that he went from Italy to Asia, thence back west to Spain, and once more returned to the Levant. But all the details of his movements which we can gather from the Pastoral Epistles seem to belong to the closing year or two of his life. Then he went once more to Ephesus and Macedon ; he sailed across to Crete, of which he had caught a glimpse on his voyage to Rome, and perhaps he founded the Church there. He meant to spend the winter in a part of the Greek mainland which was new to him, on the shore of the Adriatic. Perhaps he did, and went on in the spring to Rome. But at all events he was arrested, either at Nicopolis or Rome, and thrown once more into prison : by this time to bear the name of a Christian was equivalent in the capital to a confession of membership in a criminal society. He could not hope to escape again, and he did not. As a Roman citizen, he was not liable to the sentence of crucifixion awarded to St. Peter. To him came the more merciful form of execution by beheading. Tradition says that he was taken two miles outside the Ostian gate on the south of the city to a spot afterwards known as the Aquæ Salviæ, and there suffered death by the headsmans' axe. To the west of it, on the Ostian Way and not far from the Tiber, is the Church of St. Paul-without-the-Walls, originally built by Constantine the Great. The story runs that a woman named Lucina recovered the corpse and buried it here on her own property.[1] Whether this be founded on fact or no, the great Apostle of the Gentiles, the missionary of Catholic Christianity, rests somewhere in the Imperial City which was for so long the centre of the world.

This reconstruction of the history of his last years cannot claim certainty : but it should be noticed that it does not rest on St. Paul's authorship of the Pastoral Epistles, which is doubtful ; but only on the historicity of his movements as noticed in these Epistles, which is confirmed to a considerable extent by Clement of Rome and others.

4. CHURCH ORGANISATION, IN THE PASTORAL EPISTLES.—
We have seen that in Acts 20²⁸ St. Paul, in addressing the presbyters of Ephesus, calls them " bishops " of God's Church when he is emphasising their administrative functions. " Bishop " and " Presbyter " are then two words for the same officer. Again he addresses " Philippians " to the Church at Philippi and its local officers, " the bishops and deacons " (Phil. 1¹). Thus in Greece, as late as 60 A.D., we find only two orders in the local ministry, the same two

[1] See Baedeker, *Central Italy*, pp. 350, 352.

as existed at Ephesus three years earlier. We know that St. Paul's habit was to appoint presbyters to take charge of every local Church ; yet the word "presbyter" never occurs in his writings outside the Pastoral Epistles— only the word "bishop." The reason is clear—the two terms were synonymous.

Going outside the New Testament, when we come to Clement of Rome (c. 95 A.D.) we still find the same thing. In § 42 he speaks of "bishops" and "deacons" as established by the Apostles, and notes that some of the bishops have been removed from their office at Corinth : lower down he speaks of some "presbyters" as having been removed.[1] Again, the same two orders, and only two, are found in the Didaché, which probably dates from the opening years of the second century. The first sign of a threefold order in the Christian ministry is in the letters of Ignatius to the Churches of Asia Minor (about A.D. 115). With characteristic dogmatism he insists, obviously as against people who differ from him, that the three orders are quite necessary to a Church.

The distinction of a bishop's office from a presbyter's seems to have followed, as one would expect, from the dying out of the Apostles. Law and order required that first there should be a presiding presbyter in each Church (e.g. St. James at Jerusalem) ; then that he should be given the authority wielded by the Apostles as such.

[1] The view taken here is approximately that of Bishop Lightfoot (Philippians, Dissertation 1, pp. 181–269). There are those who dispute it, and maintain that in Acts 20[28] St. Paul addresses first the whole body of presbyters, and then the bishops among them ; and they insist on the fact that Clement mentions bishop, presbyter, and deacon. But on that view St. Paul somehow slights the presbyters in Phil. 1[1]. And though it is conceivable that either Acts 20[28] or Clement or the Didaché, if it stood alone, admits of a threefold ministry ; yet it is surely inconceivable that all three authorities should agree in only requiring us to suppose the existence of two orders when there were actually three.

When we turn to the Pastoral Epistles, we find the writer giving the characteristics of the ideal " bishop " (singular number) in 1 Tim. 3² and Tit. 1⁷ ; and the passage in Titus seems decisively to imply that bishop and presbyter are synonymous terms (" bishop " being used as in Acts 20²⁸ to call attention to his administrative functions) : " You are to appoint *presbyters* in every city, such men as are above reproach. . . . For the *bishop* must be above reproach " (Tit. 1⁵⁻⁷). This conclusion is in absolute harmony with the whole trend of first-century custom, as we saw above. But it is worth noting that it carries with it the inference that the Pastoral Epistles are first-century documents.

5. NATURE OF THE FALSE TEACHING ATTACKED IN THE PASTORAL EPISTLES.—The author of these Epistles has frequent allusions to a type of teaching which he regards partly as a waste of valuable time and attention (" foolish and ignorant questions, " 2 Tim. 2²³ ; cp. 2¹⁴, Tit. 3⁹), but also as really dangerous to moral and spiritual life. He compares it to a " gangrene " (2 Tim. 2¹⁷) and frequently opposes it to the doctrine which makes for health ($\dot{v}\gamma\iota\alpha\dot{\iota}\nu\omega\nu$, $\dot{v}\gamma\iota\dot{\eta}s$ ; 1 Tim. 1¹⁰ 6³, 2 Tim. 1¹³ 4³, Tit. 1⁹⋅ ¹³ 2¹⋅ ²⋅ ⁸). But he nowhere explains it in detail or sets himself to show how it is false. Perhaps this is quite natural in private letters addressed to intimate friends who knew the writer's mind, though at the same time it is exactly what we should expect to find in the work of a forger seeking to crush opposition by an appeal to authority rather than to reason.[1]

---

[1] Cp. 2 Peter. See especially the quotation in Tit. 1¹², " The Cretans are always liars, evil beasts, lazy gluttons." It is hard to believe that St. Paul would repeat these words with approval, even in a private letter. It is difficult to resist the feeling that the denunciatory passages of the Pastorals are quite un-Pauline : they remind one of the self-chosen apostles of orthodoxy who write to our modern Church newspapers.

The general trend of this teaching is much the same at Ephesus and in Crete, though in the latter place it is less definite and well defined.

We may sum it up under the following heads : [1]

(a) They are admirers of the Jewish law (1 Tim. 1[7]), who dabble in "fables and endless genealogies" (1 Tim. 1[4]), "profane and old wives' fables" (4[7]), "Jewish fables" (Tit. 1[14]) which are "foolish" and make for "contentions about the law" (3[9]). The most probable theory about these fables is that they were Jewish legends based on the history "of the patriarchs and their descendants, akin to the Jewish Haggadoth, and illustrated by the Book of Enoch, the Book of Jubilees, and the treatise on Biblical Antiquities attributed to Philo" (Lock in Hast. *D.B.* He is following Hort, *Judaistic Christianity*, pp. 130–46.). Others find in these fables and genealogies an early development of the Gnostic speculations which became so marked in the second century and posited a whole series of "æons" or intermediate beings between the Absolute God and evil matter.

(b) They probably laid claim to a special knowledge (1 Tim. 6[20]), on which they prided themselves as opposed to the common herd of believers. Timothy is bidden to turn away from "the profane babblings and contradictions (ἀντιθέσεις) of the knowledge falsely so called." Now Marcion the Christian Gnostic wrote a book which he called Ἀντιθέσεις, *i.e.* the Contradictions between the Old and New Testaments ; and the "Gnostics" in general were so called because they arrogated to themselves a superior "knowledge." But it seems quite impossible on other grounds to assign to the Pastoral Epistles a date anything like as late as that of Marcion (middle of the second century). And if we admit the Jewish character of the false teaching, we can scarcely connect it with a school

[1] Following Lock in Hast. *D.B.*, art. "1 Timothy."

of thought (Marcion's) which was fiercely anti-Jewish.
It is safest to interpret 1 Tim. 6²⁰ as meaning "rival and
contradictory conclusions reached by men who all alike lay
claim to this superior knowledge."

(c) They probably believed, as so many in Asiatic lands
have always done (and as the Gnostics did), that matter is
radically evil. On that assumption they based an ascetic
code, requiring men to abstain from marriage and certain
kinds of food (1 Tim. 4³ 6¹⁷). But human nature is apt
to assert itself against any form of extreme asceticism
and to produce in reaction outbursts of vicious living,
sometimes defended on the theory that the body is earthy
and cannot affect the divinely given soul. We find some
of these professed ascetics at Ephesus "creeping into
families, and conquering silly women who are crushed
with sins and driven by many sorts of lust" (2 Tim. 3⁶).[1]
In 2 Timothy we find mentioned at least one distinctive
feature of the false teaching. In 2¹⁷ we hear of two men
at Ephesus who hold that the resurrection is already past.

It is natural to suppose that this belief is based on the
idea that the body is wholly evil : if so, the individual
personality of a man may be regarded as tainted and incapable of existing in the absolute perfection of heaven,
which can thus only be a sort of Nirvana or absorption of
all in God : probably they regarded the resurrection as
equivalent to the "second birth" of the human spirit
on earth. Finally, in 3¹³ the false teachers are called
γόητες or "magicians," and this is often held to imply
that they dabbled in the magic for which Ephesus was
famous ; but it is only introduced casually and probably
means no more than "cunning deceivers."

In all this there are unquestionably certain elements

---

[1] It is true that in 2 Tim. 3 this paragraph takes the form of a pre-
diction (" in the last days there shall be . . ."). But it implies that such
a state of things was already beginning.

which reappear in Gnosticism ; but it is unsafe to interpret the one by the other or to suppose that there was any close historical connexion between them. The Christian Gnostics, with their low views of matter, taught docetic ideas of the Incarnation ; *i.e.* they held that the Divine Logos or Christ was not really incarnate in the human body of Jesus, nor did He suffer on the cross. This sort of teaching is found at Ephesus as early as the time of 1 John and the letters of Ignatius. But there is not a hint of it in the Pastoral Epistles. The absence of it is one more sign that they cannot be assigned to any date much later than the death of St. Paul.

6. DID ST. PAUL WRITE THE PASTORAL EPISTLES ?—We have briefly examined the historical position implied in these letters, the development of Church organisation, and the nature of the false teaching which is attacked ; and so far we have discovered nothing which is incompatible with the Pauline authorship, and a certain amount which seems rather to point to it. For instance, there is weight in the argument that, if a later Christian had been writing in the assumed name of St. Paul, he would have taken pains to make any historical facts which he mentioned conform to the history of the Acts.

Moreover, the external evidence for their genuineness is as strong as we could reasonably expect it to be. Clement of Rome and Ignatius both use phrases which almost unquestionably are borrowed from these Epistles ; so does Polycarp, the contemporary of Ignatius and the disciple of St. John at Ephesus. And we know that in the middle of the second century the three letters were received by the Church as compositions of St. Paul. Therefore they were probably regarded as his by the three early authors just mentioned.

The real difficulty begins for us when we examine *the*

24

*style and language of the Epistles.* For though we meet some of the Apostle's favourite expressions, yet many of his characteristic phrases are absent, and it is almost true to say that there is a new and different vocabulary from anything found in the earlier Epistles.

There are 897 different words used in the three letters, of which 304 are not found elsewhere in St. Paul (*i.e.* a proportion of almost 1 in 3).

Now it is quite true that in private letters a man may be expected to employ a different vocabulary from that which he uses in a public thesis,[1] and that something like five years had elapsed since St. Paul wrote the Epistles of the first Roman imprisonment, years during which he must have read many new books and come in contact with new peoples and phrases ; and finally, that many of the unique words in the Pastorals may be explained as due to the new subjects with which he is dealing (*e.g.* the qualifications of a Christian minister). All that is true, and it explains a good deal.

But the startling feature of the Pastorals is not so much the number of new words which we find (new, that is, in St. Paul), but the fact that *some of his commonest particles and terms are changed in a most unexpected way.* A man of sixty-five years of age does not readily give up his favourite expressions. Why should he suddenly drop his oft-repeated διό [2] (" wherefore ") in a private letter and substitute for it the more clumsy and formal δι᾽ ἥν αἰτίαν (" for which reason " ; which is found three times in the Pastorals, and nowhere else in the New Testament except once in Hebrews) ? Or again, would you expect St.

---

[1] Yet it is noticeable that the language of these letters is not less formal than that of the earlier Epistles (as one would expect it to be), but if anything the opposite.

[2] Other Pauline particles not found in the Pastorals are ἄρα (drawing an inference), ἔπειτα, and ἔτι.

Paul suddenly to revert to Jewish usage and speak of
" *God* our Saviour " (six times in the Pastorals as against
four occurrences of " *Christ* our Saviour ") ?   Or to
speak of the " happy God " (μακάριος), as if he were a
heathen writer, instead of using the term " blessed "
(εὐλογητός) familiar to both Jew and Christian alike ?
It is just in this sort of expression that old men do not
suddenly change their habits ; and it is this alteration,
rather than the large number of new words, which is the
serious, and I think fatal, objection to the Pauline authorship of these letters.[1]

Again, the style as a whole arouses serious doubts in our
minds.   It is hard to put down on paper what constitutes
the difference in it ; and in these questions there must
always be a preponderating element of subjective impression, so that an absolute consensus of opinion is
probably impossible.   The present writer can only state
his strong conviction that, despite passages which have
the genuine Pauline ring [2] and probably come from the
Apostle in some way, the larger part of the letters as they
stand does not read like his work.   They lack his natural-
ness and his verve ;   they are precise and measured where
he is involved or passionate ;   they suggest the official
drawing up a schedule.   Their abuse of the false teachers
lacks both his dignity and his charity.   Their pessimistic
expectation that evil shall wax ever worse, is in strong contrast to everything he had written since " Thessalonians."

[1] The defenders of their genuineness (*e.g.* Dr. Parry) mostly seem
to me to miss this point.   They examine the new words in the Pastorals
at length, and point out that there is no inherent improbability in their
use by St. Paul.   But they do not explain why he should suddenly give
up his common and lifelong phraseology.

[2] That the writer was familiar with St. Paul's Epistles is clear in
many passages, *e.g.* 2 Tim. 2²¹.   A comparison of 1 Tim. 5¹⁸ with 1 Cor.
9⁹⁻¹⁴ suggests that he is deliberately quoting.   Other passages are
Pauline in tone, though they find no close parallel in the earlier Epistles.

The mentality of the writer seems different from that of St. Paul ; nor is it such as can be naturally explained as due to the growing conservatism of an old man. The author is a thorough ecclesiastic : he quotes five " faithful " sayings which are current in the Church, and which indeed in themselves might have had St. Paul for their author (see below, note on 1 Tim. 1¹⁵). He constantly harps on the need for " healthy " teaching, and discourages just that spirit of faith in the guidance of the Holy Spirit of which St. Paul is such a notable example : he tends to substitute " the faith " [1] concrete and external for the principle of " faith " abstract and internal (cp. παραθήκη, 1 Tim. 6²⁰, 2 Tim. 1¹²).

Some commentators seek to solve these difficulties by suggesting that he used an amanuensis to write the letters for him. In itself nothing can be more likely : St. Paul habitually dictated his Epistles. There is indeed nothing in the concluding paragraphs of the three Pastorals, no clause such as " the salutation by the hand of me Paul," to show that he added a verse or two at the end in his own handwriting ; but it is in itself quite likely that he did so. Nevertheless the suggestion that he dictated the letters obviously will not help here. We should have to suppose that he merely outlined the subject-matter to his secretary ; and that the latter, while remembering a few phrases of St. Paul, put the stamp of his own style and mentality on the letters. But it is almost incredible that the Apostle would have left so much to another, in giving important directions to Timothy and Titus as his apostolic delegates.

*The personal references and characterisation in the Epistles.* —We have reserved to the end an important consideration which must be put in the other scale against the difficulties with which we have been dealing. It is often pointed out that there are no Pauline Epistles which con-

---

[1] Cp. 1 Tim. 1¹⁹ 3⁹ 4¹⁻⁶ 6¹⁰⁻²¹, 2 Tim. 2¹⁸ 3⁸.

tain a greater proportion of personal references than these. That at any rate is true of 2 Timothy (see $1^{15\text{-}18}$ $4^{9\text{-}18}$; and cp. Tit. $1^5$ $3^{12\text{-}13}$, 1 Tim. $1^3$); and the details given do not strike one as such that a forger would invent. Again, the character of Timothy is drawn in lifelike and convincing strokes : we learn something of his weaknesses as well as his excellences, the last thing on which any forger would venture. Timothy is praised for his good record, and encouraged by the reminder that at his ordination certain prophecies had singled him out for administrative work (1 Tim. $1^{18}$ $4^{14}$ $6^{12}$, 2 Tim. $1^6$) : but he needs encouragement to overcome his timidity and self-diffidence (1 Tim. $4^{12\text{-}16}$, 2 Tim. $1^7$ $2^3$); he feels himself too young to be set over people of more advanced age (1 Tim. $4^{12}$; cp. 1 Cor. $16^{11}$); he suffers from frequent ill-health ($5^{23}$), which is probably one reason for his nervousness ; and lastly, though he holds an important position and must have been at least thirty years of age in A.D. 65, he is warned to " flee youthful lusts " (2 Tim. $2^{22}$). It is hard to resist the impression that in all this we are in touch with actual life and historic fact.

*A tentative solution.*—Thus we seem to have two lines of evidence which point to contradictory conclusions. The phraseology and general style are decidedly against the genuineness of the Epistles : the lifelike details of fact, particularly in 2 Timothy, point no less decidedly to St. Paul's authorship in certain passages. Also we have seen that the general atmosphere of the Epistles necessitates a date in the first century, not the second.

It is impossible to decide the question with any assurance. But these facts (if such they be) seem to suggest that, in the generation which followed the death of St. Paul, some one came across certain short letters of St. Paul to Timothy and Titus, and edited them with additions of his own, in the hope of crushing by an appeal to authority certain doctrines which were then spreading in Asia. The main objection to the theory is that it is impossible for us to break up the Epistles as we have them into Pauline and non-Pauline sections. There is no apparent break in the unity of any of the three. Some sections, such as Tit. $3^{12-15}$ and 2 Tim. $1^{3-12}$ $2^{3-13}$ $4^{5-22}$, read like genuine Pauline passages, though even here certain phrases suggest another hand. While we admit the difficulty, still this solution seems open to fewer objections than any other. At any rate it seems reasonable to accept the evidence of the Pastorals as to historical facts and as to the conditions of Church life between A.D. 65 and A.D. 95.

### 7. Brief Paraphrase and Notes on 1 Timothy.[1]

$1^{1-22}$. The Salutation.—Note that the writer says "God our Saviour," an expression never found in St. Paul outside the Pastorals. Its only other occurrences in the New Testament are in Luke $1^{47}$ and Jude v.[25], both being passages of a strongly Jewish colour. Again, "mercy" (v.[2]) occurs in no other salutation in the Pauline Epistles except in 2 Timothy. (It is found also in 2 John v.[3].) We have another un-Pauline and non-Jewish phrase in v.[11], "the happy God."

$1^{3-20}$. Against the Myths and Genealogies popular with some Christians at Ephesus. The "Aim of (our) Charge" to Men is Sincere Love (v.[5]). Not that the Jewish Law is not good when used in its Proper Sphere to restrain Sin (vv.[8-11]). But the Glory of the Christian Gospel, of which God called Paul the Sinner to be a Minister, is the Message of Sin forgiven (vv.[12-17]). In this Warfare Timothy has been marked out to take a Glorious Part, opposing Men who have made Shipwreck of the Faith.

---

[1] It seems unnecessary to paraphrase the three Epistles in detail. An outline analysis is given, with notes on obscure verses.

*Notes.*—(vv.[8-9]) " I do not object to their teaching the Mosaic Law : it is a good instrument in the hands of a teacher who uses it *lawfully*, that is as a warning against wickedness rather than as a sufficient guide to righteousness."

v.[15] gives us the first of the five " faithful sayings " which are found in the Pastorals. They seem to be [1] as follows :

(*a*) " Christ Jesus came into the world to save sinners " (1 Tim. 1[15]).

(*b*) " She (woman) shall be saved through her childbearing " (1 Tim. 2[15]).

(*c*) " Godliness hath promise of the life which now is and of that which is to come " (1 Tim. 4[8-9]).

(*d*) " According to His mercy He saved us through the washing of regeneration and renewing of the Holy Spirit which He poured out upon us richly through Jesus Christ our Saviour " (Tit. 3[5-6]). [Possibly v.[7] ought also to be included.]

(*e*) " For if we died with Him, we shall also live with Him. If we endure, we shall also reign with Him. If we deny Him, He also will deny us. If we are faithless, He abideth faithful " (2 Tim. 2[11-13]).

They probably are proverbial sayings among the early Christians. (*d*) suggests a liturgy, and (*e*) a hymn.

(v.[18]) He returns to his charge to Timothy, from which he had digressed in v.[4] in the Pauline manner. Certain prophecies had been uttered about the good work which Timothy should do : these ought to encourage him, whatever

[1] Opinions, as to what is included in the saying, differ in (*b*) (*c*) and (*d*).

his natural self-distrust may be. $4^{14}$ suggests that the prophecies were uttered at the time of his " ordination."

(v.$^{20}$) Alexander was a coppersmith at Ephesus (see 2 Tim. $4^{14}$). He may be the Jew mentioned in the riot at Ephesus (Acts $19^{33}$). If so, he had turned Christian. St. Paul " delivered to Satan " him and Hymenæus. For the meaning of this, see note on 1 Cor. $5^5$.

$2$–$3^{1a}$. Timothy is to instruct Men to pray for all Sorts and Conditions of Men, especially those in authority (vv.$^{1\text{-}2}$). For God's Will is that *all* Men shall be saved, and that is the Message which God has given to himself (vv.$^{3\text{-}7}$). Men therefore should pray for the Work in Public Worship. Women should wear Quiet Clothes and seek to do Good to others, in quiet subordination to their Husbands. Woman was responsible for the Fall in Eden; but her " Motherhood redeems her," as the saying runs, if she is Faithful, Loving, and Sober-minded.

*Notes.*—(vv.$^{4\text{-}6}$) " For there is one God who is Father of *all* men and yearns for *all* men ; one mediator, Himself man, Christ Jesus who died for *all* men. That is the witness I have to bear on all occasions."

(vv.$^{14\text{-}15}$) " *Hath fallen into transgression* " does not mean that women are specially sinful.[1] " Fell into sin, as Genesis says " (perfect tense) is the best rendering. " *Saved through the childbearing* " admits of several interpretations : *e.g.* Moffatt renders it, " get safely through childbirth." But the R.V. margin, which is followed above, seems to give far the

[1] As Bengel understands it : " facilius decepta, facilius decipit " ! But Bengel was an abbot.

(vv.⁷⁻⁸) " It is true that we must train for the
religious life with self-discipline. The training of the body for the games is of small service
except for the one end in view ; the religious
self-training is of service in all directions."
v.¹⁰ seems to show that " bodily training "
refers to the games rather than to ascetic
practices.

(v.⁹) The " faithful saying " probably is to be found
in the last clause of v.⁸ rather than in v.¹⁰.

(v.¹⁰) " *Strive* " (R.V.) ἀγωνιζόμεθα, read by
א A C. The A.V. translates ὀνειδιζόμεθα
(" suffer reproach ") with D₂ L and all the
Versions.

" *The Saviour of all mankind, especially of
them that believe*," is a striking phrase. It
seems to teach universalism.

4¹¹⁻¹⁶. TIMOTHY MUST NOT LET HIS YOUTHFULNESS
INTERFERE WITH HIS AUTHORITY. HE MUST MAKE HIS
LIFE AN EXAMPLE, WITH THE OBJECT OF SAVING NOT
ONLY HIMSELF BUT OTHERS.

*Notes.*—(v.¹³) " *Reading* " means public reading of
the Scriptures.

(v.¹⁴) See 1¹⁸ and 2 Tim. 1⁶. The prophet's words
at his ordination declared the fact ; the imposition of the elders' hands was the moment
that he realised its truth.

5¹⁻²⁵. TIMOTHY'S RELATIONS TO OLDER PEOPLE AND TO
YOUNGER (vv.¹⁻²) : DIRECTIONS ABOUT WIDOWS : THE
OLDER WIDOWS MUST BE MAINTAINED BY THEIR CHILDREN
IF THERE ARE ANY ; IF NOT, BY THE CHURCH, AS LONG AS
THEY ARE GIVEN TO PRAYER, NOT TO PLEASURE, AND ARE
NOT LESS THAN SIXTY YEARS OLD AND BEAR A GOOD
CHARACTER (vv.³⁻¹⁰). YOUNGER WIDOWS SHOULD MARRY
AGAIN, AND NOT LEAD A LIFE OF IDLE GOSSIP (vv.¹¹⁻¹⁵).

A CHRISTIAN WOMAN, WHO HAS A WIDOWED RELATIVE, SHOULD MAINTAIN HER (v.[16]). PRESBYTERS WHO ARE EFFICIENT IN ADMINISTRATION MUST BE PROPERLY PAID, PARTICULARLY IF THEY WORK HARD, IN ACCORDANCE WITH THE SAYING OF JESUS. ACCUSATIONS AGAINST THEM ARE NOT TO BE LIGHTLY ENTERTAINED ; BUT IF PROVED, THE GUILTY MUST BE STERNLY REBUKED. PERSONAL PREJUDICE MUST NOT ENTER INTO THE MATTER. GREAT CARE SHOULD BE TAKEN BEFORE ORDAINING A MAN TO THE OFFICE : MEN'S SINS AND THEIR GOOD DEEDS ALIKE MAY NOT BE OBVIOUS AT FIRST SIGHT.

*Notes.*—(v.[1]) " *Elder* " here does not denote " presbyter."

(vv.[9-10]) Patristic writers often mention an " order " of widows, who in return for maintenance performed such duties as the care of orphan children. " *Wife of one husband* " (see above on 3[2]). " *Washed the saints' feet,*" *i.e.* not scorned menial acts in showing loving care (cp. 1 Sam. 25[41]).

(v.[12]) " *Their first faith* " must mean their determination to give their lives to the service of others.

(v.[18]) In 1 Cor. 9[9, 14] St. Paul quotes the same verse from the Law and the same command of Jesus. Our Lord's words (Matt. 10[10] = Luke 10[7]) can scarcely be included under the term " the Scripture," if this is a first-century document.

(vv.[22-25]) " Do not consecrate to the presbyter's office any one without long and careful testing. If you ordain a man of scandalous life, you share the responsibility for the harm he does, and you must keep yourself pure. (In saying this, I do not infer that you should abstain

> from wine : you need a little for your health's
> sake.) Remember that while some men's sins
> are obvious, others keep theirs hidden ; and
> the same is true of good works."

$6^{1-2}$. ABOUT THE RELATIONS OF MASTER AND SLAVE.
(vv.$^{3-10}$) PEOPLE WHO DO NOT FOLLOW CHRIST'S TEACH-
ING ARE CONCEITED AND COME TO DOTE OVER WORDY
QUESTIONS WHICH ONLY CAUSE STRIFE : THEY THINK THEY
CAN GAIN SOME PERSONAL ADVANTAGE OUT OF THEIR
RELIGION. TRUE RELIGION, PRODUCING CONTENTMENT,
IS OF COURSE A GREAT ADVANTAGE ; BUT FOR MATERIAL
WEALTH A MAN SHOULD BE CONTENT WITH FOOD AND
CLOTHING. THE SEARCH FOR WEALTH BRINGS GREAT
TEMPTATIONS AND HARMFUL DESIRES WHICH PLUNGE
MEN IN RUIN. THE LOVE OF MONEY IS A ROOT OF ALL
KINDS OF EVIL. (vv.$^{11-19}$) THE MAN OF GOD MUST AIM AT
CHRISTIAN LOVE AND FAITH, AND FIGHT THE GOOD FIGHT.
TIMOTHY IS TO WARN THE WEALTHY AGAINST BEING
SUPERCILIOUS AND TRUSTING IN THEIR WEALTH : AND URGE
THEM TO USE IT TO HELP OTHERS. (vv.$^{20-21}$) FINALLY,
HE MUST GUARD JEALOUSLY THE FAITH ENTRUSTED TO
HIS CARE, AND BEWARE OF PSEUDO-KNOWLEDGE.

*Notes.*—(v.$^{7b}$) " *For neither* " (R.V.) is literally " because neither " (ὅτι οὐδέ), which makes no sense.
The A.V. translates the reading of some late
and inferior manuscripts which insert δῆλον ;
" it is clear that neither . . ." Hort thinks
the ὅτι ought to be deleted.

(v.$^{20}$) See above, § 5, p. 367.

8. THE EPISTLE TO TITUS.

$1^{1-4}$. THE SALUTATION. See notes on 1 Tim. $1^{1-2}$.

$1^{5-16}$. TITUS HAS BEEN LEFT IN CRETE IN ORDER TO SET
THINGS STRAIGHT AND APPOINT PRESBYTERS IN EVERY
CITY. HE IS REMINDED OF THE QUALIFICATIONS NEEDED

FOR THE OFFICE (vv.⁵⁻⁹). MANY IN CRETE, ESPECIALLY
OF THE JEWISH CHRISTIANS, ARE DISORDERLY HUMBUGS
WHO REALLY ONLY TEACH FOR THE SAKE OF MAKING
MONEY : THEY MUST BE SILENCED. (EVEN THE CRETAN
POET CALLS HIS COUNTRYMEN "LIARS AND IDLE
GLUTTONS.") TITUS MUST REBUKE THEM FOR THEIR
ABSORPTION IN JEWISH MYTHS AND COMMANDS. MEN
WHO ARE DEFILED AND UNBELIEVING FIND HARM IN
EVERYTHING AND PROGRESSIVELY DETERIORATE.

> *Notes.*—(v.⁶) "*Husband of one wife.*" See note on
> 1 Tim. 3².
>
> (v.⁸) The emphasis on "hospitable" is interesting.
>
> (v.¹²) The quotation is from the philosopher
> Epimenides.

2. ADVICE WHICH TITUS IS TO GIVE TO OLDER MEN (v.²),
AND OLDER WOMEN. THE LATTER ARE TO SET A GOOD
EXAMPLE TO YOUNGER WOMEN AND TEACH THEM TO DO
THEIR HOME DUTIES (vv.³⁻⁵). ADVICE FOR THE YOUNGER
MEN (v.⁶) : TITUS IS TO SET THEM A GOOD EXAMPLE AND
STICK TO SOUND DOCTRINE (vv.⁷⁻⁸). ADVICE TO GIVE
SLAVES (vv.⁹⁻¹⁰). EVERY ONE MUST TRY TO BE AN ORNA-
MENT TO THE RELIGION OF GOD'S SAVING GRACE, AS ONE
ALWAYS WAITING FOR THE REVELATION OF GOD AND
CHRIST (vv.¹¹⁻¹⁴).

> *Note.*—(v.¹³) "*The appearing of the glory of our great God
> and Saviour Jesus Christ.*" So R.V., but they
> are probably wrong. The R.V. margin ("the
> great God and our Saviour") is a possible
> rendering of the Greek in spite of the absence
> of the article before σωτῆρος. It is true
> that "appearing" is always used of Christ's
> Parousia elsewhere, but the insertion of the
> word "glory" makes a difference here. Cp. 3⁴
> below, where conversion to Christ is the
> "appearing" of God's goodness. If Christ is

here called " our great God," the language has
no parallel in St. Paul.

3. Titus must urge Men to be submissive to the
Powers that be, to avoid Quarrels and be meek towards all Men (vv.$^{1-2}$). For though Paul himself
and they alike were once Slaves of their Passions
and hated others, yet God revealed to them all His
Loving-kindness and saved them in the Water of
Baptism, giving His Spirit to them through Christ,
as the Well-known Saying puts it (vv.$^{3-8a}$). Such
Teaching is good, but Foolish Genealogies and Contentions about Small Points of Law are useless
(vv.$^{8b-9}$). Factious People are to be warned, but
if they persevere, avoided (vv.$^{10-11}$). Personal
Messages (vv.$^{12-14}$). Farewell (v.$^{15}$).

Notes.—(v.$^5$) Cp. Eph. 5$^{26}$. Moffatt paraphrases the
clause as follows: " by the water that means
regeneration and renewal under the Holy
Spirit."

(v.$^8$) " The saying." See on 1 Tim. 1$^{15}$.

(v.$^{12}$) Nicopolis. There was an important city of
this name in Epirus, on the south-easterly
coast of the Adriatic. In 2 Tim. 4$^{10}$ Titus
is said to be in Dalmatia, which was part of
Illyria, to the north of Epirus. But there was
another Nicopolis in Macedon which may be
meant here.

(v.$^{14}$) " Maintain good works " (R.V.) is more
probable than the R.V. margin, " profess
honest occupations," because the latter de-
parts from the common meaning of " good
works." He bids the Christians of Crete
prepare themselves in the small acts of everyday life to meet the bigger calls when they
come (" necessary uses," literally " needs ").

9. 2 TIMOTHY.

1¹⁻². SALUTATION.

1³⁻¹⁸. " It is a joy to me to pray for you constantly.   I
long to see you.   You have, I am certain, the same sincere
faith which marked your mother and grandmother (vv.³⁻⁵).
And God bestowed on you, when I ordained you, a special
gift which you must not allow to lie dormant :  God did
not give us a spirit of cowardice but of power, love, and
discipline (vv.⁶⁻⁷).   Therefore do not be ashamed of our
message nor of my imprisonment :  bear hardship for the
gospel ;  God who saved us in His grace is mighty ;  Christ
brought to naught death and brought to light life, as I
have been appointed to preach.   Therefore I suffer without shame :  I have put my faith in Him and I know He
is mighty to keep what He has committed to me.   I have
committed to you a model of sound instruction ;  keep it
safe through the Spirit which dwells in us (vv.⁸⁻¹⁴).   All
those who are now in Asia deserted me in my need :
but Onesiphorus refreshed me often and was never
ashamed of my imprisonment :  he sought me out in
Rome ;  and you know well how he served me formerly
in Ephesus."

*Notes.*—(v.⁶) See 1 Tim. 1¹⁸ 4¹⁴.

> (v.⁷) " *Discipline* " (R.V.).   σωφροσύνη and σώφρων
> are rare in St. Paul's writings, except in the
> Pastorals where they occur frequently.   They
> express the essentially Greek ideal of sane-
> minded moderation.   The word in this verse is
> σωφρονισμός, which expresses not self-control
> but the power of controlling others, *i.e.* " dis-
> ciplining," not " discipline."
>
> (v.¹²) " *That which I have committed to Him* "
> (R.V.) is a possible rendering.   But the
> usage of παραθήκη elsewhere in the Pastorals
> suggests that the R.V. margin is right in

rendering, "that which He has committed to me."

(v.[15]) We do not know the circumstances of St. Paul's arrest, and so cannot say what this verse means. He may have been arrested at Ephesus and left in the lurch by all the local Christians except Onesiphorus. But perhaps the reference is to certain Asians who were with him in the West and have now returned to Asia.

2[1-2]. "Be strong and commit to faithful men, able to teach others, the instruction you received from me. (vv.[3-6]) Christ's soldier must suffer hardship, and like any other soldier avoid being engrossed in matters of everyday life. In the games only the competitor who keeps the rules can win the crown. The farmer who has worked hard has first claim on the produce. (vv.[7-10]) Remember always the risen Christ, incarnate of David's line. For preaching Him I am shut up in prison as a malefactor, but God's revelation is not shut up. (vv.[11-13]) Remember the well-known saying that we must suffer with Christ if we would reign with Him. (vv.[14-18]) Warn men not to waste time on petty and useless disputes. Strive yourself to cut straight the true teaching. Profane babblings become a gangrene in the Church, as in the case of those who say that our resurrection has already taken place. (v.[19]) God's firm foundation is known by this mark that 'those who worship Him depart from unrighteousness.' (v.[20]) In a large house there are utensils of various materials and for nobler or baser purposes : any one who cleanses himself of the errors I have named, shall be God's vessel for an honourable use. (v.[22]) Avoid youthful lusts ; follow after righteousness ; keep away from foolish questions which gender strife. Be meek in admonishing opponents, in the hope that God may give them repentance."

25

*Notes.* — (v.[2]) "*Among many witnesses*" (E.V.) does
violence to the Greek.[1] "Through many
witnesses" must be right : apparently meaning, "Many who have heard me have empha-
sised it to you."

(v.[18]) See above, p. 368.

(v.[20]) Cp. Rom. 9[21].

(v.[26]) The literal translation is, "having been taken
captive by him (αὐτοῦ) to do the other's
(ἐκείνου) will." The "Him" must be God.
ἐκείνου is probably "of Christ," as in St.
John ἐκεῖνος, standing alone, denotes Christ
(John 19[35], 1 John 3[3] 4[17]).

3[1]. "It has been foretold that in the last days times
shall be difficult and men self-indulgent. (v.[6]) You know
how some creep into a household and take captive silly
women who are victims of various passions. (v.[8]) Like
the magicians who opposed Moses, these men oppose the
truth. (v.[10]) But you have throughout known my teaching and my Christian life ; you knew all the persecutions
which befell me in Lycaonia ; indeed all who follow the
religion of Christ Jesus shall suffer persecution. (v.[12]) Evil
men shall get worse and worse ; but you must remain
true to the teaching which you have enjoyed from your
boyhood in a Jewish home. You know the old Scriptures ;
(v.[16]) all of them are inspired and therefore meant for our
instruction in righteousness."

*Notes.*—(v.[8]) Jannes and Jambres, according to the
Targum of Jonathan on Ex. 7[11], were the
magicians who opposed Moses.

(v.[15]) The "*sacred writings*" must mean the Old
Testament, as it does in Philo and Josephus.

(v.[16]) The paraphrase given above follows the R.V.

---

[1] διά of attendant circumstances is not used of *persons* : unless indeed
διὰ τοῦ Ἰησοῦ in 1 Thess. 4[14] means "*with* Jesus" (see note, p. 130).

> margin, which is the obvious translation of the
> Greek. Inspiration entails spiritual insight
> into the significance of life.

4[1]. "Never relax your efforts in teaching, comforting,
rebuking. The time is coming when men will not tolerate
sound teaching but rush off to new teachers who tickle
their fancy with various myths. (v.[5]) You must be ready
to endure hardship in your ministry. (v.[6]) My life-blood
is soon to be shed as a libation to God. I have fought the
good fight : the Lord will give me the crown which He
promised."

(vv.[9-22]) PERSONAL MESSAGES AND FAREWELL.

*Notes.*—(v.[1]) The R.V. reading ($\kappa\alpha\iota$, for $\kappa\alpha\tau\acute{\alpha}$ of A.V.)
has overwhelming evidence on its side.

> (v.[3]) "*Having itching ears*" was a proverbial
> expression for people who "liked to hear some-
> thing to please them" (Hesychius).

> (v.[10]) Galatia may mean the Galatia in Asia Minor,
> or Gaul in Europe, which was often called
> Galatia down till A.D. 200.

> (v.[13]) $\phi\epsilon\lambda\acute{o}\nu\eta$ (Latin "pænula ") was a large out-
> door cloak. The "*books*" are papyri, the
> "*parchments*" are vellum and therefore much
> more costly (see below, p. 401).

> (v.[17]) "*Out of the mouth of the lion.*" Not to be
> taken literally, for as a Roman citizen St. Paul
> could not be thrown to the lions in the
> amphitheatre. It is probably a reminiscence
> of Ps. 22[21].

# CHAPTER XIX.

## A SUMMARY OF ST. PAUL'S RELIGIOUS
## BELIEF.

1. THE SIMPLICITY OF HIS BELIEF.—We have tried, in our study of the Apostle's life and letters, to get at the heart of his Christianity—that is, at the practical religion which pulsed in his daily life and gave him strength to meet peril, anxiety, and weariness. In this chapter we have nothing new to add : we have only to gather up briefly what has been already said in scattered fragments.

Is it all too simple to satisfy us ?  Many Christians will answer, " Yes, it is vague and elementary : it misses out some of the vital truths which St. Paul taught, such as imputed righteousness or sacramental grace."  Another school will complain that our sketch omits just those characteristic features which St. Paul introduced into the religion of Jesus Christ.

But such criticisms mostly start with the presupposition that theological dogmas, which are found in the Church two centuries later, must necessarily be read back into St. Paul.  They overlook the possibility—may we not say probability ?—that early attempts to systematise doctrine inevitably tended to parody it somewhat, partly through a too literalistic interpretation by the Western mind, and partly by hardening it into dogma.  The same danger of parody attends philosophical analysis in all ages, and not least in modern psychology.  We can at least claim this for our picture of St. Paul's religion, that it is in harmony with

the recorded teaching of our Lord in the Gospels, and
only goes beyond it in one or two details of belief about
our Lord's preincarnate work (which, however, are found
in the Fourth Gospel) and about our future life after death.

Does the simplicity of our picture in itself raise any
doubts as to its general inclusiveness ?  In some of St.
Paul's Churches, notably Colossæ, he was met with the very
complaint that his religious teaching was too simple and
elementary and that it lacked theological philosophy.
In our own day, however, nothing so much keeps men of
sincere mind and upright life from accepting the teaching
of the Church, as a conviction that her theological dogmas
are too complicated and arbitrary, and too remote from
life, to be convincing.  It is surely true that the simple
things in life, such as fatherhood and love and personality,
are always the deepest and most inexplicable :  and it is
when religion is based at every point on such simple experiences that it carries most conviction and gives the
deepest insight.  " Faith—as indeed may be said of all
truth—is like Antæus in Greek legend, who was invincible
when touching mother-earth." [1]

Be this as it may, the chief essential in approaching St.
Paul's letters to discover his religious belief is as complete
as possible a renunciation of all preconceptions, joined to
as complete as possible a knowledge of his life and environment.  We believe that, so approached, his religion
will be found to be at once very simple and very vital. [2]

2. GOD AND ATONEMENT WITH HIM IN CHRIST.
CHRISTOLOGY.—The great inheritance which St. Paul

---

[1] Carnegie Simpson, *The Fact of Christ*, p. 105.

[2] In this connexion it is worth considering his missionary method.  A
stay of about two years in a large city, such as Corinth or Ephesus,
seemed to him sufficient.  If he had taught a nucleus of people the
meaning and reality of life in Christ and given them an outline of His
recorded words, he felt he could leave them to God and go elsewhere.

received from his Jewish faith was a deep conviction of the unutterable holiness of the one transcendent God. God dwells in light unapproachable and His utter abhorrence of sin is beyond human ken. This truth was often obscured by the self-complacence of the legalistic school among the Pharisees, who regarded themselves as kept within the Covenant by ritual observances : but it was not so with a man of honest conscience like St. Paul. To him God's righteousness could not be compromised by accepting sacrifice instead of obedience. God does indeed forgive the penitent sinner, but only on condition that henceforth he shall walk perfectly in the way of holiness ; and how shall man find *power* to do that or ever be clean in his Maker's sight ? How shall he find repentance, which is not remorse but involves a shifting of one's whole attitude towards his sin (μετάνοια =change of mind) ? There was no solution to the difficulty of atonement with God for a man whose conscience refused to be beguiled by legalistic casuistry. " The evil that I would not, that I do. . . . O wretched man that I am, who shall deliver me from this body given over to death ? " Salvation by works can only bring haunting failure and despair to one who refuses to lower his vision of God's holiness.

Then Christ spoke and claimed His Apostle. St. Paul learned once for all that God is love even more than He is holiness, and that by self-sacrificing love He can redeem and do what fear can never do in men. Free redemption— utterly, absolutely free—is available for any man who can answer to God's self-sacrificing and self-stooping love, who learns to trust God and so love Him. This " redemption," " salvation," " justification " is found " *in* Christ "—that is, in union with the risen, ever-present Lord.

We considered above (p. 73) what he means by his ever-repeated phrase " in Christ." Here let us borrow a quotation from a modern writer which puts it clearly.

Dr. Carnegie Simpson writes : Christ's " moral aim and mission on earth were not simply to teach morals, or even exemplify them, but—it is His own phrase—' baptize with the spirit.' And that He succeeded in this, His transformation of a John and a Peter, a Mary Magdalene, and countless others shows. Most literally and obviously He put into them a new spirit—His own spirit of purity, love, forgiveness, and humility—and thus made them new characters. We can understand this so long as Jesus actually was living on earth. The spirit of a great personality enters into those who come into actual contact with Him. A brave man inspires the spirit of bravery in others by his presence ; a pure soul purifies us when we are with him. . . . But this has limits. This kind of influence on men's spirits demands one thing—that the author of it be himself present. It is essentially personal. . . . But it is here that we meet with by far the most remarkable phenomenon both of the New Testament and of all moral history. [Here he discusses our Lord's promises of the abiding presence of His spirit after His earthly career was closed.] . . . Let us turn now to the other writings of the New Testament. What do we find ? This pathetic sense of irreparable personal loss, the constant sigh that He were here to guide and strengthen and inspire, the sad refrain—' Now He is dead ' ? . . . We find that every page is simply throbbing with the utter opposite. Every book is filled with the witness to it that the last words of Jesus [' I am with you always, even unto the end of the world '] are found fully, literally true. His great idea had been towards the end of His earthly life that all that spiritually He had been to men—all that He was for men, above mere precept and example, in His personality— would continue a living spirit within them. The New Testament writers' chief thesis—I say it deliberately— is that this is so. The spirit of Jesus moving them, moulding them, transforming them as really, as directly, as powerfully, as personally, as when He walked on earth and spoke to them—that is unquestionably the great feature of New Testament literature." [1]

But how can this redemption make us utterly at one *with God* the absolutely Holy ? Only on one condition— that Jesus Christ, who lived on earth as man, really subject to all human limitations except sin, is Himself utterly and entirely at one with God. And, be it noticed, we have here no dialectic argument but a conclusion which keeps in touch with St. Paul's daily experience. The daily Presence, in which his whole life was wrapt up, was indeed that of Christ : but in it and in it alone he touched God, was gripped by Him. The Christian, says Dr. Carnegie Simpson, " finds in the fact of Christ all he looks to find in God. As he reads the definition of eternal life as ' to know Thee (that is, God) and Jesus Christ whom Thou hast sent,' he is quite unable religiously to maintain the distinction between the two. He finds God not beyond Christ, but in Him." [2] So with St. Paul : Christ for him is the " image " (εἰκών) of God : He has the " fulness " of the Godhead (Col. $1^{19}$), and " in Him " we are " filled full " (Col. $2^{10}$).

Theologians have erected on this the doctrine of " imputed " righteousness, though it is important to notice that St. Paul never used the word " impute " in this connexion ! If by this they mean that, according to the Apostle, God sees the seed of life growing in us and knows to what fulness it will some day attain, and therefore He " justifies " us, their term expresses what St. Paul says over and over again : but in that case it were better to speak of " imparted " righteousness—imparted here on earth in measure, but some day to be imparted in full. But too often they give a further connotation to the term " im-

[1] Carnegie Simpson, *The Fact of Christ*, pp. 71–6.  [2] *Ibid.* p. 112.

puted righteousness," and one which it is hard to find in St. Paul's writings. They think of a God like some human lawgiver, who has attached a penalty to the breach of law : the majesty of the law must be vindicated, or God's holiness would be besmirched ; and it has been vindicated by the perfect obedience and voluntary sacrifice of our Lord for us. This theory seems to bring religious satisfaction to some people : but we search for it in vain in the letters of St. Paul. In this connexion it is worth while to study closely the passage in Rom. $3^{24\text{-}26}$. We shall not attempt here to reiterate what was said above on these verses (see p. 255). But we may emphasise the leading thought in the writer's mind. God, in His tolerance, " passed by " the former sins of men ; but in Christ He showed at once His own absolute righteousness and His will to treat as righteous the man who has faith in Jesus. How, we may ask, did God in Christ show forth His own absolute righteousness ? Simply by proving to men that He the all-Holy cannot forgive sin without an incalculable cost—the cost *to Himself, paid by Himself,* of yearning suffering over His erring children (cp. Rom. $8^{26\text{-}27}$). So God suffers always for the sins of the world ; and the price proves His utter Holiness as well as the infinity of His redemptive love. God is the absolutely righteous and loving Father, in whose heart the lives of all His children are always present and who treats them in perfect wisdom, so as to make them, by their own choice, seek after and share His own righteousness : and the way for men, the only way, is to put in the background of their minds the external duties which He would have them perform, and seek Him, the living Person, in their union with Christ, to win His mind and His standpoint. This is " justification by faith," not " by works." [1]

[1] It may be felt that the interpretation here offered does less than justice to St. Paul's connexion of the Atonement with the Crucifixion

Yet it is noteworthy that St. Paul, like other New Testament writers, avoids saying explicitly that God suffers for the sins of the world, though he comes very near to it in Rom. $8^{26-27}$ and Eph. $4^{30}$. Probably this fact is due to the belief which seems to have arisen at an early date in the Christian Church that Christ is to be regarded as the Divine Logos (Word or Reason of God). This conception is a meeting-point of Jewish speculation and Greek philosophy. Some of the Jewish prophets (*e.g.* Isaiah and Ezekiel) attributed superhuman qualities to the coming Messiah ; in later times he was identified by some with Israel's guardian angel, spoken of in Dan. 7, and with the "Wisdom" of God which is almost personified in the Wisdom literature. In the "Similitudes" of the Book of Enoch, the Messiah to come is regarded as a heavenly "Son of man," already existing *in idea* with Jehovah. It was inevitable that the early Christian Church should apply all this to our Lord. Moreover, at Alexandria the intellectual school of Jews were trying to harmonise Greek philosophy with their own religion ; and they spoke of the Logos of God as denoting, not only the rational principles which underlie the material world and give it meaning, but more generally the human—facing finite-wards—aspect of God as distinguished from His infinite and absolute qualities, God's self-revelation to man. This, of course, is highly speculative, however satisfying it may be to the Christian who knows from his experience

of Christ. But the death of our Lord is regarded by him as the supreme point of His self-sacrifice for us (Phil. $2^8$). He gave Himself so utterly that He submitted even to a criminal's execution, facing the uttermost that human sin and cruelty entail. And the Crucifixion is the gage of His self-identification with us by which He bears our sins. Moreover, St. Paul speaks of our being redeemed "*in* Christ" and being saved by "the blood" of Christ (*i.e.* His Divine life poured out for us) far oftener than he connects it with the Crucifixion alone. The Resurrection is an integral part of the meaning of the Crucifixion.

that Jesus Christ is Divine.   St. Paul regarded our Lord's
pre-existence as almost self-evident, and therefore it was
natural that he should believe in Him as God's agent in
creation and subsequently as the sustainer of the whole
world ;  He is its final cause, its efficient power and meaning, its future goal (Col. 1$^{16-17}$, 1 Cor. 8$^6$).

3. THE INDIVIDUAL AND THE CHURCH.   THE MEANS OF
GRACE.—Christ or " the Spirit of Christ " or " the Spirit
of God " (for he uses the three terms interchangeably,
Rom. 8$^{9-10}$) is ever present with the Christian to guide him
into truth in all his thoughts and plans and deeds.   Our
part is but to seek Him constantly in prayer and worship
and meditation and active life.

But is this guidance granted primarily to the individual
or the Church as a whole ?   St. Paul would unquestionably say, " to the Church through the individuals of whom
it is composed."   When he gave advice to the Corinthians
on difficult problems in their lives, he said, " Judge ye
yourselves what I say " (1 Cor. 10$^{15}$).   When he took his
line about the admission of the Gentiles without circumcision, he did so independently of the consent of the Church.
He insisted strongly that his commission had been given
him by Christ Himself, not through man nor by man.

Yet the life of the whole body, the Church, is much
richer than the life of any member of it.   The Holy Spirit
gives different gifts to every individual.   They are har-
monious, for they all come from the same Spirit, and there
is but one Lord Christ working in all Christians (1 Cor.
12$^{4-6. 11}$).   The whole has a meaning and force which the
component parts lack.   St. Paul himself uses two metaphors to express it :  first, that of a temple consisting of
many different parts ;  secondly, that of the human body,
and this is his favourite comparison because it is living
and gives an analogy to the one spiritual life-force, Jesus

Christ. Catholicity implies the gathering into one of every man's gift and revelation ; it is all-inclusive, not exclusive.

Such is his idealistic view ; but in practice there are found to be excrescences in the parts, which forbid their perfect fitting together, and which therefore cannot be in conformity with God's plan. The only thing to do is to go forward in humility, believing that, where a man has faith, there God will reveal to him his errors (Phil. 3$^{15}$). All Christians *are* members of the body of Christ, *are* one in Him (1 Cor. 1$^{12}$). By acts of brotherly love, such as the collection of funds among the Gentiles for the poor Christians at Jerusalem, they can be made to realise their essential unity.

But there were two external acts of ritual which, instituted by Christ Himself, were regarded with special reverence in the early Church—namely, Baptism and Holy Communion. That they were held to be uniquely sacred is evident from 1 Cor. 10$^{1\text{-}13}$, where we find that the Corinthians, in accordance with a tendency always present in human nature, had begun to look on them as magical charms which secured God's favour without regard to their moral lives.

St. Paul's attitude to the two sacraments is much the same as that of the great Jewish prophets to sacrifice ; they are only of help to those who come with a humble and sincere heart. Jesus, who had discarded all the elaborate ritual of the Jews as burdensome and exorbitant, seems deliberately to have based these two Christian symbols on the commonest acts of daily life—washing and feeding. And to the early Christians the prime significance of each sacrament resided in the fact that the Lord is actually present : as He took children in His arms and blessed them when on earth, so still He receives the child or man who comes to the symbolic act of washing away sin ; and as He gave the bread and wine to the Apostles at the Last Supper, so He still does to " God's merry men " (to use

St. Francis' term). Does the sacrament effect what it
symbolises for those who come conscious of His presence ?
As much, perhaps, as a mother kissing her child as a sign
and symbol of affection feeds its love for her. Matter is
but a parable, a vesture of God, to those who have eyes
to see. Humanity, being limited by time and space, is
necessarily subject to the influence of definite moments and
specific acts. The very simplicity of the two sacraments
instituted by Christ is a proof that we are meant to raise
all the common acts of life to their level and potentiality.
All things uncontaminated by sin are God's sacraments
to man. If in one sense Christ left but two sacraments,
in another and real sense He left us thousands of them—
marriage (Eph. 5$^{32}$), ordination, a beautiful sunset, a
spiritual face, all these and countless others.

So much *at least* St. Paul held and believed, and such
truths were perhaps more obvious in an age when Holy
Communion was still part of the common Love-Feast of
the community, a copy of the Last Supper. But does he
mean no more when he writes about Baptism such a
passage as Rom. 6$^{3-5}$, where he pursues a favourite thought
and says that we are baptized into Christ's death and
resurrection ? Does this language imply that he found in
the Sacrament some magic efficacy, uniting us with Christ
almost as if it were physically ? Such a belief in the
external potency of a symbol would surely be strangely
out of keeping with the whole trend of his mind in religion.
If he held it, he must have given to Baptism a far more
prominent place in his teaching about justification by
faith ; instead of which he only mentions it incidentally
in this connexion, as an illustration of the inward spiritual
faith which gives union with the Lord. In 1 Cor. 10$^2$ he
can say that the Israelites at the Exodus were " all baptized
into Moses," meaning that they put their whole trust in
their leader to rescue them from a seemingly desperate

impasse : it is the quality of faith that makes the comparison real. The Sacraments by their external elements make this faith easier and increase it.

4. ESCHATOLOGY.—St. Paul's doctrine of the last things may be called speculative, like some points in his Christology ; but it is more directly based on his religious experience. And here he shows his originality : while much of the eschatology of the early Church was still confined in the swaddling clothes of Jewish belief about the life beyond death, he came to the great conclusion that to die means to go and be with Christ immediately, and he formulated the great conception of a spiritual body.

Our Lord's argument to the Sadducees, to prove personal existence beyond death, is that God was in a real sense *the God* of the patriarchs ; if Abraham, Isaac, and Jacob could hold commune with Him, it could only be because they had in them something of His Divine spirit, which is indestructible. In confirmation of this, the Christian could turn to the fact of Christ's Resurrection as a pledge of his own : if he was *in* Christ, he would be with Christ in eternity, but only if he had received of God's life and become Christlike (this is the argument of 1 Cor. 15). As to the fate of the wicked and unfaithful, the early Christians had no more knowledge than we have : only Christ had said emphatically that there is a sure and certain hell for all who deliberately turn their backs on God. Whether this hell was to be retributive and everlasting (as the Jews held) or redemptive and temporary, they had no clear opinion. St. Paul, as we have seen, came at last to the great hope of the ultimate redemption of all mankind.

Now Christ had taught that the kingdom of heaven and eternal life are to be found on earth since His coming, partial but real : and that they shall grow, like the mustard seed, to a great consummation in the day when God shall

be all in all.  Heaven and hell therefore are not places
but states of mind (as the Fourth Gospel insists so emphatically).  Death is but the great promotion, the throwing off of the limits of time and space : but personality
endures (the " spiritual body "), personality more full and
real than here on earth, not naked and stripped ; because,
as St. Paul says, we shall be with Christ, the great creator
of personality, walking by sight, not faith (Phil. 1²³, 2 Cor.
5⁶⁻⁹).  He will inevitably make us Christlike, even as light
floods a dark place (Eph. 5¹³ ; cp. 1 John 3²).  So, after
speaking of the bitterest sufferings and most heart-searching fears that earth can offer, St. Paul can burst into his
great song of triumph (Rom. 8³¹⁻³⁹) : " neither death nor
life . . . will be able to separate us from the love of God
which is in Christ Jesus our Lord."

5. His Message for our Age.—It has only been
possible, in the space at our disposal, to sketch in very
rough outline St. Paul's religious belief.

"Paulinism (writes Harnack, *History of Dogma*, I. 135),
is a religious and Christocentric doctrine, more inward
and more powerful than any other which has ever
appeared in the Church.  It stands in the clearest
opposition to all merely natural moralism, all righteousness of works, all religious ceremonialism, all Christianity
without Christ. . . . ' The Pauline reactions describe the
critical epochs of theology and the Church ' (Bigg). . . .
Paulinism has proved to be a ferment in the history of
dogma ; a basis it has never been.  Just as it had that
significance in Paul himself, with reference to Jewish
Christianity, so it has continued to work through the
history of the Church."

St. Paul has a thousand messages for our age, and they
would fill many books.  But if we may choose one, it is

surely that of unfaltering faith in the Risen Christ and in the Father. The infallibilities of Bible or Church, in which our ancestors believed, have gone, and the pendulum has swung to the other extreme. Even in our religious world there is a note of uncertainty and timidity which can never achieve the victory of God. But nothing can touch the fact of the Risen Christ who is the Jesus of history. The attempt to prove that men make their own religious experience by auto-suggestion may have a small element of truth in it ; but when it is brought forward to explain the fact of Christ and all our belief in God, it is nothing but a gigantic bluff, attributing to human nature a creative power immeasurably greater than anything we possess. Such an attack on religion is surely a counsel of despair.

We have an " anointing " from the anointed Christ, or (to use St. Paul's term) an " earnest," a first instalment of God's Holy Spirit. Nothing can shake or alter that fact. And so in an age distraught with the cruelties of war, when human nature is revealing at once its glorious heroism and its animal ferocity, faith in Christ and in the power of love as opposed to force still brings the hope " which putteth not to shame." We think of the little Jew of Tarsus setting out to storm the strongholds of the heathen world which were entrenched behind its vested interests and its centuries of dark superstition, its materialism, and its world-empire : we see him dogged perpetually by the unscrupulous hatred of his own people ; yet never despairing, and in the end carried on by God to a victory such as an Alexander or a Napoleon never knew. God is working His purpose out through " men of good will," and the " weak things " of the world still have power to subdue the strong. " Wherefore, my beloved brethren, be ye stedfast, unmovable, always abounding in the work of the Lord, inasmuch as ye know that your labour is not in vain in the Lord."

# APPENDIX.

## NOTE ON THE TEXTUAL CRITICISM OF THE NEW TESTAMENT AND ON MANUSCRIPTS AND VERSIONS WHICH CONCERN THE ACTS AND PAULINE EPISTLES.

*[Only for readers who know nothing of the subject.]*

### 1. THE MATERIAL FOR ANCIENT BOOKS.

FOR two thousand years and more before Christ the ordinary material used for books was papyrus [1]—that is, the stem of the papyrus reed cut into slices (about 15 by $2\frac{1}{2}$ inches). Three or four such slices were placed side by side longitudinally, and backed with others transversely, to make a " page." These " pages " were then made up into a circular roll, some 30 feet long at the most. But papyrus becomes fragile and friable except in very dry places, and books were not long-lived.

Necessity is the mother of invention. In the second century B.C. Eumenes, King of Pergamus, was a book-collector : his rival, Ptolemy, cut off from him the supply of papyrus which grew by the Nile, in order to give priority to his own library at Alexandria. Eumenes circumvented him by inventing a method of dressing leather to form " vellum," for writing on, which became known as ' charta Pergamene " or " parchment." It was durable but very

[1] Short private letters were often written on wax-tablets with a metal pen, but St. Paul probably used papyrus always.

costly,[1] and the early Christians could not afford it until the Roman Empire became officially Christian in A.D. 313 under Constantine. Consequently our New Testament books were written on papyrus and new copies were frequently made.

## 2. TRANSCRIPTIONAL ERRORS.

In any book copied by hand there must be a percentage of errors. This percentage is higher when the original was dictated. Again in the earlier days the words of the New Testament were not treated with so much reverence as later. Men often did not hesitate to change a word or a construction to give what they thought was greater clearness or better style, particularly in private pocket Bibles.[2] In some cases they added a detail of geography or some traditional story which had come to their knowledge. Thus there exists a large number of variant readings, due to unintentional or intentional alterations, in the manuscripts. Westcott and Hort's text differs even from that followed by the Revised Version in about six thousand cases, though the vast majority of these differences do not materially alter the sense.

Fortunately we have so many manuscripts of the New Testament, as well as early " Versions " (particularly the translations into Latin, Syriac, and Coptic), that in practically every case we may be confident that the original text is preserved somewhere among them.

[1] One of our leading manuscripts (א) has in its present mutilated form 346½ leaves : each leaf is half the skin of an antelope.

[2] Papyri were sometimes made up into book form, though their brittleness made this generally inadvisable. It is noticeable that in our earliest vellum manuscripts of the Bible (א and B, dating from about A.D.330), which, of course, are in book form, we have reproduced exactly the " pages " of the papyri from which they were copied ; i.e. they have respectively four and three narrow vertical columns of writing on each page.

### 3. Methods of Judging between Two Variant Readings.

We may consider any variation in reading under two headings :

(a) On grounds of INTERNAL EVIDENCE, we may ask (1) which reading seems *intrinsically* the more probable, as giving the better sense ; and (2) which seems preferable on grounds of *transcriptional probability, i.e.* which looks more like a copyist's unintentional error of ear or eye, or again which is the copyist more likely to have altered intentionally.[1]

In some cases internal evidence settles the question. But in the majority its voice is indecisive : commentators differ in opinion ; and it is obviously necessary to find if possible some external scientific criterion which will be independent of any one's individual judgment.

(b) So we look for it in EXTERNAL EVIDENCE, or the evidence of our documents (Greek manuscripts, early versions, and quotations of Scripture by the early fathers).

### 4. Scientific Use of Manuscript Evidence.

The primitive method of using manuscript evidence was simply to count the number of authorities which supported each variant reading and to follow the majority. But a hundred manuscripts may all be copied from one original in the same locality ; their evidence is then worth no more than that of the one. Nor will it suffice simply to count heads among the older or the more trustworthy manuscripts. Sometimes one of late date gives a better text than one much earlier : and the most trustworthy still has a percentage of errors.

---

[1] The reading, which *at first sight* looks the harder, is often found to give really a better sense. A copyist, not understanding it, has altered the text.

At last it became obvious that there is only one method which promises greater scientific accuracy, and that is known as the *genealogical* method. Manuscripts of the N.T. are found to fall roughly into three big groups characterised by broadly recognisable types of text, and we can more easily assess the value of a group than of an individual.

In the space available here we can only summarise the conclusions of Westcott and Hort about these groups.

(*a*) The first, which they call THE NEUTRAL because they think it diverges least from the original text, is a type definitely connected with Alexandria and Cæsarea and traceable as far back as about A.D. 200. It only numbers among its supporters two first-grade manuscripts, ℵ and B, though they are the two most ancient in existence and differ very little from each other. Their text is often the same as that used by Origen (*c.* 200), the most learned investigator of the early Church into the text of Scripture.

(*b*) The second, which they call THE WESTERN, can be traced back at least to A.D. 150, and was widely known from Gaul to Syrian Antioch.[1] But it is not a homogeneous whole : its members differ widely among themselves, though they share salient characteristics. The leading authorities which give this type of text are : (1) Among Greek manuscripts D and $D_2$, with some kindred South French or Sardinian manuscripts. D is on the extreme left wing : a number of its readings are universally rejected, though the residue is important. (2) The many old Latin Versions, the oldest of which go back to A.D. 150. (3) The old Syriac Versions (except the Sinaitic Syriac, which is largely Neutral).

Westcott and Hort consider that the Western Text contains so many deliberate changes of the original text,

[1] " Western " is now known to be a misnomer.

that they refuse almost everywhere [1] to accept its evidence.
Recent opinion is inclined to hold that they were too
drastic in rejecting Western readings, considering the
early date and wide spread of this type of text.[2]

(c) The third group they called THE SYRIAN, because it is
probably due to a revision of the New Testament text in
Syria in the fourth century. An overwhelming majority
of the later Greek manuscripts belong to this type, which is
followed in our Authorised Version (the Textus Receptus).
It has no claim to be primitive or accurate : it is simply
the product of an attempt to secure a fixed text along
cautious conservative lines in an unscientific age.

[In critical apparatus the sign ω is sometimes used
(e.g. in Souter's Greek Testament) to denote the mass of
manuscripts of this type.]

5. NOTES ON THE CHIEF GREEK MANUSCRIPTS AND ON
THE MOST ANCIENT VERSIONS WHICH CONTAIN THE
ACTS AND PAULINE EPISTLES.

### (A) Neutral Type Manuscripts.

‫א‬ (i.e. Aleph) is the Codex Sinaiticus. The Saxon
Tischendorf found it in the middle of the last century
at the monastery of St. Catharine on Mount Sinai. He
abducted it and gave it to the Czar : it is in Petrograd
now. It contains the whole New Testament : its date is
about A.D. 330, and its birthplace probably Cæsarea.

---

[1] The chief exception is a group of passages which they call the
" Western non-interpolations," i.e. clauses which they consider to
be later additions interpolated into other texts, but lacking in the
"Western." These are specially frequent in the last three chapters of
St. Luke, where they are printed by W.H., but enclosed between double
brackets.

[2] For those who desire to have a Greek New Testament based
eclectically on the " Western " text, there is the excellent and inex-
pensive text edited by Nestle.

B is the Codex Vaticanus, in the Vatican Library at Rome. Its date and birthplace are approximately the same as those of ℵ. It contains the whole New Testament. Its text in the Gospels and Acts is more purely Neutral even than ℵ, but in the Pauline Epistles it incorporates some readings of a Western type.

Lesser Neutral authorities are the manuscript L (the Codex Regius now at Paris, eighth century) ; and two tenth-century " minuscules " (i.e. manuscripts written in a " cursive " hand, with the letters of each word ligatured together) known as 1 and 33 (=17 in the Pauline Epistles).

## (B) *Western Type Manuscripts.*

D is the Codex Bezæ, a sixth-century manuscript of the Gospels and Acts. The Huguenots took it at the sack of Lyons in the sixteenth century, and Beza, who was Calvin's disciple, sent it to the Cambridge University Library, where it still is. It was copied, or ultimately derived, from a private pocket Bible in which the owner had felt himself free to make innumerable alterations in the Greek text. It is unique among manuscripts in its readings. It is bilingual, with the Greek text on one page and the Latin opposite.

Its chief characteristic consists in innumerable verbal changes, most of which need no consideration. But a much more interesting feature is its introduction of clauses which are not found anywhere else and are particularly frequent in the Acts. These additions [1] fall mainly under two heads : first, words added to emphasise the guidance of the Holy Spirit (cp. Acts 19[1-2]) ; secondly, explanations inserted by some one obviously familiar with the topography of St. Paul's travels (e.g. Acts 19[9] 21[16], etc.). On

---

[1] The most striking of them will be found in the Appendix at the end of W.H.'s Greek Testament (*List of Noteworthy Rejected Readings*).

the whole D is much too freakish to be a safe guide, except where it is associated with more respectable witnesses.

[For the Acts $E_2$, the Codex Laudianus, a seventh-century Græco-Latin manuscript now in the Bodleian Library, gives a text akin to D.]

$D_2$ is the Codex Claromontanus, a sixth-century manuscript containing only the Pauline Epistles. It belongs to a Græco-Latin group (of which $G_3$ is the other most striking member). Its text is very much less extreme than that of D, though it shows the same tendencies.

### (C) We have Two Outstanding Manuscripts of a " Mixed " Character.

A is the Codex Alexandrinus, now in the British Museum. Its date is fifth century. Its text in the Acts and Pauline Epistles has a good deal in common with the Neutral.

C is the Codex Ephraemi rescriptus (i.e. the Biblical text was scraped off with pumice-stone and the works of Ephraem were written over it on the same vellum; in technical language it is a " palimpsest "). It also dates from the fifth century and is now at Paris. In the Acts and Pauline Epistles it has a certain element in common with the Neutral group.

### (D) Versions.

1. Of the old Latin Versions space forbids us to give any account. Their manuscripts are denoted by the *small* letters of the English alphabet (*a*, *b*, *c*, *d*, etc.). They are referred to as a whole by the abbreviation *Lat.*[vet.] (i.e. Latina vetus). The Vulgate (*Vulg.*) is Jerome's revision of the old Latin Bibles, made shortly before A.D. 400; it gives a later (i.e. Syrian) type of text.

2. Of the old Versions in the Syriac language (*Syr.*[vet.])

we have no copies which contain the Acts and Pauline Epistles.

3. Of the Coptic or Egyptian Versions (*Egg.*) we have a complete edition in the Northern dialect called Bohairic (*Boh.*). Its text is mainly Neutral.

There are fragments of an older Version which comes from South Egypt in a dialect called Sahidic (*Sah.*). Its text is mainly Western.

# INDEX.

[*N.B.*—This Index gives references to salient facts only, and is not intended to be exhaustive. It is hoped that the list of St. Paul's ideas and phrases may serve, in some measure, as a guide to his teaching.]

Entries in **bold type** are the most important.

Figures in square brackets refer to kindred topics or uncertain parallels.

f. denotes following page.

ff. denotes following pages (two or more).